About Island Press

Island Press is the only nonprofit organization in the United States whose principal purpose is the publication of books on environmental issues and natural resource management. We provide solutions-oriented information to professionals, public officials, business and community leaders, and concerned citizens who are shaping responses to environmental problems.

In 1998, Island Press celebrates its fourteenth anniversary as the leading provider of timely and practical books that take a multidisciplinary approach to critical environmental concerns. Our growing list of titles reflects our commitment to bringing the best of an expanding body of literature to the environmental community throughout North America and the world.

Support for Island Press is provided by The Jenifer Altman Foundation, The Bullitt Foundation, The Mary Flagler Cary Charitable Trust, The Nathan Cummings Foundation, The Geraldine R. Dodge Foundation, The Ford Foundation, The Vira I. Heinz Endowment, The W. Alton Jones Foundation, The John D. and Catherine T. MacArthur Foundation, The Andrew W. Mellon Foundation, The Charles Stewart Mott Foundation, The Curtis and Edith Munson Foundation, The National Fish and Wildlife Foundation, The National Science Foundation, The New-Land Foundation, The David and Lucile Packard Foundation, The Surdna Foundation, The Winslow Foundation, The Pew Charitable Trusts, and individual donors.

To Heal the Earth

To Heal the Earth

Selected Writings of Ian L. McHarg

Edited by Ian L. McHarg and
Frederick R. Steiner

Foreword by Robert D. Yaro

ISLAND PRESS
Washington, D.C. ♦ Covelo, California

Library of Congress Cataloging-in-Publication Data
McHarg, Ian L.
    [Selections.   1998]
    To heal the earth : the selected writings of Ian L. McHarg /
edited by Ian L. McHarg and Frederick R. Steiner : foreword by Bob
Yaro.
        p.   cm.
    Includes bibliographical references (p.   ) and index.
    ISBN 1-55963-573-8
    1. Landscape ecology. 2. Land use—Planning—Environmental
aspects. 3. Landscape design—Environmental aspects.   I. Steiner,
Frederick R.   II. Title.
QH541.15.L35M38   1998   98-3337
577.5'5—dc21   CIP

Printed on recycled, acid-free paper

Manufactured in the United States of America
10 9 8 7 6 5 4 3 2 1

Contents

Part IV. Revealing the Genius of the Place: Methods and Techniques for Ecological Planning   203

Part V.   Linking Knowledge to Action   265

Foreword

When historians in the next millennium look back at the second half of the twentieth century, in all likelihood the wars, revolutions, and internecine struggles of this violent period will fade in significance. But one revolutionary movement that emerged in this century, the global environmental movement, will continue to shape events in the next.

The products of this international movement and its underlying ethic have already profoundly changed the way the world manages its environment, as witnessed by the 1992 Rio conference, Agenda 21, and the 1997 Kyoto climate accords. In the United States and other developed countries, national environmental protection agencies and environmental impact review procedures have been established. And in a growing number of countries, effective national, regional, state, and local plans, as well as a rapidly expanding legion of environmental advocacy groups now protect landscapes and communities from the destructive effects of urban sprawl. Perhaps most important, polls in the United States and other developed countries show environmental protection to be immensely popular with the general public. Although much remains to be done to heal the planet, at least now we understand the extent of the environmental threats we face, and we have a growing number of tools to protect them.

How did this movement and these tools emerge? They certainly are not inevitable. In 1949 Aldo Leopold proposed a new environmental ethic and a new relationship between people and the land in *A Sand County Almanac*. In the 1960s Rachel Carson popularized scientific concerns about the destruction of the environment in her 1962 classic, *Silent Spring*.

But it was Ian McHarg, a University of Pennsylvania professor and practicing landscape architect who, hearing the environmental alarm sounded by Carson and others, brought it home to the general public, and in particular, to the design and planning professions. McHarg made it clear that as a terrestrial species, we homo sapiens have to be at least as concerned about destruction of the land as we were about the destruction of the atmosphere, the seas, and the habitats of other species.

McHarg popularized his views through his classic 1969 book *Design with Nature* and through dozens of professional articles. His CBS television series *The House We Live In* reached a mass audience and was surely the most verdant oasis in the "vast wasteland" that television was termed at the time. McHarg further promoted his vision for a new relationship between humans and their environment through hundreds of lectures to professional and lay audiences. As a result, since the 1960s, every design professional, environmentalist, and most thinking adults in the United States and much of the industrialized world has at some point had a first-hand opportunity to experience Ian McHarg's passion for combating the threats that face the planet.

McHarg had a particularly profound impact on the nearly two generations of students he taught at the University of Pennsylvania. Many of them became leaders in the design professions as government officials, consultants, and teachers, and most have put Ian's environmental dogma and practices to work in their own careers. And, probably more than any other group, McHarg's Penn graduates have for decades dominated the planning and landscape architecture faculties at leading universities in the United States and abroad.

But the direct impact of McHarg's teaching and writing has reached far beyond Penn. He made a particularly deep and lasting impression on the outlooks and careers of the generation of environmentalists, planners, and landscape architects who came of age in the heady period following the first Earth Day which took place on April 22, 1970, and which McHarg helped instigate.

I can write from personal experience on his impact on my own life and career. Like thousands of others, I helped organize Earth Day observances and activities. While McHarg was keynoting the Earth Day gathering at Fairmount Park in Philadelphia, I was helping to organize and lead a clean-up along the Connecticut River in Middletown, Connecticut, where I was a student at Wesleyan University. As a newly minted environmentalist, I knew I wanted to save my piece of the planet, but it was only when I brought my own copy of *Design with Nature* that spring that I realized how I was going to do it.

Within a year I was working as a professional city planner, first in Connecticut and then in Boston, trying to put Ian's concepts and techniques to work. Among other things, I wrote some of the first iteration of environmental assessments under the National Environmental Policy Act (NEPA) and MEPA, Massachusett's own environmental impact statement process.

Although I was already a disciple, it was not until 1973 that I experienced McHarg in person. That year he lectured at the Harvard Graduate School of Design, where Ian had received degrees in city planning and landscape architecture two decades earlier and where I would receive a master's degree in city and regional planning. I will always remember the intensity and passion of Ian's presentation that day, as well as his persistent optimism and sardonic wit. These combined with his thick Scottish accent, tweedy suit, and sometimes bawdy humor to make his presentation even more enthralling, like a shot of single-malt scotch. (Indeed, as a life-long chain smoker he had the smoky aroma of Islay scotch, and he probably did loosen up his presentation with a "wee dram" prior to his talk.) Ian's colorful characterization of suburban sprawl as a "cancerous excrescence on the landscape" was particularly memorable.

Not since Frederick Law Olmsted, the great nineteenth-century pioneering city planner and landscape architect, has one person had such a profound effect on the theory and practice of city planning and city building. And like Olmsted, McHarg has moved seamlessly and effectively between theory, advocacy, and practice.

As a theorist, McHarg is part of the tradition of environmental thinking that relates human progress to the quality of its environment, one that begins with George Perkins Marsh and builds upon the writings of Aldo Leopold and Lewis Mumford. It is worthwhile to note that McHarg promoted his view of the planet and all its species as representing a single living organism a decade before James Lovelock and Lynn Margulis advanced the Gaia theory.

Through dozens of professional projects around the world, McHarg has demonstrated the techniques needed to transform our relationship with the natural world. His plans for the valleys outside Baltimore, New York's Battery Park City and West Side Waterfronts, the new town of The Woodlands in Texas, and others set the standard for community and environmental planning in the 1960s and 1970s and beyond. Consequently, McHarg not only helped instigate and lead, but also shaped the outcome of the great environmental revolution of the late twentieth century.

What is perhaps his most lasting impact, however, came as a result of his advisory role to the federal government during the Johnson administration. In this capacity, McHarg successfully promoted the establishment of the National Environmental Policy Act and the world's first institutionalized system of environmental impact reviews. McHarg also advocated the creation of a biological survey at the federal level that could parallel the work of the U.S. Geological Survey. In the mid-1990s Interior Secretary Bruce Babbitt finally established the U.S. Biological Survey, although its power as an analytical tool led to its near-destruction at the hands of a growth-at-any-cost-Congress.

McHarg's plans for the federal highway administration in the 1960s demonstrated the value of suitability analyses, in which layers of environmental data were overlayed on each other to identify suitable sites or corridors for highway projects. This overlay mapping process established a procedure for the siting of major facilities that has been the standard in the United States and abroad since the 1970s. This process also inspired the early geographic information systems, laying the foundations for today's advanced computerized GIS analyses.

It is ironic that, despite his enormous contribution to the fields of landscape architecture and urban and environmental planning, few of McHarg's many scholarly articles, book chapters, or presentation papers, have had a wide audience. Many of the pieces were written for obscure professional journals or for public clients and did not receive much attention after their initial publication. Other papers were prepared for presentations at conferences, and although they may have had an important impact on the audience at the time, were not published except in ephemeral proceedings. This book serves to remedy that situation. For the first time many of McHarg's theoretical and applied papers are compiled and edited in book form. This allows the reader to see how the author's thinking evolved over time, and to see how his theories were later applied in McHarg's professional practice. Frederick Steiner's thoughtful introductory essays provide the reader with the context for each article or presentation, creating a continuity that pulls you through the book.

Robert D. Yaro

Preface

This book is a result of a relationship which developed into a friendship between teacher and student that began in 1972 and stemmed from interwoven concerns about civil rights, war and peace, and the environment. The environmental interests of the student, Frederick Steiner, prompted him to read *Design with Nature*, one of the clarion works of those times. This reading led the student to attend a speech by the author in a standing-room-only Cincinnati conference hall, then to graduate school at the University of Pennsylvania (called Penn) in the department that the teacher then chaired.

The teacher, Ian McHarg, had begun his quest much earlier; for the student Penn was just the beginning of the journey. Years passed and their relationship matured and evolved. Eventually, the student assisted the teacher with his autobiography. In the process, the student discovered that the teacher had produced a body of published work that had become eclipsed by his most famous publication, *Design with Nature*.

This book is a collection of those works of the teacher, connected and introduced by essays by the student. To create a useful retrospective of McHarg's work, we (teacher and student, and please excuse us for drifting in and out of the third person, but it seems the only comfortable and honest way to introduce this collaboration) set ourselves the task of selecting writings from McHarg's extensive oeuvre that do not duplicate his major publications *Design with Nature* and *A Quest for Life*. Some overlap, of course, is inevitable, as ideas explored in papers or lectures found full expression years later in a book. We included those papers that exhibit the evolution of key ideas, while attempting to keep redundancies to a minimum. The selections span much of McHarg's career from the 1950s to the present. An original essay, "Landscape Architecture," as well as section introductions, and a "Prospectus" were written for this collection.

The essays in this selection have been edited for consistency. For example, we have adopted consistent systems for citations and headings. A few errors that occurred in the originals have been corrected and some information has been updated. Several illustrations from the originals have been replaced or omitted, but otherwise the essays have not been changed.

We owe several debts of gratitude to those who assisted with this book. First, a grant from the Graham Foundation allowed us to prepare the manuscript. We appreciate the support for the Graham proposal which we received from Deborah Dalton, William McDonough, and Dan Sayre.

The University of Pennsylvania provides Professor Emeritus Ian McHarg office space, which has been essential to the completion of this work. The Arizona State University School of Planning and Landscape Architecture has provided considerable support. In particular, we are thankful for the contribution of Chris Duplissa, who was responsible for scanning the original publications and organizing them in a consistent format. She also typed original material which required many revisions. John Meunier, Gary Hack, and John Dixon Hunt are responsible for the institutional support at ASU and Penn. Their ongoing encouragement and support is valued.

We greatly appreciate the comments on draft manuscripts by Lynn Miller, Meto Vroom, Danilo Palazzo, Ward Brady, Bill Miller, Sung-Kyun Kim, and Joochul Kim. Michael Clarke, Ignacio San Martin, Kim Shetter, Michael Rushman, Paul Smith, and Dan Sirois provided helpful advice and information. We are grateful to the publishers and co-authors who granted us permission to reprint the papers here. They are listed in the acknowledgments on pages 361–362. Co-authors are identified in the table of contents as well as with each paper. Jonathan Sutton was especially helpful and provided original slides from The Woodlands project.

We thank Bob Yaro of the Regional Plan Association for his insightful foreword. Heather Boyer, Cecilia González, Christine McGowan, and Dan Sayre of Island Press have been wonderful collaborators with this effort. We value their professionalism and attention to detail. We highly value the support and critical advice of our families and thank Anna, Halina, and Andrew Steiner, and Carol, Ian, and Andrew McHarg for their love and encouragement.

Frederick Steiner
Tempe, Arizona

Ian L. McHarg
Philadelphia, Pennsylvania

Introduction

Two landscape architects/city planners stand alone in their contribution to American culture and to how we view landscapes. One was Frederick Law Olmsted, who pioneered both landscape architecture and city planning in the last half of the nineteenth century. Olmsted was responsible for, among other things, New York City's Central Park, the preservation of Yosemite State Park and of Niagara Falls, the design of many college campuses and city parks, and the layout of the Chicago Columbian Exposition of 1893. The other is Ian L. McHarg, who advanced landscape architecture and planning in the last half of the twentieth century. Both Olmsted and McHarg sought to generate healthy, creative environments.

Frederick Law Olmsted initiated the American professions of landscape architecture and city planning in the nineteenth century. He was influenced by the leading American writings of his time. The transcendentalists Emerson and Thoreau advanced the concepts of self-awareness and freedom through interaction with Nature. Whitman sang of himself, rewriting that song over and over to clarify his place in the world. Whitman pondered the uniqueness of our Nation of teeming nations. Olmsted was a writer before he was a planner or landscape architect. Like the transcendentalists, he believed interaction with nature was a prerequisite for freedom. Like Whitman, Olmsted was concerned about nation building, especially in a country divided by war.

Influenced by his visit to Britain's Birkenhead Park in 1850, Olmsted saw the concept of the urban park as an antidote for the demoralizing aspects of nineteenth-century American city life brought about by the industrial revolution. The eighteenth-century English landscape gardeners (or landscape improvers, as they called themselves) had developed a rehabilitation concept for the estates of the rich and eventually began to apply these same design principles to parks. This English landscape concept is often referred to as the pastoral aesthetic. Olmsted imported the pastoral vision, first to urban parks, then to suburbs and campuses. From Central Park in Manhattan to the Biltmore Estate in rural North Carolina, Olmsted imprinted the pastoral aesthetic into the American consciousness.

Olmsted's vision became institutionalized through the efforts of his son and nephew as well as several protégés and followers, most notably Charles

1

Eliot and John Nolen. These individuals established organizations, such as the American Society of Landscape Architects, the Trustees of Public Reservation, and the American Planning and Civic Association, as well as academic programs in landscape architecture and planning at leading American universities, such as Harvard and the University of Illinois. They also influenced American policy for national parks and national forests, wrote numerous plans and zoning ordinances for towns and cities, and published books and articles.

Although Americans enjoyed the pastoral aesthetic in grassy lawns and massed tree clumps, the institutions fractured in the decades following the deaths of the senior Olmsted and of Eliot. City planning separated from landscape architecture and after World War II, began promoting itself as an applied social science rather than an environmental design art. Planning grew in prominence, but eventually lost its effectiveness in improving human communities. Planners became engaged in many of the most pressing political issues of our day, from social equity to environmental quality. However, they distanced themselves from the creation and rehabilitation of the places where people live. An emphasis on process, quantitative analysis, and policy improved the capacities of planners in many ways, but this improvement came at the expense of physical plan-making. While policies for engaging citizens in public decisions proliferated, the quality of communities deteriorated.

Meanwhile, landscape architecture retreated from the social advocacy of the Olmsteds. Notable exceptions existed, such as Jens Jensen's promotion of native plants in park design in Chicago, Alfred Caldwell's vision for a living city, also in Chicago, and Frank Waugh's concern for rural communities and for national forests and parks in the American West from his Amherst, Massachusetts, base. But, largely landscape architects were engaged in applying the pastoral aesthetic to the country homes of the wealthy, to golf courses, and to exclusive subdivisions (that frequently excluded people because of their race or religion). During and after World War II, academic programs in landscape architecture began to disappear or become marginalized.

In the 1960s a landscape architect-planner emerged to challenge the *status quo* and to establish a new direction. Ian McHarg revived, redirected, and re-created the professions of landscape architecture and planning in the late twentieth century. Like Olmsted, McHarg was influenced by the leading American environmental writings of his time. Aldo Leopold and Rachel Carson had related the science of ecology to the quality of the world we live in. Lewis Mumford had advanced the notion that planning and design could be viewed as forms of social criticism and that the regional, ecological city could improve our quality of life.

McHarg was a landscape architect and planner before he became a writer and theorist. Like Carson and Leopold, he believed ecology could be used to understand complex interactions between people and their environments and that the science could be employed to guide actions. Like his mentor Mumford, McHarg came to see planning and design as means for criticism of the environments we had created. McHarg was also profoundly influenced by the new view of Earth that was provided from space. A veteran of war, he sought means for peacefully inhabiting the planet by greening and healing it.

Like the English landscape gardeners before him, McHarg went beyond the garden wall and discovered through his work all nature to be a garden. McHarg transcended disciplinary boundaries, and by making this leap the limits of his own fields were extended. A new theory was advanced:that we should plan and design with nature, that we should use ecology to inform the environmental design arts, that we should follow nature's lead. McHarg presented this theory at a time when the nation and the world were receptive to creating better environments—a time when we were beginning to recognize the limits to growth and our dependence on our surroundings for our well-being.

McHarg's *Design with Nature* was not published in a vacuum. Compatible ideas about the use of ecology were being presented by others in the 1960s, most notably by the Israeli-Dutch planner Artur Glikson (another protégé of Mumford), the Canadian Angus Hills, and the American landscape architect Philip Lewis.

But McHarg emerged as the principal spokesman. He was more colorful, blunter, and wittier than his peers. He had hosted his own network television program, produced a documentary for PBS, and was a frequent guest on that American institution—the talk show. The nation was looking for representatives for the environment and at the same time had become enamored by the culture of the British Isles, from the Beatles and the Rolling Stones, to the Scot Sean Connery and Ian Fleming's 007, on to Twiggy and Carnaby Street. McHarg, a Scot like Connery, was a former commando and paratrooper, a British red beret who showed no fear either to the Fortune 500 or to thousands of hippies at an Earth Day rally.

Design with Nature was not the only channel through which McHarg relayed his message. As an American academic, he was required to publish, and publish he did in scholarly and professional journals and in edited volumes. McHarg was also an academic practitioner. He founded a company with David Wallace which became an international business. Wallace-McHarg Associates grew into Wallace, McHarg, Roberts, and Todd and, then after McHarg's departure, the present Wallace Roberts and Todd. McHarg also pursued numerous design and planning projects under the auspices of his home institution, the University of Pennsylvania (Penn). At Penn, he promoted a multidisciplinary, collaborative approach to planning and design. The team-based studio became a vehicle to combat the reductionism of the science, while drawing on scientific knowledge, to create new syntheses.

McHarg, the scholar and the academic practitioner, produced a body of writings, selections of which are gathered here. For readers familiar with *Design with Nature*, this collection will provide a context for the work that preceded that classic text and for the writings that flowed after it. For others unfamiliar with Ian McHarg's work, this collection will provide a comprehensive introduction to his ideas.

Although all of his ideas were certainly not new, McHarg cultivated theories of ecology and, in doing so, was able to present them in a way that changed the very nature of landscape architecture and planning. This collection also relates the study, practice, and theory of landscape architecture to the broader conceptions of ecology, architecture, and the built environment.

The book is divided into five parts, representing five different themes from McHarg's work: First, McHarg's theoretical writings and their influence on the basic nature of design and planning; second, planning the ecological region; third, the interrelationship between ecology and design; fourth, methods and techniques related to design and planning; and, fifth, links between theory and action through McHarg's innovative planning projects.

Each part begins with a short essay that provides the "connective tissue" for the book, context for the works represented, and continuity for the book as a whole. A short comment introduces each work. The comments attempt to frame each piece and to provide further context.

A lesson from the pragmatism of John Dewey is that philosophy works best when eternal questions are connected to everyday practice. An eternal question facing us is how best to live on earth in a sustaining manner. The writings of Ian McHarg can help us heal the planet by making better decisions about how we plan and design our surroundings.

Frederick R. Steiner

Part I

Changing the Nature of Design and Planning: Theoretical Writings

Design with nature is an elegant theory. Both simple and direct, it is as much a proposition as a principle. Design with nature is a normative theory, an ideal to be achieved. A process is suggested to reach that goal. The conception that we should design with nature is deeply rooted in the Western arts and sciences; some would argue it is a universal theme underlying all cultures. Certainly nature as represented by our material surroundings and our own human character underlies all art and science. In Western societies knowledge about our surroundings has too often been used "to multiply and to subdue" nature. A grand canyon exists between the values espoused and the reality created.

A better fit between the ideal and the actual, between our surroundings and our interventions, has long been promoted in design theory. From ancient to modern times, architects have worked to fit buildings to a given site. In the first century B.C., the Roman architect and engineer Marcus Vitruvius Pollio devoted much of his ten books on architecture to understanding sites and to the primordial elements of air, fire, earth, and water. In the planning of a city, he noted the need to "consider and observe the natures of birds, fishes, and land animals" and suggested that the designs of houses should "conform to the nature of the country and to diversities of climate." Two thousand years later, the American architect Frank Lloyd Wright advocated an "organic" approach to architecture, seeking to blur the distinction between the inside and the outside of a building. Such wisdom should be used in the planning of groups of houses that form communities as well as communities that comprise cities and their regions.

Landscape architects and planners have also promoted environmental understanding to guide their arts. Jens Jensen advocated the use of native plants in park design. Patrick Geddes promoted the idea of a regional survey of environmental factors to precede planning, a concept embraced by Lewis Mumford, Benton MacKaye, and others.

With his contribution of connecting the science of ecology to the environmental design and planning arts, McHarg is an important part of this tradition. He linked the Vitruvius–Wright–Jensen–Mumford tradition with that of Aldo Leopold, Paul Sears, and Rachel Carson.

The following five papers represent the core of McHarg's theoretical ideas. They overlap with the topics of the subsequent sections of the book on planning and design, but focus more on the theoretical than the applied aspects (although McHarg has always jumped back and forth). The earliest essay was published in 1963 and the most recent in 1997. There is a gap between the four theoretical papers from the 1960s and the 1997 article in this section. This gap is filled with the four subsequent sections that illustrate how his theories were transformed into actions.

McHarg has identified "Man and Environment" as his first serious theoretical writing that set the stage for those that followed, including the themes of religion, science, and creativity that emerge and reappear throughout his work. What may surprise some readers and some of the critics who lump McHarg in the American antiurban tradition is the attention McHarg gives to city life and his desire to seek out an alternative urban morphology. His interest in, and knowledge of, urban history is also impressive and due in part to the mentorship of Mumford.

McHarg's 1964 "The Place of Nature in the City of Man" explicitly addresses "the place of nature" in our urban habitat. The prose exhibits McHarg's often sardonic humor as well as his clever way with words, for example, "that anarchy which constitutes urban growth" and "the place where man and nature are in closest harmony in the city is the cemetery." The essay clearly defines the urban environmental agenda that still dominates planning debates: the loss of prime farmland "by the most scabrous housing," the pollution of air and water, the paving over of precious green spaces within the city, the filling in of marshes that we now call wetlands, and the gradual uglification of everything. These processes occur worldwide from Phoenix to Madrid, from Mexico City to Seoul. McHarg lays the blame of the "urban growth anarchy" on economic determinism and he provides a theoretical antidote.

In the 1966 article, "Ecological Determinism," McHarg proposed the use of ecology in planning and design to avert the necropolis predicted by Mumford. The Mumford influence on McHarg's 1960s writings is evident. So too is the thinking of the great minds he invited to his *The House We Live In* television program and his "Man and Environment" course at Penn, especially, I think, Paul Sears, Paul Shepard, and Ruth Patrick. He also learned much from his interactions with his Penn colleagues, such as David Goddard and the wonderful Loren Eiseley, whom McHarg once described as "a large, wise, round, magnificent man."

In "Ecological Determinism" McHarg pushes his ideas for a new urban morphology, one determined by ecology to counter the prevailing economic determinism, which McHarg masterfully critiques. Ecological determinism differs from environmental determinism as it was developed by geographers and other social scientists early in the twentieth century. These social scientists were strongly influenced by biological ideas, and briefly the prospects for a synthetic human ecology were bright. Unfortunately these ideas were appropriated by individuals seeking to advance racist notions about the influence of surroundings on human physiology. These theories were rightly debunked, but an unfortunate drifting began of the social scientists away from the natural scientists that is only recently being bridged. McHarg's ecological determinism focuses on the importance of interactions and rather exclusively on the role of surroundings.

Another contribution of the "Ecological Determinism" paper is McHarg's treatment of the English landscape movement. Before McHarg's analysis, the English landscape school was viewed mainly as a period of garden history populated by funny, eccentric people doing bold things. He observed that "Nature itself produced the esthetic" of the landscapes designed by William Kent, Capability Brown, Humphry Repton, and others. McHarg recognized the complexity of their work, which contrasted the simplicity (or "simple-mindedness") of French Renaissance garden design. Since McHarg's 1966 observations, the English landscape school has been viewed as an applied ecology that formed the basis for creating functional landscapes with a new aesthetic.

McHarg was quite clear early on, even before the publication of *Design with Nature* about his quest. In the 1968 "Values, Process and Form," he wrote: "We need a general theory which encompasses physical, biological, and cultural evolution; which contains an intrinsic value system; which includes criteria of creativity and destruction and, not least, principles by which we can measure adaptations and their form." The theory was to be based on an understanding of ecology: "The place, the plants, the animals, and man and the orderings which they have accomplished over time, are revealed in form." Our role, then, was to be creative agents of change, that is, "The role of man is to understand nature, which is to say man, and to intervene to enhance its creative processes."

Creativity was one of McHarg's central and recurring themes. His persistent optimism is impressive. McHarg became mildly disillusioned about the state of the earth without being embittered. His optimism provides a counterbalance to the pessimism, the necropolis of Mumford. "There are the challenges. What are the opportunities?" is a question posed by McHarg frequently.

The writings from the 1960s are as contemporary as if they were written today, except for his use of "man" instead of "human" or "people," an indication of his time when "man" was used in its Greek sense to refer to humanity. They address contemporary, perhaps timeless, topics. That we should "understand nature, which is to say man" is a response to critics of environmentalists who claim ecological designers and planners ignore people. In fact, McHarg's themes from the 1960s foreshadow Neil Evernden's ideas in his insightful *The Social Creation of Nature* (1992) as well as Daniel Botkin's in *Discordant Harmonies* (1990). Like Evernden, McHarg indeed recognizes that nature is a social creation. Like Botkin in his "New Ecology for the Twenty-First Century," McHarg has long acknowledged people as part of ecology, as active agents who interact with and bring about change in their environments. Similar, too, are McHarg's ideas to those of the Dutch geobiochemist Peter Westbroek (1991) that life, including human life, is a geological force.

He proposed the concept of the biosphere as a superorganism a decade before James Lovelock (1979) and Lynn Margulis put forth their Gaia hypothesis. Although his focus in the 1960s was more on local and regional landscapes, even then McHarg offered a global view, graphically displayed in the early use of the portrait of the Earth from space on the cover of *Design with Nature*. Early on, he provocatively compared people to "a global pathogen, an agent of planetary disease." Simultaneously he recognized the potential for people to become the Earth's physicians.

His reflective 1997 "Natural Factors in Planning" challenges the human race to transform itself from being a "global pathogen" to that of a catalyst for maintaining crucial processes. After presenting the consequences for not becoming such catalysts, McHarg summarizes the challenges to more effective ecological planning. First, there is the fragmentation of knowledge. "Integration requires bridging between separate sciences," McHarg observes.

A second challenge is the fragmentation of government. "There are redundant and often conflicting policies, evidence of cross purposes" that handicap governmental environmental management efforts. McHarg also identifies the inadequacies of planning initiatives to respond to the environmental challenge, but, he provides hope.

McHarg observes the emergence of the environment in public policy since the 1970s. He gives several reasons for optimism, including the environmental literacy of today's children. Scientific knowledge about the environment, although still fragmented, has grown. He urges us to "direct our energies toward synthesis." Such synthesis of environmental knowledge is necessary "to improve the human condition."

Design the nature of the planet: heal it, restore its health. This is our challenge, this is our opportunity. In these five chapters, McHarg provides a foundation. Ecology is the basis for that foundation—ecology, the subversive science, as Paul Sears (1964) called it. Sears speculated that if ecology was "taken seriously for the long-run welfare of mankind, [then it would] endanger the assumptions and practices accepted by modern societies, whatever their doctrinal commitments" (1964, p. 11). Ian McHarg has indeed taken ecology seriously and, in doing so, changed how we approach planning and design.

References

Botkin, Daniel. 1990. *Discordant Harmonies, A New Ecology for the Twenty-First Century*. New York: Oxford University Press.

Evernden, Neil. 1992. *The Social Creation of Nature*. Baltimore: The Johns Hopkins University Press.

Lovelock, J. E. 1979. *Gaia, A New Look at Life on Earth*. Oxford: Oxford University Press.

Sears, Paul. 1964. "Ecology—A Subversive Subject." *BioScience* 14 (7, July):11.

Westbroek, Peter. 1991. *Life as a Geological Force*. New York: Norton.

1

Man and Environment (1963)

Ian McHarg considers the writing of this paper, published in The Urban Condition *edited by Leonard Duhl, as "a threshold in my professional life and . . . the first summation of my perceptions and intentions." It began when McHarg was invited by Duhl to join his Committee on Environmental Variables and Mental Health. Duhl, a medical doctor, was director of research for the National Institute of Mental Health. He selected the members of the committee, which included Herbert Gans, J. B. Jackson, and Melvin Webber.*

For McHarg the paper represented a "tremendous leap in scale." He changed his focus from small-scale urban concerns to a larger regional vision. He wrote "Man and Environment" at the time when he was organizing his The House We Live In *television program for CBS. The influence of the guests from that program is evident in this paper. Not only did the scale of McHarg's concerns change, but also the nature of his audience. Prior to 1962, his lectures outside of Penn had been limited to state associations of garden clubs, where he agreed to devote half his speech to garden design history if he could spend the other half speaking about the environment. This paper is a "coming out," where the half garden designer is shed for the complete environmentalist. It was, according to McHarg, "my most embracing address on the subject of the environment to that point."*

The nature and scale of this enquiry can be simply introduced through an image conceived by Loren Eiseley. Man, far out in space, looks back to the distant earth, a celestial orb, blue-green oceans, green of verdant land, a celestial fruit. Examination discloses blemishes on the fruit, dispersed circles from which extend dynamic tentacles. The man concludes that these cankers are the works of man and asks, "Is man but a planetary disease?"

There are at least two conceptions within this image. Perhaps the most important is the view of a unity of life covering the earth, land and oceans, interacting as a single superorganism, the biosphere. A direct analogy can be found in man, composed of billion upon billion of cells, but all of these operating as a single organism. From this the full relevance of the second conception emerges, the possibility that man is but a dispersed disease in the world-life body.

The conception of all life interacting as a single superorganism is as novel as is the conception of man as a planetary disease. The suggestion of man the destroyer, or rather brain the destroyer, is salutary to society which has traditionally abstracted brain from body, man from nature, and vaunted the rational process. This, too, is a recent view. Yet the problems are only of yesterday. Pre-atomic man was an inconsequential geological, biological, and ecological force; his major power was the threat of power. Now, in an instant, post-atomic man is the agent of evolutionary regression, a species now empowered to destroy all life.

In the history of human development, man has long been puny in the face of overwhelmingly powerful nature. His religions, philosophies, ethics, and acts have tended to reflect a slave mentality, alternately submissive or arrogant toward nature. Judaism, Christianity, Humanism tend to assert outrageously the separateness and dominance of man over nature, while animism and nature worship tend to assert total submission to an arbitrary nature. These attitudes are not urgent when human societies lack the power to make any serious impact on environment. These same attitudes become of first importance when man holds the power to cause evolutionary regressions of unimaginable effect or even to destroy all life.

Modern man is confronted with the awful problem of comprehending the role of man in nature. He must immediately find a *modus vivendi*, he must seek beyond for his role in nature, a role of unlimited potential yet governed by laws which he shares with all physical and organic systems. The primacy of man today is based more upon his power to destroy than to create. He is like an aboriginal, confronted with the necessity of operating a vast and complex machine, whose only tool is a hammer. Can modern man aspire to the role of agent in creation, creative participant in a total, unitary, evolving environment? If the pre-atomic past is dominated by the refinement of concern for man's acts towards man, the inauguration of the atomic age increases the dimension of this ancient concern and now adds the new and urgent necessity of understanding and resolving the interdependence of man and nature.

While the atomic threat overwhelms all other considerations, this is by no means the only specter. The population implosion may well be as cataclysmic as the nuclear explosion. Should both of these threats be averted there remain the lesser processes of destruction which have gathered momentum since the nineteenth century. In this period we have seen the despoliation of continental resources accumulated over aeons of geological time, primeval forests destroyed, ancient resources of soil mined and sped to the sea, marching deserts, great deposits of fossil fuel dissipated into the atmosphere. In the country, man has ravaged nature; in the city, nature has been erased and man assaults man with insalubrity, ugliness, and disorder. In short, man has evolved and proliferated by exploiting historic accumulations of inert and organic resources, historic climaxes of plants and animals. His products are reserved for himself, his mark on the environment is most often despoliation and wreckage.

The Duality of Man and Nature

Conceptions of man and nature range between two wide extremes. The first, central to the Western tradition, is man-oriented. The cosmos is but a pyramid erected to support man on its pinnacle, reality exists only because man can observe it, indeed God is made in the image of man. The opposing view, identified with the Orient, postulates a unitary and all-encompassing nature within which man exists, man in nature.

These opposing views are the central duality, man and nature, West and East, white and black, brains and testicles, Classicism and Romanticism, orthodoxy and transnaturalism in Judaism, St. Thomas and St. Francis, Calvin and Luther, anthropomorphism and naturalism. The Western tradition vaunts the individual and the man-brain, and denigrates nature, animal, non-brain. In the Orient nature is omnipotent, revered, and man is but an aspect of nature. It would be as unwise to deny the affirmative aspects of either view as to diminish their negative effects. Yet today this duality demands urgent attention. The adequacy of the Western view of man and nature deserves to be questioned. Further, one must ask if these two views are mutually exclusive.

The opposition of these attitudes is itself testimony to an underlying unity, the unity of opposites. Do our defining skin and nerve ends divide us from environment or unite us to it? Is the perfectibility of man self-realizable? Is the earth a storeroom awaiting plunder? Is the cosmos a pyramid erected to support man?

The inheritors of the Judaic-Christian-Humanist tradition have received their injunction from Genesis, a man-oriented universe, man exclusively made in the image of God, given dominion over all life and non-life, enjoined to subdue the earth. The naturalist tradition in the West has no comparable identifiable text. It may be described as holding that the cosmos is unitary, that all systems are subject to common physical laws yet having unlimited potential; that in this world man is simply an inhabitant, free to develop his own potential. This view questions anthropocentrism and anthropomorphism; it does not diminish either man's uniqueness or his potential, only his claims to primacy and exclusive divinity. This view assumes that the precursor of man, plant and animal, his co-tenant contemporaries, share a cosmic role and potential.

From its origin in Judaism, extension in Classicism, reinforcement in Christianity, inflation in the Renaissance, and absorption into the nineteenth and twentieth centuries, the anthropomorphic-anthropocentric view has become the tacit view of man versus nature.

Evolution of Power

The primate precursors of man, like their contemporary descendants, support neither a notably constructive, nor a notably destructive role in their ecological community. The primates live within a complex community which has continued to exist; no deleterious changes can be attributed to the primate nor does his existence appear to be essential for the support of his niche and habitat. When the primates abandoned instinct for reason and man emerged, new patterns of behavior emerged and new techniques were developed. Man acquired powers which increased his negative and destructive effect upon environment, but which left unchanged the possibility of a creative role in the environment. Aboriginal peoples survive today: Australian aborigines, Dravidians and Birbory in India, South African Bushmen, Veda in Ceylon, Ainu in Japan, Indians of Tierra del Fuego; none of these play a significantly destructive role in the environment. Hunters, primitive farmers, fishermen—their ecological role has changed little from that of the primate. Yet from aboriginal people there developed several new techniques which gave man a significantly destructive role within his environment. The prime destructive human tool was fire. The consequences of fire, originated by man, upon the ecology of the world cannot be measured, but there is reason to believe that its significance was very great indeed.

Perhaps the next most important device was that of animal husbandry, the domestication of grazing animals. These sheep, goats, and cattle, have been very significant agents historically in modifying the ecology in large areas of the world. This modification is uniformly deleterious to the original environment. Deforestation is perhaps the third human system which has made considerable impact upon the physical environment. Whether involuntary, that is, as an unconscious product of fire, or as a consequence of goat and sheep herding, or as an economic policy, this process of razing forests has wrought great changes upon climate and microclimate, flora and fauna. However, the regenerative powers of nature are great; and while fire, domestic animals, and deforestation have denuded great areas of world surface, this retrogression can often be minimized or reversed by the natural processes of regeneration. Perhaps the next consequential act of man in modifying the natural environment was large-scale agriculture. We know that in many areas of the world agriculture can be sustained for many centuries without depletion of the soil. Man can create a new ecology in which he is the prime agent, in which the original ecological community has been changed, but which is nevertheless self-perpetuating. This condition is the exception. More typically agriculture has been, and is today, an extractive process in which the soil is mined and left depleted. Many areas of the world, once productive, are no longer capable of producing crops. Extractive agriculture has been historically a retrogressive process sustained by man.

The next important agent for modifying the physical environment is the human settlement: hamlet, village, town, city. It is hard to believe that any of the pre-classical, medieval, Renaissance, or even eighteenth-century cities were able to achieve a transformation of the physical environment comparable to the agents mentioned before—fire, animal husbandry, deforestation, or extensive agriculture. But with the emergence of the nineteenth-century industrial city, there arose an agent certainly of comparable consequence, perhaps even of greater consequence, even more destructive of the physical environment and the balances of ecological communities in which man exists, than any of the prior human processes.

The large modern metropolis may be thirty miles in diameter. Much, if not all, of the land which it covers is sterilized. The micro-organisms in the soil no longer exist; the original animal inhabitants have largely been banished. Only a few members of the plant kingdom represent the original members of the initial ecology. The rivers are foul; the atmosphere is polluted; the original configuration of the land is only rarely in evidence; climate and microclimate have retrogressed so that the external microclimate is more violent than was the case before the establishment of the city. Atmospheric pollution may be so severe as to account for 4,000 deaths in a single week of intense "fog," as was the case in London. Floods alternate with drought. Hydrocarbons, lead, carcinogenic agents, carbon dioxide, carbon monoxide concentrations, deteriorating conditions of atmospheric electricity—all of these represent retrogressive processes introduced and supported by man. The epidemiologist speaks of neuroses, lung cancer, heart and renal disease, ulcers, the stress diseases, as the badges of urban conditions. There has also arisen the specter of the effects of density and social pressure upon the incidence of disease and upon reproduction. The modern city contains other life-inhibiting aspects whose effects are present but which are difficult to measure: disorder, squalor, ugliness, noise.

In its effect upon the atmosphere, soil as a living process, the water cycle, climate and micro-climate, the modern city represents a transformation of the original physical environment certainly greater over the area of the city than the changes achieved by earlier man through fire, animal husbandry, deforestation, and extensive agriculture.

Indeed, one can certainly say that the city is at least an ecological regression, although as a human institution it may represent a triumph. Whatever triumphs there are to be seen in the modern city as an institution, it is only with great difficulty that one can see any vestige of triumph in the modern city as a physical environment. One might ask of the modern city that it be humane; that is, capable of supporting human organisms. This might well be a minimum requirement. In order for this term to be fully appropriate—that is, that the city be compassionate and elevating—it should not only be able to support physiological man, but also should give meaning and expression to man as an individual and as a member of an urban society. I contend that far from meeting the full requirements of this criterion, the modern city inhibits life, that it inhibits man as an organism, man as a social being, man as a spiritual being, and that it does not even offer adequate minimum conditions for physiological man; that indeed the modern city offers the least humane physical environment known to history.

Assuredly, the last and most awful agent held by man to modify the physical environment is atomic power. Here we find post-atomic man able to cause evolutionary regressions of unimaginable effect and even able to destroy all life. In this, man holds the ultimate destructive weapon; with this, he can become the agent of destruction in the ecological community, of all communities, of all life. For any ecological community to survive, no single member can support a destructive role. Man's role historically has been destructive; today or tomorrow it can be totally, and for all life existent, irrevocably destructive.

Now, wild nature, save a few exceptions, is not a satisfactory physical environment. Where primitive peoples exist in a wild nature little adapted by man, their susceptibility to disease, life expectancy, vulnerability to climatic vagaries, and to the phenomena of drought and starvation is hardly ideal. Yet the certainty that man must adapt nature and himself does not diminish his dependence upon natural, non-human processes. These two observations set limits upon conceptions of man and nature. Man must adapt through both biological and cultural innovation but these adaptations occur within a context of natural, non-human processes. It is not inevitable that adapting nature to support human congregations must of necessity diminish the quality of the physical environment.

Creation of a physical environment by organisms as individuals and as communities is not exclusively a human skill. The chambered nautilus, the beehive, and the coral formation are all efforts by organisms to take inert materials and dispose them to create a physical environment. In these examples the environments created are complementary to the organisms. They are constructed with great economy of means; they are expressive; they have, in human eyes, great beauty; and they have survived periods of evolutionary time vastly longer than the human span. Can we hope that man will be able to change the physical environment to create a new ecology in which he is primary agent, but which will be a self-perpetuating and not a retrogressive process? We hope that man will be able at least to equal the chambered nautilus, the bee, and the coral—that he will be able to build a physical environment indispensable to life, constructed with economy of means, having lucid expression, and containing great beauty. When man learns this single lesson he will be enabled to create by natural process an environment appropriate for survival—the minimum requirement of a humane environment. When this view is believed, the artist will make it vivid and manifest. Medieval faith, interpreted by artists, made the Gothic cathedral ring with holiness. Here again we confront the paradox of man in nature and man transcendent. The vernacular architecture and urbanism of earlier societies and primitive cultures today, the Italian hill town, medieval village, the Dogon community, express the first view, a human correspondence to the nautilus, the bee, and the coral. Yet this excludes the Parthenon, Hagia Sofia, Beauvais, statements which speak of the uniqueness of man and his aspirations. Neither of these postures is complete, the vernacular speaks too little of the consciousness of man, yet the shrillness of transcendence asks for the muting of other, older voices.

Perhaps when the achievements of the past century are appraised, there will be advanced as the most impressive accomplishment of this period the great extension of social justice. The majority of the population of the Western world moved from an endemic condition of threatening starvation, near desperation, and serfdom, to relative abundance, security, and growing democratic freedoms. Human values utilized the benison of science, technology, and industry, to increase wealth absolutely and to distribute it more equitably. In the process, responsibility and individual freedom increased, brute hunger, bare suppression, and uncontrolled disease were diminished. It is a paradox that in this period of vastly increased wealth, the quality of the physical environment has not only failed to improve commensurately, but has actually retrogressed. If this is true, and I believe that there is more than ample evidence to support this hypothesis, then it represents an extraordinary failure on the part of Western society. The failure is the more inexplicable as the product of a society distinguished by its concern for social justice; for surely the physical environment is an important component of wealth and social justice. The modern city wears the badges which distinguish it as a product of the nineteenth and twentieth centuries. Polluted rivers, polluted atmosphere, squalid industry, vulgarity of commerce, diners, hot dog stands, second-hand car lots, gas stations, sagging wire and billboards, the whole anarchy united by ugliness—at best neutral, at worst offensive and insalubrious. The product of a century's concern for social justice, a century with unequaled wealth and technology, is the least humane physical environment known to history. It is a problem of major importance to understand why the nineteenth and twentieth centuries have failed in the creation of a physical environment; why the physical environment has not been, and is not now, considered as a significant aspect of wealth and social justice.

Renaissance and Eighteenth Century

If we consider all the views in our Western heritage having an anti-environmental content, we find they represent a very impressive list. The first of these is the anthropomorphic view that man exclusively is made in the image of God (widely interpreted to mean that God is made in the image of man). The second assumption is that man has absolute dominion over all life and non-life. The third assumption is that man is licensed to subdue the earth. To this we add the medieval Christian concept of other-worldliness, within which life on earth is only a probation for the life hereafter, so that only the acts of man to man are of consequence to his own soul. To this we add the view of the Reformation that beauty is a vanity; and the Celtic, and perhaps Calvinistic, view that the only beauty is natural beauty, that any intent to create beauty by man is an assumption of God's role, is a vanity, and is sacrilegious. The total of these views represents one which can only destroy and which cannot possibly create. The degree to which there has been retention of great natural beauty, creation of beauty and order, recognition of aspects of natural order, and particularly recognition of these aspects of order as a manifestation of God, would seem to exist independently of the Judaic-Christian view. They may be animist and animitist residues that have originated from many different sources; but it would appear, whether or not they are espoused by Christian and Jews, that they do not have their origins in Judaism or Christianity. It would also appear that they do not have their origins in classical or humanist thought, or even in eighteenth-century rationalist views.

These two opposed views of man's role in the natural world are reflected in two concepts of nature and the imposition of man's idea of order upon nature. The first of these is the Renaissance view most vividly manifest in the gardens of the French Renaissance and the projects of André le Nôtre for Louis XIV. The second is the eighteenth-century English picturesque tradition. The gardens of the Renaissance clearly show the imprint of humanist thought. A rigid symmetrical pattern is imposed relentlessly upon a reluctant landscape. If this pattern was, as is claimed, some image of a perfect paradisiac order, it was a human image which derived nothing from the manifest order and expression of wild nature. It was rather, I suggest, an image of flexed muscles, a cock's crow of power, and an arrogant presumption of human dominance over nature. Le Roi Soleil usurped none of the sun's power by so claiming. Art was perverted to express a superficial pattern while claiming this as an expression of a fundamental order.

If the Renaissance sought to imprint upon nature a human order, the eighteenth-century English tradition sought to idealize wild nature, in order to provide a sense of the sublime. The form of estates in the eighteenth century was of an idealized nature, replacing the symmetrical patterns of the Renaissance. The form of ideal nature had been garnered from the landscape painting of Nicolas Poussin and Salvator Rosa; developed through the senses of the poets and writers, such as Alexander Pope, Abraham Cowley, James Thomson, Joseph Addison, Thomas Gray, the third earl of Shaftesbury, and the Orientalist William Temple—a eulogy of the *campagna* from the painters; a eulogy of the natural countryside and its order from the writers; and from Temple, the occult balance discovered in the Orient. However, the essential distinction between the concept of the Renaissance, with its patterning of the landscape, and that of eighteenth-century England was the sense that the order of nature itself existed and represented a prime determinant, a prime discipline for man in his efforts to modify nature. The search in the eighteenth century was for creation of a natural environment which would evoke a sense of the sublime. The impulse of design in the Renaissance was to demonstrate man's power over nature; man's power to order nature; man's power to make nature in his human image. With so inadequate an understanding of the process of man relating to nature, his designs could not be self-perpetuating. Where the basis for design was only the creation of a superficial order, inevitably the consequence was decoration, decay, sterility, and demise. Within the concepts of eighteenth-century England, in contrast, the motivating idea was to idealize the laws of nature. The interdependence of micro-organisms—plants, insects, and animals, the association of particular ecological groupings with particular areas and particular climates— this was the underlying discipline within which the aristocrat-landscape architect worked. The aim was to create an idealized nature which spoke to man of the tranquillity, contemplation, and calm which nature brought, which spoke of nature as the arena of sublime and religious experience, essentially speaking to man of God. This represents, I believe, one of the most healthy manifestations of the Western attitude toward nature. To this eighteenth-century attitude one must add a succession of men who are aberrants in the Western tradition, but whose views represent an extension of the eighteenth-century view—among them, Wordsworth and Coleridge, Thoreau and Emerson, Jonathan Edwards, Jonathan Marsh, Gerald Manley Hopkins, and many more.

Natural Science and Naturalism

It might be productive to examine the natural scientist's view of the evolution of nature and certain aspects of this order. The astronomer gives us some idea of immensity of scale, a hundred billion galaxies receding from us at the speed of light. Of these hundred billion galaxies is one which is our own, the Milky Way. Eccentric within the immensity of the Milky Way, the inconspicuous solar system exists. Within the immensity of the solar system, revolves the minute planet Earth. The astronomer and geologist together give us some sense of the process during which the whirling, burning gases increased in density, coalesced with cooling, condensed, gave off steam, and finally produced a glassy sphere, the Earth. This sphere with land and oceans had an atmosphere with abundant carbon dioxide, with abundant methane, and little or no free oxygen. A glassy sphere with great climatic ranges in temperature, diurnal and seasonal, comparable to an alternation between Arctic and Equatorial conditions. From the biologist, we learn of the origins of life. The first great miracle of life was this plant-animal in the sea; the emergence of life on land, the succession of fungi, mosses, liverworts, ferns. The miracle beyond life is photosynthesis, the power by which plants, absorbing carbon dioxide, give out oxygen and use the sun's energy to transform light into substance. The substance becomes the source of food and fuel for all other forms of life. There seems to be good reason to believe that the Earth's atmosphere, with abundant oxygen, is a product of the great evolutionary succession of plants. On them we depend for all food and fossil fuels. From the botanist we learn of the slow colonization of the Earth's surface by plants, the degree to which the surface of the Earth was stabilized, and, even more significantly, how plants modified the climatic extremes to support the amphibian, reptilian, and subsequent mammalian evolutionary sequence.

The transcendental view of man's relation to nature implicit in Western philosophies is dependent upon the presumption that man does in fact exist outside of nature, that he is not dependent upon it. In contemporary urban society the sense of absolute dependence and interdependence is not apparent, and it is an extraordinary experience to see a reasonably intelligent man become aware of the fact that his survival is dependent upon natural processes, not the least of which are based upon the continued existence of plants. This relationship can be demonstrated by experiment with three major characters: light, man, and algae. The theater is a cylinder in which is a man, a certain quantity of algae, a given quantity of water, a given quantity of air, and a single input, a source of light corresponding to sunlight (in this case a fluorescent tube). The man breathes the air, utilizes the oxygen, and exhales carbon dioxide. The algae utilize the carbon dioxide and exhale oxygen. There is a closed cycle of carbon dioxide and oxygen. The man consumes water, passes the water, the algae consume the water, the water is transpired, collected. and the man consumes the water. There is a closed water cycle. The man eats the algae, the man passes excrement, the algae consume the excrement, the man consumes the algae. There is a closed cycle of food. The only input is light. In this particular experiment the algae is as dependent upon the man as the man is upon the algae. In nature this is obviously not true. For some two billion years nature did exist without man. There can, however, be absolutely no doubt about the indispensability of the algae or plant photosynthesis to the man. It is the single agent able to utilize radiant energy from the sun and make it available as products to support life. This experiment very clearly shows the absolute dependence of man on nature.

Man has claimed to be unique. Social anthropologists have supported this claim on the ground that he alone has the gift of communication, and again that he alone has values. It might be worthwhile considering this viewpoint. A very famous biologist, David Goddard, said that a single human sperm, weighing one billionth of a gram, contains more information coded into its microscopic size than all of the information contained in all of the libraries of all men in all time. This same statement can be made for the seed of other animals or plants. This is a system of communication which is not rational, but which is extraordinarily delicate, elegant, and powerful, and which is capable of transmitting unimaginable quantities of information in microscopic volume.

This system of communication has enabled all species to survive the evolutionary time span. All forms of extant life share this system of communication; man's participation in it is in no sense exceptional.

Man also claims a uniqueness for himself on the grounds that he alone, of all of the animals, has values from which cultural objectives are derived. It would appear that the same *genetic* system of communication also contains a *value system*. Were this not so, those systems of organic life which do persist today would not have persisted; the genetic information transmitted is the information essential for survival. That information ensures the persistence of the organism within its own ecological community. The genetic value system also contains the essential mutation; that imperfection essential for evolution and survival. This system of communication is elegant, beautiful, and powerful, capable of sifting enormous numbers of conflicting choices. Man participates in and shares this system, but his participation is in no sense exceptional.

Yet another aspect of man's assumption that he is independent of natural processes is the anthropomorphic attitude which implies a finite man who is born, grows, and dies, but who during his life is made of the same unchanging stuff—himself. Not so. If we simply measure that which man ingests, uses, and rejects, we begin to doubt this premise. Hair, nails, skin, and chemical constituents are replaced regularly. He replaces several billion cells daily. The essential stuff of man is changed very regularly indeed. In a much more fundamental way, however, man is a creature of environment. We have learned that he is absolutely dependent upon stimuli—light, shadow, color, sound, texture, gravity; and upon his sense of smell, taste, touch, vision, and hearing.

These constantly changing environmental conditions are his references. Without them there would be hallucination, hysteria, perhaps mental disintegration, certainly loss of reality.

The Ecological View

It remains for the biologist and ecologist to point out the interdependence which characterizes all relationships, organic and inorganic, in nature. It is the ecologist who points out that an ecological community is only able to survive as a result of interdependent activity between all of the species which constitute the community. To the basic environment (geology, climate) is added an extraordinary complexity of inert materials, their reactions, and the interaction of the organic members of the community with climate, inert materials, and other organisms. The characteristic of life is interdependence of all of the elements of the community upon each other. Each one of these is a source of stimulus; each performs work; each is part of a pattern, a system, a working cycle; each one is to some lesser or greater degree a participant and contributor in a thermodynamic system. This interdependence common to nature—common to all systems—is in my own view the final refutation of man's assumption of independence. It appears impossible to separate man from this system. It would appear that there is a system, the order of which we partly observe. Where we observe it, we see interdependence, not independence, as a key. This interdependence is in absolute opposition to Western man's presumption of transcendence, his presumption of independence, and, of course, his presumption of superiority, dominion, and license to subdue the earth.

A tirade on the theme of dependence is necessary only to a society which views man as independent. Truly there is in nature no independence. Energy is the basis for all life; further, no organism has, does, or will live without an environment. All systems are depletive. There can be no enduring system occupied by a single organism. The minimum, in a laboratory experiment, requires the presence of at least two complementary organisms. These conceptions of independence and anthropocentrism are baseless.

The view of organisms and environment widely held by natural scientists is that of interdependence—symbiosis. Paul Sears of Yale University has written:

> Any species survives by virtue of its niche, the opportunity afforded it by environment. But in occupying this niche, it also assumes a role in relation to its surroundings. For further survival it is necessary that its role at least be not a disruptive one.

Thus, one generally finds in nature that each component of a highly organized community serves a constructive, or, at any rate, a stabilizing role. The habitat furnishes the niche, and if any species breaks up the habitat, the niche goes with it. . . . That is, to persist they [ecological communities] must be able to utilize radiant energy not merely to perform work, but to maintain the working system in reasonably good order. This requires the presence of organisms adjusted to the habitat and to each other, so organized as to make the fullest use of the influent radiation and to conserve for use and re-use the materials which the system requires. The degree to which a living community meets these conditions is therefore a test of its efficiency and stability (Sears 1956).

Man, too, must meet this test. Sears states:

Man is clearly the beneficiary of a very special environment which has been a great while in the making. This environment is more than a mere inert stockroom. It is an active system, a pattern and a process as well. Its value can be threatened by disruption no less than by depletion.

The natural scientist states that no species can exist without an environment, no species can exist in an environment of its exclusive creations, no species can survive, save as a non-disruptive member of an ecological community. Every member must adjust to other members of the community and to the environment in order to survive. Man is not excluded from this test.

Man must learn this prime ecological lesson of interdependence. He must see himself linked as a living organism to all living and all preceding life. This sense may impel him to understand his interdependence with the microorganisms of the soil, the diatoms in the sea, the whooping crane, the grizzly bear, sand, rocks, grass, trees, sun, rain, moon, and stars. When man learns this he will have learned that when he destroys he also destroys himself; that when he creates, he also adds to himself. When man learns the single lesson of interdependence he may be enabled to create by natural process an environment appropriate for survival. This is a fundamental precondition for the emergence of man's role as a constructive and creative agent in the evolutionary process. Yet this view of interdependence as a basis for survival, this view of man as a participant species in an ecological community and environment, is quite contrary to the Western view.

I have reminded the reader that the creation of a physical environment by organisms, as individuals and as communities, is not exclusively a human skill; it is shared with the bee, the coral, and the chambered nautilus, which take inert materials and dispose them to create a physical environment, complementary to—indeed, indispensable to—the organism.

When man abandoned instinct for rational thought, he abandoned the powers that permitted him to emulate such organisms; if rationality alone sufficed, man should at least be able to equal these humble organisms. But thereby hangs a parable:

> The nuclear cataclysm is over. The earth is covered with gray dust. In the vast silence no life exists, save for a little colony of algae hidden deep in a leaden cleft long inured to radiation. The algae perceive their isolation; they reflect upon the strivings of all life, so recently ended, and on the strenuous task of evolution to be begun anew. Out of their reflection could emerge a firm conclusion: "Next time, no brains."

Reference

Sears, Paul B. 1956. "The Process of Environmental Change by Man." In W L. Thomas, Jr. ed., *Man's Role in Changing the Face of the Earth*. Chicago: University of Chicago Press.

2

The Place of Nature
in the City of Man (1964)

In the early 1960s McHarg's interest in values toward nature and the physical envi-
ronment increased. Published in a special issue on urban revival in The Annals of
the American Academy of Political and Social Science *edited by Robert Mitchell,*
this article directs that interest toward the topic of nature in the city. McHarg proposes
a theory for a "simple working method for open space." Essentially, he suggests that envi-
ronmentally sensitive areas be used as open space. Such areas usually have multiple
benefits. For example, by protecting wetland areas, floods can be controlled and safe
drinking water supplies may be ensured. This theory for a "simple working method
for open space" has had considerable influence since McHarg presented it in 1964.

Abstract

Unparalleled urban growth is pre-empting a million acres of rural lands each
year and transforming them into the sad emblems of contemporary urbanism. In that anarchy which constitutes urban growth, wherein the major
prevailing values are short-term economic determinism, the image of nature
is attributed little or no value. In existing cities, the instincts of eighteenth-
and nineteenth-century city builders, reflected in the pattern of existing
urban open space, have been superseded by a modem process which disdains
nature and seems motivated by a belief in salvation through stone alone. Yet
there is a need and place for nature in the city of man. An understanding of
natural processes should be reflected in the attribution of value to the constituents of these natural processes. Such an understanding, reflected in city
building, will provide a major structure for urban and metropolitan form, an
environment capable of supporting physiological man, and the basis for an

art of city building, which will enhance life and reflect meaning, order, and purpose.

Introduction

"Before we convert our rocks and rills and templed hills into one spreading mass of low grade urban tissue under the delusion that, because we accomplish this degradation with the aid of bulldozers and atomic piles and electronic computers, we are advancing civilization, we might ask what all this implies in terms of the historic nature of man" (Lewis Mumford 1956, p. 142).

The subject of this essay is an inquiry into the place of nature in the city of man. The inquiry is neither ironic nor facetious but of the utmost urgency and seriousness. Today it is necessary to justify the presence of nature in the city of man; the burden of proof lies with nature, or so it seems. Look at the modern city, that most human of all environments, observe what image of nature exists there—precious little indeed and that beleaguered, succumbing to slow attrition.

William Penn effectively said, Let us build a fair city between two noble rivers; let there be five noble squares, let each house have a fine garden, and let us reserve territories for farming. But that was before rivers were discovered to be convenient repositories for sewage, parks the best locus for expressways, squares the appropriate sites for public monuments, farmland best suited for buildings, and small parks best transformed into asphalted, fenced playgrounds.

Charles Eliot once said, in essence, This is our city, these are our hills, these are our rivers, these our beaches, these our farms and forests. I will make a plan to cherish this beauty and wealth for all those who do or will live here. And the plan was good but largely disdained. So here, as elsewhere, man assaulted nature disinterestedly, man assaulted man with the city; nature in the city remains precariously as residues of accident, rare acts of personal conscience, or rarer testimony to municipal wisdom, the subject of continuous assault and attrition while the countryside recedes before the annular rings of suburbanization, unresponsive to any perception beyond simple economic determinism.

Once upon a time, nature lay outside the city gates a fair prospect from the city walls, but no longer. Climb the highest office tower in the city, when atmospheric pollution is only normal, and nature may be seen as a green rim on the horizon. But this is hardly a common condition and so nature lies outside of workaday experience for most urban people.

Long ago, homes were built in the country and remained rural during the lives of persons and generations. Not so today, when a country house of yesterday is within the rural–urban fringe today, in a suburb tomorrow, and in a renewal area of the not-too-distant future.

When the basis for wealth lay in the heart of the land and the farms upon it, then the valleys were verdant and beautiful, the farmer steward of the landscape, but that was before the American dream of a single house on a quarter acre, the automobile, crop surpluses, and the discovery that a farmer could profit more by selling land than crops.

Once men in simple cabins saw only wild nature, silent, implacable, lonely. They cut down the forests to banish Indians, animals, and shadows. Today, Indians, animals, and forests have gone and wild nature, silence, and loneliness are hard to find.

When a man's experience was limited by his home, village, and environs, he lived with his handiworks. Today, the automobile permits temporary escapes from urban squalor, and suburbanization gives the illusion of permanent escape.

Once upon a time, when primeval forests covered Pennsylvania, its original inhabitants experienced a North Temperate climate, but, when the forests were felled, the climate became, in summer, intemperately hot and humid.

Long ago, floods were described as Acts of God. Today, these are known quite often to be consequences of the acts of man.

As long ago, droughts were thought to be Acts of God, too, but these, it is now known, are exacerbated by the acts of man.

In times past, pure air and clean abundant water were commonplaces. Today, "pollution" is the word most often associated with the word "atmosphere," drinking water is often a dilute soup of dead bacteria in a chlorine solution, and the only peoples who enjoy pure air and clean water are rural societies who do not recognize these for the luxuries they are.

Not more than two hundred years ago, the city existed in a surround of farmland, the sustenance of the city. The farmers tended the lands which were the garden of the city. Now, the finest crops are abject fruits compared to the land values created by the most scabrous housing, and the farms are defenseless.

In days gone by, marshes were lonely and wild, habitat of duck and goose, heron and egret, muskrat and beaver, but that was before marshes became the prime sites for incinerator wastes, rubbish, and garbage—marshes are made to be filled, it is said.

When growth was slow and people spent a lifetime on a single place, the flood plains were known and left unbuilt. But, now, who knows the flood plain? *Caveat emptor.*

Forests and woodlands once had their own justification as sources of timber and game, but second-growth timber has little value today, and the game has long fled. Who will defend forests and woods?

Once upon a time, the shad in hundreds of thousands ran strong up the river to the city. But, today, when they do so, there is no oxygen, and their bodies are cast upon the shores.

The Modern Metropolis

Today, the modern metropolis covers thousands of square miles, much of the land is sterilized and waterproofed, the original animals have long gone, as have primeval plants, rivers are foul, the atmosphere is polluted, climate and microclimate have retrogressed to increased violence, a million acres of land are transformed annually from farmland to suburban housing and shopping centers, asphalt and concrete, parking lots and car cemeteries, yet slums accrue faster than new buildings, which seek to replace them. The epidemiologist can speak of urban epidemics—heart and arterial disease, renal disease, cancer, and, not least, neuroses and psychoses. A serious proposition has been advanced to the effect that the modern city would be in serious jeopardy without the safeguards of modern medicine and social legislation. Lewis Mumford can describe cities as dysgenic. There has arisen the recent specter, described as "pathological togetherness," under which density and social pressure are being linked to the distribution of disease and limitations upon reproduction. We record stress from sensory overload and the response of negative hallucination to urban anarchy. When one considers that New York may well add 1,500 square miles of new "low-grade tissue" to its perimeter in the next twenty years, then one recalls Loren Eiseley's image and sees the cities of man as gray, black, and brown blemishes upon the green earth with dynamic tentacles extending from them and asks: "Are these the evidence of man, the planetary disease?"

Western Views: Man and Nature

Yet how can nature be justified in the city? Does one invoke dappled sunlight filtered through trees of ecosystems, the shad run or water treatment, the garden in the city or negative entropy? Although at first glance an unthinkable necessity, the task of justifying nature in the city of man is, with prevailing values and process, both necessary and difficult. The realities of cities now and the plans for their renewal and extension offer incontrovertible evidence of the absence of nature present and future. Should Philadelphia realize its comprehensive plan, then $20 billion and twenty years later there will be less open space than there is today. (A prediction which, indeed, came to pass, with the single sad exceptions of the numerous "brownfield" sites of abandoned industry as well as deserted and derelict houses and businesses.) Cities are artifacts becoming ever more artificial—as though medieval views prevailed that nature was defiled, that living systems shared original sin with man, that only the artifice was free of sin. The motto for the city of man seems to be: salvation by stone alone.

Within the Western tradition exists a contrary view of man and nature which has a close correspondence to the Oriental attitude of an aspiration to harmony of man in nature, a sense of a unitary and encompassing natural order within which man exists. Among others, the naturalist tradition in the West includes Duns Scotus, Joannes Scotus Erigena, Francis of Assisi, Wordsworth, Goethe, Thoreau, Gerald Manley Hopkins, and the nineteenth- and twentieth-century naturalists. Their insistence upon nature being at least the sensible order within which man exists or a manifestation of God demanding deference and reverence is persuasive to many but not to the city builders.

Are the statements of scientists likely to be more persuasive?
David R. Goddard:

> No organism lives without an environment. As all organisms are depletive, no organism can survive in an environment of its exclusive creation (1960).

F. R. Fosberg:

> An ecosystem is a functioning, interacting system composed of one or more organisms and their effective environment, both physical and biological. All ecosystems are open systems. Eco-systems may be stable or unstable. The stable system is in a steady state. The entropy in an unstable system is more likely to increase than decrease. There is a tendency towards diversity in natural ecosystems. There is a tendency towards uniformity in artificial ecosystems or those strongly influenced by man (1958).

Paul Sears:

> Any species survives by virtue of its niche—the opportunity afforded it by environment. But in occupying this niche, it also assumes a role in relation to its surroundings. For further sur-vival it is necessary that its role at least be not a disruptive one. Thus, one generally finds in nature that each component of highly organized community serves a constructive, or at any rate a stabilizing, role. The habitat furnishes the niche, and, if any species breaks up the habitat, the niche goes with it . . . to

persist [organic systems] must be able to utilize radiant energy
not merely to perform work, but to maintain the working system in reasonably good order. This requires the presence of
organisms adjusted to the habitat and to each other so organized to make the fullest use of the influent radiation and to
conserve for use and reuse the materials which the system
requires (1956, p. 472).

Complex creatures consist of billions of cells, each of which, like any
single-celled creature, is unique, experiences life, metabolism, reproduction,
and death. The complex animal exists through the operation of symbiotic relationships between cells as tissues and organs integrated as a single
organism. Hans Selyé describes this symbiosis as intercellular altruism,
the situation under which the cell concedes some part of its autonomy
towards the operation of the organism and the organism responds to cellular
processes.

Aldo Leopold has been concerned with the ethical content of symbiosis:

Ethics so far studied by philosophers are actually a process in
ecological as well as philosophical terms. They are also a
process in ecological evolution. An ethic, ecologically, is a limitation on freedom of action in the struggle for existence. An
ethic, philosophically, is a differentiation of social from anti-
social conduct. These are two definitions of one thing which
has its origin in the tendency of interdependent individuals
and groups to evolve modes of cooperation. The ecologist calls
these symbioses. There is as yet no ethic dealing with man's
relation to the environment and the animals and plants which
grow upon it. The extension of ethics to include man's relation
to environment is, if I read the evidence correctly, an evolutionary possibility and an ecological necessity. All ethics so far
evolved rest upon a single premise that the individual is a
member of a community of interdependent parts. His instincts
prompt him to compete for his place in the community, but his
ethics prompt him to cooperate, perhaps in order that there
may be a place to compete for (1949).

The most important inference from this body of information is that interdependence, not independence, characterizes natural systems. Thus,
man–nature interdependence presumably holds true for urban man as for his
rural contemporaries. We await the discovery of an appropriate physical and
symbolic form for the urban man–nature relationship.

Natural and Artificial Environments

From the foregoing statements by natural scientists, we can examine certain extreme positions. First, there can be no conception of a completely "natural" environment. Wild nature, save a few exceptions, is not a satisfactory physical environment. Yet the certainty that man must adapt nature and himself does not diminish his dependence upon natural, nonhuman processes. These two observations set limits upon conceptions of man and nature. Man must adapt through both biological and cultural innovation, but these adaptations occur within a context of natural, nonhuman processes. It is not inevitable that adapting, nature to support human congregations must of necessity diminish the quality of the physical environment. Indeed, all of preindustrial urbanism was based upon the opposite premise, that only in the city could the best conjunction of social and physical environment be achieved. This major exercise of power to adapt nature for human ends, the city, need not be a diminution of physiological, psychological, and aesthetic experience.

While there can be no completely natural environments inhabited by man, completely artificial environments are equally unlikely. Man in common with all organisms is a persistent configuration of matter through which the environment ebbs and flows continuously. Mechanically, he exchanges his substance at a very rapid rate while, additionally, his conceptions of reality are dependent upon the attribution of meaning to myriads of environmental stimuli which impinge upon him continuously. The materials of his being are natural, as are many of the stimuli which he perceives; his utilization of the materials and of many stimuli is involuntary. Man makes artifices, but galactic and solar energy, gases of hydrosphere and atmosphere, the substance of the lithosphere, and all organic systems remain elusive of human artificers.

Yet the necessity to adapt natural environments to sustain life is common to many organisms other than man. Creation of a physical environment by organisms as individuals and as communities is not exclusively a human skill. The chambered nautilus, the beehive, the coral formation, to select but a few examples, are all efforts by organisms to take inert materials and dispose them to create a physical environment. In these examples, the environments created are complementary to the organisms. They are constructed with great economy of means; they are expressive; they have, in human eyes, great beauty; and they have survived periods of evolutionary time vastly longer than the human span.

Simple organisms utilize inert materials to create physical environments which sustain life. Man also confronts this necessity. Man, too, is natural in that he responds to the same laws as do all physical and biological systems. He is a plant parasite, dependent upon the plant kingdom and its associated microorganisms, insects, birds, and animals for all atmospheric oxygen, all food, all fossil fuel, natural fibers, and cellulose, for the stability of the water cycle and amelioration of climate and microclimate. His dependence upon the plant and photosynthesis establishes his dependence upon the microorganisms of the soil, particularly the decomposers which are essential to the recycling of essential nutrients, the insects, birds, and animals which are in turn linked to survival of plant systems. He is equally dependent upon the natural process of water purification by microorganisms. The operation of these nonhuman physical and biological processes is essential for human survival.

Having concluded that there can be neither a completely artificial nor a completely natural environment, our attention is directed to some determinants of optimal proportions. Some indication may be inferred from man's evolutionary history. His physiology and some significant part of his psychology derive from the billions of years of his biological history. During the most recent human phase of a million or so years, he has been preponderantly food gatherer, hunter, and, only recently, farmer. His urban experience is very recent indeed. Thus, the overwhelming proportion of his biological history has involved experience in vastly more natural environments than he now experiences. It is to these that he is physiologically adapted.

According to F. R. Fosberg:

> It is entirely possible that man will not survive the changed environment that he is creating, either because of failure of resources, war over their dwindling supply, or failure of his nervous system to evolve as rapidly as the change in environment will require. Or he may only survive in small numbers, suffering the drastic reduction that is periodically the lot of pioneer species, or he may change beyond our recognition. . . . Management and utilization of the environment on a true sustaining yield basis must be achieved. And all this must be accomplished without altering the environment beyond the capacity of the human organism, as we know it, to live in it.(1957, p. 160).

Human Ecosystems

There are several examples where ecosystems, dominated by man, have endured for long periods of time; the example of traditional Japanese agriculture is perhaps the most spectacular. Here an agriculture of unequaled intensity and productivity has been sustained for over a thousand years, the land is not impoverished but enriched by human intervention: the ecosystem, wild lands, and farmlands are complex, stable, highly productive, and beautiful. The pervasive effect of this harmony of man–nature is reflected in a language remarkable in its descriptive power of nature, a poetry succinct yet capable of the finest shades of meaning, a superb painting tradition in which nature is the icon, an architecture and town building of astonishing skill and beauty, and, not least, an unparalleled garden art in which nature and the garden are the final metaphysical symbol.

In the Western tradition, farming in Denmark and England has sustained high productivity for two or more centuries, appears stable, and is very beautiful; in the United States, comparable examples exist in Amish, Mennonite, and Pennsylvania Dutch farming.

Understanding of the relationship of man to nature is more pervasive and operative among farmers than any other laymen. The farmer perceives the source of his food in his crops of cereal, vegetables, roots, beef, fish, or game. He understands that, given a soil fertility, his crop is directly related to inputs of organic material, fertilizer, water, and sunlight. If he grows cotton or flax or tends sheep, he is likely to know the source of the fibers of his clothes. He recognizes timber, peat, and hydroelectric power as sources of fuel; he may well know of the organic source of coal and petroleum. Experience has taught him to ensure a functional separation between septic tank and well, to recognize the process of erosion, runoff, flood and drought, the differences of altitude and orientation. As a consequence of this acuity, the farmer has developed a formal expression which reflects an understanding of the major natural processes. Characteristically, high ground and steep slopes are given over to forest and woodland as a source of timber, habitat for game, element in erosion control, and water supply. The more gently sloping meadows below are planted to orchards, above the spring frost line, or in pasture. Here a seep, spring, or well is often the source of water supply. In the valley bottom, where floods have deposited rich alluvium over time, is the area of intensive cultivation. The farm buildings are related to conditions of climate and microclimate, above the flood plain, sheltered and shaded by the farm woodland. The septic tank is located in soils suitable for this purpose and below the elevation of the water source.

Here, at the level of the farm, can be observed the operation of certain simple, empirical rules and a formal expression which derives from them. The land is rich, and we find it beautiful.

Clearly, a comparable set of simple rules is urgently required for the city and the metropolis. The city dweller is commonly unaware of these natural processes, ignorant of his dependence upon them. Yet the problem of the place of nature in the city is more difficult than that of the farmer. Nature, as modified in farming, is intrinsic to the place. The plant community is relatively immobile, sunlight falls upon the site as does water, nutrients are cycled through the system in place. Animals in ecosystems have circumscribed territories, and the conjunction of plants and animals involves a utilization and cycling of energy and materials in quite limited areas. The modern city is, in this respect, profoundly different in that major natural processes which sustain the city, provide food, raw materials for industry, commerce, and construction, resources of water, and pure air are drawn not from the city or even its metropolitan area but from a national and even international hinterland. The major natural processes are not intrinsic to the locus of the city and cannot be.

Nature in the Metropolis

In the process of examining the place of nature in the city of man, it might be fruitful to consider the role of nature in the metropolitan area initially, as here, in the more rural fringes, can still be found analogies to the empiricism of the farmer. Here the operative principle might be that natural processes which perform work or offer protection in their natural form without human effort should have a presumption in their favor. Planning should recognize the values of these processes in decision-making for prospective land uses.

A more complete understanding of natural processes and their interactions must await the development of an ecological model of the metropolis. Such a model would identify the regional inventory of material in atmosphere, hydrosphere, lithosphere, and biosphere, identify inputs and outputs, and both describe and quantify the cycling and recycling of materials in the system. Such a model would facilitate recognition of the vital natural processes and their interdependence which is denied today. Lacking such a model, it is necessary to proceed with available knowledge. On a simpler basis, we can say that the major inputs in biological systems are sunlight, oxygen–carbon dioxide, food (including nutrients), and water. The first three are not limiting in the metropolis; water may well be limiting both as to quantity and quality. In addition, there are many other reasons for isolating and examining water in process. Water is the single most specific determinant of a large number of physical processes and is indispensable to all biological processes. Water, as the agent of erosion and sedimentation, is causal to geological evolution, the realities of physiography. Mountains, hills, valleys, and plains experience a variety of climate and microclimate consequent upon their physiography; the twin combination of physiography and climate determines the incidence and distribution of plants and animals, their niches, and habitats. Thus, using water as the point of departure, we can recognize its impact on the making of mountains and lakes, ridges and plains, forests and deserts, rivers, streams and marshes, the distribution of plants and animals. Lacking an ecological model, we may well select water as the best indicator of natural process. In any watershed, the uplands represent the majority of the watershed area. Assuming equal distribution of precipitation and ground conditions over the watershed, the maximum area will produce the maximum runoff. The profile of watersheds tends to produce the steeper slopes in the uplands with the slope diminishing toward the outlet. The steeper the slope, the greater is the water velocity. This combination of maximum runoff links maximum volume to maximum velocity—the two primary conditions of flood and drought. These two factors in turn exacerbate erosion, with the consequence of depositing silt in stream beds, raising flood plains, and increasing intensity and incidence of floods in piedmont and estuary.

The natural restraints to flooding and drought are mainly the presence and distribution of vegetation, particularly, on the uplands and their steep slopes. Vegetation absorbs and utilizes considerable quantities of water; the surface roots, trunks of trees, stems of shrubs and plants, the litter of forest floor mechanically retard the movement of water, facilitating percolation, increasing evaporation opportunity. A certain amount of water is removed temporarily from the system by absorption into plants, and mechanical retardation facilitates percolation, reduces velocity, and thus diminishes erosion. In fact, vegetation and their soils act as a sponge restraining extreme runoff, releasing water slowly over longer periods, diminishing erosion and sedimentation, in short, diminishing the frequency and intensity of oscillation between flood and drought.

Below the uplands of the watershed are characteristically the more shallow slopes and broad plains of the piedmont. Here is the land most often developed for agriculture. These lands, too, tend to be favored locations for villages, towns, and cities. Here, forests are residues or the products of regeneration on abandoned farms. Steep slopes in the piedmont are associated with streams and rivers. The agricultural piedmont does not control its own defenses. It is defended from flood and drought by the vegetation of the uplands. The vegetation cover and conservation practices in the agricultural piedmont can either exacerbate or diminish flood and drought potential; the piedmont is particularly vulnerable to both.

The incidence of flood and drought is not alone consequent upon the upland sponge but also upon estuarine marshes, particularly where these are tidal. Here at the mouth of the watershed at the confluence of important rivers or of river and sea, the flood component of confluent streams or the tidal component of floods assumes great importance. In the Philadelphia metropolitan area, the ocean and the estuary are of prime importance as factors in flood. A condition of intense precipitation over the region combined with high tides, full estuary, and strong onshore winds combines the elements of potential flood. The relation of environmental factors of the upland component and the agricultural piedmont to flood and drought has been discussed. The estuarine marshes and their vegetation constitute the major defense against the tidal components of floods. These areas act as enormous storage reservoirs absorbing mile-feet of potentially destructive waters, reducing flood potential.

This gross description of water-related processes offers determinism for the place of nature in the metropolis. From this description can be isolated several discrete and critical phases in the process. Surface water as rivers, streams, creeks, lakes, reservoirs, and ponds would be primary; the particular form of surface water in marshes would be another phase; the flood plain as the area temporarily occupied by water would be yet another. Two critical aspects of groundwater, the aquifer and its recharge areas, could be identified. Agricultural land has been seen to be a product of alluvial deposition, while steep slopes and forests play important roles in the process of runoff. If we could identify the proscriptions and permissiveness of these parameters to other land use, we would have an effective device for discriminating the relative importance of different roles of metropolitan lands. Moreover, if the major divisions of upland, piedmont, and estuary and the processes enumerated could be afforded planning recognition and legislative protection, the metropolitan area would derive its form from a recognition of natural process. The place of nature in the metropolis would be reflected in the distribution of water and flood plain, marshes, ridges, forests, and farmland, a matrix of natural lands performing work or offering protection and recreational opportunity distributed throughout the metropolis.

This conception is still too bald; it should be elaborated to include areas of important scenic value, recreational potential, areas of ecological, botanical, geological, or historic interest. Yet, clearly, the conception, analogous to the empiricism of the farmer, offers opportunity for determining the place of nature in the metropolis.

Nature in the City

The conception advocated for the metropolitan area has considerable relevance to the problem of the place of nature in the city of man. Indeed, in several cities, the fairest image of nature exists in these rare occasions where river, flood plain, steep slopes, and woodlands have been retained in their natural condition—the Hudson and Palisades in New York, the Schuylkill and Wissahickon in Philadelphia, the Charles River in Boston and Cambridge. If rivers, flood plains, marshes, steep slopes, and woodlands in the city were accorded protection to remain in their natural condition or were retrieved and returned to such a condition where possible, this single device, as an aspect of water quality, quantity, flood and drought control, would ensure for many cities an immeasurable improvement in the aspect of nature in the city, in addition to the specific benefits of a planned watershed. No other device has such an ameliorative power. Quite obviously, in addition to benefits of flood control and water supply, the benefits of amenity and recreational opportunity would be considerable. As evidence of this, the city of Philadelphia has a twenty-two-mile waterfront on the Delaware River. The most grandiose requirements for port facilities and water-related industries require only eight miles of waterfront. This entire waterfront lies in a flood plain. Levees and other flood protection devices have been dismissed as exorbitant. Should this land be transformed into park, it would represent an amelioration in Philadelphia of incomparable scale.

Should this conception of planning for water and water-related parameters be effectuated, it would provide the major framework for the role of nature in the city of man. The smaller elements of the face of nature are more difficult to justify. The garden and park, unlike house, shop, or factory, have little "functional" content. They are, indeed, more metaphysical symbol than utilitarian function. As such, they are not amenable to quantification or the attribution of value. Yet it is frequently the aggregation of these gardens and spaces which determines the humanity of a city. Values they do have. This is apparent in the flight to the suburbs for more natural environments—a self-defeating process of which the motives are clear. Equally, the selection of salubrious housing location in cities is closely linked to major open spaces which reflects the same impulse. The image of nature at this level is most important, the cell of the home, the street, and neighborhood. In the city slum, nature exists in the backyard ailanthus, sumac, in lice, cockroach, rat, cat, and mouse; in luxury highrise, there are potted trees over parking garages, poodles, and tropical fish. In the first case, nature reflects "disturbance" to the ecologist; it is somewhat analogous to the scab on a wound, the first step of regeneration towards equilibrium, a sere arrested at the most primitive level. In the case of the luxury highrise, nature is a canary in a cage, surrogate, an artifice, forbidden even the prospect of an arrested sere.

Three considerations seem operative at this level of concern. The first is that the response which nature induces, tranquillity, calm, introspection, openness to order, meaning and purpose, the place of values in the world of facts, is similar to the evocation from works of art. Yet nature is, or was, abundant; art and genius are rare.

The second consideration of some importance is that nature in the city is very tender. Woodlands, plants, and animals are very vulnerable to human erosion. Only expansive dimensions will support self-perpetuating and self-cleansing nature. There is a profound change between such a natural scene and a created and maintained landscape.

The final point is related to the preceding. If the dimensions are appropriate, a landscape will perpetuate itself. Yet, where a site has been sterilized, built upon, buildings demolished, the problem of creating a landscape, quite apart from creating a self-perpetuating one, is very considerable and the costs are high. The problems of sustaining a landscape, once made, are also considerable; the pressure of human erosion on open space in urban housing and the inevitable vandalism ensure that only a small vocabulary of primitive and hardy plants can survive. These factors, with abnormal conditions of groundwater, soil, air, atmospheric pollution, stripping, and girdling, limit nature to a very constricted image.

The Future

Perhaps, in the future, analysis of those factors which contribute to stress disease will induce inquiry into the values of privacy, shade, silence, the positive stimulus of natural materials, and the presence of comprehensible order, indeed natural beauty. When young babies lack fondling and a mother's love, they sometimes succumb to moronity and death. The dramatic reversal of this pattern has followed simple maternal solicitude. Is the absence of nature—its trees, water, rocks and herbs, sun, moon, stars, and changing seasons—a similar type of deprivation? The solicitude of nature, its essence if not its image, may be seen to be vital.

Some day, in the future, we may be able to quantify plant photosynthesis in the city and the oxygen in the atmosphere, the insulation by plants of lead from automobile exhausts, the role of diatoms in water purification, the amelioration of climate and microclimate by city trees and parks, the insurance of negative ionization by fountains, the reservoirs of air which, free of combustion, are necessary to relieve inversion pollution, the nature-space which a biological inheritance still requires, the stages in land regeneration and the plant and animal indicators of such regeneration, indeed, perhaps, even the plant and animal indicators of a healthy environment. We will then be able to quantify the necessities of a minimum environment to support physiological man. Perhaps we may also learn what forms of nature are necessary to satisfy the psychological memory of a biological ancestry.

Today, that place where man and nature are in closest harmony in the city is the cemetery. Can we hope for a city of man, an ecosystem in dynamic equilibrium, stable and complex? Can we hope for a city of man, an ecosystem with man dominant, reflecting natural processes, human and non-human, in which artifice and nature conjoin as art and nature, in a natural urban environment speaking to man as a natural being and nature as the environment of man? When we find the place of nature in the city of man, we may return to that enduring and ancient inquiry—place of man in nature.

References

Fosberg, F. R. 1958. "The Preservation of Man's Environment." In *Proceedings of the Ninth Pacific Science Congress*, 1957, 20.

Goddard, David F. 1960. *The House We Live In*. Transcript of the program broadcast on WCAU-TV (CBS), Channel 10, Philadelphia, Sunday, October 23, hosted and edited by Ian McHarg.

Leopold, Aldo. 1949. *A Sand County Almanac*. Oxford: Oxford University Press.

Mumford, Lewis. 1956. "Prospect." In William L. THomas, Jr., ed., *Man's Role in Changing the Face of the Earth*. Chicago: The University of Chicago Press, pp. 1132–52.

Sears, Paul B. 1956. "The Processes of Environmental Change by Man." In William L. Thomas, Jr., ed., *Man's Role in Changing the Face of the Earth*. Chicago: The University of Chicago Press, pp. 471–84.

3

Ecological Determinism (1966)

During the 1960s, McHarg directed his own efforts as well as those of his graduate students toward ways ecological principles could be applied to landscape architecture and environmental planning. This paper was presented at a conference convened by The Conservation Foundation in April, 1965, at Airlie House, Warrenton, Virginia. Subsequently it appeared in the book Future Environments of North America *edited by F. Fraser Darling and John P. Milton and published by The Natural History Press (the eventual publisher of* Design with Nature*). Darling, a distinguished British ecologist, pioneered the study of human ecology in the Scottish highlands. He showed how small technological innovations changed human settlements and landscapes. This paper is an early discussion of McHarg's theory for an ecological planning method.*

Introduction

In the Western world during the past century transformation of natural environments into human habitats has commonly caused a deterioration of the physical environment. However, much improvement to the social environment has been accomplished in these transformations; city slurb and slum are less attractive physical environments than forest, field, and farm that preceded them. In earlier times, because of the slow rate of change, unity of materials, structural method and expression, this was not so. Few among us regret the loss of ancient marshes on which Venice and Amsterdam sit, the loss of even more ancient hills which now seat Athens and Rome. History testifies to human adaptations, accomplished with wisdom and art, which were and are felicitous. Yet the principles which ensured these successes are inadequate for the speed, scale, and nature of change today. In the seventeenth century it required a third of the treasury of France, the mature life of Louis XIV, and the major effort of André Le Nôtre to realize Versailles. Three centuries later greater New York will urbanize at the rate of 50,000 acres and absorb 600,000 people into its perimeter each year without any plan. In the interim the classical city has been superseded by the industrial city, by metropolis, megalopolis, and now, in the opinion of Lewis Mumford, is en route to Necropolis. Paradoxically in this period of change the city plan has remained the Renaissance archetype which motivated Versailles, a poor symbol of man–nature in the seventeenth century, an inexcusable prototype for the twentieth century.

It is clear that the principles which contributed to historic successes in urban form have failed dismally since the industrial revolution. The success of the subsequent city as provider of employment and social services is its best testimony, but as a physical environment it has continually retrogressed. New principles must be developed for human adaptations, for city, metropolis, and megalopolis.

The problem is an enormous one both in extent and speed of change. Three hundred million Americans are expected to populate the United States in the year 2000. If indeed 80 percent of these will live in urban places, then this involves the urbanization of 55 million acres of non-urbanized land. If one extrapolates from the present megalopolis to this future population, then 10 percent of the land area of the United States, 200 million acres, will fall within urban influence, comparable to megalopolis, in a mere 35 years.

Today, the prescriptions for urban location, form, and growth derive almost exclusively from the social sciences. Both analytic and predictive models are based upon economics. The natural sciences have remained aloof from the problem, yet the understanding of physical and biological processes, which reposes in these sciences, is indispensable for good judgment on the problems of human adaptations of environment.

Many central questions can best be answered by natural scientists but at the onset one alone can suffice. What are the implications of natural process upon the location and form of development? The answer to this is vital to administrators, regional and city planners, architects and landscape architects. For the last it is the indispensable basis for their professional role. As the representative of a profession with a historic concern for the relation of man to nature and the single bridge between the natural sciences and the artificers of the urban environment, it is not inappropriate that the spokesperson for this group ask for the formulation of an ecological determinism.

Landscape Architecture

In the Western tradition, with the single exception of the English eighteenth century and its extension, landscape architecture has been identified with garden making, be it Alhambra, Saint Gall, the Villa d'Este, or Versailles. In this tradition decorative and tractable plants are arranged in a simple geometry as a comprehensible metaphysical symbol of a benign and orderly world.

Here the ornamental qualities of plants are paramount; no concepts of community or association becloud the objective. Plants are analogous to domestic pets, dogs, cats, ponies, canaries, and goldfish, tolerant to man and dependent upon him; lawn grasses, hedges, flowering shrubs and trees, tractable and benign, man's cohorts, sharing his domestication.

This is the walled garden, separated from nature, a symbol of beneficence, island of delight, tranquillity, introspection. It is quite consistent that the final symbol of this garden is the flower.

Not only is this a selected nature, decorative and benign, but the order of its array is, unlike the complexity of nature, reduced to a simple and comprehensible geometry. This is then a selected nature, simply ordered to create a symbolic reassurance of a benign and orderly world, an island within the world and separate from it. Yet the knowledge prevails that nature reveals a different form and aspect beyond the wall. Loren Eiseley has said that "the unknown within the self is linked to the wild." The garden symbolizes domesticated nature, the wild is beyond.

The role of garden making remains important. Man seeks a personal paradise on earth, a unity of man and nature. The garden is such a quest for a personal oasis, a paradise garden. In these, man can find peace and in tranquillity discover, in Kenneth Rexroth's words, "the place of value in a world of facts." He can respond to natural materials, water, stone, herbs, trees, sunlight and shadow, rain, ice and snow, the changing seasons, birth, life and death. This is a special microhabitat, a healthy cell in the organism of the city, a most humane expression, yet clearly its relevance, depending upon ornamental horticulture and simple geometry, is inadequate for the leap over the garden wall.

In the eighteenth century in England landscape architects "leap't the wall and discovered all nature to be a garden." The leap did not occur until a new view of nature dispelled the old and a new esthetic was developed consonant with the enlarged arena.

Starting with a denuded landscape, a backward agriculture, and a medieval pattern of attenuated land holdings, this landscape tradition rehabilitated an entire countryside, making that fair image persisting today. It is a testimony to the prescience of William Kent, Lancelot "Capability" Brown, Humphry Repton, and their followers that, lacking a science of ecology, they used native plant materials to create communities which so well reflected natural processes that their creations endured and are self-perpetuating.

The functional objective was a productive, working landscape. Hilltops and hillsides were planted to forest, great meadows occupied the valley bottoms in which lakes were constructed and streams meandered. The product of this new landscape was the extensive meadow supporting cattle, horses, and sheep. The forests provided valuable timber, the lack of which Evelyn had earlier deplored, and supported game, while free-standing copses in the meadows provided shade and shelter for animals.

The planting reflected the necessities of shipbuilding but the preferred trees, oak and beech, were climax species and they were planted *de novo*. On sites where these were inappropriate, northern slopes, thin soils, elevations, pine and birch were planted. Watercourses were graced with willows, alders, osiers, while the meadows supported grasses and meadow flowers. As long as the meadow was grazed, a productive sere was maintained and meanwhile the forests evolved.

The objective, however, was more complex than function alone. Paintings of the *campagna* by Claude Lorrain, Nicolas Poussin, and Salvator Rosa, a eulogy of nature which obsessed poets and writers, had developed the concept of an ideal nature. Yet it clearly did not exist in the raddled landscape of eighteenth-century England. It had to be created. The ruling principle was that "nature is the gardener's best designer," applied ecology of yesteryear. Ornamental horticulture, which had been obtained within garden walls, was disdained and a precursory ecology replaced it. The meadow was the single artifice, the remaining components were natural expressions, their dramatic and experiential qualities exploited, it is true, but deriving in the first place from that observed in nature.

Nature itself produced the esthetic; the simple geometry, not simplicity but simple-mindedness, of the Renaissance was banished. "Nature abhors a straight line" was declaimed. The discovery of an established esthetic in the Orient based upon occult balance, asymmetry, confirmed this view. In the eighteenth century, landscape began the revolution which banished the giant classicism and the imposition of its geometry as a symbol of man–nature.

This tradition is important in many respects. It founded applied ecology as the basis for function and esthetics in the landscape. Indeed before the manifesto of modern architecture had been propounded, "Form follows function," it had been superseded by the eighteenth-century concept wherein form and process were seen to be indivisible facets of a single phenomenon. It is important because of the scale of operation. One recalls that Capability Brown, when asked to undertake a project in Ireland, retorted, "I have not finished England yet." Another reason for its importance lies in the fact that it was a creation. Here the landscape architect, like the empiricist doctor, found a land in ill-health and brought it into good heart and to beauty. Man the artist, understanding nature's laws and forms, accelerated the process of regeneration so well indeed that who today can discern the artifice from the untouched?

It is hard to find fault with this tradition but one must observe that while the principles of ecology and its esthetic are general, the realization of this movement was particular. It reflects in agricultural economy, principally based upon cattle, horses, and sheep. It never confronted the city, which in the eighteenth century remained the Renaissance prototype. Only in the urban square, parks and circuses, in natural plantings, was the eighteenth-century city distinguishable from its antecedents.

The successes of this tradition are manifest. No other movement has accomplished such a physical regeneration and amelioration. Its basis lies in applied ecology. It is necessary that modern ecology become the basis for modern interventions particularly at the scale of city, metropolis, and megalopolis, if we are to avert Necropolis.

Ecological Determinism

Processes are expressive; morphology is a superficial expression of the process examined. The creation of a twentieth-century tradition requires an understanding of natural process and the morphology of the artifacts of man as process. Thus, natural processes are deterministic, they respond to laws; they then give form to human adaptations which themselves contain symbolic content.

Beehive huts, igloos, stilt homes on marshes are morphologically determined. We need today an understanding of natural process and its expression and, even more, an understanding of the morphology of man–nature, which, less deterministic, still has its own morphology, the expression of man–nature as process. The eighteenth century developed a morphology for a pastoral landscape in England. What are the prerequisites for discerning the appropriate morphologies for our time?

I believe that there are six elements which are required:

1. Ecosystem inventory
2. Description of natural processes
3. Identification of limiting factors
4. Attribution of value
5. Determination of prohibitions and permissiveness to change
6. Identification of indicators of stability or instability

The final for the artificers is then the perception of the revealed morphology and its realization.

Ecosystem Inventory

The eighteenth-century landscape architects were only fair taxonomists, but, by using collected material, transferring from site to like site and planting in communities, they avoided the errors of caprice, ornamental horticulture, and much traditional forestry. In the intervening years descriptive ecology has developed the concept of community. In the Philadelphia region the identification of open water, reed swamp, sedge meadow, secondary succession, mixed mesophytic forest, and pine barrens has great utility. Recent work which refines these descriptions by identifying gradients adds value to this technique. The conception of range from hydrosere to zerosere is of great value but it is the conception of succession, sere, and climax which adds dynamics to the eighteenth-century view. The first prerequisite for the application of ecology to the planning process is the preparation of ecosystem inventories. This involves the creation of ecological maps at various scales in which communities are identified. The inventory should also include the city. The ailanthus-pigeon-starling "community" is quite as important as the oak-beech-hickory forest. The ecosystem inventory is the basis for planning related to natural processes.

Description of Natural Processes

Inventories and ecological maps have to be supplemented by explanation of natural processes. In particular the stability or instability stage in succession of ecosystems must be described. While this is important for all communities it is particularly necessary for major physiographic regions—coastal plains, piedmont, uplands, etc—and for certain discrete environments—pine barrens, estuarine environment, mixed mesophytic forest, sand dunes, etc. In the city the relation of atmospheric pollution to isolation photosynthesis CO_2 consumption is typical of a human process which affects ecosystems. Transformation of farmland to subdivision and erosion-turbidity-reduced photosynthesis and natural water purification are other examples. Descriptions of natural processes and the degree to which they are affected by man are a vital component of this body of information.

Identification of Limiting Factors

It is important to establish what factors are necessary to ensure the perpetuation of any ecosystem; apart from factors in abundance, which elements are critical—water-plane-table elevation, alkalinity, acidity, fire, first and last frost, etc. This category must be extensive enough to include limiting factors external to the ecosystem under study such as, for example, transformation of a fresh-water into a salt-water marsh through channel deepening and river widening.

Attribution of Value

In eighteenth-century England the land was thought to be the arena for the creation of a metaphysical symbol—all nature is a garden. Nature was attributed a value which transcended any concept of productivity, the landscape was also productive. In the twentieth century, when nature desperately needs a defense in the face of disdain, disinterest, and remorseless despoliation, the first defense is certainly non-economic, the insistence that man is a co-tenant of the universe, sharing the phenomenal world of living and inert processes, an organism in an interacting biosphere. From this some people will conclude that nature is a manifestation of God, others that the cosmos is unitary, all processes subject to physical law yet having infinite potential, that man is an inhabitant free to develop his potential. Each of these views contains an inherent deference, a posture of serious inquiry, and the instinct to exercise care, intelligence, and art in accomplishing human interventions. Such a view characterized eighteenth-century landscape architects, nineteenth-century naturalists, and today is associated with conservationists.

The search for a theology of man–nature–God does not exclude exchanges which involve the coinage of the time and place. This requires that the proponents of nature also attribute values to nature processes so that these may be recognized as parameters in the planning process. Indeed, given ecological inventories, explanation of natural processes, and identification of limiting factors, the next increment of knowledge essential for an applied ecology is precisely the attribution of value to these natural processes.

Four major divisions of value can be discerned: intrinsic value, value as productivity, value as work performed, and, finally, negative value as discouragement to use.

Intrinsic value is thought to exist wherein the landscape neither is "productive" nor "performs work" but simply is. Areas of wilderness, scenic beauty, scientific value, and educational value might fall into this category.

Productivity would include agriculture, forestry, fisheries, extractive minerals, recreation, gamelands, a concept in common usage.

The attribution of value based upon work performed might include water catchment, water purification and storage, flood, drought and erosion control, hydroelectric power generation, "airshed," climate, and microclimate amelioration.

Negative value would include those areas wherein there is a hazard and whence occupancy should be discouraged. No occupancy would avert costs and damages. Thus areas subject to earthquakes, volcanism, hurricanes, avalanches, floods, drought, subsidence, and forest fires should fall into this category.

All of these subdivisions can be subject to the concept of replacement value, a most useful concept which can apply at several scales. For example, in the case of a city park planned for an expressway intersection, the value is not "land value" alone but rather the entire cost of replicating the park including the cost of equally mature trees, shrubs, etc. Where it is intended to fill a marsh, the replacement value would include the cost of equal flood protection, water equalization, and wildlife habitats on another site. In the case of transforming prime agricultural land to housing, replacement value would include the cost of upgrading poorer soils to prime capability. Given attribution of value to natural processes, the concept of replacement value provides an important measuring device for alternative choices. No other device offers a comparable restraint to thoughtless despoliation.

Clearly the concept of value poses many difficulties, the change of value over time is one. Low-grade ores, presently marginal farmland, undistinguished rural areas can increase in value with increased demand and shrunken supply. In addition, value is relative. If, as in the Netherlands, survival is linked to the stability of the dunes, then marram and sedge are valuable. If no such a role exists, then dune grasses are merely decorative. If diatoms are needed for water treatment, then they have value. If water is treated with coagulants, rapid sand filter, and chlorine, then diatoms have, in this local case, no value. Marshes can be seen either as costly obstructions to development or as invaluable defenses against flood; in one case they represent costs, in another they represent values. Another problem arises from the geographic scale of natural process and interdependence. The Mississippi watershed unites suburban Chicago with New Orleans; effects upon water quality will affect values in the entire downstream area. The requirements of clean air unite western and eastern United States. There is no method of accounting which relates snowfall in the Rockies to the value of water in California, no accounting which attributes value to forests of upstream watersheds and flood control in the lower Mississippi. The final difficulty in attribution of value lies in unmeasurable qualities. Who will attribute value to the whooping crane, grizzly bear, or pasque flower? Yet the inability to attribute value to serenity, happiness, and health has not deterred economic determinism. In spite of difficulties, the attribution of value to natural process is a necessary precondition for applied ecology as a basis for determining non-intervention, intervention, and the nature, scale, and location of such intervention.

Determination of Prohibitions and Permissiveness to Change

Given descriptive ecological inventories, supplemented by descriptions of natural process and limiting factors, with a scale of values, the necessary information is available to establish the constraints inherent in natural process which should affect the location and nature of development.

This finally produces the program. No longer is nature an undifferentiated scene, lacking values, defenseless against transformation; it is seen to be a complex interrelated system, in process, having discernible limiting factors, containing values, present or prospective, and, finally, containing both constraints and opportunities. For example, the Arctic and Antarctic; bare mountains, oceans, and perhaps beaches are highly tolerant to human use. Other systems are highly intolerant, wild animals retreat or succumb, natural plant communities are erased and superseded by man's cohorts in the processes of agriculture, industry, and urbanism. Can we select environments, more suitable than these extremely tolerant examples, which, satisfactory for man, are unusually tolerant to him? Can one set limits on transformation of natural habitats implicit in the processes themselves? Thus, how much housing can a forest absorb and still perform an attributed role in the water regimen? How much development can occur on a marsh without destroying its role of water equalization, emergency flood storage, or wildlife habitat? What proportion of an aquifer can be waterproofed by urbanism before its percolation performance is diminished below a required level? The answer to such questions, and many others, is prerequisite to the application of ecology to the planning process.

For the regional planner, landscape architect, city planner, and architect, the development of concepts of prohibition and permissiveness inherent in natural process is the beginning of a modern applied ecology, the gift of natural form, the program for intervention which has relevance to the house and its site, the subdivision, hamlet, village, town, city, metropolis, megalopolis, and the nation.

Identification of Indicators of Stability or Instability

The concept of ecological determinism requires criteria of performance. For pond ecosystems it may be possible to determine stability or instability from the entropy in the system. It seems unlikely that this concept will be capable of dealing with extensive geographic areas or with the problem of the city. Clearly for the moment some simpler devices are necessary by which stability or instability, succession, sere or climax can be discerned; indeed, there is a desperate need for a concept of a "healthy" and "healthful" environment. We need analogies to litmus paper, the canary in the cage, indicators of health and change. Ruth Patrick has developed histograms from which the "state of health" of Pennsylvania streams may be discerned. Luna Leopold has propounded the measure of a "duration curve" against which stability or instability of stream processes can be examined. This writer has advocated the use of the "coefficient of runoff" as a planning determinant for land use relative to the water regimen. "Sky blue" is a measure of the relative presence of atmospheric pollution. The presence of trace metals in the environment is being investigated as an indicator of health. The technique of indicators is established, but it must be extended, not only to "natural" environments, but also to include those dominated by man.

Can we proceed from broad presumptions which have utility while evidence is collected and analyzed? Can one say that where trees cannot live, then man should not try? Can one say that when the most abundant inhabitants, with man, are pigeons, starlings, and rats, a threshold has been crossed and either evacuation or redevelopment is necessary?

It is important that stable and healthy forests, marshes, deserts, rivers, and streams can be defined, that succession and retrogression can be identified, but it is even more necessary to find comparable definitions and indicators for the city. This moves the subject from the orthodoxy of ecology yet those concerned with the environment are the cohorts of medicine. Pathology is the concern of the medical sciences, the environment of health must be the concern of the artificers, but they require from ecologists an identification of healthy and healthful environments.

The role of the ecologists would include the identification of "healthy environments"—that is, for example, a forest wherein trees, shrubs, animals, and fish were conspicuously healthy and a determination of those factors which were contributory to this condition. Healthy natural environments could then be used as criteria against which adjacent urban environments could be compared.

In the city, examination of health or pathology devolves upon the social and medical sciences. It is necessary to determine stressors, the pathology of stress, and the environment of stress. Among stressors the poisons of food, atmosphere and water, density, noise, sensory overload, and sensory deprivation would be included. The pathology of stress—mortality, cancer, heart disease, suicide, alcoholism, crime, neuroses, and psychoses—might be mapped as isobars, and from the incidence and distribution of both stressors and stress disease the environments of stress may be located.

Given identification of healthy "natural" environments and the urban environments of stress pathology, diagnosis of environments becomes possible and therapy can be prescribed. There are environmental variables linked to most urban stressors. In this search for health and pathology in environments, indicators could serve a valuable role in diagnosis. In Philadelphia does the presence of hemlock indicate a tolerable level of particulate matter in the atmosphere? What plant pathology indicates a dangerous level of lead? Are there indicators of sulphur dioxide or nitrogen dioxide at "safe" levels? What creatures can coexist with levels of noise preferred by man? What indicators can be found for the optimum distribution of trace metals? Which reveal optimal concentrations? What can be inferred of human environments when trees degenerate?

This line of inquiry might well be unproductive yet there are now no operative standards of environmental quality, no limits are placed upon density, poisons, noise, no criteria are available as measures of existing environments or as programs for new environments.* It is clear that criteria are need-

---

*Since this essay was written, the Clean Air Acts, the Clean Water Acts, and several other laws have established standards for environmental quality and have placed limits on pollution.

ed, and for the empiricist planner, indicators could be a vital tool. The conception of succession or retrogression, stability and instability must be utilized in the examination not only of wild environment, but of those environments dominated by man.

Where does the canary expire, the litmus change color? Where is the disgenic zone, the area of apathetic survival, the environment of full health—and what are the indicators?

The Morphology of Ecological Determinism

Each year a million acres of rural land succumb to hot-dog stands, sagging wires, billboards, diners, gas stations, split-levels, ranches, asphalt, and concrete. Most of this is accomplished without benefit of planning, landscape architecture, or architecture. Where these professionals intervene they utilize some part of available knowledge, the best of them are pressing for better information, yet action must occur even when information is inadequate.

This apologia precedes a description of three experiences in which the writer has been involved, each crude in terms of the available information and the interpretations made, yet, for all of their crudity, so effective in giving form as to justify description. These experiences permit extrapolation on the form of ecological determinism.

New Jersey Shore

From the fifth to the eighth of March 1962 a violent storm lashed the northeast coast from Georgia to Long Island. For three days sixty-mile-per-hour winds whipped high spring tides across 1,000 miles of ocean. Forty-foot waves pounded the shore and vast stretches of barrier islands and bay shore were flooded. In New Jersey alone, 2,400 houses were wrecked, 8,300 partially damaged, and eighty million dollars' worth of direct damages incurred over a three-day period. Almost all of this damage was caused by ignorance of natural process and the resultant destruction of the natural defenses against flood. In this case an ecological inventory existed, natural processes in the beach-bay-shore communities had been described and limiting factors identified, the values involved could be inferred from damages and costs. The requirements requested by this chapter for all ecosystems were satisfied in this one situation.

The theory of dune formation is well understood, as is stabilization by vegetation. The ecological communities from beach dune to bay shore have been identified, as have been their limiting factors. In the Netherlands the value of dunes and their stabilizing grasses, and the important role of groundwater are known and attributed value, but not, however, in New Jersey. It is common knowledge that beaches are highly tolerant to human use but that dunes and their grasses are not. Development of the Jersey shore included breaching of dunes for many purposes—home building, beach access, etc. No constraints were placed upon use of dunes so that vegetation died and the dunes became unstable; no effective restraints were placed upon withdrawals of groundwater which inhibited vegetation growth. Considerable areas were waterproofed by buildings, roads, parking areas, which diminished recharge of the aquifers. The consequences were inevitable: With its natural defenses destroyed, the shore was vulnerable and was extensively damaged.

Had development responded to an understanding of natural process, ecological determinism, much if not all of the damage could have been averted. The form of development, however, would have been quite different. The beach, highly tolerant, would have been intensively utilized; the dunes, generally two in number between sea and bay, would have been inviolate, protected, stabilized by marram; access to the beach would have been made possible by bridges over the dunes; woody vegetation would have been protected in the trough; development would have been excluded from dunes and located only in wide areas of trough and on the bay side. Roads and parking would have been constructed of flexible, permeable materials; drainage would have been used for aquifer recharge; buildings would have been of columnar construction; withdrawals of groundwater would have been regulated. The application of this determinism, responsive to natural process, would have located buildings, roads, and drainage systems and determined their form. It would have been the principal determinant of planning, landscape architecture, and architecture. It would indeed produce the morphology of man-dune-bay for the New Jersey shore.

The Green Springs and Worthington Valleys

Seventy square miles of beautiful farmland adjacent to Baltimore were made accessible by the construction of a new expressway. The present population [in 1966] of 17,000 was predicted to rise to 75,000 by 1980, to 110,000 by the year 2000. It became necessary to determine where best this development would be located to ensure the conjunction of optimum development and optimum preservation. The conception of ecological determinism was invoked.

The area is characterized by three major valleys contained by wooded slopes with a large intervening plateau. It transpired that the valley bottoms were coterminous with the major aquifers in the region, that in the valleys were the major surface water systems, flood plains, and extensive soils unsuitable for development using septic tanks. The major source of erosion lay in the slopes defining the valleys. The plateau in contrast contained no major aquifers or minor streams; flood plains were absent, as were soils unsuitable for development using septic tanks.

Ecological determinism suggested prohibition of development in the valleys, prohibitions of development on bare slopes, development limited to one house per three acres on wooded slopes. In contrast, development was concentrated upon the plateau in a hierarchy of country town, villages, and hamlets, related in response to physiography. Development in wooded plateau sites was limited to one house per acre; this standard was waived on promontory sites, where high-rise apartments were recommended.

In this example, ecological analysis revealed the morphology of development; it selected the plateau as most tolerant, the valley bottoms and side slopes as least tolerant. It suggested densities of use appropriate to natural process. When this analysis was carried to a more detailed examination of the plateau, this, too, demonstrated variability in both opportunity and intolerance which suggested a hierarchy of communities, hamlets, villages, and a country town instead of pervasive suburbanization. Here the utilization of a very few determinants—surface water, groundwater, flood plains, alluvial silts, steep slopes, forest cover, and an interpretation of their permissiveness and prohibitions, revealed the morphology of man and the Maryland piedmont.

Metropolitan Open Space from Natural Processes

The Urban Renewal Agency and the states of Pennsylvania and New Jersey supported a research project to establish criteria for the selection of metropolitan open space. The hypothesis advanced was that such criteria can best be discerned by extending the inquiry to examine the operation of the major physical and biological processes in the region. It was suggested that when this is understood, and land-use policies reflect this understanding, not only will the values of natural process be ensured, the place for nature in the metropolis of man, but also there will be discerned a structure of natural process in the metropolitan area, form-giving for metropolitan growth, and the identification of areas for metropolitan open space, recreation, and amenity.

In the country at large and even in metropolitan areas, open space is seen to be absolutely abundant. In the Philadelphia Standard Metropolitan Statistical Area (PSMSA) only 19.1 percent of the area is urbanized; twenty years hence this may reach 30 percent, leaving 2,300 square miles of open space.

The problem of metropolitan open space lies, then, not in absolute area, but in distribution. The commodity concept of open space for amenity or recreation would suggest an interfusion of open space and population. The low attributed value of open space ensures that it is transformed into urban use within the urban area and at the perimeter. Normal process excludes interfusion and consumes peripheral open space.

Yet as the area of a circle follows the square of the radius, large open-space increments can exist within the urban perimeter without major increase in the radius or in the time distance from city center to urban fringe.

The major recommendation of this study was that the aggregate value of land, water, and air resources does justify a land-use policy which reflects both the value and operation of natural processes. Further, that the identification of natural processes, the permissiveness and prohibitions which they exhibit, revealed a system of open space which directs metropolitan growth and offers sites for metropolitan open space.

The characteristics of natural processes were examined; an attempt was made to identify their values, intrinsic value, work performed, and protection afforded. Large-scale functions were identified with the major physiographic divisions of uplands, coastal plain, and piedmont; smaller-scale functions of air-water corridors were identified; and finally, eight discrete parameters were selected for examination. These were: surface water, marshes, flood plains, aquifers, aquifer recharge areas, steep slopes, forests and woodlands, and prime agricultural lands.

For each of the discrete phenomena, and for each successive generalization, approximate permissiveness to other land uses and specific prohibitions were suggested. While all were permissive to a greater or lesser degree, all performed their natural process best in an unspoiled condition. Clearly, if land is abundant and land-use planning can reflect natural process, a fabric of substantially natural land can remain either in low-intensity use or undeveloped, interfused throughout the metropolitan region. It is from this land that metropolitan open space can best be selected.

When this concept was applied to the PSMSA, the uplands were discerned as performing an important role in natural process and offering a specific range of recreational opportunity. The coastal plain was observed to perform an equally important but very different role and offered another range of recreational potential. Uniting uplands and coastal plain to the central city are major air-water corridors, while at the lowest level exist the distribution of the eight parameters selected.

In general, planning for natural process would select uplands, coastal plains, and air-water corridors to remain relatively undeveloped; it would confirm urbanization in the piedmont. It would protect surface water, and riparian lands, exempt flood plains from development by land uses other than those unimpaired by flooding or inseparable from waterfront locations, exclude development from marshlands and ensure their role as major water storage areas, limit development on aquifer resources and their recharge areas, protect prime farmland as present and prospective resources of agricultural productivity and scenic beauty, ensure the erosion-control function of forested steep slopes and ridges, and ensure their role, with forests and woodlands, in the water economy, and as a scenic-beauty and recreational potential.

Land Type	Recommended Uses
Surface water and riparian lands	Ports, harbors, marinas, water-treatment plants, water-related industry, certain water-using industry, open space for institutions and housing, agriculture, forestry, recreation.
Marshes	Recreation.
Fifty-year flood plain	Ports, harbors, marinas, water-treatment plants, water-related and water-using industry, agriculture, forestry, recreation, institutional open space, open space of housing.
Aquifers	Agriculture, forestry, recreation, industries that do not produce toxic or offensive effluents. All land uses within limits set by percolation.
Aquifer recharge areas	As aquifers.
Prime agricultural lands	Agriculture, forestry, recreation, open space of institutions, housing at one house per twenty-five acres.
Steep lands	Forestry, recreation, housing at maximum density of one house per three acres.
Forests and woodlands	Forestry, recreation, housing at densities not higher than one house per acre, other factors permitting.

Certain environmentally sensitive lands can be used for some purposes with restrictions. For example, recommended uses for such lands in the Philadelphia metropolitan area are as follows:

This concept, if realized, would ensure a structured system of open space within the metropolitan area within which only limited development would occur. It would produce the "natural" morphology of the metropolis. Due to the small number of parameters examined, this is a coarse-grain study. By increasing the number of phenomena and replacing the descriptive account of natural process by accurate quantitative analysis, the value of this information could be compounded.

The importance of these three examples lies simply in the fact that the commonplaces of natural science, where applied to planning, can be intensely illuminating and provide form in a most dramatic way from the level of the house on the shore to the form of metropolis.

Conclusion

Today, in the face of momentous change in which urbanization is one of the most dramatic phenomena, nature is seen to be defenseless against the positive acts of transformation. The proponents of nature emphasize preservation: a negative position, one of defense, which excludes positive participation in the real and difficult tasks of creating noble and ennobling cities in fair landscapes. Meanwhile, the positive acts of urbanism proceed without perception of natural process, blind to its operation, values, and form-giving rules, scarcely modified by appeals for preservation and protection, remorseless in destruction, and impotent in constructive creation.

The negative view of conservation and the disinterest of natural science in problems of planning and urbanism are disservices to society. The redirection of concern to include not only wild environments, but also those dominated by people is a challenge which the natural sciences and their public arm—conservation—must confront and accept. Understanding of natural process is of central importance to all environmental problems and must be introduced into all considerations of land utilization.

The burden of this chapter is a request to natural scientists, particularly ecologists, to provide the indispensable information which the artificers require—ecological inventories, explanation of natural processes and identification of their limiting factors, the attribution of value, the indicators of healthy and unhealthy environments, and, finally, the degree of permissiveness or prohibition to transformation, implicit in natural processes.

Given this information, those who bring goodwill to the problems of resource planning and urbanism may add knowledge. This information can provide the basis for persuasion in both private and public domains; it can indeed provide the basis for a federal land-use policy based upon natural processes.

Such information can identify roles with geographic locations and attribute values to them. Thus, catastrophe-prone and danger areas would be prohibited to development—earthquake, volcanic, hurricane, avalanche, flood, drought, fire, and subsidence zones; areas having great intrinsic value—wilderness areas, wildlife habitats, areas of great scenic beauty, areas having important scientific and educational value, would be identified and exempted from development; the concept of "work performed" would permit identification of constituent roles—water-catchment areas, dunes, flood, drought-and erosion-control areas, flood plains, airsheds, etc., on which only limited development, responsive to natural process, could occur. Positively this information could select areas suitable for development, tolerant to man. The final component, the indicator, would permit diagnosis and prescription for existing environments.

This ecological information is thus deterministic and might well be called ecological determinism. It reveals the megaform of natural processes at the national level, the mezoform of the region, the microform of the city. From the city down to the level of its parts, ecological determinants become participant parameters in the planning process, but still influential as form-giving.

Precursory ecology made possible the leap over the garden wall in the eighteenth century, but the landscape created was a pastoral one. Modern ecology can enable us to leap more surely into many different environments, reserving some, intervening with deference in others, accomplishing great and wise transformations for human habitats in certain selected locations. When the program is developed and understood, when pervasive, then the artist will make it manifest. His interventions will become metaphysical symbols revealed in art.

The search is then for the place of nature in the city of man and, even more profoundly, for the place of man in nature.

References

McHarg, Ian L., Roger D. Clemence, Ayre M. Dvir, Geoffrey A. Collins, Michael Laurie, William J. Oliphant, and Peter Ker Walker. 1963. *Sea, Storm and Survival, A Study of the New Jersey Shore* (mim.). Philadelphia: Department of Landscape Architecture, University of Pennsylvania.

McHarg, Ian L., David A. Wallace, Ann Louise Strong, William Grigsby, Anthony Tomazinis, Nohad Toulan, William H. Roberts, Donald Phimister, and Frank

Shaw. 1963. *Metropolitan Open Space from Natural Processes* (mim.). Philadelphia: Department of Landscape Architecture, University of Pennsylvania.

Wallace, David A., and Ian L. McHarg. 1964. *Plan for the Valleys*. Philadelphia: Wallace-McHarg Associates.

4

Values, Process and Form (1968)

This paper was published while Design with Nature *was being written. McHarg first tested his theoretical concepts on applied ecology in this article, to an audience at the Institute for Advanced Study at Princeton University. He was "absolutely terrified" because of the stature of the audience. McHarg was so gratified by the positive response that he gave the paper again at the Smithsonian Institution, the version that appears here and that was published in* The Fitness of Man's Environment *(Harper and Row). Essentially, McHarg was seeking confirmation for his ideas about ecology and was able to present theories, which he considered risky coming from a landscape architect, to audiences of distinguished scientists at Princeton and the Smithsonian.*

It is my proposition that, to all practical purposes, Western man remains obdurately pre-Copernican, believing that he bestrides the earth round which the sun, the galaxy, and the very cosmos revolve. This delusion has fueled our ignorance in time past and is directly responsible for the prodigal destruction of nature and for the encapsulating burrows that are the dysgenic city.

We must see nature and man as an evolutionary process which responds to laws, which exhibits direction, and which is subject to the final test of survival. We must learn that nature includes an intrinsic value-system in which the currency is energy and the inventory is matter and its cycles—the oceans and the hydrologic cycle, life forms and their roles, the cooperative mechanisms which life has developed, and, not least, their genetic potential. The measure of success in this process, in terms of the biosphere, is the accumulation of negentropy in physical systems and ecosystems, the evolution of apperception or consciousness, and the extension of symbioses—all of which might well be described as creation.

This can be pictured simply in a comparison between the early earth and the present planet. In the intervening billions of years the earth has been transformed and the major change has been in the increase of order. Think of the turbulence and violence of the early earth, racked by earthquakes and vulcanism, as it evolved toward equilibrium, and of the unrestrained movements of water, the dust storms of unstabilized soils, and the extreme alternations of climate unmodified by a green, meliorative vegetative cover. In this early world physical processes operated toward repose, but in the shallow bays there emerged life and a new kind of ordering was initiated. The atmosphere which could sustain life was not the least of the creations of life. Life elaborated in the seas and then colonized the earth, thus increasing the opportunities for life and for evolution. Plants and decomposers created the soils, anchored the surface of the earth, checked the movements of soil particles, modified water processes, meliorated the climate, and ordered the distribution of nutrients. Species evolved to occupy and create more habitats, more niches, each increase requiring new cooperative relationships between organisms—new roles, all of which were beneficial. In the earth's history can be seen the orderings which life has accomplished: the increase to life forms, habitats and roles, symbiotic relationships, and the dynamic equilibrium in the system—the total an increase in order. This is creation.

In the early earth, the sunlight which fell upon the planet equaled the degraded energy which was radiated from it. Since the beginning of plant life, some of the sun's energy has been entrapped by photosynthesis and employed with matter to constitute the ordered beings of plants; thence, to the animals and decomposers, and all of the orderings which they have accomplished. This energy will surely be degraded, but the entrapped energy, with matter, is manifest in all life forms past and present, and in all of the orderings which they have accomplished. Thus, creation equals the energy which has been temporarily entrapped and used with matter to accomplish all of the ordering of physical, biological, and cultural evolution. This, physicists describe as negentropy, in contrast with the inevitable degradation of energy which is described as entropy.

By this we see the world as a creative process involving all matter and all life forms in all time past and in the present. Thus, creation reveals two forms: first, the physical entrapment and ordering which is accomplished primarily by plants and by the simplest animals; and, second, apperception and the resulting ordering for which an increased capacity is observed as species rise in the phylogenetic scale. In this, man is seen to be especially endowed. This view of the world as a creative process involving all of its denizens, including man, in a cooperative enterprise, is foreign to the Western tradition that insists upon the exclusive divinity of man, his independent superiority, dominion, and license to subjugate the earth. It is this man in whose image was God made. This concept of nature as a creative, interacting process in which man is involved with all other life forms is the ecological view. It is, I submit, the best approximation of the world that has been presented to us, and the indispensable approach to determining the role of man in the biosphere. It is indispensable also for investigation, not only of the adaptations which man accomplishes, but of their forms.

The place, the plants, the animals, and man, and the orderings which they have accomplished over time, are revealed in form. To understand this it is necessary to invoke all physical, biological, and cultural evolution. Form and process are indivisible aspects of a single phenomenon: being. Norbert Weiner described the world as consisting of "To Whom It May Concern" messages, but these are clothed in form. Process and fitness (which is the criterion of process) are revealed in form; form contains meaning. The artifact, tool, room, street, building, town or city, garden or region, can be examined in terms of process, manifest in form, which may be unfit, fit, or most fitting. The last of these, when made by man, is art.

The role of man is to understand nature, which is also to say man, and to intervene to enhance its creative processes. He is the prospective steward of the biosphere. The fruits of the anthropocentric view are in the improvement of the social environment, and great indeed are their values, but an encomium on social evolution is not my competence, and I leave the subject with the observation that, while Madison, Jefferson, Hamilton, and Washington might well take pride in many of our institutions, it is likely that they would recoil in horror from the face of the land of the free.

An indictment of the physical environment is too easy, for post-industrial cities are such squalid testimony to the bondage of toil and to the insensitivity of man, that the most casual examination of history reveals the modern city as a travesty of its antecedents and a denial of its role as the proudest testimony to peoples and their cultures. The city is no longer the preferred residence for the polite, the civilized, and the urbane, all of which say "city." They have fled to the illusion of the suburb, escaping the iridescent shills, neon vulgarity of the merchants, usurious slumlords, cynical polluters (household names for great corporations, not yet housebroken), crime, violence, and corruption. Thus, the city is the home of the poor, who are chained to it, and the repository of dirty industry and the commuter's automobile. Give us your poor and oppressed, and we will give them Harlem and the Lower East Side, Bedford-Stuyvesant, the South Side of Chicago, and the North of Philadelphia—or, if they are very lucky, Levittown. Look at one of these habitats through the Cornell Medical School study of Midtown Manhattan, where 20 percent of a sample population was found to be indistinguishable from the patients in mental institutions, and where a further 60 percent evidenced mental disease. Observe the environments of physical, mental, and social pathology. What of the countryside? Well, you may drive from the city and search for the rural landscape, but to do so you will follow the paths of those who preceded you, and many of them stayed to build. But those who did so first are now deeply embedded in the fabric of the city. So as you go you will transect the annular rings of the thwarted and disillusioned who are encapsulated in the city as nature endlessly eludes pursuit. You can tell when you have reached the edge of the rural scene for there are many emblems: the cadavers of old trees, piled in untidy heaps beside the magnificent machines for land despoliation, at the edge of the razed deserts; forests felled; marshes filled; farms obliterated; streams culverted; and the sweet rural scene transformed into the ticky-tacky vulgarity of the merchants' creed and expression. What of the continent? Well, Lake Erie is on the verge of becoming septic, New York suffers from water shortages as the Hudson flows foully past, and the Delaware is threatened by salt water intrusion. Smog, forest fires, and mud slides have become a way of life for Los Angeles. In San Francisco, the Bay is being filled and men build upon unconsolidated sediments, the most perilous foundations in this earthquake-prone area. DDT is in Arctic ice and ocean deeps, radioactive wastes rest on the Continental Shelf, the Mississippi is engorged with five cubic miles of topsoil each year, the primeval forests are all but gone, flood and drought become increasingly common, the once-deep prairie soils are thinner now and we might as well recognize that itinerant investment farming is just another extractive industry.

This is the face of our Western inheritance—Judaism, Christianity, Humanism, and the Materialism which is better named "Economic Determinism." The countryside, the last great cornucopia of the world's bounty, ravaged; and the city of man (God's Junkyard, or call it Bedlam) a vast demonstration of man's inhumanity to man, where existence, sustained by modern medicine and social legislation, is possible in spite of the physical environment. Yet we are the inheritors of enormous beauty, wealth, and variety. Our world is aching for the glorious cities of civilized and urbane men. Land and resources are abundant. We could build a thousand new cities in the most wonderful locations—on mountains and plains, on rocky ocean promontories, on desert and delta, by rivers and lakes, on islands and plateaus. It is within our compass to select the widest range of the most desirable lands and promulgate policies and regulations to ensure the realization of these cities, each in response to the nature of its site. We can manage the land for its health, productivity, and beauty. All of these things are within the capacity of this people now. It is necessary to resolve to fulfill the American Revolution and to create the fair image that can be the land of the free and the home of the brave. But to resolve is not enough; it is also necessary that society at large understand nature as a process, having values, limiting factors, opportunities, and constraints; that creation and destruction are real; that there are criteria by which we can discern the direction and tests of evolution; and, finally, that there are formal implications revealed in the environment which affect the nature and form of human adaptations.

What inherited values have produced this plight, from which we must be released if the revolution is to be completed? Surely it is the very core of our tradition, the Judeo-Christian-Humanist view which is so unknowing of nature and of man, which has bred and sustained his simple-minded anthropocentrism and anthropomorphism. It is this obsolete view of man and nature which is the greatest impediment to our emancipation as managers of the countryside, city builders, and artists. If it requires little effort to mobilize a sweeping indictment of the physical environment which is man's creation, it takes little more to identify the source of the value system which is the culprit. Whatever the origins, the text is quite clear in Judaism, was absorbed all but unchanged into Christianity, and was inflated in Humanism to become the implicit attitude of Western man to nature and the environment. Western man is exclusively divine, all other creatures and things occupy lower and generally inconsequential status; man is given dominion over all creatures and things; he is enjoined to subdue the earth. Here is the best of all possible texts for him who would contemplate biocide, carelessly extirpate great realms of life, create Panama Canals, or dig Alaskan harbors with atomic demolition. Here is the appropriate injunction for the land rapist, the befouler of air and water, the uglifier, and the gratified bulldozer. Dominion and subjugation, or better call it conquest, are their creeds. It matters little that theologians point to the same source for a different text, and choose rather the image of man the steward who should dress the garden and keep it. It matters little that Buber and Heschel, Teilhard de Chardin, Weigel and Tillich retreat from the literality of the dominion and subjugation text, and insist that this is allegory. It remains the literal injunction which has been so warmly welcomed and enshrined at the core of the Western view. This environment was created by the man who believes that the cosmos is a pyramid erected to support man on its pinnacle, that reality exists only because man can perceive it, that God is made in the image of man, and that the world consists solely of a dialog between men. Surely this is an infantilism which is unendurable. It is a residue from a past of inconsequence when a few puny men cried of their supremacy to an unhearing and uncaring world. One longs for a psychiatrist who can assure man that his deep-seated cultural inferiority is no longer necessary or appropriate. He can now stand erect among the creatures and reveal his emancipation. His ancient vengeance and strident cries are a product of an earlier insignificance and are now obsolete. It is not really necessary to destroy nature in order to obtain God's favor or even his undivided attention. To this ancient view the past two centuries have added only materialism—an economic determinism which has merely sustained earlier views.

The face of the city and the land are the best testimony to the concept of conquest and exploitation—the merchants' creed. The Gross National Product is the proof of its success, money is its measure, convenience is its cohort, the short term is its span, and the devil take the hindmost is its morality. The economists, with some conspicuous exceptions, have become the spokesmen for the merchants' creed and in concert they ask with the most barefaced effrontery that we accommodate our values to theirs. Neither love nor compassion, health nor beauty, dignity nor freedom, grace nor delight are true unless they can be priced. If not, they are described as nonprice benefits and relegated to inconsequence, and the economic model proceeds towards its self-fulfillment—which is to say more despoliation. The major criticism of this model is not that it is partial (which is conceded by its strongest advocates), but more that the features which are excluded are among the most important human values, and also the requirements for survival. If the ethics of society insist that it is man's bounden duty to subdue the earth, then it is likely that he will obtain the tools with which to accomplish this. If there is established a value system based upon exploitation of the earth, then the essential components for survival, health, and evolution are likely to be discounted, as they are. It can then come as no surprise to us that the most scabrous slum is more highly valued than the most beautiful landscape, that the most loathsome roadside stand is more highly valued than the richest farmland, and that this society should more highly prize tomato stakes than the primeval redwoods whence they come.

It is, in part, understandable why our economic value system is completely blind to the realities of the biophysical world—why it excludes from consideration, not only the most important human aspirations, but even those processes which are indispensable for survival. The origins of society and exchange began in an early world where man was a trifling inconsequence in the face of an overwhelming nature. He knew little of its operation. He bartered his surpluses of food and hides, cattle, sheep and goats; and valued such scarcities as gold, silver, myrrh, and frankincense. In the intervening millennia the valuations attributed to commodities have increased in range and precision and the understanding of the operation of this limited sphere has increased dramatically. Yet, we are still unable to identify and evaluate the processes which are indispensable for survival. When you give money to a broker to invest you do so on the understanding that this man understands a process well enough to make the investment a productive one. Who are the men to whom you entrust the responsibility for ensuring a productive return on the world's investment? Surely, those who understand physical and biological processes realize that these are creative. The man who views plants as the basis of negentropy in the world and the base of the food chain, as the source of atmospheric oxygen, fossil fuels and fibers, is a different man from one who values only economic plants, or that man who considers them as decorative but irrelevant aspects of life. The man who sees the sun as the source of life and the hydrologic cycle as its greatest work, is a different man from one who values sunlight in terms of a recreation industry, a portion of agricultural income, or from that man who can obscure sky and sunlight with air pollution, or who carelessly befouls water. The man who knows that the great recycling of matter, the return stroke in the world's cycles, is performed by the decomposer bacteria, views soils and water differently from the man who values a few bacteria in antibiotics, or he who is so unknowing of bacteria that he can blithely sterilize soils or make streams septic. That man who has no sense of the time which it has taken for the elaboration of life and symbiotic arrangements which have evolved, can carelessly extirpate creatures. That man who knows nothing of the value of the genetic pool, the greatest resource which we bring to the future, is not likely to fear radiation hazard or to value life. Clearly, it is illusory to expect the formulation of a precise value system which can include the relative value of sun, moon, stars, the changing seasons, physical processes, life forms, their roles, their symbiotic relationships, or the genetic pool. Yet, without precise evaluation, it is apparent that there will be a profound difference in attitude—indeed, a profoundly different value system— between those who understand the history of evolution and the interacting processes of the biosphere, and those who do not.

The simpler people who were our ancestors (like primitive peoples today) did not subscribe to anthropocentric views, nor did the eighteenth-century English landscape tradition which is the finest accomplishment of Western art in the environment, and which derives from a different hypothesis. The vernacular architecture in the Western tradition and the attitudes of the good farmer come from yet another source, one which has more consonance with the Orient than the West. But the views which ensured successes for the hunter and gatherer, for the vernacular farmer, and for the creation of a rich and beautiful pastoral landscape are inadequate to deal with twentieth-century problems of an inordinate population growth, accelerating technology, and transformation from a rural to an urban world. We need a general theory which encompasses physical, biological, and cultural evolution; which contains an intrinsic value system; which includes criteria of creativity and destruction and, not least, principles by which we can measure adaptations and their form. Surely, the minimum requirement for an attitude to nature and to man is that it approximate reality. Clearly, our traditional view does not. If one would know of these things, where else should one turn but to science. If one wishes to know of the phenomenal world, where better to ask than the natural sciences; if one would know of the interactions between organism and environment, then turn to the ecologist, for this is his competence. From the ecological view, one can conclude that by living one is united physically to the origins of life. If life originated from matter, then by living one is united with the primeval hydrogen. The earth has been the one home for all of its evolving processes and for all of its inhabitants; from hydrogen to man, it is only the bathing sunlight which changes. The planet contains our origins, our history, our milieu—it is our home. It is in this sense that ecology, derived from *oikos*, is the science of the home. Can we review physical and biological evolution to discern the character of these processes, their direction, the laws which obtain, the criteria for survival and success? If this can be done, there will also be revealed an intrinsic value system and the basis for form. This is the essential ingredient of an adequate view of the world: a value system which corresponds to the creative processes of the world, and both a diagnostic and constructive view of human adaptations and their form.

The evolution of the world reveals movement from more to less random, from less to more structured, from simplicity to diversity, from few to many life forms—in a word, toward greater negentropy. This can be seen in the evolution of the elements, the compounds, and life. It is accomplished by physical processes, as in the early earth when matter liquefied and coalesced, forming the concentric cores of the planet. Vulcanism revealed the turbulence of early adaptations toward equilibrium. So, too, did the creation of the oceans. Evaporation and precipitation initiated the processes of erosion and sedimentation in which matter was physically sorted and ordered. When, from the aluminosilicate clays in the shallow bays, there emerged that novel organization, life, there developed a new agency for accomplishing ordering. The chloroplast of the plant was enabled to transmute sunlight into a higher ordering, sustaining all life. The atmosphere, originally hostile to life, was adapted by life to sustain and protect it, another form of ordering. The emergence of the decomposers, bacteria and fungi, permitted the wastes of life forms—and their substance after death—to be recycled and utilized by the living, the return stroke in the cycle of matter in the biosphere. The increasing number of organisms in the oceans and on land represent negentropy in their beings and in the ordering which they accomplish. We can now see the earth as a process by which the falling sunlight is destined for entropy, but is arrested and entrapped by physical processes and creatures, and reconstituted into higher and higher levels of order as evolution proceeds. Entropy is the law and demands its price, but while all energy is destined to become degraded, physical and biological systems move to higher order—from instability towards steady-state—in sum, to more negentropy. Evolution is thus a creative process in which all physical processes and life forms participate. Creation involves the raising of matter and energy from lower to higher levels of order. Retrogression and destruction consist of reduction from the higher levels of order to entropy.

As life can only be transmitted by life, then the spore, seed, egg, and sperm contain a record of the entire history of life. The journey was shared with the worms, the coelenterates, the sponges, and, later, with the cartilaginous and bony fishes. The reptilian line is ours, the common ancestor that we share with the birds. We left this path to assume mammalian form, live births, the placenta, and suckling of the young; the long period of infantile dependence marks us. From this branching line the monotremes, marsupials, edentates, and pangolins followed their paths, and we proceeded on the primate way. Tree shrew, lemur, tarsier, and anthropoid, are our lineage. We are the line of man—the raised ape, the enlarged brain, the toolmaker—he of speech and symbols, conscious of the world and of himself. It is all written on the sperm and on the egg although the brain knows little of this journey. We have been through these stages in time past and the imprint of the journey is upon us. We can look at the world and see our kin; for we are united, by living, with all life, and are from the same origins. Life has proceeded from simple to complex, although the simplest forms have not been superseded, only augmented. It has proceeded from uniform to diverse, from few to many species. Life has revealed evolution as a progression from greater to lesser entropy. In the beginning was the atom of hydrogen with one electron. Matter evolved in the cosmic cauldrons, adding electron after electron, and terminating in the heaviest and most ephemeral of elements. Simple elements conjoined as compounds, thus reaching the most complex of these as amino acids, which is to say life. Life reached unicellular form and proceeded through tissue and organ to complex organisms. There were few species in the beginning and now they are myriad; there were few roles and now they are legion. There were once large populations of few species; now there is a biosphere consisting of multitudes of communities composed of innumerable interacting species. Evolution has revealed a progression from simple to complex, from uniform to diverse, from unicellular to multicelled, from few to many species, from few to many ecosystems, and the relations between these processes have also evolved toward increased complexity.

What holds the electrons to the nucleus? The molecules in rocks, air, and water may have ten atoms, but the organic molecule may have a thousand. Where is the catalytic enzyme which locks and unlocks the molecules? The single cell is very complex indeed; what orchestrates the cytoplasm and nucleus, nucleolus, mitochondria, chromosomes, centrosomes, Golgi elements, plastids, chromoplasts, leucoplasts, and, not least, chloroplasts? The lichen shows an early symbiosis at the level of the organism as the alga and the fungus unit. The plant and the decomposer enter into symbiosis to utilize energy and matter, to employ the first and recycle the latter. The animal enters the cycle, consuming the plant, to be consumed by the decomposer and thence by the plant. Each creature must adapt to the others in that concession of autonomy toward the end of survival that is symbiosis. Thus parasite and host, predator and prey, and those creatures of mutual benefit develop symbioses to ensure survival. The world works through cooperative mechanisms in which the autonomy of the individual, be it cell, organ, organism, species, or community is qualified toward the survival and evolution of higher levels of order culminating in the biosphere. Now these symbiotic relationships are beneficial to the sum of organisms although clearly many of them are detrimental to individuals and species. While the prey is not pleased with the predator or the host far from enamored of the parasite or the pathogen, these are regulators of populations and the agents of death—that essential return phase in the cycle of matter, which fuels new life and evolution. Only in this sense can the predator, parasite, and pathogen be seen as important symbiotic agents, essential to the creative processes of life and evolution. If evolution has proceeded from simple to complex, this was accomplished through symbiosis. As the number of species increased, so then did the number of roles and the symbiotic arrangements between species. If stability increases as evolution proceeds, then this is the proof of increased symbiosis. If conservation of energy is essential to the diminution of entropy, then symbioses are essential to accomplish this. Perhaps it is symbiosis or, better, altruism that is the arrow of evolution.

This view of the world, creation, and evolution reveals as the principal actors: the sun, elements and compounds, the hydrologic cycle, the plant, decomposers, and the animals. Further, if the measure of creation is negentropy, then it is the smallest marine plants which perform the bulk of the world's work, which produce the oxygen of the atmosphere, the basis of the great food chains. On land it is the smallest herbs. Among the animals the same is true; it is the smallest of marine animals and the terrestrial herbivores which accomplish the greatest creative effort of raising the substance of plants to higher orders. Man has little creative role in this realm although his destructive potential is considerable. However, energy can as well be considered as information. The light which heats the body can inform the perceptive creature. When energy is so considered, then the apperception of information as meaning, and response to it, is also seen as ordering, as antientropic. Noise to the unperceptive organism, through perception becomes information from which is derived meaning. In an appraisal of the world's work of apperception, it is seen that the simpler organisms, which create the maximum negentropy, are low on the scale of apperception which increases as one rises on the evolutionary scale. Man, who had no perceptible role as a creator of negentropy, becomes prominent as a perceptive and conscious being. We have seen that the evolution from the unicellular to the multicellular organism involved symbiotic relationships. Hans Selyé has described intercellular altruism as the cooperative mechanism which makes 30 billion human cells into a single integrated organism. He also has described interpersonal altruism. Surely one must conclude that the entire biosphere exhibits altruism. In this sense, the life forms which now exist on earth, and the symbiotic roles which they have developed, constitute the highest ordering which life forms have yet been able to achieve. The human organism exists as a result of the symbiotic relationships in which cells assume different roles as blood, tissues, and organs, integrated as a single organism. So, too, can the biosphere be considered as a single superorganism in which the oceans and the atmosphere, all creatures, and communities play roles analogous to cells, tissues, and organs. That which integrates either the cell in the organism or the organism in the biosphere is a symbiotic relationship. In sum, these are beneficial. This then is the third measure, the third element, after order and complexity, of the value system: the concession of some part of the autonomy of the individual in a cooperative arrangement with other organisms which have equally qualified their individual freedom toward the end of survival and evolution. We can see this in the alga and fungus composing the lichen, in the complex relationships in the forest, and in the sea. Symbiosis is the indispensable value in the survival of life forms, ecosystems, and the entire biosphere. Man is superbly endowed to be that conscious creature who can perceive the phenomenal world, its operation, its direction, the roles of the creatures, and physical processes. Through his apperception, he is enabled to accomplish adaptations which are the symbioses of man–nature. This is the promise of his apperception and consciousness. This examination of evolution reveals direction in retrospect— that the earth and its denizens are involved in a creative process of which negentropy is the measure. It shows that creation does have attributes which include evolution toward complexity, diversity, stability (steady-state), increase in the number of species, and increase in symbiosis. Survival is the first test, creation is the next; and this may be accomplished by arresting energy, by apperception, or by symbiosis. This reveals an intrinsic value system with a currency: energy; an inventory which includes matter and its cycles, life forms and their roles, and cooperative mechanisms.

All of the processes which have been discussed reveal form; indeed, form and process are indivisible aspects of a single phenomenon. That which can be seen reveals process. Much of this need not be superficially visible; it may lie beneath the skin, below the level of vision, or only in invisible paths which bespeak the interactions of organisms. Yet, the place, the plants, animals, men, and their works, are revealed in form.

All of the criteria used to measure evolutionary success apply to form. Simplicity and uniformity reveal a primitive stage, while complexity and diversity are evidence of higher evolutionary forms: few elements or species as opposed to many, few interactions rather than the multitude of advanced systems. Yet, there is need for a synoptic term which can include the presence or absence of these attributes in form. For this, we can use "fitness" both in the sense that Henderson employs it, and also in Darwinian terms. Thus, the environment is fit, and can be made more fitting; the organism adapts to fit the environment. Lawrence Henderson speaks of the fitness of the environment for life in the preface to his book, *The Fitness of the Environment*.

Darwinian fitness is compounded of a mutual relationship between the organism and the environment. Of this, fitness of environment is quite as essential a component of the fitness which arises in the process of organic evolution; and in fundamental characteristics the actual environment is the fittest possible abode for life.

Henderson supports his proposition by elaborating on the characteristics of carbon, hydrogen, oxygen, water, and carbolic acid, saying that "No other environment consisting of primary constituents, made up of other known elements, or lacking water and carbolic acid, could possess a like number of fit characteristics, or in any manner such great fitness to promote complexity, durability, and the active metabolism and the organic mechanism we call life."

The environment is fit for life and all of the manifestations which it has taken, and does take. Conversely, the surviving and successful organism is fitted to the environment. Thus, we can use fitness as a criterion of the environment, organisms and their adaptations, as revealed in form. Form can reveal past processes and help to explain present realities. Mountains show their age and composition in their form; rivers demonstrate their age and reflect the physiography of their passage; the distribution and characteristics of soils are comprehensible in terms of historical geology, and climate and hydrology. The pattern and distribution of plants respond to environmental variables represented in the foregoing considerations, while animals respond to these and to the nature of the plant communities.

Man is as responsive, but he is selective; the pattern and distribution of man is likely to be comprehensible in these same terms. The term "fitness" has a higher utility than art for the simple reason that it encompasses all things— inert and living, nonhuman and those made by man—while art is limited to the last. Moreover, it offers a longer view and more evidence. Nature has been in the business of form since the beginning, and man is only one of its products. The fact that things and creatures exist is proof of their evolutionary fitness at the time, although among them there will be those more or less fit. There will be those which are unfit and will not persist, those are the misfits; then, those which are fit; and finally, the most fitting—all revealed in form. Form is also meaningful form. Through it, process and roles are revealed, but the revelation is limited by the capacity of the observer to perceive. Arctic differs from rain forest, tundra from ocean, forest from desert, plateau from delta; each is itself because. The platypus is different from seaweed, diatom from whale, monkey from man . . . because. Africans differ from Asians, Eskimo from Caucasoid, Mongoloid from Australoid . . . because; and all of these are manifest in form.

When process is understood, differentiation and form become comprehensible. Processes are dynamic, and so coastlines advance and recede as do ice sheets, lakes are in the process of filling while others form, mountains succumb to erosion and others rise. The lake becomes marsh, the estuary a delta, the prairie becomes desert, the scrub turns into forest, a volcano creates an island, while continents sink. The observation of process, through form and the response, represents the evolution of information to meaning. If evolutionary success is revealed by the existence of creatures, then their fitness will be revealed in form; visible in organs, in organisms, and in communities of these. If this is so, then natural communities of plants and animals represent the most fitting adaptation to available environments. They are most fitting and will reveal this in form. Indeed, in the absence of man, these would be the inevitable expression. Thus, there is not only an appropriate ecosystem for any environment, and successional stages toward it, but such communities will reveal their fitness in their expression. This is a conclusion of enormous magnitude to those who are concerned with the land and its aspect: that there is a natural association of creatures for every environment. This could be called the intrinsic identity of the given form.

If this is so, then there will be organs, organisms, and communities of special fitness, and these will, of course, be revealed in form. This might well be described as the ideal. The creation of adaptations which seek to be metaphysical symbols is, in essence, the concern with representing the ideal. Adaptation of the environment is accomplished by all physical processes and by all life. Yet, certain of these transformations are more visible than others, and some are analogous to those accomplished by man. Throughout the natural world, many creatures are engaged in the business of using inert material to create adaptive environments. These reveal the individual, a society, or a population. Can the criteria of fitness be applied then to the artifact? We can accept that the stilt's legs, the flamingo's beak, and the mouth of the baleen whale are all splendid adaptations, and visibly so. It is no great leap to see the tennis serve, the left hook, and the jumping catch, as of the same realm as the impala's bound, the diving cormorant, or the leopard's lunge. Why then should we distinguish between the athletic gesture and the artifacts which are employed with them: the golf club, bat, glove, or tennis racquet? The instrument is only an extension of the limb.

If this is so, then we can equally decide if the hammer and saw are fit, or the knife, fork, and spoon. We can conclude that the tail-powered jet is more fit for the air than the clawing propellers. If we can examine tools, then we can as well examine the environments for activities: the dining room for dining, the bedroom for sleeping or for loving, the house, street, village, town, or city. Are they unfit, misfit, fit, or most fitting? It appears that any natural environment will have an appropriate expression of physical processes, revealed in physiography, hydrology, soils, plants, and animals.

There should then be an appropriate morphology for man-site, and this should vary with environments. There will then be a fitting-for-man environment. One would expect that as the plants and animals vary profoundly from environment to environment, this should also apply to man. One would then expect to find distinct morphologies for man–nature in each of the major physiographic regions. The house, village, town, and city should vary from desert to delta, from mountain to plain. One would expect to find certain generic unity within these regions, but marked differentiation between them.

If fitness is a synoptic measure of evolutionary success, what criteria can we use to measure it? We have seen that it must meet the simplicity-complexity, uniformity-diversity, instability-stability, independence-interdependence tests. Yet, in the view of Ruth Patrick, as demonstrated by her study of aquatic systems, these may all be subsumed under two terms: ill-health and health. A movement towards simplicity, uniformity, instability, and a low number of species characterizes disease. The opposites are evidence of health. This corresponds to common usage: ill-health is unfit; fitness and health are synonymous. Thus, if we would examine the works of man and his adaptations to the countryside, perhaps the most synoptic criteria are disease and health. We can conclude that which sustains health represents a fitting between man and the environment. We would expect that this fitness be revealed in form. This criterion might well be the most useful to examine the city of man: wherein does pathology reside? What are its corollaries in the physical and social environment? What characterizes an environment of health? What are its institutions? What is its form? Know this, and we may be able to diagnose and prescribe with an assurance which is absent today.

What conclusions can one reach from this investigation? The first is that the greatest failure of Western society, and of the post-industrial period in particular, is the despoliation of the natural world and the inhibition of life which is represented by modern cities. It is apparent that this is the inevitable consequence of the values that have been our inheritance. It is clear, to me if to no one else, that these values have little correspondence to reality and perpetrate an enormous delusion as to the world, its work, the importance of the roles that are performed, and, not least, the potential role of man. In this delusion the economic model is conspicuously inadequate, excluding as it does the most important human aspirations and the realities of the biophysical world. The remedy requires that the understanding of this world which now reposes in the natural sciences be absorbed into the conscious value system of society, and that we learn of the evolutionary past and the roles played by physical processes and life forms. We must learn of the criteria for creation and destruction, and of the attributes of both. We need to formulate an encompassing value system which corresponds to reality and which uses the absolute values of energy, matter, life forms, cycles, roles, and symbioses.

We can observe that there seem to be three creative roles. The first is the arresting of energy in the form of negentropy, which offers little opportunity to man. Second is apperception and the ordering which can be accomplished through consciousness and understanding. Third is the creation of symbiotic arrangement, for which man is superbly endowed. It can be seen that form is only a particular mode for examining process and the adaptations to the environment accomplished by process. Form can be the test used to determine processes as primitive or advanced, to ascertain if they are evolving or retrogressing. Fitness appears to have a great utility for measuring form: unfit, fit, or most fitting. When one considers the adaptations accomplished by man, they are seen to be amenable to this same criterion but, also, synoptically measurable in terms of health. Identify the environment of pathology; it is unfit, and will reveal this in form. Where is the environment of health— physical, mental, and social? This, too, should reveal its fitness in form. How can this knowledge be used to affect the quality of the environment? The first requirement is an ecological inventory in which physical processes and life forms are identified and located within ecosystems, which consist of discrete but interacting natural processes. These data should then be interpreted as a value system with intrinsic values, offering both opportunities and constraints to human use, and implications for management and the forms of human adaptations.

The city should be subject to the same inventory and its physical, biological, and cultural processes should be measured in terms of fitness and unfitness, health and pathology. This should become the basis for the morphology of man–nature and man–city. We must abandon the self-mutilation which has been our way, reject the title of planetary disease which is so richly deserved, and abandon the value system of our inheritance which has so grossly misled us. We must see nature as a process within which man exists, splendidly equipped to become the manager of the biosphere; and give form to that symbiosis which is his greatest role, man the world's steward.

5

Natural Factors in Planning (1997)

The idea for this essay came from Lloyd Wright, then director of conservation and ecosystem assistance for the U.S. Natural Resources Conservation Service (NRCS). A dedicated member of the federal bureaucracy, Lloyd Wright believed other government employees needed inspiration and challenge in light of the harsh criticism that had been leveled against them beginning with the Ronald Reagan administration and perhaps culminating in the bombing of the Alfred P. Murrah Federal Office Building in Oklahoma City.

Wright identified McHarg as the best person for such inspiration and challenge. McHarg's charge was to provide a theoretical framework for using natural resource information in planning. The NRCS provided support through a cooperative agreement with the Arizona State University School of Planning and Landscape Architecture to commission McHarg to write this essay. It was subsequently published in the Journal of Soil and Water Conservation, *which is widely read by NRCS staff and other governmental natural resource managers. The paper was also translated into Italian by Danilo Palazzo and published in* Urbanistica, *an Italian planning journal.*

In earlier times, in predominantly agricultural societies, conventional wisdom and folklore included an understanding of the region, its phenomena, processes, and calendar—time to plow, farrow, seed, harvest, first and last frosts, the probability of precipitation. Cultural memories recalled past events, flood and drought, pestilence, earthquakes, hurricanes, tornadoes. Given the crucial importance of this knowledge, essential to survival and success, it seems pointless to restate the obvious, but, sadly, it is increasingly necessary, more so than in earlier, simpler times. The phenomenal increase in urban concentrations, combined with exponential population growth and the reduction of the agricultural component in society and economy, have produced asphalt people who know little of nature and care less. To such people, knowledge of nature is apparently irrelevant to their success or future.

This view is not merely wrong. It is diametrically opposed to need. The greater the population and the greater the urban concentration, the greater the need to understand nature and to act prudently, using the best available knowledge.

The world population is growing exponentially; five billion now, doubling how soon? This enlargement is increasingly concentrated; megacities of 30 million, unknown only decades ago, are commonplace now. Mexico City, São Paulo, Calcutta, Tokyo are the most conspicuous examples and more will follow. The presence of such mammoth populations, of unprecedented size and concentration, is a recipe for disaster.

Surely the combination of massive populations in such urban concentrations should be warning enough but the situation is exacerbated by location—the annual flooding in the Gangetic flood plain takes an enormous toll now; the view of the circle of volcanoes, surrounding Mexico City, is not reassuring.

But this is not enough; it appears that the future includes increased frequency and violence in climatic events. Warm a pot of water, see activity increase with temperature until boiling occurs. So too with the earth. Whether or not from the accumulation of greenhouse gases, world temperatures rise and with them climatic violence. This is thought to include not only flood and drought, hurricanes, tsunamis, and tornadoes but earthquakes and volcanoes too. So we have actively increased the threat of death, disaster, pain, and loss by those concurrent processes, population increase, concentration, and now climatic violence.

The consequences of national disasters are awesome now. What of the future? A flood in Bangladesh and an earthquake in the Crimea accounted for half a million deaths. Two hundred thousand lives were lost from twenty events in the last forty years. There are also damages. In 1989, Hurricane Hugo incurred over $6 billion in damages and 80 lives were lost. In the same year, the Loma Prieta earthquake caused $10 billion in damages. Hurricane Andrew caused another $25 billion in 1992, approximately seven percent of Florida's Gross State Budget. The 1994 Midwest floods in the Mississippi River basin and the Northbridge earthquake the same year together resulted in over $50 billion in destruction. Insurance claims for the first three years of this decade exceeded claims for the entire earlier one. These are significant costs, only exceeded by the U.S. Department of Defense budget and the national debt. These costs can be reduced significantly.

In the face of this massive indictment, it would seem impossible to disregard natural calamities in the planning process. The burden of discussion paper is that natural factors have for too long been either excluded or inadequately incorporated in planning. Surely, you say, this is a restatement of the obvious. How can effective planning proceed without the inclusion of this crucial realm? It has, can, and does, and the absence of such data causes planning to be either irrelevant, exclusionary, or inconsequential. How did this paradoxical situation come to be? How can it be corrected?

There are many reasons. The first reposes in the historic disinterest of leading scientists and institutions in the environment. Fashions tend to vary, but for half a century particle physics has dominated the physical sciences, molecular biology has preempted attention in the biological sciences. As recently as the 1950s, the environment was barely an accepted term. I recall when in the 1950s the Audubon Society was preoccupied with birds, the Sierra Club concentrated on preserving the scenic American West. Then the only organization concerned with the national environment was the Conservation Foundation, housed in a one-room office in New York City. In the 1960s, there were few writers or speakers prepared to discuss the environment: Rachel Carson, Ralph Nader, Paul Ehrlich, Barry Commoner, René Dubos, and me.

Rachel Carson was the first spokesperson for the environment: Her message was that we were poisoning natural systems and ourselves; Ralph Nader brought the subject of the environment to national attention and illustrated the impact of the issue on the consumer; Paul Ehrlich gave vivid attention to the population problem; Barry Commoner emphasized chemical pollutants; René Dubos, pathologist, the most humane of the group, insisted that the way the French peasant lived with the environment provided the appropriate answer; my theme was design with nature.

The Fragmentation of Knowledge

Science itself was fragmented. Reductionism held sway. Integration requires bridging between separate sciences, an attitude resisted by universities and governmental institutions. Meteorologists study climate, geologists rocks, hydrologists address water, pedologists focus on soils. Vegetation is addressed by ecologists, limnologists, and marine biologists; animals and wildlife have their appropriate investigators: animal ecologists, ethnologists, fish and wildlife scientists. For almost every discipline there will be an associated institution. National Oceanic and Atmospheric Adminstration (NOAA) links to climate, the U.S. Geological Survey controls rocks and water, soils repose in USDA Natural Resources Conservation Service, fish and wildlife are located in the National Biological Survey and in the U.S. Fish and Wildlife Service. The U.S. Environmental Protection Agency (EPA) limits itself to regulation while natural vegetation alone has no institutional sponsor. The Smithsonian Institution seems to have no niche.

Each of these elements, either in universities or in government, is like a piece of a jigsaw puzzle which has never been assembled. Is there anyone with the wit, capability, and energy to do this? Unlikely

> Humpty Dumpty sat on a wall;
> Humpty Dumpty had a great fall;
> All the king's horses and all the king's men;
> Couldn't put Humpty together again.

The environment is like a pile of eggshell fragments. Not only has the environment been disdained by all but a handful of our leading scientists but inevitably by the most prestigious institutions. There the mandarins scorned the workmen of the environment with their black rimmed fingernails, soiled shirt collars, inhabiting land-grant colleges in declining programs in agriculture and forestry. And moreover, the single integrative science, ecology, absent or little represented in the Ivy League, was housed in broom closets in the land-grant and state colleges.

The Fragmentation of Government

In addition, of course, there are redundant and often conflicting policies, evidence of cross purposes. The U.S. National Park Service is charged with the preservation and interpretation of national scenic wonders but the U.S. Forest Service is charged with exploiting our national forests, the U.S. Bureau of Land Management (BLM) fills a comparable role for rangeland. While the U.S. Geological Survey (USGS) studies geological and hydrological systems, the U.S. Army Corps of Engineers concentrates on intervention in riverine systems, as does the BLM. Regulation mainly reposes in the EPA, but the Army Corps of Engineers is charged with managing wetlands; the agent which supervised the filling of wetlands is now charged with protecting them! The study of climate by NOAA is very impressive. Satellites, sensors, and computers have advanced meteorology. This advance is not paralleled in hydrology. The massive midwestern floods of 1994 may well have been enhanced by public actions—floods as a public gift at great public cost.

As molecular biology assumed dominance biology became a crucial component of medicine. Organismic and community biology was abandoned. Generalists were cytologists, preoccupied with the cell. Organismic biology declined with the retirement or death of the nineteenth-century naturalists in biology—never to be replaced. In geology this same interest focused physical sciences on carbon dating and planetary physics. It was only the discovery of plate tectonics which brought geology back to spatial studies. But here the disdain of geologists for hydrologists or soil scientists remains an important obstruction to integration.

Natural Processes Affect Our Health and Safety

If science has been indifferent to the environment, victims of natural calamities certainly have not been. These natural disasters—flood, drought, hurricanes, tsunamis, tornadoes, volcanoes, and earthquakes—have caused enormous loss of life, plus considerable damage, suffering and pain, and promise more. Indeed, it would appear that the sum of global behavior is to increase this damage, pain, suffering, and loss of life.

This is particularly poignant because so much of it could be avoided. Surely it is neither wise nor necessary to locate populations in areas prone to natural disasters. Nor is it necessary to exacerbate them. One example might suffice.

The 1994 Mississippi flooding was exacerbated by failure to understand the role of river ecologies in mitigating flooding and by years of engineering practices that neutralized much natural protection.

The explanation for the lack of interest in natural processes in planning began with the long-term rejection of the environment as a fitting subject of research by both prestigious academic institutions and governmental agencies. The commitment to reductionism and the fragmentation of science provide other reasons. The passion for obtaining data as a commonplace obsession is paralleled by a disinterest in integration. A widespread public belief that natural calamities are acts of God and must be endured is also a culprit. Yet management of natural disaster is one area where profound advances have been made. The understanding of tectonic and meteorological processes, improved monitoring and prediction, and better communication have reduced the consequences of natural calamities.

The Inadequacies of Planning to Respond to the Environmental Challenge

Yet another explanation lies in the composition of those engaged in city and regional planning. In the postwar years planning was described as an "applied social science," certainly in the dominant planning schools, such as the University of Pennsylvania, the University of North Carolina, the Massachusetts Institute of Technology, the University of California-Berkeley, and Harvard University. Such a description had a profound effect on the planning operation.

Go into a local city or county planning office, anywhere in the United States. Establish that you have been commissioned to write an article on the importance of natural factors in the processes of planning and community design. Speak to the staff. You will find that their training has been predominantly in the applied social sciences. They are likely to have studied economics, sociology, computation, statistics, perhaps (hopefully) land-use and zoning law. Only the planners with an education in geography are likely to have received any training in physical and biological science. So your investigation will not assure you of the central importance of natural science in planning and community design. Indeed, the absence of planners trained in the natural sciences is an explanation for the exclusion of environmental science.

The Emergence of the Environment in Public Policy

Since the 1970s, the environment has emerged as a significant subject. However, the science departments of most prestigious universities still focus on molecular biology and subatomic physics. While the environment may have emerged from oblivion in the public consciousness it is still not prominent. Agencies continue in their ad hoc, reductionist ways, although there are timid efforts of integration—the National Science Foundation-Environmental Protection Agency combined focus on watersheds is a welcome and belated innovation; the creation of the National Biological Survey (NBS) in the U.S. Department of Interior is an attempt at integration. The U.S. Fish and Wildlife Service Gap Analysis Program and the Clinton administration's Interagency Ecosystem Management Task Force are other hopeful efforts.

But in sum, it is a lugubrious review. What is the remedy? Well, clearly there must be widespread recognition of the necessity for all of the sciences to address the problems of the environment. In this fragmented and reductionist world it is necessary to recognize and to acknowledge that the greatest progress can be accomplished, not by providing additional data (we already have quantities beyond our ability to use them). No, the greatest advance will occur when it is recognized that integration and synthesis constitute the greatest challenge and provide the greatest promise of success.

On the positive side the increase in scientific knowledge, the availability of sensors, not the least global positioning systems (GPS), offer great opportunities for ecological planning. As important are computers, their ability to digitize massive data sets, retrieve data, analyze them, and undertake automatic analytic procedures and finally perform complex planning syntheses.

Human Ecological Planning

I have called such a process human ecological planning. It includes data and precepts from the relevant physical, biological, and social sciences. In the 1970s, the Ford Foundation made grants to support ecology at Princeton University, the University of Georgia, and the University of Pennsylvania. At Penn, we designed a new curriculum in ecologically based regional planning, recruiting persons with undergraduate qualifications in the natural sciences. An integrated, ecology-based curriculum was developed, a natural scientist faculty was hired, including such luminaries as Ruth Patrick, a 1996 recipient of the National Medal of Science. This program prospered for twenty years. It produced 15 deans, 38 chairmen and directors, and 150 professors worldwide. From this cadre came 15 new programs emphasizing ecological planning and design. The Penn program ultimately shrank in parallel with the opposition to planning and the environment initiated by former Presidents Ronald Reagan and George Bush and continued by the current U.S. Congress.

Ecological planning, developed at Penn and employed in instruction and research, produced over a thousand graduates who employ ecological planning in many academic institutions and government agencies in North America and around the world. This initiative should receive massive support. It represents an unmatched degree of integration, the incorporation of all of the environmental sciences—physical, biological, and social—combined with advanced computational capability. Descriptions of human ecological planning have been published elsewhere but can be presented in synopsis here. First, it requires that all of the environmental sciences be included and unified by chronology and depicted as a "layer cake." These would include meteorology, geology, physical oceanography, surficial geology, geomorphology, groundwater and surficial hydrology, soils, vegetation, wildlife (including marine biology), and limnology. The social sciences should be included in ecological inventories too with ethology, ethnography, cultural anthropology, economics, sociology, and geography, particularly computational science.

Our faculty teams undertook numerous studies with the landscape architecture and regional planning students at Penn. From that work, we identified the baseline natural resource data necessary for a layer-cake inventory of a place (table 1).

In addition to being comprehensive and inclusive, the integrating device recommended is chronology. That is, all studies should involve a historic recapitulation ordered by time. Information from the sciences should be organized in a "layer cake" fashion, with older components including rocks at the bottom of the cake and younger layers, such as soil and vegetation above. The completion of such a human ecological study presents an understanding of how the region came to be, what it is, how it works, and where it tends to go. A human perspective is essential—how people relate to their environments both historically and today. The ethnographic history should describe the populations, structured in constituencies, having characteristic values, settlement patterns, resource utilization, and specific issues and attitudes to them. When the inventory is complete, and the data accumulated chronologically, and thus meaningfully, the history of the region under study, its constituent processes, its past, its current form, and its tendencies for the future

Table 1. Baseline Natural Resource Data Necessary for Ecological Planning

The following natural resource factors are likely to be of significance in planning. Clearly the region under study will determine the relevant factors but many are likely to occur in all studies.

Climate. Temperature, humidity, precipitation, wind velocity, direction, duration, first and last frosts, snow, frost, fog, inversions, hurricanes, tornadoes, tsunamis, typhoons, Chinook winds

Geology. Rocks, ages, formations, plans, sections, properties, seismic activity, earthquakes, rock slides, mud slides, subsistence

Surficial geology. Kames, kettles, eskers, moraines, drift and till

Groundwater hydrology. Geological formations interpreted as aquifer with well locations, well logs, water quantity and quality, water table, flood plains

Physiography. Physiographic regions, subregions and features, contours, sections, slopes, aspect, insulation, digital terrain model(s)

Surficial hydrology. Oceans, lakes, deltas, rivers, streams, creeks, marshes, swamps, wetlands, stream orders, density, discharges, gauges, water quality

Soils. Soil associations, soils series, properties, depth to seasonal high water table, depth to bedrock, shrink-swell, compressive strength, cation and anion exchange, acidity-alkalinity

Vegetation. Associations, communities, species, composition, distribution, age and conditions, visual quality, species number, rare and endangered species, fire history, successional history

Wildlife. Habitats, animal populations, census data, rare and endangered species, scientific and educational value

Human. Ethnographic history, settlement patterns, existing land use, existing infrastructure, population characteristics

will become apparent. The product should be an interacting biophysical model on which a human population is causally located.

Determining Suitability

This database is now available for queries. One realm of such queries will involve correlation. Where are hurricane-prone zones? Where is landslide susceptibility? Tornado zones? What aspects of elevation, geology, climate, soil, slope are associated with vegetation types? What environmental aspects combine to proffer a habitat for, let us say, an endangered species? One can say that the richer the data set, the better the answers.

There is a process which I have called suitability analysis. This requires that prospective land uses be identified. Normally this would include forestry, agriculture, extractive minerals, recreation, and urbanization. Each of these can be further subdivided, urbanization might include housing of various densities, commerce, and industry. When the consumers have been identified, the inventory is reviewed to identify all factors on the legends of all maps and to determine those which are propitious, neutral, or detrimental for each prospective land use. Maps, either manually or computer produced, will depict all propitious factors for each land use. They will also depict all detrimental attributes. Finally, the computer will solve the command "show me those locations where all or most propitious factors are located, and where all or most detrimental factors are absent" by superimposing the propitious and detrimental factors. A reasonable convention is to colour all propitious factors in shades of green, all detrimental ones in oranges and reds. Dominant green shows the intrinsically suitable locations.

Of course, the method can be enhanced by weighting and scaling each of the factors. I have generally produced a map entitled "protection" which depicts all factors and regions wherein exist hazards to life and health. These environmentally sensitive areas will vary from location to location but are likely to include the following: flood plains, ocean surges, hurricane zones, tornadoes, tsunamis, earthquakes, vulcanism, wildfires, and subsidence. This protection map and associated text should identify the degrees of hazard represented by these processes and recommend a prudent response. As a result, suitability analysis suggests both constraints and opportunities for future land uses.

Reasons for Optimism

There are reasons for optimism. The subject of the environment has been embraced by the media, surely more for vicarious thrill than for science and understanding. Children's books and television carry much superior information about the environment than they did in your or my childhood. Indeed, I have an excellent sample: my older two sons, in their thirties and forties now, are sympathetic to the environment and lived in a household where ecology was a common word, but their stepbrothers, fourteen and eight, have experienced richer insights into the environment from *Nova*, *National Geographic* specials, *The Planet Earth*, and more. There is an emerging generation, well informed on the environment, indignant at pollution and destruction. They may follow the lead of the 1970s which gave us the flood of environmental legislation. The environmental groups—the World

Wildlife Fund, Audubon, Sierra Club, Friends of the Earth, The Nature Conservancy, the National Resources Defense Fund, the Soil and Water Conservation Society—should all constitute youth clubs to embrace these young potential soldiers for the environment.

Scientific knowledge of the environment has grown. The study of plate tectonics alone have advanced our knowledge of the environment; the world warming hypothesis and accompanying research have expanded our knowledge of the atmosphere and meteorology. The development of sensors has added to our ability to monitor the environment, not least GPS which has so simplified surveys and thus landscape inventories. The continuing advances in computation may be the greatest reason for optimism. More data can be ingested, evaluated, synthesized faster, more accurately than ever before.

There are also some sinister reasons for optimism. I would assert that the greatest impetus to improved ecological planning is the last disaster. A disaster amplifies awareness. The succession of alphabetic hurricanes, Edward, Fran, added to Hugo, Agnes, and Andrew have sensitized coastal communities to incipient disaster. Increased population, increased concentration combined with greater climatic violence guarantees more and bigger disasters. If the assertion is true, then each increment of pain and suffering should lead to the greater application of knowledge and wisdom to the planning process.

Can we use our massive brain, augmented by the great prosthesis of sensors and computers, to diminish such pain? Let us hope so.

The last and most important steps begin with resolve. Let us applaud the benefits of analysis and reductionism. They have contributed much to modern science which because of its fragmented nature clearly is not enough. It need not be superseded, but certainly it must be augmented to include synthesis and holism. The environment is now subdivided by science and language. We must direct our energies toward synthesis. There is a vital role here for all scientific institutions, all government departments and agencies. There should be a serious effort to reorganize contradictory views, programs at cross purposes, above all exclusionary myopia, and initiate cooperative procedures. Can we study watersheds, physiographic regions, oceans, tectonic plates, ecosystems? There is a new instrument which does not insist upon scientific disciplines or boundaries, which can accomplish synthesis. It is GIS, geographic information systems, capable of handling immense quantities of data, describing processes and undertaking planning. Not only can GIS undertake the most complex of planning studies undertaken manually it is possible to do studies which cannot be manually done.

Moreover, the computer and the GIS fraternity are already constituencies with magazines, conferences, vendors of hardware and software, oriented to the computer world, irrespective of university, agency, or country. Can this new constituency accomplish the integration which orthodox science has so resolutely rejected? Will GIS provide the belated integration required for planning? Will it spur an integration of inter- and intradisciplinary research and application? Will it lead to integration and synthesis?

The availability of GIS makes inventories a necessity. These should be extensive. A few years ago, I wrote a report with John Radke, Jonathan Berger, and Kathleen Wallace for the EPA entitled "A Prototype Database for a National Ecological Inventory." Our proposal includes a demonstration 40-km^2 sample, the Washington Crossing Hexagon. We chose this to examine two states, with different counties each with distinct nomenclature of geology, soils, vegetation, land use, and zoning. We mapped geology, produced sections, a digital terrain model, digitized aquifers, wells, well logs, discharge gauges, rivers, streams, marshes, wetlands, flood plains, and soils. We digitized 1929 and 1992 vegetation. We mapped all properties, land uses, and zones. It should be noted that making inventories is also an integrative process, particularly if extensive, employing the layer-cake method and using chronology as the underlying principle for organization.

In sum the opportunities for integration, organization of rich data, its analysis and planning using GIS are true, they are available. Will they be used to fulfill their promise, meet society's needs, and give government a larger role in understanding, planning, and regulating the environment and by so doing diminish death, damage, pain, and enhance human health and well-being? Let us hope so—even more, resolve to make it so.

Conclusion

Newt Gingrich, speaker of the house, archcritic of bureaucracy, insists upon across-the-board reductions of 33 percent for USGS, NBS, EPA, and many more agencies. This approach is unable to distinguish excellence from indolence; it mutilates, rather than accomplishes remedial surgery. Yet there are bums, fools, incompetents, failed programs galore, many in competition. Can we not dispose of surplus, failures, incompetence and, above all, eliminate cross-purposes and ensure integration? But can programs be seen as complementary, contributing to our national purpose?

A White House Task Force should be convened to investigate the integration of scientific perceptions of the environment by accomplishing the following:

- Propose a uniform ecological planning method to be employed by all agencies
- Propose a process to develop and monitor the sets of environmental data that must be employed by all agencies
- Create a master agency devoted to assembling, updating, and interpreting all digital environmental data; it should develop a national GIS

- Produce a uniform policy to handle "greenhouse gases" and plan for carbon fixing
- Develop government-wide strategies to improve biodiversity
- Develop plans to minimize the losses from environmental disasters
- Produce a plan to construct a national ecological inventory

The White House Task Force should design a training process to be offered by selected institutions to instruct senior officials from all agencies on the ecological planning process. A further training program should be designed as a prerequisite for existing junior staff and for all new employees on all environmental agencies.

So, the natural sciences have either been excluded or lightly incorporated in the planning process. As we have seen, natural calamities cost thousands of lives annually, billions of costs, and enormous insurance claims. There is a mood for economy present in Congress but economies in environmental protection are not popular so, why not achieve economies by diminishing the pain and cost of hurricanes, floods, tornadoes, fires, and other catastrophes? To accomplish such real economies, we should undertake a national ecological inventory, monitor the environment and improve both understanding and prediction of natural phenomena, employ these data in ecological planning processes. Announce the intention to convene a White House Task Force to address the subjects of the environment, reorganization of government, a commitment to integration, address the problems of world warming, biodiversity, greater climatic violence, the increased threats from megacities and the necessity of bringing the environmental sciences into an improved planning process.

Let us plan to save lives, to protect the environment, to achieve savings from appropriate ecological planning, to improve prediction and placement, and to improve the human condition.

Part II

Planning the Ecological Region

Ian McHarg is part of the organic tradition of American planning that has two clear, although somewhat overlapping, lineages. The first is that of landscape architecture from Frederick Law Olmsted, Sr., to Charles Eliot, Frederick Law Olmsted, Jr., John C. Olmsted, and today's John Lyle, Julius Fabos, Anne Spirn, Forester Ndubisi, Donna Erickson, Glenn Eugster, Catherine Brown, and Rob Thayer. The second line is that of planning, from Patrick Geddes, Lewis Mumford, Benton MacKaye, Artur Glikson to today's Bob Yaro, Randall Arendt, Deborah Popper, Frank Popper, and Tim Beatley. McHarg is the heir to and propagator of both lines. He also cross-pollinates both strains with that of the naturalist-scientist-conservationist tradition, that of George Perkins Marsh, John Wesley Powell, and Gifford Pinchot, the Leopolds and the Odums, Loren Eiseley and Paul Sears, and Rachel Carson and Ruth Patrick.

The connection with Mumford is especially strong. Mark Luccarelli provides a thoughtful analysis of Lewis Mumford's contributions to planning in *Lewis Mumford and the Ecological Region* (1995). Luccarelli's description of Mumford's efforts "to reorient urban life, to address the crisis of over urbanization, and to recontextualize cities in relation to nature" nicely captures McHarg's work as well:

> Mumford cultivated the possibility of a third way: not rural or urban—at least not as these have been defined as polar opposites in the modern era—and certainly not the "middle landscape" of the pastoral suburb; rather, a city as polis in relation to the organic complexities of the regional ecosystem (p. 3).

Mumford used regionalism as a unifying principle to combine ideas about neotechnics, organicism, and community. He drew much from the work of the Scottish botanist-sociologist-town planner Patrick Geddes as well and the French sociologist and biogeographer Frédéric Le Play. According to Luccarelli (1995, see also Wojtowicz 1996), "Mumford was concerned with planning an ecological and regional restructuring of the city and its environs, *he insisted that regional planning be informed cultural criticism*" (p. 35, emphasis added).

To this end, Mumford joined with several other intellectuals to form the Regional Planning Association of America (RPAA) in 1923. This small group included forester Benton MacKaye, architect Clarence Stein, landscape architect Henry Wright, housing advocate Catherine Bauer, architect Frederick Ackerman, and a few others. The RPAA in general and Mumford especially sought to expand Ebenezer Howard's garden city idea. According to Luccarelli, "Mumford believed the garden city could be a 'regional city': a new kind of modern city in creative relationship with the surrounding countryside" (1995, p. 77). Mumford's colleague MacKaye contributed ideas about the *processes* needed to achieve such a "creative relationship": planning as exploration and as applied science for charting the future from an understanding of natural processes and patterns.

Benton MacKaye (1940) explicitly linked regional planning to ecology. He defined regional planning as "a comprehensive ordering or visualization of the possible or potential movement, activity or flow (from sources onward) of water, commodities or population, within a defined area or sphere, for the purpose of laying therein the physical basis for the 'good life' or optimum human living" (p. 351).

According to MacKaye, a comprehensive ordering referred to "a visualization of nature's permanent comprehensive 'ordering' as distinguished from the interim makeshift orderings of man" (1940, p. 350). MacKaye quoted Plato to emphasize this thought, "To command nature we must first obey her." MacKaye felt that what he called the "good life" or "optimum human living" was expressed by what the U.S. Congress has called the "general welfare" and what Thomas Jefferson called the "pursuit of happiness." He concluded that "regional planning is ecology" and gave the following definition:

> Human ecology: its concern is the relation of the human organism to its environment. The region is the unit of environment. Planning is the charting of activity therein affecting the good of the human organism, its object is the application or putting into practice of the optimum relation between the human and the region. Regional planning in short is applied human ecology (MacKaye, 1940, p. 351).

In his introduction to McHarg's *Design with Nature* (1969) Mumford clearly passed the regional ecological planning torch to McHarg, who would link the new knowledge derived from ecology to action. Mumford wrote: "he demonstrates, by taking difficult concrete examples, how this new knowledge may and must be applied to actual environments, to caring for natural areas, like swamps, lakes and rivers, to choosing sites for further urban settlements, to reestablishing human norms and life-furthering objectives in metropolitan conurbations."

To accomplish this purpose, McHarg realized that he had to change planning education. He addresses this topic in "Regional Landscape Planning," a 1963 paper based on a talk given at the University of Massachusetts during a conference on natural resources. The talk addressed open space concerns and how to create systems of open spaces. McHarg's approach differs from putting "a stencil over the land and saying that a Green Belt should surround the city." McHarg illustrated his approach through actual projects, a reflection of his design training. He created a model for applied, or action, research where hypotheses were developed and methods tested. In essence, he laid the foundation for a case study approach to planning education and research. In his writings and speeches, he would then narrate the case studies or projects as "stories."

His systems approach was interdisciplinary and had teams of talented individuals. One of the "stories" related in his 1963 paper notes the involvement of Ann Strong, who later emerged as one of the most significant environmental attorneys of our time. The study included early explorations of important concepts such as development rights, wetlands zoning, conservation easements, and preferential taxation for open space lands.

In his quest to redefine the planning profession, McHarg recognized that "the normal professional training of the landscape architect is totally inadequate" for the elevated mission he was proposing. He felt that planning education in the 1960s was equally inadequate. Regional landscape planning is what today would be called ecological planning or environmental planning.

A revealing aspect of that day's talk can be seen in the comments by the two discussants from two different disciplines. Professor Lawrence Hamilton, from the Cornell University Department of Conservation, offered the perspective of a natural scientist engaged in professional resource management education. Professor John Friedmann, then of the Harvard-MIT Joint Center for Urban Studies and later of UCLA, commented from the point of view of a social scientist concerned with graduate education and research in the planning discipline.

Professor Hamilton provides McHarg with a hearty endorsement. John Friedmann, who became one of the leading planning theorists from an applied social scientist perspective, is more skeptical: "my colleagues [Hamilton and McHarg] and I are taking utterly different approaches to pursuing the subject of resource development on a regional scale." Professor Friedmann attributes this difference to their disparate disciplinary origins (i.e., forestry, landscape architecture, and economics), overlooking (or unaware of) McHarg's academic background in city planning and the social sciences at Harvard or that the forester was quick to grasp McHarg's arguments for a new approach to regional planning. Furthermore, Friedmann notes that one "of the great difficulties in planning is that the social scientist finds it nearly impossible to talk with the physical planners." As the planning movement followed Friedmann this schism was exacerbated, and problems of communication developed between social scientists and architects and landscape architects.

Still, Friedmann did advocate "a common orientation, a common outlook, a common vocabulary, and a common concern" for planners both in education and practice. To establish such a base, he argued that three major subject areas should form the core of planning curricula: (1) resource analysis and policies; (2) the politics, process, and theory of planning decisions; and (3) social values and goals. I believe that McHarg followed Friedmann's ideas for both a common orientation and the three major subject areas. In the Master of Regional Planning curriculum McHarg developed at Penn, the common outlook and vocabulary revolved around ecology. The curriculum was structured to address (1) environmental inventories and analysis; (2) the planning process and environmental law; and (3) social values. A basic understanding of ecological science and geology was considered a prerequisite.

The planning of open space is also the topic of his 1970 "Open Space from Natural Processes," which appeared in a book on the topic edited by McHarg's then-partner, the innovative planner David Wallace. McHarg promotes a positive role for open space, one that complements rather than avoids the built environment. The optimum result would be a system of two intertwining webs, one composed of developed land and the second consisting of open space in a natural, or near natural, state.

In that article McHarg evokes Mumford and MacKaye again. He also begins to identify his work with that of Charles Eliot, the brilliant son of the Harvard president and the protégé of Frederick Law Olmsted. McHarg discovered Eliot in the early 1960s and mentioned him in 1964 in "The Place of Nature in the City of Man" (see chapter 2). As the 1970 article illustrates, McHarg remained a champion of Eliot throughout his career.

It also shows that McHarg was well aware of the work of his contemporaries, such as the pioneering river corridor plans of Philip Lewis in Wisconsin and Illinois (Lewis 1996). McHarg also provides an insightful discussion about the merits of using either hydrological or physiographic structure for regional open space planning. (McHarg clearly prefers the use of physiographic structure.) The open space work of Lewis and McHarg during the 1960s provided the foundation for subsequent greenways planning from the late 1970s to the present.

McHarg's article also introduces the intriguing concept of using open space and "airsheds" to ameliorate air pollution problems. Pollution-free areas, "tributary to the city," such as parks and other open spaces, help to create airsheds. McHarg suggests that planning such airsheds at the regional scale would reduce air pollution. For cities with "high pollution days," such as Denver, Los Angeles, and Phoenix, this concept is even more timely today than in 1970. Airsheds, in a more narrow sense, are used by the U.S. Environmental Protection Agency to implement federal clean air laws. Air quality could be improved by implementing open-space systems.

Like the 1963 "Regional Landscape Planning" article, "Must We Sacrifice the West?" is based on a speech. The paper provides insight into Ian McHarg's provocative speaking style as well as his self-depreciating wit. A distinguishing aspect is his ability to adapt his rather consistent main themes to various specific times and places. "Must We Sacrifice the West?" was delivered at the height of the "energy crisis" of the 1970s. His talk was given in Colorado, where at the time an energy development boom threatened the quality of the Rocky Mountain environment. As a result, Ian McHarg provides cogent advice for energy planning.

Because it argues that calculations of energy expenses should include social costs, the paper demonstrates the social concerns that underlie McHarg's ecological planning approach. Planning is advocated as a means to address social issues, "the device" by which people "confront the future." Such confrontation requires that human values be explicit. McHarg holds that such values, when clarified and linked to the environment, have considerably more influence on planning than any amount of data.

Throughout his academic career, McHarg continued to rub up against the "orthodox" city planning tradition, frequently irritating planning theorists but also influencing and changing their ideas about planning. His 1978 "Ecological Planning" was included in an orthodox, but comprehensive, planning theory text. He calls the planner who pursued the traditional approach attempting to come from out of town to help people solve problems "a menace." The role envisioned by McHarg is that of catalyst. He views such a role as a creative activity. Planning, then, is an art, but one based on the predictability that science provides. Science helps the planner understand "the consequences of different courses of action."

McHarg argues that planners should not impose their values on a people or a place. Rather, values should be derived from those who inhabit the landscapes. Developing values from a local perspective based on regional biophysical processes differs from importing values from outside the region.

Determining, identifying, and making explicit values are central to McHarg's planning theory. The value system determines the planning process.

His 1981 "Human Ecological Planning at Pennsylvania" returns to the topic of planning education. Regional Landscape Planning has been replaced by Human Ecological Planning in this *Landscape Planning* essay. However, the actual degree that was implemented at Penn in 1965 was a Master of Regional Planning. Between the early 1960s and the early 1980s interest in regional planning waned in the United States. Meanwhile, interest in environmental and even ecological planning increased, partially as a result of McHarg's influence. His 1981 article offers a reflection on the goals for planning (and for McHarg *ecological* was increasingly the correct modifier) that he established in the 1960s.

In spite of McHarg's influence, the term environmental planning has gained wider acceptance in the United States than ecological planning. Why? There are at least three reasons. First, environmental design and environmental planning are terms that have enjoyed much popularity within the influential California academic circles since the 1960s. For example, the University of California-Berkeley, the University of California-Davis, the California State Polytechnic University-Pomona, and the California Polytechnic State University-San Luis Obispo have colleges or schools of environmental design, and California-Berkeley offers a Ph.D. in environmental planning. Second, the National Environmental Policy Act of 1970 mandated the use of "the environmental design arts" in federal decision making. As a result, environmental design became institutionalized in the federal bureaucracy.

Third, the concepts of environmental design and environmental planning evolved from architecture and planning. The design disciplines have a long history of intervening in and manipulating our surroundings and in creating places. Architects give form to built urban environments. Planners suggest policy options for human settlements. Environments have a strong visual connotation. Architects are comfortable with visual aesthetics. Ecology, the understanding of interactions, is more unsettling, even subversive.

In contrast to environmental design and planning, *ecological* design and planning developed in the United States within academic programs of landscape architecture. Landscape architecture education began in the mid-nineteenth century in agricultural and horticulture colleges that were established as a result of land-grant legislation signed by Abraham Lincoln in 1862. This law provided land grants to the states to establish public agricultural and technical colleges. A strong supporter of this system was the pioneer landscape architect Frederick Law Olmsted, Sr., who was involved in planning several land-grant college campuses. The Olmsted brothers' firm (Frederick, Jr., and John C.) subsequently carried on this tradition of campus planning, especially at growing land-grant schools.

A second tradition of landscape architecture education was established when Harvard University founded a landscape architecture program in 1900 with close ties to architecture. In contrast to the land-grant system, Harvard's program emphasized design instead of agriculture and horticulture. Under Frederick Law Olmsted, Jr., and John Nolen's leadership, Harvard initiated a city planning program in the early twentieth century. Many American universities followed the Harvard example of landscape architecture closely aligned with architecture and planning. As a result, two traditions in landscape architecture were established: one emphasizing rural concerns and natural resources; the other more focused on design and urban planning.

Ecological design and planning are a fusion of those traditions. For McHarg ecological planning is a method "to promote human health and well being." He distinguishes ecological planning from economics, transportation, and orthodox city planning. The key, noted in the 1981 human ecological planning article, is McHarg's advocacy to understand the locality, that is, the natural and social processes of a specific region, a specific place. A role of the planner is to synthesize information from the various sciences about a locality to develop hypotheses about its possible futures.

In several other publications, McHarg explains how to organize biophysical information chronologically and arrange it in a "layer cake" model to display causality and to reveal landscape patterns. He also discusses, in many places, how to incorporate the human values of such information to reveal opportunities and constraints for future land uses. The 1981 *Landscape Planning* (now called *Landscape and Urban Planning*) article is his most complete work on the relevance of human ecological information in the planning process.

Human ecology dominated the Penn Department of Landscape Architecture and Regional Planning research agenda throughout the 1970s. With the publication of *Design with Nature* McHarg received some criticism for ignoring social factors in the planning process. He openly admitted that the focus of *Design with Nature* was on natural processes, on ecological determinism, because such information had been ignored by most traditional planning, design, and decision-making processes. To balance that one-sided approach, he began in the 1970s to incorporate social factors into ecological planning.

At the time anthropology was a strong discipline at Penn, and McHarg was a friend and admirer of Loren Eiseley of the anthropology department. Anthropologists also had strong interest in ecology and, at Penn, they had discovered the city. Because of criticism for sending ethnographers to exotic Third World nations ("cultural imperialism") while ignoring the contemporary urban settlements in developed nations, the Center for Urban Ethnography was founded at Penn. Led by John Szwed, it attracted anthropologists interested in urban America (see Dan Rose's wonderful *Black American Street Life* [1987], for example).

As a result, McHarg imported anthropologists into his department during the 1970s as he had a decade earlier with ecologists, geologists, hydrologists, and soil scientists (as well as architects, landscape architects, the economist Nick Muhlenberg, and the attorney-city planners Ann Strong and John Keene). Anthropologists Yehudi Cohen and Setha Low taught courses that introduced planners and landscape architects to the basic concepts of ecological and medical anthropology. Even more significantly, ethnographer Dan Rose collaborated with regional planner Jon Berger on a series of human ecology projects that were patterned after McHarg's work.

The essential contribution of the discipline of anthropology to environmental planning is the idea that an ethnographic history of a place should be included in the inventory phase of the planning process. Like a layer-cake diagram of the biophysical processes, the chronology provided by an ethnographic history can help to explain causality. The result is a combination of Patrick Geddes' folk–work–place with ideas about randomness and order reminiscent of chaos theory (see Prigogine and Stengers 1984, for example).

John Friedmann includes a table—a family tree—of the intellectual influences on American planning theory in his *Planning in the Public Domain* (1987). He commented on McHarg's 1963 paper at the University of Massachusetts, so obviously he is aware of him, but McHarg, Patrick Geddes, Charles Eliot are not included in the family tree. The organicists are generally excluded, except for Mumford, who is listed on the far right branch under the category "Utopians, Social Anarchists and Radicals." From an orthodox perspective this is probably an accurate placement. "Sociology" and "Scientific Management" (i.e., Emile Durkheim, Max Weber, and Frederick Taylor) are placed in the center of Friedmann's table. Ian McHarg, like his mentor Mumford, indeed offered a radical view of planning, one based on ecology.

One younger theorist, Manuel Castells, whom Friedmann identifies as a neo-Marxist (the neo-Marxists also fall on the far right of Friedmann's table) has begun to espouse an ecological view. Castell's observations of 1992 are similar to those expressed by McHarg two decades earlier, especially as they relate to the destructiveness of planning systems based on economic determinism as well as to the importance, even prominence, of environmentally based planning. According to Castells, "The danger of total environmental destruction under the new worldwide economic dynamism imposes a new, more comprehensive conception of land use. Environmental planning will be the most rapidly expanding planning frontier in the United States in the next decade" (1992, p. 77). If the neo-Marxists have adopted such ideas, perhaps the organic, ecological tradition of Eliot–Geddes–Mumford–McHarg belongs at the center of planning's intellectual influences, not the margins.

References

Castells, Manuel. 1992. "The World Has Changed: Can Planning Change?" *Landscape and Urban Planning* 22:73–78.

Friedmann, John. 1987. *Planning in the Public Domain: From Knowledge to Action.* Princeton: Princeton University Press.

Lewis, Philip H., Jr. 1996. *Tomorrow by Design: A Regional Design Process for Sustainability.* New York: Wiley.

Luccarelli, Mark. 1995. *Lewis Mumford and the Ecological Region: The Politics of Planning.* New York: The Guilford Press.

MacKaye, Benton. 1940. "Regional Planning and Ecology." *Ecological Monographs* 10:349–53.

McHarg, Ian. 1969. *Design with Nature.* Garden City, N.Y.: Doubleday, Natural History Press. 1992. Second edition, New York: Wiley.

Prigogine, Ilya and Isabelle Stengers. 1984. *Order Out of Chaos.* Toronto, Ontario: Bantam.

Rose, Dan. 1987. *Black American Street Life: South Philadelphia, 1969–1971.* Philadelphia: University of Pennsylvania Press.

Wojtowicz, Robert. 1996. *Lewis Mumford and American Modernism.* New York: Cambridge University Press.

6

Regional Landscape Planning (1963)

In 1997 the comment by John Friedmann at the end of this chapter was confirmed for accuracy. In the book Resources, the Metropolis and the Land-Grant University, *where the essay appeared, his name was misspelled, so it may have been another John Friedmann, one with a single "n" in his family name, who commented. Now retired in Australia, Professor Friedmann confirmed by e-mail that, yes, indeed, he was the author of the remarks in question. University of Massachusetts conference organizer and book editor Andrew Scheffey was a friend of Friedmann. From Australia, Professor Friedmann made the following observations:*

> *Thank you for this piece of forgotten history in my academic life. Andy Scheffey was an old buddy of mine from Korea days, and it was he who put the conference together. Rereading my commentary and your [Steiner's] historical introduction, I confess that I was quite intolerant of the "organic" school of regional planning at the time. Intolerant and somewhat ignorant of its contributions. The two probably go together. Today, I have become more tolerant, but I have not become an ecologically informed regionalist. Although I admire the work of (some) landscape architects, I have not found a way to integrate their work with the approach to regional planning (or spatial planning) that comes out of the socio-economic tradition with which you are familiar. The discourse on "sustainable development" has helped to highlight the importance of environmental/ecological dimensions of economic growth, but the idealism implicit in Ian McHarg's and Mumford's formulations is altogether absent from the discourse.*

> *So: two streams that touched in 1963 but had little to share and ultimately went their separate ways.*

No, I do not wish to add anything to my commentary at the time. I would put things differently today, but it wouldn't put me any closer to Ian than I was thirty-four years ago.

Professor Friedmann's candid observations reveal the gap between "orthodox" planning theory and the Mumford–McHarg "organic" tradition. As Friedmann reveals, this gap persists, although interest in "sustainability" and "sustainable development" may indeed create a bridge. McHarg's quest then was, with the advice and encouragement of Mumford, to re-create the field of planning. This chapter represents a first step.

I differentiate the professions of regional planning and regional science from that of regional landscape planning which we hope to develop at the University of Pennsylvania. Although there are as yet no specific accomplishments to refer to, I want to talk with you about the direction of this prospective curriculum. I have been asked, wisely I believe, to approach this subject indirectly by describing some of the research work being carried out in the Department of Landscape Architecture at the University of Pennsylvania, as well as some of the research projects which I am involved in as a private practitioner. From a discussion of these projects one can discern some of the skills which are required for Regional Landscape Planning. This discussion hopefully will have some value to you for its generality, although quite obviously it is based upon several particular experiences within a particular context.

The first project concerns open space. When the open space provisions of the 1961 Housing Act were made law, the Urban Renewal Administration confronted the necessity of producing criteria for guiding the purchase of sites within metropolitan areas. As you may recall, the law contains provisions under which 20 percent of the cost of open space land acquisition would be made available from a $50 million fund established for this purpose, or 30 percent in the event that the open space sought was part of a comprehensive metropolitan plan. But the act contained no regulations or criteria concerning the type of land areas to be acquired for such open space purposes.

While my department knew nothing of this particular quandary, we had just finished a year-long study of the Delaware River Basin carried out by twelve graduate landscape architecture students. We had conducted this study in cooperation with the U.S. Army Engineers, the Soil Conservation Service, and various state departments of conservation, economic development, and so forth. In a memorandum describing the preliminary results of this study, sent to the Director of the Institute for Urban Studies at the University of Pennsylvania, I had stated several tentative conclusions of the study. These were not revolutionary findings or concepts in any sense of the term, and they will probably appear relatively simple to those of you who are natural scientists by training and profession, but within our own academic planning departments they had the aspect of original innovations.

The purpose of the study was to develop criteria for land-use planning in the Delaware River Basin. It was obvious that the criteria should be based upon an understanding of the natural processes in the region. Criteria used within this penumbra selected discreet natural processes which performed work, which had intrinsic value, or which offered protection in their natural state. These land classifications were mapped and measured. In addition a panoply of legal tools was related to the selected classifications as prospective instruments of land-use planning.

The Institute for Urban Studies was interested in the ideas presented, and took the matter up with the Urban Renewal Administration, which ultimately decided to support a research project designed to test these various concepts, and to come up with qualitative measurements of these functional values. The unit of study was determined to be the eight-county Philadelphia-Camden metropolitan area.

The criteria advanced were, again, fundamentally quite simple: surface water, marshes, flood plains, wetlands, aquifers-recharge areas, forests, agricultural land, ridges, and steep land. We advanced the concept that the upland sponge has a preponderant role in matters of flood control and water supply, particularly low-flow problems. The disproportionate role of estuary marshes in the diminution of the tidal component of floods was discussed, and beyond that the concept that the coefficient of runoff within a flood control plan might be an appropriate determinant of land use. A final concept was presented, that of an urban airshed. It assumes that atmospheric pollution is going to stay with us, and that inversion conditions will continue at the normal incidence, but that the increasing growth, increasing combustion, and increasing pollution, will make the quality of the air-relieving inversion more important. Thus, in the future we may want to know more about the area of clear air, without combustive processes, that will be required in any metropolitan area to ensure that the air which replaces the foul air is significantly cleaner than that which it replaces.

It is not difficult to discern the wide range of professional competencies necessary to provide the basic information required to establish such criteria—information on water-based classifications, surface waters in various forms, the aquifers and their aquifer recharge areas, the flood plains, the marshes, the wetlands. The basic information on these topics was provided by the U.S. Geological Survey and the U.S. Army Corps of Engineers by their hydrologists. The information on alluvium and flood plains was secured from the Soil Conservation Service county soil surveys. A correlation of alluvium to cyclical floods will be done in collaboration with hydrologists of the Army

Corps of Engineers relating these direct observations to the deposition of alluvium as recorded in the various soil surveys.

Having mapped these factors in the study areas, the next problem was the measurement of each of the parameters of which there were eight. With eight counties and four hundred municipalities involved, overlapping two states, this could have become a fantasy of planimetry, and perhaps the only real innovation of this research project was the discovery that the photo electric cell is adaptable, and can be used to measure reflected and incident light. By making a negative of each of these parameters, of which the parameter itself is black against a white background, and knowing the total area of the metropolitan region, it is possible to determine the area covered by the parameter. This proved to be a most inexpensive and accurate method.

The next problem involved the calculation of land values, and this required an economist. It proved to be an extremely difficult physical problem indeed, because of the disparate quality and quantity of available information. In addition, properties are seldom assessed on the basis of constituent parts, for example, in one farm the constituent value of flood plain, steep lands, woodlands, and so forth. Clearly this investigation falls to the economist.

The final step in this first project involved an analysis of existing and proposed legislation. This called for legal skills. We secured the services of a lawyer, Ann Louise Strong, and her role was to consider a sequence of means including tax exemptions, tax deferrals, preferential assessments, development rights, scenic easements, recreational easements, various types of zoning—wetland zoning, aquifer zoning, agricultural zoning, steep land zoning, forestry zoning, and so on, with the final possibility of outright purchase.

This process, then, included the definition of a range of criteria, mapping of these criteria, their measurement, assembly of legislative tools, and analysis of costs. Many disciplines were involved in this process. In this case the landscape architect was the coordinator. Equally clear, the normal professional training of the landscape architect is totally inadequate in preparation for such a role. Hydrology and geology, agriculture and forestry, zoology, botany and ecology, economics and law were all integral to this process.

This project was done for a total cost of $15,000. The second project I want to mention is being done in cooperation with the states of Pennsylvania and New Jersey, each providing $10,000, and the federal government which is providing $42,000. The purpose of this project is to go beyond the steps already described, to determine the future recreational demand, and to produce a primer on the selection of metropolitan open space land areas. A number of elements are involved.

The first is to interpret and modify and adopt the estimates of recreation demand made by the Outdoor Recreation Resources Review Commission. We believe that these figures are good, but must be refined and elaborated. The calculations on demand will be the responsibility of economists with the involvement of persons qualified in transportation. In this region we have data from the Penn-Jersey Transportation Study which permit us to construct a transportation model related to recreational demand.

The next thing we shall have to do, after determining the location of all available lands now used for open space purposes, and assessing the utilization in these facilities, will be to calculate the degree to which these areas might be further developed to permit more intensive use. It is quite apparent that these existing areas will not meet future demand. Therefore, we shall have to examine all the natural areas which have been defined, many of which are permissive to various types of recreational uses, and indicate the extent to which these areas can support some of this recreational load, consistent with their other functions. Again, it is reasonable to presume that these two resources collectively will not fully satisfy future demands, and so the final step in this project will be to determine that increment of unsatisfied demand which will have to be met through the acquisition of additional open space. These will be determined by the types of demand anticipated, physical location of the sites, and economic criteria—the values of the land. The latter will be the task of the economist and transportation expert. The determination of the appropriateness of the land in terms of scenery and its suitability for various recreation functions will be the role of the landscape architect.

At that point we shall be confronted with the problem of reconciling a number of different criteria: existing open space which has been acquired for a number of different reasons, few of them rational; a number of natural areas, the selection of which has been based upon various different criteria, none of which were really recreational; and finally, those areas of open space which will have to be acquired to meet the residual recreational demand. We shall be confronted with the necessity of deciding whether or not these should be systematic. It must be realized that the prototype of most regional planning of this sort, certainly in Great Britain, is to put a stencil over the land and say that a Green Belt should surround the city. We do not believe that this idea of simply proscribing a Green Belt is very valuable or appropriate for the needs of today. We are concerned with producing metropolitan open space for the Philadelphia metropolitan area, but we are also concerned with the criteria which should produce systems of open space.

From this brief discussion it should be clear that the skills and professional qualifications of many persons other than the landscape architect are called for in research projects of this nature. Yet this is the type of regional planning that will become increasingly needed in the future. I suspect that there is no single person who could be trained to do it alone.

Let me now tell you about another project which is quite different, but which in a sense is focused on the same objective. This project happens to be in the private domain rather than the public.

Some time ago a colleague of mine and I were asked to be consultant planners by a group of inhabitants in two valleys in Baltimore County, Maryland. The problem these people face is a very common one. They are located on the outskirts of Baltimore, and they are soon going to be overwhelmed by the excremental type of development. They are reluctant to have this beautiful land ruined. And it is beautiful land, typical hunt country, covered with beech and hickory, a lovely landscape which they do not want despoiled. The problem facing these people is to avoid the cataclysm of development, while at the same time reaping some of the fruits of this development.

The project which we have proposed, in bare outline, involves the following elements. First, we shall make an economic and physical projection based upon the status quo. That is, if nothing else intervenes, if the only future intervention is the existing zoning power, which is to say no intervention whatsoever, then what will be the result? We propose to make an economic projection of the changes in land value, changes of building values, the type and location of development which can be anticipated under prevailing circumstances. We know already, of course, that such development will be catastrophic, and that it will cause everybody who has been there and made the area what it is to leave.

The next step will be to determine the best possible solution to this. What of this land is actually indispensable to the image which the present inhabitants have of it? What parts of it are in effect amenable to development and should be developed?

Answering these questions will require a number of steps. First will be a particular analysis of the physiography of the region, of the flood plains, of the agricultural land and the forests, the marshes and streams, and an analysis of the degree to which parts of the valley are indivisible to other parts. Following upon an analysis of the *genius loci* there is the task of developing alternative plans which locate development without despoilation. This is the orthodox task of the landscape architect-planner. By far the more difficult task is to develop a method through which a plan may be realized. This area contains some 500 landowners. They must act in concert to ensure realization of the plan. We can heighten their willingness by demonstrating the specter of despoilation resulting from unplanned development. Our proffered solution is the creation of a Development Corporation. We suggest that the landowners concede the development rights of their land to the corporation in exchange for stock. This method has a number of merits. It will tend to halt prodigal development creating low values and it will thus induce intensive development and high values. This device will also produce a higher increment of development profits, which permits giving payments to members of the corporation whose lands should not, in the plan, be developed. This process calls for the services of the tax lawyer, the corporation lawyer, the land-use lawyer, and the economist. The earlier portions of this project will be the province of geologists, hydrologists, agriculturalists, soil conservationists, and landscape architects. And in the very first stage the economist will predominate. So here again, dealing with quite a different sort of problem, we have the same wide spectrum of professionals.

One purpose in telling you about this is to show what is involved, not only in doing landscape planning jobs, but also in finding these jobs and persuading people that they have to be done! In this sense the architect is lucky, because people really have to keep the rain out, and so there will always have to be buildings. But the landscape architect is really involved in purveying a metaphysical symbol, and purveying it to a society which really doesn't give a damn about metaphysical symbols. And so, he not only has to be propagandist for metaphysical symbols, but he has to do this in a materialistic society; he has to show them that they can have metaphysical symbols and Cadillacs, too!

We have in Philadelphia a comprehensive plan which envisions spending $12.5 billion in 20 years to acquire open space, at which time there will be less open space then, than there is now. This struck me as rather expensive retrogression and I was somewhat distressed by this finding. After thinking about it I hit upon the idea of creating new usable open space. We have in Philadelphia some 300 piers, all but a few of which are derelict. I thought that perhaps the area between the bulkhead and the pierhead might be filled in and converted into riverside parks. The Philadelphia Planning Commission retained me to prepare a preliminary investigation of this hypothesis.

This again involved a great number of scientific investigations. First came the hydrologic work. Would the diminution of the water perimeter affect the flood capacity of the Delaware River? Here we obviously turned to the hydrologists of the U.S. Army Corps of Engineers. The next consideration concerned the problems of building foundations, and for this we went again to the Army Corps of Engineers, and also to the Netherlands to discuss the problem with the people at the Soil Mechanics Institute at Delft. Then there was the question of aquifers and the aquifer recharge areas on both sides of the Delaware. The question of sediment yield came up, and it was learned that sediment deposition would in fact be diminished by reducing the friction by bulkheading instead of having a whole set of finger piers.

Another important consideration was the potential source of fill material. The Army Corps of Engineers were at the time widening and deepening the Delaware channel, and were producing literally hundreds of millions of tons of gravel, sand, and organic silt. At the same time, it transpired that the city sanitation department had the problem of disposing of one million cubic yards of incinerator waste a year. They have a $10 million capital investment program to buy barges, build water transfer stations, and to transfer this material to the marshes of New Jersey, which of course they would then despoil.

A cost-benefit analysis showed that the City of Philadelphia could bulk-head 6 ½ miles of waterfront, create 436 acres of new park land, and spend $10 million on the development of parks, at costs identical to that required to barge incinerator wastes to destroy the marshes of New Jersey. Here again, quite a varied spectrum of professionals was involved, and hardly a landscape problem, but certainly a metropolitan resource situation.

I can conclude very quickly by turning to the question of regional landscape planning at Pennsylvania. We now have a Department of Regional Science, under Walter Isard. We have a Department of City Planning with a faculty of about fifty, primarily social scientists. There is active discussion about the development of a Department of Regional Planning, based largely upon the proclivities and attitudes of the present Department of City Planning, but in conjunction with the Department of Regional Science. This is all very well, and such a development would fit very smoothly into our situation. However, both of these existing departments are staffed almost exclusively by social scientists. *Both* would like very much to have natural scientists present.

Strangely enough, in my university, where there is no forestry, no agriculture, and where the natural scientists are primarily the biological scientists, concerned with cytology and microbiology, landscape architecture constitutes the only bridge to the natural sciences. This is fortuitous, and we have, therefore, received the assent of the Departments of Regional Science, City Planning, the Dean, and the Provost to investigate creating a Department of Regional Landscape Planning which will be the third department of this triad—regional science, regional planning, regional landscape planning. The last would be the bridge to the natural sciences. The first two departments would include people from statistics, economics, planning, sociology, law, and the latter would attract natural scientists interested in planning problems. We would hope to receive people with at least a master's degree proficiency in their own field, and to this we would add one and perhaps two years of work in planning itself, done in conjunction with courses in regional science and regional planning. Of course, we would hope that the regional scientists and planners would take at least several courses with us.

I think that this new direction is a great adventure. I am very glad that the natural scientists are beginning to be concerned with the problems confronting the physical planner. I believe that the absence of the natural scientists in planning up to this point is very, very sad indeed. I do not think this is due to any exclusion by the social scientists, but rather to the indifference of the natural scientists themselves.

I am delighted that the day has come when the natural scientists are beginning to become interested in this field. I think that their contributions are fundamental and that this interaction will be beneficial in complementing the existing body of planning knowledge, and leading us to fruitful innovation.

Comments—Lawrence S. Hamilton

I want to take this opportunity to re-emphasize, from the standpoint of the so-called natural sciences, the imperative for action which I see in this open space question generally. Secondly, I wish to stress the need for greater participation by the natural scientists in regional planning activities. I then want to make a few remarks about what we have been doing at Cornell in our graduate training program in trying to produce resource professionals who might meet this need.

With regard to the second of these—the need for greater participation by natural sciences—if I heard Professor McHarg correctly, all that I can do is to say Amen to his plea. He has demonstrated this point so well that I wish I had said it that way.

And now to the first point. In New York State we find the problems of open space planning mounting at a phenomenal rate. The changes in land use are occurring at a bewildering pace. We have the paradox, which I am sure you in Massachusetts have also, of a state that is becoming both increasingly urbanized and increasingly forested at one and the same time. We see something like 200,000 acres passing out of agriculture each year into this wild domain called open space. Some land is going into urban uses, but much is starting down the successional path toward forest. In this forest, along with the floral and fauna constituents, there will, of course, be weekend hideaways, summer residences, and even year-round homes. These present land-use planning problems of new dimensions.

In no place is the change more rapid than on the cutting edge of the urban or metropolitan fringe— this tension zone of rural-urban interpenetration. A group such as this meeting, or any educational institution concerned with natural resources, might well focus its attention on the problems being generated in this fringe area. The problems are legion, and they are on a new scale, making obsolete our traditional tools, techniques, and approaches. This is where the landscape of America is being most drastically altered. We need research directed towards these problems, and we need to have persons with an ecological comprehension of the problems involved in our resource planning and development activities. Again, I strongly concur with the sentiments expressed by Professor McHarg, and with his plea for greater participation by the natural scientists.

It is important, as we decide what we are going to do with this open space, that we recognize that the various components—trees, grasses, sedges, gullies, water, and so forth—are not just there, but that they are part of a process going on, part of a number of processes—life and death, weathering and erosion migration and invasion, deposition—all these and others, contributing to some kind of energy system. I am talking about the ecosystem. These processes tend to become exceedingly complex, and what we do to one element has repercussions which echo around the entire system.

Resource professionals trained to understand the biological and physical environment (some of them do not at the present time), geologists, foresters, wildlife managers, soil scientists or hydrologists, are in a position to identify the natural resource development opportunities which exist, as well as the natural resource or environmental constraints which are operative. Portions of the environment having unique natural characteristics often fall before unplanned or ill-planned urban and suburban uses because they are beyond the ken of subdividers, politicians, real estate developers, lot purchasers, and perhaps even some urban and regional planners who have come primarily from the social sciences.

We are all familiar with the everyday examples of these ill-planned uses of land. There are the gravel deposits of high value that may be lost to commercial exploitation because we put residences on them, or near enough to them that the owners feel gravel exploitation to be a nuisance, and pass ordinances against them. Or, the unique recreation site, important waterfowl areas, key areas for future water storage, that become lost to use, or become too expensive to reclaim, because of ill-advised development. Resources such as these must be identified in advance so that certain types of non-compatible uses generated by urban forces may be guided, wherever possible, to more appropriate and equally satisfactory areas. Similarly, areas of highly productive soils, uniquely adapted to low-cost agricultural production, should be identified and perhaps reserved from development until absolutely needed for building sites, airports, residences, and industrial zones. The evaluation and proper interpretation of soil resources can result in better planning for transportation, industrial location, subdivision development, landscaping, and other functions. A soil survey can identify various soils appropriate for particular uses, thus avoiding such costly ecological consequences as soil slippage, flooded basements, waste disposal problems.

I believe that this aspect of the regional planning process can best be met by persons trained in disciplines dealing with the use and management of natural resources. In addition to professional specialized resource training of undergraduate programs, such persons should receive additional training in ecology and economics. This is what we are trying to do at Cornell. Those resource professionals who come to us with an interest in land-use planning are given an ecological basis by appropriate work in soils, geology, air photo interpretation (which is really understanding the environment from a picture of it), plant and animal ecology. In addition to this they are given work in planning theory. The methods provided by economics for weighing and analyzing alternative possibilities are equally important ingredients. Since this is frequently lacking in the training of many resource specialists, we encourage either a major or minor concentration in economics.

This sort of broad-brush graduate training admittedly has some real dangers. We have tried to hold these to a minimum by insisting that persons coming into the program have depth training in one of the natural sciences, and that they have had professional work experience. By observing these criteria we have been successful in securing mature graduate students, who know why they have come back, and who feel a commitment to making this kind of academic endeavor. They realize that an understanding of the natural environment is necessary if they are to work effectively in their particular field. They are concerned about making the environment a more pleasant place for human occupancy.

An institution such as the University of Massachusetts would be well advised to capitalize on the strengths that currently exist at the institution. Where a strong college of agriculture with competency in natural sciences is within the university, it would seem to me that land-use planning orientation might well have an ecological foundation. Our program of resource training originated within such a framework, although we have established good working relationships with the social sciences and the urban-oriented planning of the college of architecture.

These remarks refer to the training provided for natural resource specialists interested in working in the planning phases of this field. It seems to me that as these people move away from the hinterland and become more involved in metropolitan fringe problems they will become more closely associated with people now trained in regional planning. This is not to say that they will become one and the same, but merely to observe that they will more closely resemble their social science counterparts.

Comments—John Friedmann

It is of great interest to me to find that my colleagues and I are taking utterly different approaches in pursuing the subject of resource development on a regional scale, reflecting no doubt the three disciplines of our separate origins—Professor McHarg from landscape architecture, Professor Hamilton from forestry and conservation, and I from economics and geography. I think there is a lesson in this to be learned about educating young people who will go out into the world to engage in the practical tasks of regional planning and resource development.

The kinds of programs that Professor McHarg described for us are typical examples, although they are clearly not the only ones that might be cited. They are especially typical in that they all make use of a large number of different specialists. And so, when we speak of training for resource development and consider the problem of devising appropriate courses of study for those who wish to gain expertise in this area, we are confounded, because we know that, in actual development situations, the resource specialists will have to work, shoulder to shoulder, with professionals representing many different backgrounds and skills and exhibiting altogether different ways of thinking.

I have been closely associated with two major regional development programs, one with the TVA, and another in Venezuela. I have found all sorts of people working on these programs—engineers, agronomists, sociologists, lawyers, and so on down the list. But generalists in resource development and management were not among them. This experience, which I believe is not unique, suggests that we cannot really expect to train generalists who will be competent in the total spectrum of specializations required for resource development. We cannot expect to combine, within a single person, the skills of a hydrologist, ecologist, soil specialist, city designer, urban designer, sociologist, and economist. It is a sheer impossibility for any one person in a single lifetime to acquire the knowledge necessary to absorb the very specialized and diversified knowledge in each of these professions.

What we can expect, however, is that students who have an interest in resource development acquire, partly from their formal education and partly from their working experience, a common orientation, a common outlook, a common vocabularly, and a common concern. One of the great practical difficulties in planning is that the social scientist finds it nearly impossible to talk with the physical planners. This is especially true in the newly developing regions of the world, where the economic and physical planners clearly go their own and separate ways. Although they should be working in close coordination with one another, they don't, simply because they do not command the same scientific language.

It seems, therefore, that one of the great tasks confronting a university is to create this universal language for people who are concerned with problems of resource development. The spectrum of specializations which might be involved is so broad that there is no need to put any limit upon it. You have had one roster of specializations brought before you this afternoon.

How then, specifically, can we go about creating this common feeling and understanding, this common vocabulary and knowledge, within a university? It seems to me, in a field so fluid as this one, which is in a continuing state of flux, and in which there is no great body of literature to refer to, that we cannot begin to teach resource development except by associating such teaching with research. Perhaps this is true of all fields which today are characterized less by a received stock of knowledge than by a process of study. But it applies particularly to the field of resource development. I believe that very little progress can be made by teaching that is not closely related to research.

Therefore, I would put first emphasis on that aspect, though I realize that much of the teaching will be done at the undergraduate level, where research has not traditionally been part of the curriculum. However, there is a need for change toward this kind of orientation, and we must begin, even at the undergraduate level, to introduce students to research, and to provide more time for their professors to engage in research.

Another aspect that I would stress in this connection is the need to ensure that research in resource development be undertaken across the broad spectrum of disciplinary specializations. This in itself will help to build up a common vocabulary, to create some common understanding, and perhaps new theoretical insights. It is not going to be done by one specialist thinking ". . . how can I be cross-disciplinary. . . ." It can be done only by keeping up a constant stream of communication, information, and conversation among a group of concerned specialists, scientists, and researchers working on a common problem. This is the way in which a common stock of experience, knowledge, and language can be built up. In this sense I look upon the teaching of resource development not merely as a job of communicating knowledge, but as participation in a flow of constantly evolving knowledge.

Secondly, I want to suggest the desirability for establishing, in addition to this research phase, a common core curriculum for students interested in resource development. We can, of course, have lengthy arguments as to what this core should consist of. This is not the place to enter into such a discussion. Since I am of the conviction that we must, for the time at least, continue to train specialists rather than generalists in the field of resource development, the core curriculum I envision would be a rather restricted one. It should neither be all-encompassing nor take too much out of the student's total time spent at the university.

I would suggest that, as a minimum, three major subject areas should be included in a core curriculum. The first should focus on resource analysis and policies. The second should deal with the politics, process, and theory of planning decisions. The third should be in the area of social values and goals as they relate to resource development and planning. Since development is always for a purpose, we must become sensitive to the social values and objectives involved, must have some familiarity with them, and be able to talk and think about them in a reasonably sophisticated way.

There are, of course, many ways in which a core curriculum might be established. Probably the most feasible, in most situations, is to incorporate it into existing schools and departments, perhaps at the initiative of an interdisciplinary Committee on Education and Research in Resource Policy and Development. Such a committee might not only introduce new courses bearing on resources problems, but guide students in developing course sequences appropriate to their specialization and interest. Another possibility is the establishment of a separate facility or organization within the university—such as a center or an institute—which would begin to pull together related activities, and to focus on interdisciplinary resource problems and situations.

In conclusion, I wish to stress the importance, in this whole problem complex, of educating the public, that is, the consumers of resource development planning. Here your university has accumulated a great deal of relevant experience, stemming from many decades of work in agricultural extension. In considering new activities and new subject fields for adult education, emphasis might well be given to the question of resource development on a community-wide and regional scale.

There is a clear need for the public to be alerted to the sorts of issues that are being discussed here. It is important that we have an intelligent market for our planning activities, a market that knows pretty much what it wants and how it wants to get there. Ultimately, the binding decisions will have to be made by the consumers of planning, not by the specialists. It is a case of where the specialist proposes and the community disposes. I would therefore put great stress upon public education as an integral part of the total education program.

7

Open Space from
Natural Processes (1970)

*This essay resulted from a study of metropolitan open space sponsored by the U.S.
Department of Housing and Urban Development (HUD) and the states of New Jersey and Pennsylvania. McHarg's partner and colleague, David Wallace, edited the
book* Metropolitan Open Space and Natural Process *(published by the University
of Pennsylvania Press), which was based on the HUD study. Contributors to the
study and the book included McHarg and Wallace's Penn colleagues: Ann Strong,
William Grigsby, William Roberts, and Nohad Toulan.*

*McHarg's very specific study for open space in the Philadelphia metropolitan
region became the model for other open space studies. Essentially, the study was
based on the "simple working method for open space" that he had been exploring for
a decade (see, for example, chapter 2 of this book, "The Place of Nature in the City
of Man"). McHarg's concept of protecting environmentally sensitive areas (marshes,
swamps, flood plains, steep slopes, and prime habitats) was followed in many subsequent regional open space plans. For example, the 1995 Desert Open Spaces plan for
the Phoenix region undertaken by Design Workshop for the Maricopa Association of
Governments has many similarities to McHarg's efforts three decades earlier. The
concept also influenced environmental planning rule making, as for example, the elevated position wetlands (in 1970 called marches and swamps) eventually received in
environmental policy. Although the open space plan for Philadelphia was not implemented, McHarg later collaborated on a similar effort for Tulsa, Oklahoma, which
was followed.*

There is need for an objective and systematic method of identifying and evaluating land most suitable for metropolitan open space based on the natural roles that it performs. These roles can best be understood by examining the degree to which natural processes perform work for man without his intervention, and by studying the protection which is afforded and values which are derived when certain of these lands are undisturbed.

Introduction

A million acres of land each year are lost from prime farmland and forest to less sustainable and uglier land uses. There is little effective metropolitan planning and still less implementation of what is planned. Development occurs without reference to natural phenomena. Flood plains, marshes, steep slopes, woods, forests, and farmland are destroyed with little if any remorse; streams are culverted, groundwater, surface water, and atmosphere polluted, floods and droughts exacerbated, and beauty superseded by vulgarity and ugliness. Yet the instinct for suburbia which has resulted in this enormous despoliation of nature is based upon a pervasive and profoundly felt need for a more natural environment.

The paradox and tragedy of metropolitan growth and suburbanization is that it destroys many of its own objectives. The open countryside is subject to uncontrolled, sporadic, uncoordinated, unplanned development, representing the sum of isolated short-term private decisions of little taste or skill. Nature recedes under this careless assault, to be replaced usually by growing islands of developments. These quickly coalesce into a mass of low-grade urban tissue, which eliminate all natural beauty and diminish excellence, both historic and modern. The opportunity for realizing an important part of the "American dream" continually recedes to a more distant area and a future generation. For this is the characteristic pattern of metropolitan growth. Those who escape from the city to the country are often encased with their disillusions in the enveloping suburb.

The Hypothesis

This pattern of indiscriminate metropolitan urbanization dramatizes the need for an objective and systematic way of identifying and preserving land most suitable for open space, diverting growth from it, and directing development to land more suitable for urbanization. The assumption is that not all land in an urban area needs to be, or even ever is, all developed. Therefore choice is possible. The discrimination which is sought would select lands for open space which perform important work in their natural condition, are relatively unsuitable for development, are self-maintaining in the ecological sense, and occur in a desirable pattern of interfusion with the urban fabric.

The optimum result would be a system of two intertwining webs, one composed of developed land and the second consisting of open space in a natural or near natural state.

Heretofore, urbanization has been a positive act of transformation. Open space has played a passive role. Little if any value has been attributed to the natural processes often because of the failure to understand their roles and values. This is all the more remarkable when we consider the high land values associated with urban open space—Central Park in New York, Rittenhouse Square in Philadelphia being obvious examples. This lack of understanding has militated against the preservation or creation of metropolitan open space systems complementary to metropolitan growth. In this situation, governmental restraints are necessary to protect the public from the damaging consequences of private acts which incur both costs and losses to the public, when these acts violate and interrupt natural processes and diminish social values. There is an urgent need for land-use regulations related to natural processes, based upon their intrinsic value and their permissiveness and limitations to development. This in turn requires general agreement as to the social values of natural process.

Planning that understands and properly values natural processes must start with the identification of the processes at work in nature. It must then determine the value of subprocesses to man, both in the parts and in the aggregate, and finally establish principles of development and nondevelopment based on the tolerance and intolerance of the natural processes to various aspects of urbanization. It is presumed that when the operation of these processes is understood, and land-use policies reflect this understanding, it will be evidence that the processes can often be perpetuated at little cost.

The arguments for providing open space in the metropolitan region, usually dependent on amenity alone, can be substantially reinforced if policymakers understand and appreciate the operation of the major physical and biological processes at work. A structure for metropolitan growth can be combined with a network of open spaces that not only protects natural processes but also is of inestimable value for amenity and recreation.

In brief, it is hypothesized that the criteria for metropolitan open space should derive from an understanding of natural processes, their value to people, their permissiveness, and their prohibition to development. The method of physiographic analysis outlined here can lead to principles of land development and preservation for any metropolitan area. When applied as a part of the planning process, it can be a defensible basis for an open space system which goes far toward preserving the balance of natural processes and toward making our cities livable and beautiful.

Normal Metropolitan Growth Does Not Provide Open Space, Although Land Is Abundant

Without the use of such a method as described earlier, open space is infinitely vulnerable. An examination of the growth in this century of the major metropolitan areas of the United States demonstrates that urbanization develops primarily on open land rather than through redevelopment. The open space interspersed in areas of low-density development within the urban fabric is filled by more intensive uses and open space standards are lowered. Urban growth consumes open space both at the perimeter and within the urban fabric. The result is a scarcity of open space where population and demand are greatest. This phenomenon has aroused wide public concern as the growth of the cities, by accretion, has produced unattractive and unrelieved physical environments. Amenity, breathing space, recreational areas, and the opportunity for contact with nature for an expanding population are diminished. As important, it often exacerbates flood, drought, erosion, and humidity and it diminishes recreational opportunity, scenic, historic, and wildlife resources. Further, the absence of understanding of natural processes often leads to development in locations which are not propitious. When natural processes are interrupted, there are often resultant costs to society.

Demand for urban space is not only relatively but absolutely small. The 37 million inhabitants of megalopolis, constituting 24 percent of the U.S. population, occupied 1.8 percent of the land area of the continental United States (Gottman 1996, p. 26). Only 5 percent of the United States is urbanized today; it is projected that less than 10 percent will be so utilized by the year 2000. Space is abundant. Even in metropolitan regions, where large urban populations exist in a semi-rural hinterland, the proportion of urban to rural land does not basically contradict the assertion of open space abundance. For example, in the Philadelphia Standard Metropolitan Statistical Area (PSMSA), with 3,500 square miles or 2,250,000 acres, only 19.1 percent was urbanized in 1960. Here an increase in population from 4 million to 6,000,000 is anticipated by 1980. Should this growth continue and occur at an average gross density of three families per acre, only 30 percent of the land area would be in urban land use at that time. Some 2,300 square miles or 1,500,000 acres would still remain in open space.

The difficulty in planning lies in the relationship of this open space to urban uses. The market mechanism which raises the unit price of land for urban use tends to inhibit interfusion of open space in the urban fabric. Open space becomes normally a marginal or transitional use, remaining open only while land is awaiting development. The key question then is, if land is absolutely abundant, how can growth be guided in such a way as to exploit this abundance for the maximum good?

Exceptions to the General Experience

While generally metropolitan growth has been unsympathetic to natural processes, there are exceptions. In the late nineteenth- and early twentieth-century park planning, water courses were an important basis for site selection. The Capper Cromptin Act selected river corridors in Washington, D.C. The Cook County Park System around Chicago consists of corridors of forests preponderantly based upon river valleys. The first metropolitan open space plan, developed for Boston by Charles Eliot in 1893, emphasized not only rivers, but also coastal islands, beaches, and forested hills as site selection criteria. In 1928 Benton MacKaye, the originator of the Appalachian Trail, proposed using open space to control metropolitan growth in America but did not base his open space on natural process.

Patrick Abercrombie's Greater London Plan pays implicit attention to natural process in the location for the satellite towns, in the insistence on open space breaks between nucleated growth, in the recommendation that prime agricultural land should not be urbanized, and in specifying that river courses should constitute a basis for the open space system.

In recent studies conducted by Philip Lewis on a state-wide basis for Illinois and Wisconsin (e.g., State of Wisconsin 1962) physiographic determinants of land utilization have been carried beyond these earlier examples. Corridors have been identified which contain watercourses and their flood plains, steep slopes, forests, wildlife habitats, and historic areas. These characteristics are of value to a wide range of potential supporters—conservationists, historians, and the like—and the studies demonstrate the coincidence of their interests in the corridors. The expectation is that these groups will coordinate their efforts and combine their influence to retain the corridors as open space. Resource development and preservation is advocated for them. In another recent study, ecological principles were developed and tested as part of a planning process for the Green Spring and Worthington valleys, northwest of Baltimore Maryland.[1] Here the design process later described was evolved. Two more elaborate ecological studies, the first for Staten Island (McHarg 1969, pp. 103–15) and the second for the Twin Cities Metropolitan Region in Minnesota (Wallace, McHarg, Roberts, and Todd 1969), have undertaken to analyze natural processes to reveal intrinsic suitabilities for all prospective land uses. These are shown as unitary, complementary, or in competition.

The present study of metropolitan Philadelphia open space is more general in its objective. It seeks to find the major structure of open space in the PSMSA based upon the intrinsic values of certain selected natural processes to set the stage for further investigations.

Need for the Ecological Approach

There are, of course, several possible approaches. The first of these, beloved of the economist, views land as a commodity and allocates acres of land per thousand persons. In this view nature is seen as a generally uniform commodity, appraised in terms of time-distance from consumers and the costs of acquisition and development. A second approach also falls within the orthodoxy of planning, and may be described as the geometrical method. Made popular by Patrick Abercrombie, the distinguished British planner, this consists of circumscribing a city with a green ring wherein green activities, agriculture, recreation, and the like, are preserved or introduced.

The ecological approach, however, would suggest quite a different method. Beginning from the proposition that nature is process and represents values, relative values would be ascribed to certain discernible processes. Then, operating upon the presumption that nature performs services for man without his intervention or effort, certain service-processes would be identified as social values. Yet further, recognizing that some natural processes are inhospitable to human use—floods, earthquakes, hurricanes—we would seem to discover intrinsic constraints or even prohibitions to man's use or to certain kinds of use.

Objective discussion between the ecologist and the economist would quickly reveal the fallacy of the commodity approach. Nature is by definition not a uniform commodity. In contrast, each and every area varies as a function of historical geology, climate, physiography, the water regimen, the pattern and distribution of soils, plants, and animals. Each area will vary as process, as value and in the opportunities and constraints which it proffers or withholds from human use.

In a similiar discussion between ecologist and green belt advocate, the question which most embarrasses the latter is whether nature is uniform within the belt and different beyond it. The next question is unlikely to receive an affirmative answer, "Does nature perform particular roles within the belt to permit its definition?" Clearly the ecologist emerges a victor in these small skirmishes, but now the burden is upon him. What is the ecological approach to the selections of metropolitan open space?

The Value of Natural Process in the Ecosystem

There is, at present, no existing ecological model for a city or metropolitan region; it is necessary, therefore, to embark upon a theoretical analysis of natural process without the aid of such a model.[2]

Plant and animal communities require solar energy, food, nutrients, water, protection from climate extremes, and shelter. These conditions must be substantially regular in their provision. In order to ensure these optimal conditions, non-human or primitive-human systems have adapted to the natural environment and its constituent organisms to ensure a complex process of energy utilization, based upon photosynthesis, descending through many food chains to final decomposition and nutrient recirculation. In response to the problem of climatic extremes these communities do modify the microclimate. Such natural systems have mechanisms whereby water movement is modified to perform the maximum work. The aggregate of these processes is a stable, complex ecosystem in which entropy is low and energy is conserved (Odum 1959, ch. 3).

The net result is a system with high energy utilization and production, continuous soil formation, natural defenses against epidemic disease, microclimatic extremes diminished, minimal oscillation between flood and drought, minor erosion, and natural water purification. There obviously are many advantages which accrue to civilized man from this condition—a viable agriculture and forestry, abundant fish and wildlife, natural water purification, stability in the water system, defense against flood and drought, diminished erosion, sedimentation and silting, and a self-cleaning environment with high recreational potential and amenity.

The values of the natural processes far exceed the values which usually are attributed to them. Agriculture, forestry, and fisheries are taken into consideration in the evaluation of regional assets, but atmospheric oxygen, amelioration of climate and microclimate, water evaporation, precipitation, drainage, or the creation of soils tend to be disregarded. Yet the composite picture of the region's resources must include all natural processes. Beginning with the values of agriculture, forestry, and fisheries, the value of minerals and the value of the land for education, recreation, and amenity may be added. Agricultural land has an amenity which is not generally attributed, since it is also a landscape which is maintained as a byproduct. Forests equally have an amenity value and are self-cleaning environments, requiring little or no maintenance.

Water has values which transcend those related to certain discrete aspects of the hydrologic cycle. In this latter category are many important processes—water in agriculture, industry, commerce, recreation, education and amenity, consumption, cooling, hydroelectric generation, navigation, water transport and dilution, waste reduction, fisheries, and water recreation.

Value is seldom attributed to the atmosphere; yet the protection from lethal cosmic rays, insulation, the abundance of oxygen for animal metabolism and the carbon dioxide for plant metabolism which it affords, all demonstrate an indispensability equal to land and water. In terms of positive attributed value the atmosphere has been accorded virtually none. Only when atmosphere has become polluted are the cost and necessity of ensuring clean air recognized.

Even in the exceptional condition when natural processes are attributed value as in agriculture and forestry, these are generally held in such low esteem that they cannot endure in the face of competition from urban or industrial uses. It is impossible to construct a value system which includes the vast processes described. It is, however, quite possible to recognize the fundamental value of these processes, their characteristics, and their relationship to industrial and urban processes. This understanding should lead to a presumption in favor of nature rather than the prevailing disdain.

Working toward the goal of developing working principles for land-use planning in general and the selection of metropolitan open space in particular, it is advantageous to examine the degree to which natural processes perform work for man without his intervention and the protection achieved by leaving certain sub-processes in their natural state without development. While this cannot yet be demonstrated quantitatively, it can be described.

Natural processes which perform work for man include water purification, atmospheric pollution dispersal, microclimate amelioration, water storage and equalization, flood control, erosion control, topsoil accumulation, and the ensurance of wildlife populations.

Areas which are subject to volcanic action, earthquakes, tidal waves, tornadoes, hurricanes, floods, drought, forest fires, avalanches, mud slides, and subsidence, should be left undeveloped in order to avoid loss of life and property. In addition, there are other areas which are particularly vulnerable to human intervention; this category includes beach dunes, major animal habitats, breeding grounds, spawning grounds, and water catchment areas. There are also areas of unusual scenic, geological, biological, ecological, and historic importance. In each of these cases, it is apparent that wise land-use planning should recognize natural processes and respond to them. As many of these processes are water related, it would seem that water may be a useful indicator of these major physical and biological processes described as natural processes.

Water and Natural Processes

Water, as the agent of erosion and sedimentation, is linked with geological evolution to the realities of physiography. The mountains, hills, valleys, and plains which result, experience a variety of climate and microclimate consequent upon their physiography. The combination of physiography and climate determines the incidence and distribution of plants and animals, their niches and habitats.

The use of water as a unifying concept links marsh and forest, rivers and clouds, ground and surface water, all as interdependent aspects of a single process. It permits us to see that the marsh filled in the estuary and the upland forest felled are comparable in their effect, that pollution to surface water may affect distant groundwater, that building of an outlying suburb may affect the flood height in the city. Although we lack an ecological model, a gross perception of natural process may be revealed through the selection of water as a unifying process. This may suggest land-use policies reflecting the permissiveness and prohibitions of the constituent phases of water in process. By this useful method the constituent roles of open space may be seen and the optimal distribution of open space in the metropolitan region may be discerned.

Water is not the best indicator or theoretical tool for ecological planning. The physiographic region is perhaps the best unit for ecological studies since there tends to be a marked consistency within each physiographic region and distinct variations between them.

Water and the Roles of Major Physiographic Regions

In the Philadelphia metropolitan area study, the roles of the physiographic regions have been simplified to three components: the first, the uplands of the piedmont, second, the remainder of that region with the final category being the coastal plain. The area to be studied is the PSMSA three and one-half thousand square miles which constitute the metropolitan region and straddle coastal plain and piedmont, a situation typical of many cities on the eastern seaboard.

The Uplands

The uplands are the hills of the watershed, the highest elevations, wherein many streams begin, their watercourses narrow, steep, and rocky. The soils tend to be thin and infertile from long-term erosion. In the Philadelphia metropolis, the uplands consist of a broad band of low hills, 12 to 20 miles wide, bending northeast-southwest obliquely through the area. As a result of the absence of glaciation in this area the rivers and streams lack natural impoundments and are, therefore, particularly susceptible to seasonal fluctuations.

The natural restraints to flooding and drought, contributing to equilibrium, are mainly the presence and distribution of vegetation, principally forests and their soils, particularly on the uplands and their steep slopes. Vegetation absorbs and utilizes considerable quantities of water. In fact, vegetation and their soils act as a sponge restraining extreme runoff, releasing water slowly over longer periods, diminishing erosion and sedimentation—in short, diminishing the frequency and intensity of oscillation between flood and drought and operating toward equilibrium.

In the uplands, land-use policies should protect and enhance forests and other vegetative cover to diminish runoff, oscillation between flood and drought, and the insurance of natural water purification. On steep slopes, land-use management would notably include forestation programs. Land uses should then be related to permissiveness and prohibitions inherent in such a region related to the primary role of the upland sponge in the water economy.

The Piedmont

The piedmont is also non-glaciated in the study area, and consists of the gentler slope below the uplands. It sustains fertile soils which, in limestone areas, are equal in fertility to the richest in the entire United States. In the three divisions it is in the piedmont alone that fertile soils abound. Unglaciated, the piedmont, like the uplands, lacks natural impoundment and is flood prone.

Here is the land most often developed for agriculture. These lands, too, tend to be favored locations for villages, towns, and cities. Here, forests are often residues or the products of regeneration on abandoned farms. Steep slopes in the piedmont are associated with the dissected banks of streams and rivers.

The agricultural piedmont does not control its own defenses. It is either affected by or defended from flood and drought by the conditions in the uplands and coastal plain. When cropland is ploughed and lacks vegetation, when building sites are bared, they are subject to erosion and contribute to sediment yield. Even when covered with growing crops, the average runoff here exceeds the forest. Nonetheless, the vegetative cover, configuration, and conservation practices in the agricultural piedmont can either increase or diminish flood and drought. The piedmont is particularly vulnerable to both. The presence of forests and woodlands will act as ameliorative agents as they do in the uplands and the presence of vegetation will diminish runoff by absorption, friction, and through increased percolation.

The fine capillary streams of the uplands become the larger streams and rivers of the piedmont, and their volume increases proportionately, as does their flood potential and their oscillation to low flow.

In the piedmont, fertile soils should be perpetuated as an irreplaceable resource. Both agriculture and urbanization are primary contributors to erosion and sedimentation; they are also the major contributors to water pollution from pesticides, fertilizers, domestic and industrial wastes.

Planning should relate water pollution to specific stream capacities; with-drawals of water to specific capacities of surface water and groundwater; con-servation practices to erosion control for farmland and construction sites.

The Coastal Plain

The coastal plain has been, through much of geologic time, a vast depository of sediments eroded from the uplands. The soils are shallow and acid, over-laying sedimentary material. These are naturally infertile although in New Jersey such sandy soils with abundant fertilizer and water, support extensive truck farming.

The major physiographic characteristics of the coastal plain are its flat-ness, the poverty of its soils, the abundant marshes, bays, estuaries, the unique flora of the pine barrens, and finally, the great resources of groundwater in aquifers.

The incidence of flood and drought in the piedmont and coastal plains is not only consequent upon the upland sponge, but also upon estuarine marshes, particularly where these are tidal. Here, at the mouth of the water-shed, at the confluence of important rivers or river and sea, the flood com-ponents of confluent streams or the tidal components of flood assume great importance. In the Philadelphia metropolitan area, the estuary and the ocean are of prime importance as factors in flood.

A condition of intense precipitation over the region combined with high tides, full estuary, and strong on-shore winds brings together the elements that portend floods. The estuarine marshes and their vegetation constitute the major defense against this threat. These areas act as enormous storage reservoirs, absorbing mile-feet of potentially destructive waters, thus reduc-ing flood potential. This function may be described as the estuarine sponge, in contrast to the upland sponge. The water resources of these aquifers repre-sent a significant economic value.

In the coastal plain, the susceptibility to flood of these areas and the invaluable role of marshlands as flood storage reservoirs should also be reflected in land-use policies which could ensure the perpetuation of their natural role in the water economy. The value of groundwater in aquifers should be reflected in land-use policy.

Finally, the extensive forests of the pine barrens and their unique flora depend upon fire, which is an inevitable and recurrent threat. Here extensive urbanization makes such a threat actuality: pine barrens are not suitable sites for development.

These three major divisions are clearly different in their permissiveness and prohibition, and in their roles in the water regimen: the uplands should be viewed and planned as the upstream control area for water processes, flood, drought, water quality, erosion control, and an area of high recreational potential. This region is not normally selected for extensive urbanization and can be easily protected from it. But it performs its role best when extensively forested.

The coastal plain performs a primary flood control, water supply, and water-related recreation function, and is not suited to extensive urbanization. The entire region, characterized by rivers, marshes, bays, and estuaries is critical to wildlife. Properly used, it offers a great recreational potential. In contrast, the piedmont, with the exception of prime agricultural areas, is tolerant to urbanization. Although the prime farmland of this region is an irreplaceable resource, a scenic value, and requires defense against urbanization, the piedmont should be the region for major urban growth in the future.

Planning for natural processes at this scale would regulate urban development in uplands and coastal plains, concentrate it in the piedmont, on nonprime agricultural land. Connecting these regions would be an undeveloped fabric of streams, rivers, marshes, bays, and estuaries, the steep slopes of dissected watercourses, as water corridors permeating the entire metropolis.

Significant Physiographic Phenomena and Their Roles

The major physiographic divisions reveal the principal roles in the water regimen and should constitute an important generalized basis for identification of natural processes and planning. Yet it is necessary to have a greater specificity as to the constituent roles of natural process. Toward this end, eight components have been selected for identification and examination. It is clear that they are to some extent identifiable and perform discrete roles. These eight constituent phenomena are:

1. Surface water
2. Marshes
3. Flood plains
4. Aquifers
5. Aquifer recharge areas
6. Prime agricultural land
7. Steep lands
8. Forests and woodlands

The first five have a direct relationship to water; the remaining three are water-related in that they either have been determined by, or are determinants of water-in-process.

This group of water-related parameters is selected as containing the most useful indicators of natural process for a majority of metropolitan regions in the United States. They appear to be the most productive for the project area under study, but the underlying hypothesis of natural process would take precedence in these areas where other parameters prove to be more illuminating. That is, the selection of criteria for a system of metropolitan open space can best be developed from an understanding of the major physical and biological process *of the region itself.* The interconnected phenomena should be integrated into a unified system to which the planning process responds.

Varying Permissiveness to Urban Uses

Having identified certain sub-processes, it is necessary to describe their intrinsic function and value and then to determine the degree to which the performance of natural process is prohibitive or permissive to other land uses.

The terms prohibitive and permissive are used relatively. In no case does natural process absolutely prohibit development. Yet in a condition of land abundance, there is available a choice as to location of development. This being so, areas of importance to natural process should not be selected where alternative locations of lesser importance are available. Further, development of natural process areas should occur only where supervening benefits result from such development, in excess of those provided by natural process. Still further, the tolerances of natural processes to development by type, amount, and location are an important constituent of land-use policy.

Surface Water (5,671 linear miles)

In a situation of land abundance, restraints should be exercised on the development of surface water and riparian land. In principle, only those land uses which are inseparable from waterfront locations should occupy riparian lands; land uses thereon should be limited to those which do not diminish the present or prospective value of surface water or stream banks for water supply, amenity, or recreation.

In the category of consonant land uses would fall port and harbor facilities, marinas, water treatment plants, sewage treatment plants, water-related industry, and in certain instances, water-using industries.[3]

In the category of land uses which need not diminish existing or prospective value of surface water would fall agriculture, forestry, institutional open space, recreational facilities, and, under certain conditions, open space for housing.

In the category of land uses which would be specifically excluded would be industries producing toxic or noxious liquid effluents, waste dumps, non-water-related industry or commerce.

The presumption is then that surface water as a resource best performs its function in a natural state and that land uses which do not affect this state may occupy riparian land, but other functions be permitted according to the degree which their function is indivisibly water-related.

Marshes (133,984 acres; 7.44 percent)

In principle, land-use policy for marshes should reflect the roles of flood and water storage, wildlife habitat, and fish spawning grounds. Land uses which do not diminish the operation of the primary roles are compatible. Thus, hunting, fishing, sailing, recreation, in general, would be permissible. Certain types of agriculture, notably cranberry bogs, would also be compatible. Isolated urban development might also be permitted if the water storage role of marshes was not diminished by the filling and accelerated runoff that such development would entail.

Flood Plains (339,760 acres; 18.86 percent)

The flood-plain parameter must be attributed a particular importance because of its relation to loss of life and property damage. The best records seem to indicate that the incidence and intensity of flooding in metropolitan areas is on the increase (Witala 1961). The presumption is that this results from the reduction of forest and agricultural land, erosion and sedimentation, and the urbanization of watersheds. This being so, there is every reason to formulate a land utilization policy for flood plains related to safeguarding life and property.[4]

The incidence of floods may be described as recorded maxima. For the Delaware River, the maximum recorded floods are those of 1950 and 1955. The alternate method of flood description relates levels of inundation to cyclical storms and describes these as flood levels of anticipated frequency or probability.

There is, then, a conflict of use for this land between water and other types of occupancy. This conflict is most severe in areas of frequent flooding which, however, occupy the smallest flood plain. The conflict diminishes in frequency with the more severe floods, which occupy the largest flood plain. It would seem possible to relate the utilization of the flood plain to the incidence and severity of cyclical flooding.[5]

Increasingly, the 50-year or two percent probability flood plain is being accepted as that area from which all development should be excluded save those functions which are either benefited or unharmed by flooding or those land uses which are inseparable from flood plains.

Thus, in principle, only such land uses which are either improved or unharmed by flooding should be permitted to occupy the 50-year flood plain. In the former category fall agriculture,[6] forestry, recreation, institutional open space, and open space for housing. In the category of land uses inseparable from flood plains are ports and harbors, marinas, water-related industry, and under certain circumstances, water-using industry.

Aquifers (149,455 acres; 8.3 percent)

The definition of an aquifer as a water-bearing stratum of rock, gravel, or sand is so general that enormous areas of land could be so described. For any region the value of an aquifer will relate to the abundance or poverty of water resources. In the Philadelphia area the great deposits of porous material parallel to the Delaware River are immediately distinguishable from all other aquifers in the region by their extent and capacity.

Aquifers may vary from groundwater resources of small quantity to enormous underground resources. They are normally measured by yields of wells or by the height of the water table. The aquifer in New Jersey parallel to the Delaware River has been estimated by the Soil Conservation Service [currently called the Natural Resources Conservation Service] to have a potential capacity of one billion gallons per day. This valuable resource requires restraints upon development of the surface to ensure the quality and quantity of aquifer resources. Consequently, development using septic tanks and industries disposing toxic or noxious effluents should be regulated. Injection wells should be expressly prohibited. The matter of surface percolation is also important, and as percolation will be greatest from permeable surfaces there are good reasons for maximizing development at the extremes of density—either sewered high density development or very low density free standing houses. Land-use policy for aquifers is less amenable to generalized recommendation than the remaining categories, as aquifers vary with respect to capacity, yield, and susceptibility. Consequently, there will be ranges of permissiveness attributable to specific aquifers as a function of their role and character.

In principle, no land uses should be permitted above an aquifer which inhibit the primary role as water supply and reservoir regulating oscillations between flood and drought.

Agriculture, forestry, and recreation clearly do not imperil aquifers. Industries, commercial activities, and housing, served by sewers, are permissible up to limits set by percolation requirements. Sources of pollutants or toxic material, and extensive land uses which reduce soil permeability, should be restricted or prohibited.

Aquifer Recharge Areas (83,085 acres; 4.61 percent)

Such areas are defined as points of interchange between surface water and groundwater. In any water system certain points of interchange will be critical; in the Philadelphia metropolitan area the interchange between the Delaware River, its tributaries and the parallel aquifer, represents the recharge area which is most important and which can be clearly isolated. Percolation is likely to be an important aspect of recharge. Thus, two considerations arise: the location of surface-to-groundwater interchange below the ground, and percolation of surface to groundwater.

By careful separation of polluted river water from the aquifer and by the impounding of streams transecting the major aquifer recharge areas, the aquifer can be managed and artificially recharged. Groundwater resources can be impaired by extensive development which waterproofs the surfaces, by development which occupies desirable impoundments valuable for aquifer management and by pollution.

In principle, all proposed development on aquifer recharge areas should be measured against the likely effect upon recharge. Injection wells and disposal of toxic or offensive materials should be forbidden; channel widening, deepening, and dredging should be examined for their effect upon recharge as should deep excavations for trunk sewers. Surface development and sewage disposal on such an area should be limited by considerations of percolation.

Prime Agricultural Land (248,816 acres; 11.7 percent)

Prime agricultural soils represent the highest level of agricultural productivity; they are uniquely suitable for intensive cultivation with no conservation hazards. It is extremely difficult to defend agricultural lands when their cash value can be multiplied tenfold by employment for relatively cheap housing. Yet, the farm is the basic factory, the farmer is the country's best landscape gardener and maintenance work force, the custodian of much scenic beauty. Utilization of farmland by urbanization is often justifiable as the highest and best use of land at current land values, yet the range of market values of farmlands does not reflect the long-term value or the irreplaceable nature of these living soils. An omnibus protection of all farmland is indefensible; protection of the best soils in a metropolitan area would appear not only defensible, but also clearly desirable.

Jean Gottman has recommended that "the very good soils are not extensive enough in Megalopolis to be wastefully abandoned to nonagricultural uses" (1961, p. 95). The soils so identified are identical to the prime agricultural soils in the metropolitan area.

While farmland is extremely suitable for development and such lands can appreciate in value by utilization for housing, it is seldom considered that there is a cost involved in the development of new farmland. The farmer, displaced from excellent soils by urbanization, often moves to another site on inferior soils. Excellent soils lost to agriculture for building can finally only be replaced by bringing inferior soils into production. This requires capital investment. Land that is not considered cropland today will become cropland tomorrow, but at the price of much investment.

In the PSMSA by 1980 only 30 percent of the land area will be urbanized; 70 percent will remain open. Prime agricultural lands represent only 11.7 percent of the area. Therefore, given a choice, prime soils should not be developed.

In principle, U.S. Department of Agriculture (USDA) Land Capability System Type 1 soils are recommended to be exempted from development (save by those functions which do not diminish their present or prospective productive potential). This would suggest retirement of prime soils into forest, utilization as open space for institutions, for recreation, or in development for housing at densities no higher than one house per 25 acres.

Steep Lands (262,064 acres; 14.55 percent)

Steep lands and the ridges which they constitute are central to the problems of flood control and erosion. Slopes in excess of 12° are not recommended for cultivation by the Soil Conservation Service. The same source suggests that for reasons of erosion, these lands are unsuitable for development. The recommendations of the Soil Conservation Service are that steep slopes should be in forest and that cultivation of such slopes be abandoned.

In relation to its role in the water regimen, steepness is a matter not only of degree, but also of vegetation and porosity. Two ranges of slopes are identified in our study of the PSMSA: 15 to 25 percent, and greater than 25 percent. The first category of 15 percent is identified as those slopes for which major site-engineering begins to be necessary to accommodate development. Roads should be equally parallel to the slope rather than perpendicular. Coverage by houses and roads should be compensated by measures to slow down runoff. Examination of a number of examples suggests 15 percent as the danger point for any development at all, but further empiric research is necessary. Above 25 percent, however, there appears widespread agreement that no development should occur and land should be treated to decrease runoff as much as possible.[7]

In summary, erosion control and diminution of velocity of runoff are the principal water problems of steep slopes. Land uses compatible with minimizing these problems would be mainly forestry, recreation, and low-density development on the less-steep slopes. Since such slopes also tend to dominate landscapes, their planting in forests would provide great amenity.

Forests and Woodlands (588,816 acres; 32.7 percent)

The natural vegetative cover for most of this region is forest. Where present, this exerts an ameliorative effect upon microclimate; it exercises a major balancing effect upon the water regimen, diminishing erosion, sedimentation, flood, and drought. The scenic role of woodlands is apparent, as is the provision of a habitat for game. The recreational potential of forests is among the highest of all categories. In addition, the forest is a low maintenance, self-perpetuating landscape, a resource in which accrual of timber inventory is continuous.

Forests can be employed for timber production, water management, wildlife habitats, as airsheds, recreation, or for any combination of these uses. In addition, forests can absorb development in concentrations which will be determined by the demands of natural process which they are required to satisfy. Where scenic considerations alone are operative, mature forests could absorb housing up to a density of one house per acre without loss of their forest aspect.

Land uses for forests should be determined by the natural process roles which the forest is required to play in the water regimen.

As a result of analyzing the eight significant physiographic phenomena and their roles in the region, several land uses can be recommended. These land uses are summarized in table 2.

Table 2. Limited Development Areas and Recommended Land Uses

Limited Development Areas	Recommended Land Uses
1. Surface water and riparian lands	Ports, harbors, marinas, water treatment plants, water-related industry, open space for institutional and housing use, agriculture, forestry and recreation
2. Marshes	Recreation
3. 50-year flood plains	Ports, harbors, marinas, water treatment plants, water-related and water-using industry, agriculture, forestry, recreation, institutional open space, open space of housing
4. Aquifers	Agriculture, forestry, recreation, industries which do not produce toxic or offensive effluents, all land uses within limits set by percolation

(continues)

Table 2. (continued)

5. Aquifer recharge areas	As aquifers
6. Prime agricultural lands	Agriculture, forestry, recreation, open space for institutions, housing at 1 house per 25 acres
7. Steep lands	Forestry, recreation, housing at maximum density of 1 house per 3 acres, where wooded
8. Forests and woodlands	Forestry, recreation, housing at densities not higher than 1 house per acre

Open Space and Airsheds

The atmosphere of a metropolitan area has a capacity to diffuse air pollution based upon temperature, air composition, and movement. Concentration of pollution is associated with cities and industries, replacement of polluted air and its diffusion depend upon air movements over pollution free areas. These will be related to wind movements, and must be substantially free of pollution sources if relief is to be afforded to air pollution over cities. One can use the analogy of the watershed and describe the pollution free areas, tributary to the city, as the airsheds.

The central phase of air pollution is linked to temperature inversion during which the air near the ground does not rise to be replaced by in-moving air. Under inversion, characterized by clear nights with little wind, the earth is cooled by long-wave radiation and the air near the ground is cooled by the ground. During such temperature inversions with stable surface air layers, air movement is limited; in cities, pollution becomes increasingly concentrated. In Philadelphia "significant" inversions occur one night in three. Parallel and related to inversion is the incidence of "high" pollution levels, which occurred on twenty-four "episodes" from two to five days in duration between 1957 and 1959. Inversions then are common as are "high" levels of pollution. The danger attends their conjunction and persistence. Relief other than elimination of pollution sources is a function of wind movement to disperse pollution over cities, and secondly, the necessity that in-moving air be cleaner than the air it replaces.

The windrose during inversions can establish the percentage direction of winds which might relieve pollution; the wind speed, combined with wind direction, will indicate these tributary areas over which the wind will pass to relieve pollution. These areas should be substantially, free of pollution sources.

The concentration of pollution sources in Philadelphia covers an area fifteen miles by ten miles with the long axis running approximately northeast. Let us assume sulfur dioxide to be the indicator of pollution (830 tons per day produced), an air height of 500 feet as the effective dimension, an air volume to be replaced of approximately 15 cubic miles, a wind speed of four miles per hour, selected as a critical speed. Then one cubic mile of ventilation is provided per mile of windspeed and it is seen to require three and three-quarter hours for wind movement to ventilate the long axis, two and one-half hours to ventilate the cross axis. Thus, the tributary to ensure clean air on the long axis is 15 miles beyond the pollution area, ten miles beyond for the cross axis. The windrose for Philadelphia during inversions shows that wind movements are preponderantly northwest, west, and southwest, contributing 51.2 percent of wind movements, the other five cardinal points represent the remainder.

This very approximate examination suggests that airsheds should extend from 10 to 15 miles beyond the urban air pollution sources in those wind directions to be anticipated during inversion.[8] The width of these belts should correspond to the dimension of the pollution core and, in very approximate terms, would probably be from three to five miles. Such areas, described as airsheds, should be prohibited to pollution source industries.

Should this concept be realized, broad belts of land, free of industry, would penetrate radially toward the city center.

Under the heading of atmosphere the subject of climate and microclimate was raised. In the study area the major problem is summer heat and humidity. Relief of this condition responds to wind movements. Thus, a hinterland with more equable temperatures, particularly a lower summer temperature, is of importance to climate amelioration for the city. As we have seen, areas which are in vegetative cover, notably forests, are distinctly cooler than cities in summer, a margin of 10°F is not uncommon. Air movements over such areas moving into the city will bring cooler air. Relief from humidity results mainly from air movement. These correspond to the directions important for relief of inversion. We can then say that the areas selected as urban airsheds are likely to be those selected as appropriate for amelioration of the urban microclimate. However, in the case of the former, it is important only that pollution sources be prohibited or limited. In the case of microclimate control, it is essential that the airsheds be substantially in vegetative cover, preferably forested.

The satisfaction of these two requirements, the creation of urban airsheds as responses to atmospheric pollution control and microclimate control, would create fingers of open space penetrating from the rural hinterland, radially into the city. This is perhaps the broadest conception of natural process in metropolitan growth and metropolitan open space distribution. Clearly, this proposal directs growth into the interstices between the airshed corridors and suggests that metropolitan open space exists within them.

Conclusions

In summary, it is proposed that the form of metropolitan growth and the distribution of metropolitan open space should respond to natural process. The phenomenal world is a process which operates within laws and responds to these laws. Interdependence is characteristic of this process, the seamless web of nature. Man is natural, as is the phenomenal world he inhabits, yet with greater power, mobility, and fewer genetic restraints; his impact upon this world exceeds that of any creature. The transformations he creates are often deleterious to other biological systems, but in this he is no different from many other creatures. However, these transformations are often needlessly destructive to other organisms and systems, and even more important, by conscious choice and inadvertance, also deleterious to man.

A generalized effect of human intervention is the tendency toward simplification of the ecosystems, which is equated with instability. Thus, the increased violence of climate and microclimate, oscillation between flood and drought, erosion and siltation, are all primary evidence of induced instability.

Human adaptations contain both benefits and costs, but natural processes are generally not attributed values, nor is there a generalized accounting system which reflects total costs and benefits. Natural processes are unitary whereas human interventions tend to be fragmentary and incremental. The effect of filling the estuarine marshes or of felling the upland forests is not perceived as related to the water regimen, to flood or drought; nor are both activities seen to be similar in their effect. The construction of outlying suburbs and siltation of river channels are not normally understood to be related as cause and effect; nor is waste disposal into rivers perceived to be connected with the pollution of distant wells.

Several factors can be observed. Normal growth tends to be incremental and unrelated to natural processes on the site. But the aggregate consequences of such development are not calculated nor are they allocated as costs to the individual incremental developments. While benefits do accrue to certain developments, which are deleterious to natural processes at large (for example, clear felling of forests or conversion of farmland into subdivisions), these benefits are *particular* (related in these examples to that landowner who chooses to fell trees or sterilize soil), while the results and costs are *general* in effect. Thus, costs and benefits are likely to be attributed to large numbers of different and unrelated persons, corporations, and levels of government. It is unprovable and unlikely that substantial benefits accrue from disdain of natural process; it is quite certain and provable that substantial costs do result from this disdain. Finally, in general, any benefits which do occur—usually economic—tend to accrue to the private sector, while remedies and long-range costs are usually the responsibility of the public domain.

The purpose of this study is to show that natural process, unitary in character, must be so considered in the planning process that changes to parts of the system affect the entire system, that natural processes do represent values, and that these values should be incorporated into a single accounting system. It is unfortunate that there is inadequate information on cost-benefit ratios of specific interventions to natural process. However, certain generalized relationships have been shown and presumptions advanced as the basis for judgment. It seems clear that laws pertaining to land use and development need to be elaborated to reflect the public costs and consequences of private action. Present land-use regulations neither recognize natural processes, the public good in terms of flood, drought, water quality, agriculture, amenity, or recreational potential, nor allocate responsibility to the acts of landowner or developer.

We have seen that land is abundant, even within a metropolitan region confronting accelerated growth. There is, then, at least hypothetically, the opportunity of choice as to the location of development and locations of open space.

The hypothesis, central to this study, is that the distribution of open space must respond to natural process. The conception should hold true for any metropolitan area, irrespective of location. In this particular case study, directed to the Philadelphia metropolitan region, an attempt has been made to select certain fundamental aspects of natural process, which show the greatest relevance to the problem of determining the form of metropolitan growth and open space.

The problem of metropolitan open space lies then, not in absolute area, but in distribution. We seek a concept which can provide an interfusion of open space and population. The low attributed value of open space ensures that it is transformed into urban use within the urban area and at the perimeter. Normal urbanization excludes interfusion and consumes peripheral open space.

Yet as the area of a circle follows the square of the radius, large open space increments can exist within the urban perimeter without major increase to the radius or to the time distance from city center to urban fringe.

The major recommendation of this study is that the aggregate value of land, water, and air resources does justify a land-use policy which reflects both the value and operation of natural processes. Further, that the identification of natural processes, the permissiveness and prohibitions which they exhibit, reveals a system of open space which can direct metropolitan growth and offers sites for metropolitan open space.

The characteristics of natural processes have been examined; an attempt has been made to identify their values, intrinsic value, work performed and protection afforded. Large-scale functions have been identified with the major divisions of upland, coastal plain, and piedmont; smaller scale functions of air and water corridors have been identified; and, finally, eight discrete parameters have been selected for examination.

For each of the discrete phenomena and for each successive generalization, approximate permissiveness to other land uses and specific prohibitions have been suggested. While all are permissive to a greater or lesser degree, all perform their natural process best in an unspoiled condition. Clearly, if land is abundant and land-use planning can reflect natural process, a fabric of substantially natural land will remain either in low intensity use or undeveloped, interfused throughout the metropolitan region. It is from this land that public metropolitan open space may best be selected.

This case study reveals the application of the ecological view to the problem of selecting open space in a metropolitan region. It reflects the assumption that nature performs work for man and that certain natural processes can best perform this work in a natural or mainly natural condition. Clearly, this is a partial problem; one would wish that simultaneously, consideration were also given to those lands which man would select for various purposes, for settlements, recreation, agriculture, and forestry. Such a study would be more complete than the isolation of a single demand. Yet, it is likely that the same proposition would hold although the larger study would better reveal the degree of conflict. For the moment, it is enough to observe that the ecological view does represent a perceptive method and could considerably enhance the present mode of planning which disregards natural processes, all but completely, and which in selecting open space, is motivated more by standards of acres per thousand for organized sweating, than for the place and face of nature in man's world.

Notes

1. Wallace-McHarg Associates (1964). William G. Grigsby was economic consultant, Ann Louise Strong, governmental and legal consultant, and William H. Roberts, design consultant in this first practical application of the new approach. [Wallace-McHarg Associates was later Wallace, McHarg, Roberts, and Todd and is now Wallace Roberts and Todd.]

2. Ecological model is a theoretical construct, either descriptive or mathematical, by which the energy flow of an organic system can be described.

3. 5,671 linear miles in the PSMSA; surface water has been identified as all permanent streams shown on USGS (U.S. Geological Survey) 1:24,000 Series.

4. Kates, William, and White, suggest classification of flood zones into prohibitive, restrictive, and warning zones, based on physiographic analysis. The prohibitive zone would protect structures and fill to preserve the channel capacity in flood conditions; the restrictive zone would simply alert users they were

within the flood plain and the decision to accommodate would be theirs (Kates et al. 1962).

5. See Kates and William (1962) for thorough discussion of the conditions and value judgments concerning occupancy of flood plains. It is evident from this analysis that flood controls are most easily established where the certainty of flood occurrence is high.

6. See Burton (1962) for a more detailed consideration of agricultural occupancy of flood plains.

7. E.g., in Pittsburgh, 25 percent and greater slopes are now subject to an ordinance prohibiting further development.

8. Study on the Philadelphia airshed conducted under direction of the writer by Hideki Shimizu, Department of Landscape Architecture, University of Pennsylvania, 1963, unpublished.

References

Burton, Ian. 1962. *Types of Agricultural Occupancy of Flood Plains in the U.S.A.* Chicago: Department of Geography, University of Chicago.

Gottman, Jean. 1961. *Megalopolis.* New York: The Twentieth Century Fund.

Kates, C., and Robert William. 1962. *Hazard and Choice Perception in Flood Plain Management.* Chicago: Department of Geography, University of Chicago.

Kates, C., Robert William, and Gilbert F. White. 1962. "Flood Hazard Evaluation." In Gilbert F. White, ed., *Papers on Flood Problems.* Chicago: Department of Geography, University of Chicago, pp. 135–147.

McHarg, Ian. 1969. "Processes as Values." In *Design with Nature.* Garden City, N.Y: Doubleday, Natural History Press.

MacKaye, Benton. 1928. *The New Exploration: A Philosophy of Regional Planning.* New York: Harcourt Brace.

Odum, Eugene. 1959. *The Fundamentals of Ecology.* Philadelphia: Saunders.

State of Wisconsin. 1962. *Recreation in Wisconsin.* Madison: Department of Resource Development.

Wallace-McHarg Associates. 1964. *Plan for the Valleys.* Towson, Md.: Green Spring and Worthington Valley Planning Council.

Wallace, McHarg, Roberts, and Todd. 1969. *An Ecological Study for the Twin Cities Metropolitan Region, Minnesota.* Prepared for Metropolitan Council of the Twin Cities Area. Philadelphia: U.S. Department of Commerce, National Technical Information Series.

Witala, S. W. 1961. *Some Aspects of the Effect of Urban and Suburban Development on Runoff.* Lansing, Mich.: U.S. Department of Interior, Geological Survey.

8

Must We Sacrifice the West?(1975)

In the midst of the "energy crisis" of the 1970s, McHarg was invited to the fifth Vail Symposium in Vail, Colorado, on August 12–17. The theme of the symposium was growth options for the Rocky Mountain West. McHarg's paper was subsequently published in a book produced in conjunction with the University of Denver Research Institute, edited by Terrell Minger and Sherry Oaks, with an introduction by Tom McCall, the former governor of Oregon and champion of land-use planning.

The symposium was held in a relatively small room packed with leading television journalists such as Walter Cronkite and Roger Mudd. President Gerald Ford and many members of his energy and environmental staffs were in attendance. McHarg based his observations on Howard T. Odum's net energy model. He posed the question, "How much energy do you spend for the energy received and what are the environmental consequences?" This type of cost-benefit analysis seeks to understand how much energy must be employed for each unit of extracted energy. McHarg observed that the energy that could be derived from oil shale in Colorado would be less than that expended to extract it. Subsequently, plans to exploit oil shale in Colorado were abandoned.

I know a great deal about the sacrifices that people are required to make for energy. For I was born outside of Glasgow, and energy exploitation, mineral exploitation, and sacrifice have been synonymous for at least two hundred years in that part of the world. It was in Scotland, my native country, that broadbank coal and iron were discovered. We wondered what to do with all those metallic lumps. Then somebody discovered how to process the iron into a useful form—and the industrial revolution began.

This revolution started in Scotland, moved to northeastern England, South Wales, Germany, the Lorraine, and finally to the United States. With the advent of heavy equipment, strip mining was made possible, allowing us to steal more minerals from the earth while simultaneously wreaking greater havoc on the environment. Now, the industrial revolution is poised for the attack on the West. You may be the next victim of "progress."

So the real question is: "How can we solve our energy needs without obliterating the landscape, destroying our civilization, and then, in the long run, finding our energy supplies exhausted?" This is a complex question; not one that merits a simple answer. But I think I have sufficient time to outline what we should be doing, lest we find that we have exhausted our energy resources. I shall talk about policies for ranking our energy supplies, measuring the true costs of different energy sources, and the concept of computing the net energy consumed. Since I am a "planner" by training, I'm obliged to throw in a plug for planning in America. And finally, I'll try to be obnoxious and contentious by proposing a strategy for implementing some of these concepts.

For us to organize our energy sources in terms of high and low priorities, we must look to nature for direction. We must realize that we are actually confronting a biological imperative that nature has been solving for 2 ½ billion years. Evolution has an incredible energy component: A surviving organism has to be able to find a habitable environment, one that produces the support ingredients necessary to sustain the organism and ensure its survival. Energy is an important ingredient.

The requirement of finding and utilizing energy efficiently has been a precondition for evolutionary success. Nature has always provided ample energy resources for the organisms. Their survival has been determined by their ability to effectively use the energy while expending a minimum amount of work to process it.

The problem we are experiencing now—that of using non-renewable resources—was also the situation during the earth's formative years before photosynthesis existed. During that time, all organisms were engaged in consumptive, depletive processes. Then came the miracle of photosynthesis. I see it now in my mind's eye: a chloroplastic plant in the ocean has just discovered photosynthesis. It says to the sun, "Sun, do you mind if I have some of your energy?" And the sun says, "Sure, but you know the second law of thermodynamics: you've got to give it back." The little plant says, "Sure, I just want to keep some of the sunlight for a little while, then I'll give it back in the form of infrared." So, in the presence of carbon dioxide and water, the little old chloroplast holds its hands up to the sun, and the sunlight falls upon it and is transmuted into its being. In this process, heat is lost. Here we have a miracle, based on the capability of chloroplast to entrap energy and use it for living.

Now that's the solution to the energy problem—using the renewable energy supplies that nature has been using for billions of years. Simply picking up coal (which is really ancient, stored sunlight) is not the answer because someday we will exhaust the supplies. I sometimes wonder who gave the franchises to utility companies to burn the stored sunlight, blowing it up their smokestacks, watching it being wasted. That's not the way nature works. That's not what successful evolution depends on. Successful evolution depends upon meeting the thermodynamic tests, of utilizing the least necessary amount of energy by recycling and conserving it to ensure its continued supply. How can we learn from nature's example? What sort of policies can we develop that would use biological analogies for providing energy? The first would be to array all energies just the way all plants and animals have always done: by mutation and natural selection. That is, we would array available energies by the degree to which production or utilization imposes a stress upon the producer or consumer of the environment. Now that sounds so bloody simple. Basically, it is very simple. And when we array these energies, we'd find no question about which is the least stressful or most abundant, it is sunlight.

Only 1 percent of all available sunlight is captured by plants and this sunlight really fuels the world. We have a fantastic situation where not only do we have a mechanism by which very diffused radiation is encapsulated in plants and in animals, but we also have no environmental stresses as a result of the energy production. And we benefit from atmospheric oxygen upon which the metabolism of all animals exists.

But I don't think we can do anything as clever as photosynthesis. That took perhaps about 2 ½ billion years to develop and we're not going to do that in the thirty years before we run out of oil. But we can do something a little simpler—like developing photovoltaic cells.

Every satellite is powered by photovoltaic cells. And every exploding meteor is a little miniature photovoltaic cell. We should be spending our time and money on projects like producing low-cost efficient photovoltaic cells for our homes.

Why don't we spend our money on solar energy? The answer is very simple: because we've got an oil lobby, a gas lobby, a coal lobby, and they're all vociferous and powerful. Where is the lobby for solar energy? There isn't one. But we desperately need one. We need to throw vast quantities of money into making photovoltaic cells available so that everybody would put some on his house. Nothing would please me more than to put some on my house, and run the energy through my meter, and at the end of the month send a bill to the Philadelphia Electric Company.

We already have some systems for using the sun's energy, such as heating and cooling our buildings. Although this modest technology is rather unrefined, it is, none the less, an important opportunity. We must further our efforts in this area.

There are several other energy sources that we haven't taken full advantage of, such as the wind. The whole Midwest was once covered with windmills, using this power to great benefit. And tidal surge and geothermal energy are both alternatives that we've yet to optimize. Even if these don't offer the Rocky Mountain West potentially direct applications, they can relieve the demands for your coal, oil shale, and oil—and that will surely help forestall the "Rape of the West."

As we order our energy sources, we eventually have to look at the non-renewable supplies that presently constitute our primary energy banks. You know as much about these as I do. You know they produce enormous costs to the physical environment and serious costs to the social environment. I won't even attempt to prioritize these, except for mentioning the most controversial and potentially destructive of them all: the atomic fuels.

I've followed the developments of atomic energy for a long time, since 1945. I have observed one thing: when the Atomic Energy Commission begins to be frightened by nuclear reactors, we had better be frightened too. I am frightened because the errors in the use of atomic energy don't simply attack the living, they attack the genetic inheritance of all life. So I say, here is an area where the circle costs are incalculably high and where errors are of such dimension as to be absolutely insupportable.

And this very nicely leads into my second point, one that has been implicit in my comments, but definitely should be explicit. Calculations of our energy needs cannot only be measured in BTU's and dollars, but must include all of the social expenses too. Traditionally, we haven't included the social costs in our formulas. For example, the present economic problems of Britain, in my opinion, are traceable to the brutality and oppression imposed on British workers, particularly in the mines. I want you to think of these long and enduring social costs. In our computation, in which we first consider the gradient of the environmental stress imposed by the utilization of energy types, we should also include all social costs before pricing energy.

Unfortunately, we don't include social costs in the price of our energy. Whenever I get my bill from the Philadelphia Electric Company, I have the illusion I am paying *all* the costs that are incurred. Of course, that is not true at all. Philadelphia Electric has never paid all of the costs; therefore, I am not being required to pay all of the costs. And no one has been required to even compute, let alone pay, all of the costs. You see, my costs for electricity should include the destruction of Appalachia—the depravity, hopelessness, misery, black lung disease, and injuries. The cost of remedy should be included. Then, the price I pay the Philadelphia Electric Company would be fair.

So, as we confront the "Rape of the West," let us compute all of the social costs before we determine what the price of energy will be. To do this, we need to employ what may become one of our most important concepts—the concept of net energy. Nature doesn't have any problem with this; it only can deal with net energy. But man has avoided the responsibility of dealing with net energy. Let me explain.

There are many "hidden" costs in the oil we buy from the Middle East. These include the energy necessary to drill 2,000 or 3,000 feet into the earth, to produce the steel, iron, and metals used to build the super tankers, the fuel for the ships to cross the Atlantic, storage and refinement of the oil, and energy for transporting it to the consumer. It's very important to calculate the total amount of energy used in the transaction. The fact of the matter is, we use a large amount of energy in the transaction which reduces the net energy. The deeper we have to drill, the further we have to transport, the more we use in the process, the smaller the net production.

Now, although being able to define the energy priorities, compute the social costs, and measure the net energy point us in the right direction, they don't organize the necessary future strategies. What we need to know is what the consequences of certain acts might be. With that knowledge it would be possible to select certain acts on the grounds that they will not only ensure our survival, but help us achieve the appropriate ends. Unfortunately, we have no such process now. The best we can do is called "planning," and in the United States, it is held in low esteem. Actually, planning is the most enduring biological process.

Planning is an absolutely ancient process and it's an indispensable one. It is the device by which man confronts the future. I define planning as the ability to understand the dichotomy between man and nature with sufficient perception to predict the consequences of contemplated acts, and to select those alternatives likely to guarantee survival. We've established that there are two things going on. There is an environment (biological, physical, and cultural) on one hand, and the consumers on the other hand. As discussed earlier, the thermodynamic test requires that the consumers seek the environment requiring the least energy employment. So if that is the formula, it tells us what the program should be.

First, we have to increase our knowledge of the environment. We've got a host of people who can help us with this. We must call upon these scientists of the environment. We must ask them to array the information so as to display *chronology* and *causality*, allowing us better to understand reality.

Chronology is a very good unifying device. First, we have the scientist identify bedrock geology, which is the most ancient and enduring of all subsequent events. Next, we add geomorphology, hydrology, and physiography. And then we look at the climatic impingement which explains soils and distribution of plants and animals. Through this process, the scientist has made a layer cake of chronology helping us to understand the place as an interacting biophysical process.

Next, we ask the scientists to describe the region in terms of dynamic and interacting processes, understanding that everything is in the process of interacting with everything else. Every region is in fact one single interacting region. So the scientists describe the region as an interacting biophysical system. At that point you have a descriptive model. If you can go beyond that, you have a fully or partially predictive model. Then you're in the position to make some sort of predictions about the consequences likely to result from certain human acts.

Next, we would like to understand why people are where they are and doing what they are doing. Of course, this is difficult, but it can be done through an ethnographic history. Begin with the ecological layer cake of the region, and very carefully populate it with primeval flora and fauna and some indigenous population. Carefully place man and all of his artifacts and institutions on this primeval landscape. Working up to the present, we will have a greater understanding of why people made some of the decisions they made.

Armed with all of this information, there are two things to be done: Make some predictions about the future, requiring some hypothesis about the larger setting, such as the region and the country; and at the same time, listen to people's needs, desires, and expectations of their environment. These are just as good as geologist's statements about rocks. If a man says to me, "I care more about the future of this land than about the money that can be taken out as coal," it is a piece of important data. This must be computed in any calculation comparing contemplated acts against potential consequences.

Setting up a system under which the people of the region have the best understanding of the physical and biological system of the region through the collection and interpretation of the data is critical. These data should be available through public libraries, public cable television, educational institutions, and elsewhere. You must be able to solicit the needs, desires, perceptions, affections, and expectations of all the constituencies in the region. The solution to any problem is going to involve the identification of constituencies that have set needs, desires, and expectations from the environment.

But even with all of these data, the critical thing that will determine the solution will be the *value system* of the problem solver. The solution to any planning problem of utilization of resources will vary not with respect to data, but with respect to the value system. I would like to end on a funny note which I think epitomizes this point.

Once upon a time the State Highway Department of Delaware confronted the intractable problem of putting a beltway around Wilmington. They needed a patsy—a patsy with an environmental name tag. And I fit the bill perfectly. I may be stupid, but I'm not that stupid. I realized I was being set up, so I wrote the contract in such a way that I would produce a method, not a solution.

We studied an area of 30,000 acres, digitized in one-acre cells. We not only had all the geophysical data, but all the socio-economic data, cultural data, and so on. So we took all of the information to the State Highway Department's civil engineers. I said, "Gentlemen, this is the most complete description of this region that you could possibly have. All you must do to locate the highway is weigh all the factors according to their positive or negative effect on the highway—and the highway's effect on the community. Then we'll have a computer print out the solution resulting from your value system." And of course, each did it—and each produced a different solution. I had some of my colleagues do it and they produced yet different solutions. And the State Highway Department said, "Which solution should we use?" "Oh," I said, "don't ask me. Who would I be, a Scottish immigrant living in Philadelphia, to represent myself as a surrogate for the value systems of all the people affected? But, if *you* are arrogant enough to believe that you could represent the value system for all these complex people, from the Chicano mushroom farm workers to the pre-revolutionary Blacks to the DuPonts, and all the rest in between, the best of luck to you, but I certainly wouldn't do it!"

The moral of the story is that the solution varies with respect to the value system of the person who solves the problem. So you have to identify the interactive biophysical culture system under study. You have to identify all the prospective consumer's needs, desires, and expectations. And then you have to allow each constituent to get a resolution to his particular problems. At that point in the democratic process, the resolution is the will of the majority, the rights of minorities are respected, and the conclusion lies in the courts. I would be content with this. At least those who did it would know what they're doing.

The technology exists. We can use technology as a slave, not as a master. In most cases the thing that obstructs us is not the absence of data or technology, but the absence of an integrated device or institution to utilize, to disseminate the information.

My recommendation is simple (and probably not even as obnoxious or contentious as I promised): Establish a national environmental lab for the United States. Divide the United States into eleven physiographic divisions, each of which includes homogenous environments with respect to geology, physiography, hydrology, soil, etc. Locate an environmental lab in each division and require them to be staffed with appropriate scientists, collect and digitize data, and make models. These people then become the surrogates of each region. They produce the data which allows the constituents to identify their value systems. The process is opened to public debate through cable TV hearings and publicity, making it possible for people to negotiate with each other about the value systems to be used.

If we develop this system and are able to predict the consequences of contemplated events, if we're able to choose between these consequences in terms of short-term or long-term so that our choices guarantee survival and fulfillment, then this indeed would be the way to prevent the sacrifice of the West.

You must in fact find such instruments and institutions because you are guardians, custodians, stewards, not only of a beautiful bit of Colorado, but of a wonderful, rich, and cherished part of the earth. So I commend you to this quest, for you, for me, for all Americans, for children yet unborn.

9

Ecological Planning: The Planner as Catalyst (1978)

Although McHarg challenged orthodox planning theory, especially the economic-social science deterministic approach of theorists such as John Friedmann and Britton Harris, he embraced the notion of the planner as catalyst for positive change. One role model was his partner David Wallace, who had helped transform Baltimore's downtown through his activism. In many ways, McHarg favored an activist place-making approach to environmental planning over more bureaucratic rule making, although he certainly recognized rules that are necessary to prevent environmental pollution, destruction, and degradation.

This paper was written for Robert Burchell and George Sternlieb for a conference at Rutgers University on planning theory. Other contributors to the conference and the later book included the crème of the orthodox planning theory crop, including Friedmann, Harris, Robert Beauregard, David Harvey, William Grigsby, and the most notable change agent-catalyst from the planning community, Paul Davidoff.

By and large the virtues of the planning I was taught were orderliness and convenience, efficiency and economy. The first set contains minor virtues, and the second set contains less than noble ones. These virtues have little to do with survival or success of plants, animals, and men in evolutionary time.

A fallacy is that planners plan for people. Actually this is not an assumption at all; it is a presumption. The planner who comes from out of town and is prepared to solve problems is a menace.

I prefer to think of planners as catalysts. The planner suppresses his own ego and becomes an agent for outlining available options. He offers predictability that science gives him about the consequences of different courses of action. He helps the community make its values explicit. He identifies alternative solutions with attendant costs and benefits. These vary with different constituencies, as do their needs and values.

This sort of planning might be called ecological. It is based on an understanding of both biophysical and social systems. Ecological planners operate within the framework of a biophysical culture.

Ecological planning addresses itself to the selection of environments. Ecological planners help institutions and individuals adapt these and themselves to achieve fitness.

For example, when I prepare a planning study, I insist that scientists of the environment study the region in terms of the processes which produce the phenomena constituting the region. They describe the phenomena of the region as an interacting biophysical model. Such a model can then be seen to have intrinsic opportunities and constraints to all existing and prospective users. Fitness is defined as the presence of all or most propitious attributes with none or few detrimental areas.

This notion of planning stems from two fundamental characteristics of natural processes: creativity and fitness. Creativity provides the dynamics that govern the universe. There is a tendency for all matter to degrade to entropy, but in certain energetic transactions there is a process by which some matter is transformed to a higher level or order. All of biology subscribes to this law: entropy increases but a local syntropy can be achieved. It is seen in both energetic transactions, in the evolution of matter, life, and man. This biological "creativity" enables us to explain the rich and diverse world of life today, as opposed to the sterile world of yesterday.

The second concept—fitness—stems partially from Darwinian notions about how organisms adapt and survive. Equally important is the thought that the surviving organisms are fit for the environment. The world provides an abundance of environmental opportunity. This teaches us that the world is environmentally variable, offering variable fitness. This results from the most basic elements—hydrogen, nitrogen, oxygen, and carbon—and the earth itself provides environmental opportunity.

All systems are required to seek out the environment that is most fit, to adapt these and themselves, continuously. This is a requirement for survival. This is called adaptation. It is an imperative of all life, it has been, and it always will be. Fitness can best be described as finding an environment—physical, biological, or social—in which the largest part of the work of survival is done by the environment itself. There is then an energetic imperative for evolutionary success. Systems which are "fit" are evolutionary successes; they are maximum success solutions to fitness.

Planning, of course, is more than understanding environments and explaining why they are what they are, and where they are going. It is also explaining why people are where they are, doing what they are doing. An ecological planner would look at this over time, through an ethnographic history: Where did the first people who occupied a given place come from? Why did they leave? Why did they choose the environment they did? What adaptive skills determined their location? What adaptive skills did they practice? What modifications did they make to the environment? What institutions did they develop? What plans?

The social value of a given environment is an amalgam of the place, the people, and their technology. People in a given place with opportunities afforded by the environment for practicing a means of production, will develop characteristic perceptions and institutions. These institutions will have perceptions and values that feed back to an understanding of the environment—both national and social—and that have a modification of technology. Thus, I believe, we have a continuous model, which emanates from the physical and biological, and extends to the cultural.

The most critical factor is the value system, for it determines the planning solution. I strongly object to much of the current planning philosophy as it is emerging in both teaching and practice, for it assumes that the planner imposes values and exercises for the "good of the people." I resist this. Given a set of data, the planning solutions will vary, not with respect to the set, but with respect to the value systems of the people who seek to solve the problem. Most of the important values are particular and there is no substitute for eliciting them from the constituents themselves. These values themselves become the data, whether it be for describing rocks, soils, animals, people, or institutions. Planners must elicit these data from their client if they are going to help solve the problems posed by the particular system within which the client functions. This, in fact, is the planner's most important role. After he has done it, he should step aside, and the resolution of the problem of the explicit system will be found through the political process, and ultimately, in some cases, through the courts.

In sum, the planner is a catalyst and a resource. He determines what skills and branches of knowledge are appropriate to solutions, and what institutions. He helps to describe the interactions of systems. He describes probable alternative courses of action and assists his constituents in making their value system explicit. The planner then helps his clients understand what the consequences of applying that value system are in terms of their costs and benefits. He participates with them in negotiations among different constituencies over the relaxation or change of values in order to come to some agreement about the allocation of resources.

If the process is successful the constituencies will select the fittest environments, adapting these and themselves to achieve a creative fitting. As health can be described as the ability of persons, families, or institutions to seek and solve problems, so planning is not only a measure of the health of a group or institution, but, is health-giving to such agents.

It could make planning more fitting, perhaps even healthier.

10

Human Ecological Planning at Pennsylvania (1981)

In 1981 Arthur Johnson, a faculty member at Penn, edited a special issue of Landscape Planning *(now called* Landscape and Urban Planning, *published by Elsevier). The special issue was devoted to the Penn Department of Landscape Architecture and Regional Planning. McHarg's article described the human ecological approach. He incorporates an understanding of the ecologies of people to the natural-resource approach, described in* Design with Nature. *To that end, he had encouraged colleagues such as Dan Rose, Jon Berger, and Setha Low, as well as graduate students, to pursue such an approach.*

Abstract

A theory of human ecological planning is presented which is based on the premise that all social and natural systems aspire to success. Such a state can be described as "syntropic-fitness-health." Understanding the process of interaction between the landscape and the people who inhabit it provides a basis for assessing the opportunities and constraints afforded by the environment, and the needs and desires of the population which can be combined to present alternative futures. Such a model allows examination of the impact of any plan upon the health of the inhabitants and the well-being of the social and natural systems.

Introduction

It is first necessary to define terms. The simplest term is the last in the title of this paper. Pennsylvania is a contraction for the Department of Landscape

Architecture and Regional Planning at the University of Pennsylvania (also called Penn). Here a faculty described in *Science* (Holden 1977) as one of the very few multi-disciplinary and interdisciplinary faculties in the United States, is committed to the development and teaching of human ecological planning. The faculty comprises physical, biological, and social scientists, architects, landscape architects, and city and regional planners.

It is next necessary to define human ecological planning. The central word in this compound noun has primacy: ecology has been defined as the study of the interactions of organisms and environment (which includes other organisms). The word human is adequately defined in standard dictionaries but human ecology is not. While ecology has traditionally sought to learn the laws which obtain for ecosystems, it has done so by investigating environments unaffected or little affected man; it has emphasized biophysical systems. Yet clearly no systems are unaffected by man, indeed studies of the interactions of organisms and environment are likely to reveal human dominance. Hence, ecology simply must be extended to include man. Human ecology can then be defined as the study of the interactions of organisms (including man), and the environment (including man among other organisms). However, if man is assumed to be implicit in both definitions of organisms and environment then the standard definition for ecology can apply to human ecology.

The possibilities for creating a human ecology seem to be afforded by a new extension and integration of existing scientific disciplines. Ecology has been used to integrate the sciences of the biophysical environment. If we extend ecology by adding ethology we introduce the subject of behavior as an adaptive strategy. If we extend further into ethnography and anthropology we can include the study of human behavior as adaptation. If, finally, we extend into medical anthropology and epidemiology we can close the cycle by examining the natural and human environment in terms of human health and well-being.

Planning cannot be defined succinctly. Planning consists of the formulation of hypothetical alternative futures. These are constituted into component actions comprising courses of action. These are subsequently measured in terms of costs and benefits (employing the value system of the initiator of the alternative futures). The least cost—maximum benefit solution selects the preferred hypothetical future.

When "planning" is linked to "ecological" the primacy of goals is modified. Goals are derived from the region. Ecological planning is an instrument for revealing regions as interacting and dynamic natural systems having intrinsic opportunities and constraints for all human uses. Preferred hypothetical futures will be proffered by locations where all or most propitious factors exist with none or few detrimental ones for any and all prospective uses. What constitutes detrimental or propitious is derived from the prospective use and the value system of the initiating person or group.

When the term is compounded into "human ecological planning" the region is expanded into a physical, biological, and cultural region wherein opportunities and constraints are represented in every realm. Geophysical and ecological regions are identified as cultural regions in which characteristic people pursue means of production, develop characteristic settlement patterns, have characteristic perceptions, needs and desires and institutions for realizing their objectives. Hypothetical future alternatives are derived from expressed needs and desires of groups. These are matched against the physical, biological, and cultural resources. Preferred hypothetical futures can be derived for each group with its associated value system.

Human ecological planning is a cumbersome and graceless title. Remedy, however, while possible, is distant. When it becomes accepted that no ecosystem can be studied without reference to man then we may abandon the "human" descriptor and revert to "ecological planning." Better still, when planning always considers interacting biophysical and cultural processes, then we can dispense with the distinction of "ecological" and simply employ the word "planning." However, that state is far in the future, as most planning today excludes physical and biological sciences, ecology, ethnography, anthropology, epidemiology, and concentrates upon economics and sociology. It remains necessary, not only to advance planning to become ecological, but even more, to develop a human ecological planning.

Theory

Having defined terms it is next necessary to describe the theory which impels human ecological planning. Clearly, as it incorporates the physical, biological, and social sciences it can also employ the theory of these sciences. Planning is not rich in theory, and no statement on a theory of human ecological planning has yet been propounded. In order to initiate this quest I offer the following as a tentative beginning.

It would appear that all living systems tend to oscillate between two extreme states. These can be described as: (1) syntropic-fitness-health; and (2), entropic-misfitness-morbidity. Entropy is the tendency for energy and matter to degrade from higher to lower levels of order in any energetic transaction. All energetic transactions result in an increase in entropy. However, while the preceding is true, certain energetic transactions produce a product of matter and energy at a higher level of order than at the onset. This process is described by Buckminster Fuller as syntropic. The explosion of super novae in a primeval universe composed of hydrogen resulted in an increase in entropy but there was a residuum, not only of hydrogen but also helium, lithium, beryllium, boron, on up the periodic table of elements, each more ordered than hydrogen. The evolution of matter in the universe is syntropic. In life forms, all of which constitute energetic transactions, photosynthesis is the most notable example of syntropy. Given continuous energy, in the presence of carbon dioxide and water, the chloroplast creates glucose, a higher level of order than the ingredients. The evolution of life forms itself is syntropic whereby successive forms represent increased capability, a higher level of ordered energy and matter in their beings.

Fitness has two definitions, each complementary. Charles Darwin (1859) stated that "the surviving organism is fit for the environment." Much later Lawrence Henderson (1913) augmented this proposition by showing that the actual world consists of an infinitude of environments, all exhibiting fitness for appropriate organisms. These two propositions can be linked into an evolutionary imperative. Every organism, system, or institution, is required to find the fittest environment, adapt that environment and itself in order to survive. This imperative is linked to the syntrophy-entropy criteria. An environment is defined as fit for an organism by the degree to which the environment, as found, provides the largest amount of needs for that organism. The corollary, then, is that the organism is required to import and employ the least amount of energy and time to modify the environment and itself to make it more fitting. Thus there is a condition of syntropic fitness. Entropic misfitness would be represented by an organism unable to find a fit environment and/or unable to adapt that environment and/or unable to adapt itself. Its fate would be non-survival, death, and extinction.

All creatures as individuals, species, or ecosystems, aspire to survival and success. The mechanism for achieving this state is adaptation. This has three modes: physiological adaptation by mutation and natural selection used by all life forms; innate behavior, shared by animals and man; and, the unique human instrumentality, cultural adaptation. Until recombinant DNA is employed, physiological adaptation will remain beyond voluntary control; innate behavior is similarly resistant to manipulation. Adaptation through modification of culture is the most plastic instrument for voluntary action leading to survival and success.

While the verb, "to fit," applies to the active selection of environments, adapting those and the self, the noun "fitness" has another meaning. It implies health. From another direction, the definition of a healthy person is one who solves and seeks problems. Yet a second definition of health is the ability to recover from insult or assault. Both definitions accord with evolutionary biology; they could be subsumed by adaptation, particularly the latter. It appears that fitness and health are states linked in a more profound way than is suggested by common usage. Fitness is defined as problem solving, i.e., finding fit environments, adapting these and the self. Health is similarly defined as seeking and solving problems. It would appear that not only is fitness syntropic, but so is health. There seems to be a state of syntropic-fitness-health. The antithesis confirms this assumption. Morbidity reveals a process moving from higher to lower levels of order, decomposition after death is its most complete expression. Morbidity is also a failure in adaptation: the environment is not fit for the cells, tissue, organ or organism; or the system is unable to make it or itself fit, and finally, the system is unable to recover from insult or assault, unable to solve problems resulting in entropic-misfit-morbidity. There is one further observation of significance. Health, it would appear, not only reveals evidence of the presence of syntropic fitness, but, if health is defined as problem seeking and solving, then the quest for fitness is also health-giving. This long preamble finally reaches planning. Of all the instrumentalities available through cultural adaptation (language, religion, symbol, art, philosophy, etc.), it would seem that one above all is most directly connected to the evolutionary imperative of finding fit environments and adapting these, of accomplishing syntropic-fitness-health. This instrument is planning, in particular human ecological planning, or planning for human health and well-being.

The theory of human ecological planning can now be summarized: all systems aspire to survival and success. This state can be described as syntropic-fitness-health. Its antithesis is entropic-misfitness-morbidity. To achieve the first state requires systems to find the fittest environment, adapt it and themselves. Fitness of an environment for a system is defined as that requiring the minimum work of adaptation. Fitness and fitting are indication of health and the process of fitting is health giving. The quest for fitness is entitled adaptation. Of all of the instrumentalities available to man for successful adaptation, cultural adaptation in general and planning in particular, appear to be the most direct and efficacious for maintaining and enhancing human health and well-being.

Method

Theory produces an objective which requires a method to achieve it. We are required to promote human health and well-being by planning, specifically to select fit environments for all users; to participate in the adaptation of that environment and the user. We must be able to describe regions as interacting physio-bio-cultural systems, reconstitute them as resources and hence as social values, array these attributes as either costs or benefits for prospective consumers, and select the maximum benefit—least cost solution. Thus, we must be able to model regions, insofar as science permits, at least descriptively, at best quantitatively; we must employ all of the predictive skill which science provides to forecast the consequences of contemplated actions on the interacting systems.

Before describing the method employed there is one important observation to be made. Human ecological planning incorporates the physical, biological, and social sciences and in so doing it utilizes the universal laws which those sciences employ. However, the distinction of ecological planning, unlike economic, transportation, or orthodox city planning, is that this planning theory and method emphasize locality. As with ecosystems and bioclimatic zones, it is believed that each region or locality is spatially determined. While responding to universal laws, each region is believed to comprise unique attributes of place–folk–work, as first identified by Patrick Geddes, and these will determine the capabilities, opportunities, and constraints of the region and thus the potential hypothetical futures.

The first objective of the method is to create a model of the region under study. As all of the sciences of the environment agree that things, creatures, places, and people are only comprehensible through the operation of laws and time, it is appropriate that the modeling exercise should employ evolution and history. Matter preceded life which preceded man. We should begin the construction of the model with its physical evolution, continue with biophysical evolution, and conclude with the addition of cultural history. This method selects the participants. Physical evolution is the province of meteorology, geology, hydrology, soil science, and where applicable, physical oceanography. Biophysical evolution adds botanists and marine biologists where appropriate. Human evolution requires anthropologists—physical, cultural and medical ethnographers, and such economists, sociologists, and political scientists as are compatible with the ecological view. The final participant is the planner, the person willing to undertake synthesis, oriented towards problem solving.

As science has divided this "one world" into discrete areas of concern, we are required to accept this situation, although the objective is to unite all of the discrete perceptions into a description of a single interacting system. While we must employ all disciplines which describe the environment we can collect and array their data in a way which employs history and causality to assist in the portrayal of reality. Let us build a layer-cake representation of the region with the oldest evidence on the bottom and new, consequential layers superimposed in place and in time.

We can properly begin with the oldest evidence, bedrock geology, as the basement and superimpose meteorology above. We ask that the geologist, mindful of meteorological history, reconstruct geological history to explain the phenomena of the region and its dynamics. Upon bedrock geology surficial geology is added with meteorology remaining on top. We ask a geomorphologist to add his more recent data and explain physiography in terms of bedrock and surficial geology. The next scientist, a groundwater hydrologist, interprets the previous data to explain historic and contemporary phenomena. A surface water hydrologist follows. Together they describe hydrological processes, contemporary phenomena, and tendencies. The next layer is the domain of the soils scientist. He, as with others, is required to invoke the data of all prior sciences to explain the processes and phenomena within his realm. However, he must also invoke the effect of life forms historically. The plant ecologist follows. He describes plants in terms of communities occupying habitats. The descriptions of these employ geology, meteorology, hydrology, and soils. He recapitulates vegetational history to explain the existing flora and its dynamics; the limnologist populates aquatic systems using a similar method, and finally, the animal ecologist, depending most upon plant ecology, constructs a history of wildlife and explains the contemporary populations and their environments. Arrayed as a cross-section, the layer cake is complete—bedrock geology, surficial geology, groundwater hydrology, physiography, surface-water hydrology, soils, plants, wildlife, micro-, meso- and macro-climate. The layer cake has evolved over time and continues to do so. The entire formulation of the ecological model has emphasized interacting processes and time. All phenomena have been, are now, and are in the process of becoming. The layer cake is an expression of historical causality. It is possible to peer from the surface to the bottom and explain process, reality, and form. We have, at once, a discipline and (to the degree science provides it) a predictive model.

The study of the evolutionary history of the region has revealed that all processes are interacting with each other: geological and meteorological history are expressed in surficial geology which, in turn, are expressed in hydrology and soils. The sum of these is reflected in environments populated by appropriate plant communities while these last are occupied and utilized by consonant animals. It becomes clear that physical processes are synthesized in physiography while biophysical processes are synthesized by ecosystems.

The next task is to populate the region with its inhabitants. Here we confront the threshold between ecological and human ecological planning. The physical and biological sciences assume the operation of order. While there is randomness in systems, randomness cannot explain them. In short, we accept that nature is systematic. Can we also assume that man and nature are systematic, or is man random with respect to a systematic nature? It seems more reasonable to believe that man and nature are systematic and to continue to employ the evolutionary method to explain folk–work–place. We wish to know who the people are, why they inhabit the region, why they are where they are, doing what they are doing.

In order to explain people, place, and work, using an evolutionary method, we need to undertake the study of ethnographic history. We can begin with the biophysical representation of the region before the advent of Western man. The primeval environment is then occupied by its aboriginal people. However, it is necessary to explain the anthropological model which underlies the ethnographic history before we proceed. This construct affirms that, while a region may be described as an interacting biophysical system, it is simultaneously, a social value system, i.e., it contains resources. However, what constitutes a resource is determined by the perception of the inhabitants or observers, and the available technology and capital. Given certain perceptions, technology, and capital, certain natural phenomena will be perceived as resources and exploited. These resources, e.g., minerals, lumber, wildlife, will be locationally determined by the natural history of the region. Thus the means of production, utilizing resource or resources, will also be locationally determined. The means of production implies labor selection, generally persons skilled in the appropriate kinds of employment, e.g., fishing, mining, lumbering, farming. In American history the exploitation of resources, in selecting accomplished practitioners, often attracted ethnic groups who had practiced similar skills in Europe. So we see Scots miners, Portuguese fishermen, Italian masons, Basque shepherds, Russian and Swedish farmers in the northern Great Plains, Spanish farmers in the arid Southwest, French Canadian and Swedish lumbermen, and others. People sharing an occupation tend to have similar perceptions of themselves, particularly when this is accompanied by shared ethnicity and religion. Each occupational type is likely to have characteristic land uses and settlement patterns, and, finally, groups associated with a particular means of production are likely to develop characteristic institutions to promote and enhance their success and well-being, both in the private and public domain.

Thus, we can anticipate that changes in land-use and settlement patterns respond to two causes: the first is technological change and the second includes massive social events, e.g., wars, immigration, and the like.

The method can proceed. It begins with the layer cake occupied by its aboriginal inhabitants, plants, animals and people, their settlement patterns, land uses, transportation corridors. The next land-use map should portray colonial settlement responsive to then-current perceptions and technology, and should explain the differences from the original map in terms of resource, technology, and social events. For example, in the age of sail, the colonizers of the eastern seaboard of the United States sought safe harbors and estuarine and river systems permitting penetration of the interior. The Hudson, Delaware, Christiana, Susquehanna, Potomac, and James rivers provided safe harbors, but penetration of the interior posed serious problems—waterfalls on the main rivers and their tributaries. All of the waterfalls occurred on the same geological phenomenon, the interface between the crystalline piedmont and the coastal plain. At this point, settlement occurred on each of the rivers Albany, Trenton, Philadelphia, Wilmington, Baltimore, Washington, D.C., and Richmond, Virginia. New York City was a special case of a granite island located in a drowned tidal estuary.

At the time of the American Revolution, iron for cannon and cannon balls was important. Iron was obtained from bogs, which were abundant in the coastal plain of New Jersey, but scarce elsewhere. This is comprehensible from natural history: the bogs located the bog iron which located the foundries which located settlement and which located operators. So with the grist and saw mills, ports, harbors, fisheries, and farming. Each successive map shows changes responsive to new options presented by technological innovation and/or impelled by social events, revolutions, war, immigration being the most notable. Throughout the ethnographic history, attention is also paid to nonphysical instruments of adaptation, e.g., laws, ordinances, and mores, the evolution of institutions, public and private. Finally, the last product is one of current land use, a document gravid with meaning, as ordered as a map of rocks, soils, or vegetation.

It transpires that people are who they are, where they are, doing what they are doing for good and sufficient reasons. Moreover, they are not reticent to describe themselves, in economic, ethnic, occupational, religious, and spatial terms. They have no doubt about the territory they occupy. They can define themselves, their territory, and their neighbors. The process of eliciting this people-place description is called "consensual mapping." When regions defined by inhabitants are compared to "natural" regions and features, a great conformity becomes apparent. In many cases there are physiographic-social regions and subregions. This applies not only to rural and metropolitan areas but also to urban neighborhoods in the City of Philadelphia. The discovery that people, far from being random with respect to the natural environment, are highly ordered, simplifies the next task. We wish to ascertain the needs and desires of the population. The theory presumes that health and well-being attend the task of finding fit environments, adapting these and the self. In order to ascertain what values constitute "fitness" and "misfitness" we must elicit those values because they are not objective; they cannot be attributed, but only elicited. But as it transpires that populations reveal discrete self-defined groups and locations, it is not necessary to interview large numbers to obtain this information. Key informant interviews with a small-sample questionnaire for each group will suffice. We wish to know what perceptions groups have of themselves and their environment. What are their needs and desires? In order to ascertain the values they apply, subjects are asked to reveal their positions on certain contemporary issues. This method proves more efficacious than direct questions on values.

When groups have been identified, it becomes necessary to ascertain their values and the instruments through which they seek to attain their objectives. Obviously, the formal political arena receives investigation, but informal institutions receive even greater attention. Voluntary associations, e.g., con-servation groups, fraternal organizations, voluntary fire companies, parent-teacher associations, the League of Women Voters, the Grange, Mushroom Institute, Shell Fisherman's Association, each reveals its values, its position on issues, its membership, its financial capabilities, its strategies in its publications and public statements. This analysis, combined with one on kinship, reveals the social system as a complex network with a mosaic of overlapping constituencies, each having characteristic needs and desires, with varying capabilities of realizing them through the market, private and public institutions. However, there is a danger that the social data can become so complex as to be unusable. The ordering principle employs land use. Using matrices and maps, discrete social groups, e.g., Italian Catholic mushroom farmers, are located. Next, issues are identified and positions on these issues are also represented on matrices and maps. A conformity becomes apparent between land uses, occupants, locations and positions on issues. All of the preceding data are mapped on a single four-way matrix entitled Community Interaction. One ordinate enumerates the inhabitants as self-described constituencies. At right angles are shown the issues. Opposite constituencies are listed all land uses. The final quadrant identifies all agencies, private and public, through which the constituencies operate to achieve their ends. This matrix can also be employed to show which constituencies suffer or benefit from different reactions to any issue. The data are now ordered and comprehensible. As human ecological planning is future-oriented, it cannot be content with the existing population as the client group. It must make either assumptions or predictions about its size and composition at future times. This is the area of growth modeling and market analysis dominated by economists. The economy of the region is reviewed historically and, in conjunction with assumptions made for the national and regional economy, predictions of growth or decline are made for population, employment categories, and public facilities. This analysis includes the levels of private investment which can be anticipated in different sections of private enterprise and fiscal expenditures on the various levels of government.

We have come to the point where the elements of the Darwin-Henderson imperative can be resolved. We have modeled the natural region as an interacting system in which values repose. We have asked the occupants and users to describe their needs and desires, their conception of benefits (which also reveals dislikes, aversions, and costs). We can now search for fit environments for all users, present and prospective. Fitness remains unchanged—a fit environment requires the least work of adaptation. In other words, where all or most propitious factors co-exist with none or few detrimental ones, is, by definition, "most fitting." This requires a two-part process. First, we must interpret the data maps for their opportunities and constraints for all prospective land uses. For example, the geology map might be interpreted for seismic activity, landslide hazard, fault zones, economic minerals, subsidence, compressive strength, and more. The physiography map will be interpreted to show physiographic regions and features, elevation categories, slope categories, and so on, for each map. The sum of all of the legends on all maps constitutes the sum of attributes to be employed in the allocation process. Obviously, any single phenomenon can be an opportunity for one user and a constraint to another. The users must now be defined, either in terms of self-identified social groups, e.g., Italian mushroom farmers, or more broadly, agricultural types. The appropriate user-category will be determined from the anthropological study. When known, all of the relevant attributes in every data set are compiled in terms of opportunities and constraints for that land use. The region is then shown as a gradient of maximum to minimum suitability (fitness) for each and every land use, i.e., agriculture, industry, commerce, recreation, and housing all by type. In addition, one further map is generally prepared, entitled "Protection." This identifies and delimits all hazards to life and health from physical phenomena in flood plains, hurricane zones, seismic areas, and the like. It also identifies areas which can be made hazardous by human use, e.g., by induced subsidence by withdrawal of water, gas, oil, or by mining. It also locates all rare, endangered, scarce, or valuable species of plants and animals, and all buildings, places, and spaces deemed to be of historic, scenic, or scientific value. At this point, it is possible to synthesize all of the optima for all prospective land uses showing the intrinsic suitability (fitness) of the region for all existing and prospective uses. This should show locations where more than one land use can coexist compatibly in a single area. It should also show where co-existing uses would be in conflict. The preceding procedure is appropriate for government planning as an objective statement on intrinsic fitness of the region. However, planning decisions are not made on objective criteria alone. It is also possible to allocate resources using the value system of the discrete constituencies which constitute the region. The major variable in any allocation process in planning is the value system of the problem solver. Hence, there can be as many plans as there are groups. Moreover, for every allocation one can analyze who suffers and who benefits. The availability of such data would allow groups to see the consequences of the employment of their value system in terms of resource allocation. It would permit groups to see where values would have to be modified to achieve objectives which they sought. In short, it provides the opportunity for an overt, explicit and replicatable planning process, and indeed for planning as a truly informed democratic process.

Ecological planning seeks to fit consumer and environment. This problem-solving and problem-seeking quest conforms to the definition of health. Ecological planning should be health giving. Success in such planning or fitting should be revealed in the existence of healthy communities, physical, biological, and social systems in dynamic equilibrium. However, many persons and institutions may satisfy the definition of health by seeking and solving problems but still succumb to disease and death from causes of which they were ignorant or causes beyond their control. As a result a specialization in health planning has been developed within the realm of human ecological planning. This subscribes to the ecological theory and method which has been described but uses as its viewpoint the degree to which actions by persons, groups, or institutions enhance or diminish human health and well-being.

The first category of such actions comprises natural phenomena and processes which constitute a hazard to life and health. This would include areas susceptible to volcanism and earthquakes, floods, tsunamis, avalanches, landslides, fire, subsidence, and the like. It would also include vectors of disease inducing malaria, yellow fever, schistosomiasis, river blindness, sleeping sickness, cholera, amoebic dysentery, etc.

The subsequent category would comprise those situations where certain human actions would transform a benign situation into a hazardous one, e.g., where earthquakes may be induced by injecting wastes into faults, or subsidence induced by underground mining or the withdrawal of water, natural gas, and oil, the exacerbation of flood or drought, disposal of toxins into the environment, or contemplated inhabitation of environments wherever hazards existed.

A third category would include the hazards to life and health related to resources and occupations. This would include uranium, lead, mercury, zinc, asbestos, and beryllium, among others. It would include occupations which extracted these minerals, processed, and used them. This category of occupational diseases associated with resources would include the effect of pesticides and herbicides both upon farm workers and consumers.

A further realm of investigation would focus upon regions impacted by hazardous processes, e.g., a population subtended by a plume of air pollution from one or more sources, a population utilizing contaminated water sources, or one served by an unsanitary food distribution facility, etc.

The final area is social epidemiology, where populations are analyzed to discern their degree of health/morbidity attributable to multiple factors with an emphasis on behavior.

In all of these cases the human ecological presumption holds. Individuals and society can achieve health and well-being by seeking and solving problems. In the special case of health planning, the connection is visible and incontrovertible. Persons are assisted in identifying problems to which they would otherwise be oblivious and are therefore enabled to confront and resolve them.

As one reviews the amount of work to be undertaken to accomplish human ecological planning, the first response is that it is beyond the financial or human resources of most communities. Indeed, given present priorities it probably is. Yet, if the quest for health and well-being necessarily involves planning as the agent for accomplishing syntropic-fitness-health, is this not the single most important activity of persons, families, institutions and, not least, government? All units of government are enjoined by the U.S. Constitution to promote the health and well-being of citizens. Indeed, if this is the most powerful agency available to man, can he avoid employing it? It has multiple benefits. It requires that all activities, public and private, be reviewed in terms of the degree to which they promote and enhance well-being. The acquisition of both the natural inventory and the ethnographic history, if assimilated, provides the basis for an informed citizenry capable of exercising good judgment. In addition, access to the ecological model gives the opportunity for predicting the consequence of contemplated actions, both in the public and private realm. In terms of costs the initial cost of undertaking an ecological inventory and interpretation, an ethnographic history supplemented by interviews, would be high, but they would only have to be done once. The task of keeping the inventory current and enriched would not be demanding.

I have elsewhere (Wallace, McHarg, Roberts, and Todd, 1973) described a process whereby this conception could be employed as national policy. It was recommended that a National Environmental Laboratory be created to model the ecosystem of the United States and provide a depository of integrated and interpreted data available to all, either in published form, mapped form, or through a display terminal facility, located in all public libraries. In addition there would be thirty-four Regional Environmental Laboratories, one for each of the homogenous physiographic regions comprising the United States. These would provide data at scales appropriate to the nation and its regions. Those data should also be available at scales appropriate to states, countries, and finally, cities and towns.

Of course, university departments do not engage in national policy. While this subject is of intense interest to planners, the purpose of the Penn Department of Landscape Architecture and Regional Planning is to engage in research and instruction to train professional landscape architects and regional planners. The faculty have concluded that it is presumptuous to plan without knowledge of place and people and that planning involves fitting them together, mindful of the thermodynamic imperative of fitness and the supervening criterion of enhancing human health and well-being.

The evolution of the department at Penn over the past quarter century has been from a preoccupation with design in the absence of any scientific prerequisites or training to a continuous increase in the content of both physical and biological science, integrated by ecology. The present phase aspires to extend ecological planning and design into an applied human ecology. It is the hope of this author that this issue will help bring together others engaged in this and similar quests in order that there will be mutual benefit.

References

Darwin, C. 1859. *On the Origin of Species by Means of Natural Selection, or the Preservation of Favoured Races in the Struggle for Life*. London: Murray.

Henderson, L.J. 1913. *The Fitness of the Environment*. New York: The Macmillan Company.

Holden, C. 1977. "Champion for Design with Nature." *Science*, 195:379–382.

Wallace, McHarg, Roberts, and Todd. 1973. *Towards a Comprehensive Plan for Environmental Quality*. Washington, D.C.: American Institute of Planners for the U.S. Environmental Protection Agency.

Part III

Form and Function
Are Indivisible

Ian McHarg pursued design before planning and, in many ways, remained a designer, at least he retained the flair, the attitude, of the designer. His major contributions to the environmental design arts are theoretical. Like many young people, he was attracted to landscape architecture because of overlapping interests in the outdoors and in drawing. Before the second world war, he apprenticed as a landscape architect while studying in colleges of art and agriculture. At the end of the war, he became exposed to planning through a correspondence course. But, it was his quest to be a landscape architect, a designer, that brought him to study in the United States at Harvard University.

Those were heady times at Harvard, which, with the arrival of Walter Gropius at the Graduate School of Design, had become the center of the modern movement. McHarg fell very much under the spell of modernism and was especially attracted to the Bauhaus philosophy of interdisciplinary interaction as well as its optimistic view of the promise of design for shaping a better future. He formed friendships at Harvard with leading designers that would last a lifetime. In fact, McHarg knew well all of the leading architects of the postwar era from Walter Gropius and Lou Kahn to Robert Venturi and Romaldo Giurgola. Denise Scott Brown was a member of McHarg's faculty very early in her career, just one of many distinguished designers associated with the Penn Department of Landscape Architecture and Regional Planning.

Using ecological knowledge to design and to create forms and space, is an especially difficult task. As a student at Penn, I was required to take a geomorphology course. The regular professor, Bob Giegengack, was on sabbatical, and he had been replaced by a young postdoctoral scholar from Cambridge who was puzzled why his course was filled with landscape architecture and regional planning students. After clarifying that we were not landscape gardeners, we explained that we had come to Penn to study with Ian McHarg and to learn how to design with nature.

The instructor was a flexible Englishman, so he assigned us to identify places on the Penn campus where geological materials were misused, where design was not with nature. Several of us identified the Woodland Avenue Gardens, where a grey, glazed brick in exposed aggregate concrete had been used that did not fit the Philadelphia climate. Frosts would spall the faces off the glazed bricks, resulting in ugly, pockmarked walls. The instructor was thrilled with this and other examples. We were shocked to learn that the Woodland Avenue Gardens had been designed by none other than Ian McHarg.

I do not believe any of us mentioned it to him at the time. Years passed. I left Philadelphia, returned again to teach and to pursue a Ph.D., left again, and would return from time to time. I would always walk through the Woodland Avenue Gardens because it was strategically located above a subway stop and at connecting points to West Philadelphia sidewalks. Although the walls remained ugly, I noticed that the tree canopy was quite pleasant, even room-like, and the connection between the subway stop and pedestrian routes functioned well. Eventually the area was redesigned by, among others, Hanna-Olin, and the walls were remade.

I eventually mentioned the geomorphology assignment to Professor McHarg. He explained the program was to convert a street into a park and to reinforce pedestrian connections to the subway. He had given considerable thought to the trees and, yes, it was his goal to create a room. And, yes, he remembered the grey, glazed bricks. He had been inspired to use them because of a Philip Johnson project, a small bank at 30th and Market in Philadelphia. McHarg is a great admirer of Philip Johnson, who had been McHarg's first guest critic at Penn. Johnson came to Penn at his own expense. Every criticism by Johnson was "a history lesson," according to McHarg. McHarg had also offered Johnson some site-planning advice on his famous Glass House in New Canaan. Specifically, he suggested to Johnson that he purchase the neighboring property to protect the setting of the house and suggested some selective pruning of the grounds. The landscape architect for the Glass House was Dan Kiley. Certainly, the landscape contributes to the quality of the Glass House in numerable ways.

McHarg's explanation about the Woodland Avenue design impressed me on several levels. First, I was only familiar with the "after," which, in spite of the walls, worked well. Designers transform spaces which we often take as a given after the fact. Second, McHarg described the details of the project as a designer. His critics underestimate his commitment to design. Third, the image of Ian McHarg copying the materials of Philip Johnson was fascinating. The problem of the grey, glazed bricks was that before McHarg's use at Woodland Avenue, they had only been used on buildings, not retaining walls. On buildings the inside wall was insulated. On the retaining wall both sides were exposed to the cold, which resulted in the glazing being popped off.

Early in his career Ian McHarg was indeed a modernist, and his ideas were influenced by modernism throughout his career. His process for ecological planning and design is an affirmation that we can use knowledge to build a better future, a central tenet of modernism. But McHarg also was instrumental in challenging the *style* of modernism.

I believe Nan Ellin's (1996) analysis of the fall of modernism is especially clear and accurate. She credits Mumford with laying the basis for the critique, as does McHarg (1996). Furthermore, Ellin points to the landscape critique that argued for more emphasis on both vernacular and regional ecology. The leaders of this view were J. B. Jackson and Ian McHarg. The second major body of criticism of modern design, according to Ellin, came from the social planners, mainly centered at Penn, such as Herbert Gans, Paul Davidoff, and Linda Davidoff.

Denise Scott Brown and Robert Venturi provided the synthesis, which resulted in a misnamed, that is, "postmodernism," movement and an even sillier style than that which preceded it. Both Scott Brown and Venturi have wisely proclaimed themselves not to be postmodernists. Neither is McHarg. He leapfrogged from modernism over postmodernism to something else. No one wants to live in a "post" anything era. If we do indeed live in an Information Age or an Ecological Era or both, an Eco-Information Age, then McHarg has articulated more than anyone else a theory for design for this new age.

What he advocated, as did Scott Brown and Venturi, was anti-style. What emerged in Philadelphia, in no small part because of the populist influences of Mumford, Gans, and the Davidoffs was an approach to design and planning derived from place. Scott Brown and Venturi, borrowing from J. B. Jackson among others, elevated and celebrated the vernacular. McHarg advocated understanding places through interactions, that is, its ecology. This view rejected fashion. Style from modernism to deconstructionism to whatever-is-next-ism became irrelevant.

The first essay in this section, originally published as a 1957 article in *Architecture Record*, is connected directly to both Philip Johnson and modernism. McHarg exhibits his knowledge of modernism and his concerns about the future of the city and the housing needs of its residents. During the postwar era, housing was a pressing issue for many architects and planners. McHarg had worked with the Scottish new town program in the early 1950s and was certainly familiar with English and other European housing pro-

grams. His wife, Pauline, was Dutch. Among the most extensive postwar redevelopment efforts were those in the Netherlands. Many new communities
were planned, designed, and built by the Dutch (Van der Wal 1997).

McHarg brought his firsthand European experience to the New World
and attempted to advocate a third housing form between Le Corbusier's high
rises and Frank Lloyd Wright's prairie houses. McHarg's solution to urban
housing was the town house with an interior courtyard. He observed "no
modern town house has been produced to replace the traditional seventeenth
and eighteenth century town house."

Although McHarg clearly admires traditional town houses, from Amsterdam to Philadelphia, he also finds much inspiration in Greek, Roman, North
African, and Hispanic prototypes. In addition, McHarg identified many of his
contemporaries as making advancements in court house design, most notably
Johnson, whose work he praises three times in the article.

McHarg suggests the use of town houses with courtyards as a design strategy to return people to the city. He makes a number of very specific suggestions for court house design, based on an analysis of both designed exemplars
and vernacular spaces. He displays his familiarity with and his interest in
modern architecture. He also draws on his travels during World War II
through North Africa, Italy, and Greece.

In the article, McHarg mentions that he taught design studios in which his
students explored the court house concept. He also was involved as a practitioner in urban renewal projects in Society Hill in Philadelphia and in Southeast Washington, D.C. In both instances McHarg promoted a low-rise, town
house design with public and private green spaces. Visiting Southeast Washington, D.C., today one can see how his work provides a strong contrast to the
more dominant style of public housing during the 1950s, the high-rise apartment.

There is considerable optimism for design, urbanism, and modernism in
"The Court House Concept." McHarg was still hopeful that modern designers could solve urban ills. This optimism about modernism had faded by 1970
and had been replaced by a faith in ecology and the possibilities of ecological
design.

McHarg is a storyteller. One of his favorites is the Generals Overkill story.
Because he has spent seven years in the army, it is a tale told with enthusiasm
and rebellion. His criticisms of the Generals Overkill and the "lesser
Philistines" also reveals his concern about atomic weapons as well as his criticism to the war in Vietnam. Clearly, McHarg was declaring himself a retired
warrior who wanted to ban the bomb and make peace, not war.

In the case of "Architecture in an Ecological View of the World" the Generals Overkill story was adapted to an audience of architects initially at an
American Institute of Architects (AIA) convention in Boston then in a 1970

AIA Journal article. This version differs somewhat from others, including the one published in *A Quest for Life*. Employing the device of a fantasy, McHarg attempts to explain to architects "how the world really works and demonstrates that it is an interdependent, interacting biosphere."

In this article, McHarg refutes his modernist design education and especially challenges the goal of modern architecture that simplicity should be achieved at any cost. By embracing ecology, McHarg also urges us to view the world as complex and diverse. By seeking the simple, important aspects are omitted or ignored. Complex and diverse designs have a greater chance of being sustainable.

Instead of "less is more" McHarg states that a role of design is to fit buildings to the site, which requires greater involvement with a place, a more complex approach, rather than abstraction. He notes, "Architecture should not be called architecture; it should be called fitting," or "adaptation for survival."

McHarg also addresses the subject of form, which is fundamental in design. "Every form," he states, "reflects processes engaged in the business of creative adaptation toward the end of survival; form is only one superficial expression of the processes." In short, he advocates "adaptive architecture."

His brief 1990 "Nature Is More Than a Garden" addresses the topic of garden design. Gardens are a basic design type of the landscape architect. A garden is symbolic nature: A peaceful symbol for phenomena that can be violent. As a result, gardens are a simplification. Again in this article, McHarg promotes complexity in design.

He uses the coral reefs of the South Pacific as an exemplar for designers of gardens. I am reminded of Umberto Eco's protagonist in *The Island of the Day Before* (1995). The seventeenth-century mariner marooned on an abandoned ship adjacent to an uninhabited Pacific Island discovers a new world, an alternative reality, in the coral reef between the ship and the island. The new life, forms, and patterns of this underwater living landscape forces the castaway to see the world anew, to discover new possibilities for his existence, his place in his environments. Designers need a similar alternative vision. Perhaps, a visit to a coral reef should become a requirement for a degree in design.

Garden design is but one type of landscape design. Landscape architects are capable of much more, as McHarg discusses in his 1997 "Landscape Architecture." In this essay the rise of landscape architecture as an art and as a profession is summarized. It is a discipline where "so few persons have accomplished so much." Landscape architecture is also a field which could contribute much more. To achieve its potential, landscape architects should adapt an ecological approach to "justify a more central and consequential role."

McHarg returns to the theme of the English landscape school which he had addressed in his "Ecological Determinism" essay in 1966. Again, he suggests that the work of Kent, Brown, and Repton should be viewed as "an important precursor" for ecological design.

In his 1997 "Ecology and Design" he challenges designers to use ecology in their work. Important contributions are the definitions of ecological planning and ecological design, the latter being the selection "for creative fitting revealed in intrinsic and expressive form."

McHarg clearly expresses sadness that the art of ecological design has not progressed more rapidly. He identifies only three landscape practices advancing ecological design: Andropogon and Coe Lee Robinson Roesch of Philadelphia and Seattle's Jones & Jones. All three practices include principals educated in both landscape architecture and architecture. This combination of an environmentally based design education with form-based education appears crucial for the development of ecological design.

I would add to McHarg's list a few architects engaged in ecological design or, at least, advocating it. Susan Maxman, Bill McDonough, Sim van der Ryn, and Peter Calthorpe are among the few ecological architects or "adaptive architects." From my own region I suggest the architects and/or landscape architects Steve Martino, Christine Ten Eyck, Laura Bowden, John Douglas, and Joe Ewan. The influence of *Design with Nature* on planning, environmental management, and geographic information systems is indisputable. Its influence on design has been stronger in theory than in practice. No doubt the reader can add a few more names. But, the list would remain short. We need many more designers who are capable of making creative fittings which are revealed in expressive forms. With more architects, engineers, and landscape architects advocating sustainable, and even regenerative, design, perhaps this will change.

References

Eco, Umberto. 1995. *The Island of the Day Before*. New York: Harcourt Brace & Co.

Ellin, Nan. 1996. *Postmodern Urbanism*. Cambridge, Mass.: Blackwell.

McHarg, Ian L. 1996. *A Quest for Life*. New York: Wiley.

Van der Wal, Coennard. 1997. *In Praise of Common Sense, Planning the Ordinary, A Physical Planning History of the New Towns in the IJsselmeerpolders*. Rotterdam, The Netherlands: 010 Publishers.

11

The Court House Concept (1957)

A Penn landscape architecture student in the late 1950s was much more likely to design a town house in Ian McHarg's studio than a regional plan. McHarg had become fascinated with the court house concept in Scotland, where he had been granted permission to build a separate house, rather than live in an apartment, because of his tuberculosis. He designed a 1,200-square-foot, L-shaped house. Although he never built it, McHarg became intrigued with the concept that he later pursued with both Philip Johnson and his graduate students.

McHarg's interests in housing and open space are interwoven. His investigations into open space sought to recognize the rate and value of both public and private spaces. Privacy is critical for the latter. While this can be achieved by using house walls, free-standing walls, fences and hedges, court house design can also result in privacy. The benefits of court houses include improved microclimate and the efficient, economic use of building materials in addition to privacy. McHarg first published his ideas in the 1957 Architect's Year Book, then later the same year in this 1957 Architecture Record article.

The 1957 article seems to have lasting value. In 1997 an architecture masters thesis student pursuing housing design for Phoenix, Arizona, was given a copy. The ideas in the article influenced his design for a complex of three models of court houses ranging in size and price range. Certainly, court houses are an appropriate, environmentally responsive alternative to conventional tract houses in the Southwest United States. They offer an option for urban living in other regions, too.

The free-standing, single-family house in suburb and countryside from such hands as Frank Lloyd Wright, Mies van der Rohe, Le Corbusier, Philip Johnson, or Richard Neutra undoubtedly represents the greatest contribution of modern architecture to art and environment. Bear Run and the Farnsworth House, Villa Savoie, and the Johnson New Canaan House offer a superlative environment for the exurbanite but what of the city dweller? Is not the urgent challenge to modern architecture to provide a new town house, as humane as those designed for the suburbs and country, as urbane as is consonant with the forms and values of the city?

A glance at the palette of urban housing types will only assure us of their conventionality—and their continuing inadequacy—the multi-story flat, no more than a bigger Roman *insula* with water, sewer, heating, and elevator, the walk-up apartments but the insula without disguise, the terrace house shorn of nobility. This vocabulary sufficed until the city was befouled by industry, congested by traffic, despoiled by philistinism, and abandoned to dereliction. These traditional housing types have been exploited since industry changed the nature of the city—and without success. No single present housing type is capable of arresting the flight to the suburbs, no single housing type offers the prospect of a new recentralization, no single present housing type offers an environment which can equal the salubrity of the suburb. Is there an urban house which, exploiting the advantages of city life, offers in addition a residential environment at least equaling the sum of advantages and disadvantages of the house in suburb or country? Can the essence of the free standing modern house be given an urban form?

Both questions can be answered in the affirmative. As supported by a number of projects during the past twenty years the court house, the introverted house facing upon one or more internal courts can provide the essence of the best free standing country houses; it can provide a residential environment as humane as it is urbane.

Moreover its range of application is surprisingly wide. Obviously, it permits the creation of a new town house of great luxury and elegance but it also is adaptable to the creation of a popular town house at relatively high densities. The former house has the capacity to effect a selective recentralization—the return of the civilized to the cities, while the latter can provide for a recentralization of more significant proportions by providing a milieu for family life within the city.

The claims made for the court house concept are not puny, yet in the following pages can be seen their substantiation in a number of precursory projects. These are from distinguished architects in several countries. The unanimity of their concern for this concept and their projects within its formal expression deserve a generic title—the court house concept—and an analysis of the essential quality, the range of application, the advantages and disadvantages of this concept of urban housing.

The Essential Quality of the Court House

The court house is overwhelmingly distinguished by its introversion; the house turns its back to the street and faces upon a private, internal court or courts. The historical derivation from the peristyle and atrium of Rome and

Greece, the traditional Moslem house, the traditional Chinese and Japanese house is patently obvious and these plans indicate the geometric possibilities within the court house concept. The rectangular house and single walled court, the "L" house with one court, the square house with a single internal space, "H" and "T" plans each with two courts, the "Y" plan with three courts, the cruciform house having four courts and finally the possibilities of asymmetrical plans with numerous courts, these plans are united by the single fact that the quality of experience is oriented to the private delectation of the occupants.

The major problem of modern housing and its most conspicuous failure lie in the distribution and design of open space. Modern architecture has produced classic models for the two extreme conditions and no intermediate solutions. On the one hand, as can be seen in the Farnsworth House by Mies van der Rohe and the New Canaan House by Philip Johnson, the free standing house is placed in an area of beautiful natural landscape where its geometric purity contrasts vividly with the organic sculpture and texture of ground and trees. On the other hand Le Corbusier has provided the alternative model of the tall slab rising free from a lush romantic landscape. But for the intermediate problems of central redevelopment, urban renewal, or a new town there are no adequate solutions. Indeed, in the case of the latter it is the inadequacy of the distribution and design of open space which is the key to the failure of the new towns. There open space, offered as a boon, is in fact a liability; it contributes to neither amenity nor society while it disrupts any attempt to create "town," and finally it contains no art. Open space is overprovided, usable open space is all but absent and the end product is a scene of insignificant houses lost in neutral open space.

Yet we have seen historically from Ancient Greece to the eighteenth century that good standards of open space are not antithetical to urban architecture. The eighteenth-century squares represent a convincing defense of this position. Certainly there are intermediate solutions to be discovered appropriate to the problems and expression of modern architecture.

It is interesting to observe that most of the problems of open space are solved integrally within the plan of the court house. Open space in courts is provided internally and disassociated from the street scene. These courts are private and this characteristic is the most valuable aspect of open space in housing. The courts can associate with internal functions to provide a living court, dining court, bedroom court, service court, etc. and provide a value to open space absent in all other plan types. By bringing the open space inside the house the scale of the street can be determined by traffic consideration and the height of the houses rather than being an uncontrollable sum of street and external open space. Finally the individual has a proclivity and a right to self-expression in the design of open space. In current housing where this is freely expressed the result is often anarchy, vulgarity, or both, where, as in the new towns, it is suppressed, a neutral mediocrity is the product. In the court house the individual has freedom for personal expression which cannot obtrude on the public.

The court in the Orient has long been given a formal expression representing the essence of nature and is so realized with the philosophical assumption that man and nature are indivisible, and that contemplation, soliloquy, and calm can best occur in nature, its essence if not its image, and the court then is made to represent the essence of nature. Again the Moslem court, based upon the Moslem concept of Paradise, has a religious basis for its formal expression in the Island of the Blessed and the four rivers of Paradise. The West has no comparable basis for the formal expression of courts within houses and this must yet emerge as indeed the philosophy for the formal expression of a modern landscape architecture. One direction of this expression may be seen in the court of the Rockefeller House in New York, designed by Philip Johnson. In this as in other projects by Johnson one sees an esthetic consonant with the main stream of modern architecture and perhaps the precursor of the modern expression of the court in the modern court house. In the Western court as in the Oriental, the value of this space is not alone in its functions but rather in its evocative use of natural and inert materials to induce soliloquy, calm, and an attachment to permanent values—in a humane environment.

The court house requires the expenditure of a perimeter wall to create internal open spaces. The courts are the product. These are justified by the intimate relationship established between indoor and outdoor spaces. Indeed the courts become rooms outdoors. This being so the degree of privacy accorded to internal rooms is the minimum necessary for the courts.

In every historical epoch save our own the inevitable residence for the cultivated and influential, the civilized, polite, and urbane as persons or families was the city. Today only a determined minority persists in the central city from choice and the family has been all but banished. The majority of the urban population lives in the city only because it lacks the economic mobility to escape and perforce lives in the slums, the meanness or the sanitary order of nineteenth- and twentieth-century environments. The major population movement in this century has been the flight from the city, the greater the economic mobility the further the residence from its center. The civilized, who traditionally made the city their own, the repository and the artifact of their culture, have today fled to the outermost suburbs. In Western Europe and the United States where they persist in cities they live in the reservoir of earlier historical town houses—in the Georgian and Regency squares and mews of Bloomsbury and Chelsea in London, the new town of Edinburgh, the seventeenth-century "Grachtenhuizen" of Amsterdam, the fifteenth-century Palazzo Farnese, Quartiere del Rinascimento, and via Giulia in Rome, the Marais and Isle de St. Louis in Paris, in Beacon Hill in Boston, Rittenhouse Square and Society Hill in Philadelphia, and Greenwich Village in New York. Such town houses are no longer appropriate as prototypes, changed mores have caused their adaptation to contemporary residential needs while they are continually pre-empted for office space. Yet no modern town house has been produced to replace the traditional seventeenth- and eighteenth-century town house.

The metamorphosis necessary to create the mid-twentieth century city, stimulating yet humane, representing the zenith of the regional or national art, architecture, technology, social and cultural expression, this task poses many problems, but at their heart lies the necessity of returning to the city and accommodating there that segment of society most concerned —with the problems of the city and best able to solve them. Not least then among the problems of the new city is the provision of a new town house. Such a house, while exploiting the existing advantages of city life must offer in addition a residential environment, at least equaling the sum of advantages and disadvantages of suburban environment. Without the introduction of such a new town house, that recentralization, which is the essence of the city's survival, cannot occur. Only by the provision of an urban residential environment at least equal in salubrity to that of the suburbs will the civilized, polite, urbane as persons and families return to the city to ensure its survival.

The court house represents such a town house, its merits are patent, they lie not in modernity of the concept (unless modern is used as a synonym for good) but in an intrinsic excellence which its historical persistence substantiates. The court house does meet the criteria which have been advanced. It can provide a humane urban environment, an urbane architecture, a milieu for family life within the city; it does promise that recentralization which is the prerequisite to the survival of the city.

Court House Plans

During the past five years, recurring sporadically but with increasing frequency, the court house has appeared in the architectural press. It would appear that these projects constitute a precursory movement towards widening acceptance of the court house as the new town house.

As a modern housing solution the court house concept can be loosely identified with four principal sources, only one of which is a direct extension of a historical form. The prime source stems from Mies van der Rohe and includes L. Hilberseimer and Philip Johnson; the second group, a logical extension of its Mediterranean origins, is located in Italy and, starting from the studies of Pagano, Diotallevi, and Marescotti, reached fruition in the housing at Tuscolano, Rome by Adalberto Libera. The third group, also deriving from the Mediterranean is identified with José Sert, his partner, Wiener and their collaborators in many projects for Latin American cities. The fourth group is a direct extension of the Moslem tradition in North Africa directed today by French architects. Each of these studies originated before or during the war. In the postwar period, and particularly during the past two or three years the court house concept has gathered many new advocates in a wide range of countries—Mexico, Britain, the United States, Denmark, Sweden, Germany, and Switzerland, and consequently is now advocated for other than Mediterranean and South American locations.

Mies van der Rohe–Hilberseimer–Johnson

Perhaps the first court house from the hands of a modern architect is a study by Mies van der Rohe developed in 1931. This is essentially a row house and is so described but each house is an "L" enclosing a private open court. This concept was elaborated and in 1938 Mies developed a more complex and princely group of three court houses associated in a block, each house distinct and each having a varying number of courts. This represents in the author's opinion the zenith of court house designs. Although at a density of approximately three houses to the acre, and consequently conspicuously open for urban conditions, there can be no doubt but that such development could fulfill the vital role of proffering an urban house equaling the best conditions of a suburban environment yet additionally offering the convenience of city life. A more recent project by Mies van der Rohe, the Gratiot in Detroit, falls between the studies of 1931 and 1938. In this housing complex court houses are interposed between garden apartments and multi-story flats. With one three-bedroom court house, these dwellings are conceived as middle-class, family houses. The court houses are designed in groups of six, arranged around two entrance courts which are in turn entered from a covered carport. If the 1938 project represents an urban alternative to the expressive suburban or rural house, the court houses of Gratiot offer a middle-class equivalent. These projects by Mies van der Rohe are perhaps the best evidence for the court house as a middle- and high-cost urban house. Yet the quality of the court is still not indicated.

In 1942 Philip C. Johnson, biographer and collaborator of Mies, built a simple court house in Cambridge, Massachusetts. This house did not aspire to the luxury of the court house project by Mies but, with a small and elegant structure and one private court, there was developed a conjunction of structural space and social use impossible to achieve in such an area with a conventional plan. The court in this house remained simply as lawn, shaded by large trees, but in 1949, for the Rockefeller town house in New York, Johnson created a court with one pool, a tree, a fountain, terrace, and three stepping stones. The impact of these few elements in this small space, is overwhelming in contrast to the heat, fumes, noise, overpowering scale, and tension of midtown Manhattan. This court, as a demonstration of the quality which can be achieved in a small urban space, is one of the most powerful exhibits as evidence of the validity of the court house concept and supplements the statements of Mies van der Rohe in which the court itself remains an enigma.

Prior to the projects of Philip Johnson, L. Hilberseimer, colleague of Mies van der Rohe at the Bauhaus and the Illinois Institute of Technology, had developed the court house concept as a form of popular housing. Utilizing the L-shaped, single-story house, he achieved densities of 120 persons or 20 houses per acre. This demonstration shows the court house as a popular housing solution applicable to central residential areas. In this Hilberseimer is supported by the historical precedents of Ancient Greece and Rome, ancient and modern North Africa and China.

The Court House in Italy

In 1940 the Italian architects Pagano, Diotallevi, and Marescotti made an extensive study on the court house concept which was published in *Costruzioni Casabella* (Pagano et al. 1940). The results of this examination are reflected in the writing of Eglo Benincasa today and more concretely in the housing project in the Tuscolano quarter of Rome, designed by Adalberto Libera and constructed, as low-cost housing, by Ina Casa. This project appears to be the first modern example of the court house used as a popular urban house. It has an approximate net density of 30 houses per acre and, with seven beds per house, an envisaged net density of over 200 persons per acre. The repeated block plan, which consists of four L-shaped houses, is a novel one. Three of the courts face inward while the remaining one opens to the pedestrian footpath. The courts are extremely small for the seven occupants of each house but this is in part compensated by common open space provided in the development.

The appropriateness of the court house concept to the Mediterranean would seem evident. Its appropriateness as a more general solution is indicated by Eglo Benincasa in *L'Architettura:* "Foreigners admire the 'picturesqueness' of the south, but underlying it there is a livability which the modern architect overlooks in popular housing . . . The sheltered space constitutes a challenge to modern architecture. It is a free creation linking the house to nature" (Benincasa 1955).

The Court House in South and Central America

The third line of court house development is represented by José Sert, his partner Wiener, and certain Mexican architects, notably Victor de la Lama. Sert, a Spaniard, has adapted the Moslem heritage of the court house to his native land and made this the prototype popular house in his planning and housing studies for Central and South America. In the context of Latin America with a high sun angle, high temperatures, and the Latin demand for privacy and protection the court house, its tradition, remains the most valid housing solution. In the hands of Sert and his collaborators the court house also represents an admirable means of ameliorating the micro-climate, a resource inherent in the plan but more vital in high temperature locales. Wiener and Sert are particularly distinguished by their long-established attachment to this concept and by the skill with which they have utilized it as the basis for larger planning scales—nucleus, neighborhood, and town. Indeed the distinctive contribution of these architects is that they have created a humane city in which the court house concept is the unifying element, appropriate to the climate, technology, art, and mores of South America.

The typical court house plan utilized by Wiener and Sert is the "L" house with a service court cut from the exterior angle. This house is associated in groups of four to form a rectangle with the living courts located internally. This attitude to orientation, acceptable in low latitudes, makes such a juxtaposition possible whereas it might well be questioned for other climates.

Whereas Wiener and Sert have utilized the court house as a low-cost popular house, its exploitation in Mexico has been on a more lavish scale. The projects of Victor de la Lama particularly show the court house in terms analogous to the Mies van der Rohe 1938 court house. Each house contains a number of courts with swimming pools and lush sub-tropical vegetation. These demonstrate a standard of environment, albeit for a climate distinct from either Western Europe or the United States, which compares favorably with the free-standing suburban or rural house.

The Court House in North Africa

In the eastern hemisphere the court house has persisted as a continuous concept only in the Moslem world. This housing type constitutes a vernacular form, but it has also been utilized and exploited by modern architects as a contemporary solution. Numerous French architects practicing in North Africa have used the court house as the prototype for Moslem housing projects. These developments are generally low cost with minimal standards; indeed it is apparent that while normally bedrooms, kitchen, and bathroom are provided in the house, the living room, the only living space, is the open court. The court house concept in the hands of the architect J. De La Roziere has been used not only as a house plan but as the basis for a neighborhood plan with a hierarchy of open spaces extending from the private court to larger open spaces shared by nuclei to the final open space shared by the entire community (De La Roziere in Ecochard 1955, p. 37).

Recent Court Houses

Developing from the court houses of these four groups are a large number of recent projects from a wide range of countries. From a Mediterranean and Hispano-American base the concept has entered throughout Europe and penetrated North America. Almost all the major European countries are represented in court house projects, and this housing type has been advanced for countries as distant from the Mediterranean as Denmark. These projects include L- shaped court houses by Custer, Escher, Gisel, and Weilenmann proposed as an extension to the Neubuhl in Zürich, the "atrium house" by George Schwindowski of Berlin, studies by Eske Kristensen, and John Utzon in Scandinavia, projects by Netherland students, the Smithson house for the Ideal Homes Exhibition 1956 with which a written explanation reads "all rainwater is collected and runs through a gargoyle to a container in the internal garden!" These projects, while amenable for use in urban situations, are not so proposed. In contrast, a project by the architects Chamberlin, Powell, and Bon, utilizing the court house concept aims at central urban locations and high densities. This solution, with an average height of one and a half stories provides a net density of 160 persons or about 30 houses per acre. The aim to maximize the applicability of the court house by maximizing density is laudable and the solution is extraordinarily ingenious. Particularly noteworthy is the success achieved in either eliminating or minimizing the degree of overlooking into private courts while employing a two-story bedroom unit. Yet there is some reason to believe that the density may be excessively high for this house type and that with the low sun angle of Britain the courts might well become insalubrious holes. Further, where the courts are so small it would appear vital to provide a secondary area of open space which this proposal fails to grant. With the private court provided for the family, yet another area should exist as focus and venue for social intercourse in the community. Yet this is perhaps the best example to date of the court house as a popular urban house. Densities of 160 persons per acre or even 100 persons to the acre, supplemented by tall buildings can, as the architects indicate, provide densities perfectly compatible with urban land values and building values.

Beyond the Mediterranean and Latin America, it is in the United States that the court house concept has taken the strongest hold. This is assuredly not unconnected with the presence of Mies van der Rohe, Philip Johnson, and L. Hilberseimer and their attachment to this concept. It may well also be influenced by the existence of a Hispano-American tradition in California and the southwestern United States. The preoccupation with the court house is evident but remains to date in the project phase. In addition to those architects mentioned above, Serge Chermayeff, Oskar Stonorov, Ralph Rapson, Donald Olsen, and Morse Payne have all produced court houses or court house complexes. Donald Olsen (1948) has designed a swastika house with four courts; that by Ralph Rapson has a single internal court (1948, p. 119).

The project by Morse Payne exploits the court house concept in a distinct way. The lot is a long rectangle which is divided into three or four courts—by the interposition of building volumes, usually, two or three in number—the living-dining-kitchen volume, the bedroom volume or the bedroom function divided into the master bedroom volume and the children-guest bedroom volume. By raising certain of these volumes the entire space can be continuous or divided into distinct courts associated with specific functions. This plan might well be described as the in-line court house and represents an admirable addition to the vocabulary. The density is approximately 15 houses or 90 habitable rooms per acre.

Serge Chermayeff, Oskar Stonorov, and Mies van der Rohe have during the past year developed not only court houses but have associated these in small groups. In the study which Chermayeff has conducted with students of the Harvard Graduate School of Design, the house, with a "U" plan has three courts—two external and one internal. This prototype house is associated in groups of six, but could be exploited as a row house. Before Mies van der Rohe designed his Gratiot project Stonorov prepared a scheme for this development in which he utilized court houses. This project aims for a higher net density for the court houses than does the subsequent scheme by Mies van der Rohe. To achieve this, two-story quatrefoil court houses were developed. Given the absolute necessity of building two-story structures this design is admirable, but it must be observed that all courts suffer from overlooking and the value of the court is depreciated.

The court house as a house plan has been thoroughly demonstrated and in the projects by Mies van der Rohe, Stonorov, and Chermayeff can be seen small nuclei made with four to six court houses. In the Gratiot project developed by Mies the group of houses depend upon a single-car court and each trio of houses share a common entrance court. However, save in the single project of Adalberto Libera in Rome there is no evidence of the court house as an element in a community. Toward the end of exploiting the court house as an element in the small urban community, graduate students of the University of Pennsylvania under the direction of the author made studies for a central Philadelphia city block site.

In this study the intention was not only to exploit the court house but to create a community which would be as salubrious at the community level as would be the court house at the dwelling level. The program required houses from 1,500 to 3,000 square feet with provision for one car per house. To create the court house community it was required, as in the subsequent Gratiot projects, that groups of six to ten court houses depend upon one common court acting as forecourt and that beyond that a central open space with small playground and swimming pool be provided as the venue for social intercourse in the block. The net density averaged twenty houses per acre, the gross density within the block was half that figure.

It is submitted that this final stage of utilizing the court houses around a sequence of open space as venue for social life constitutes an advance in the exploitation of the court house, that it does present an environment as urbane as it is humane, consonant with the forms and values of the city. The author, in collaboration with Philip Johnson, is in the process of designing such a project in central Philadelphia.

Conclusion

The housing solutions which have been advanced or utilized in this century fall into three main categories; the two extremes of the multi-story flat and the free-standing, single-family house, and, between these, the terrace-row semi-detached house. The multi-story flat has particularly been espoused by the leaders of modern architecture. From Le Voisin, La Ville Radieuse, The Siemensstadt, "De Plaslaon" in Rotterdam, and their derivatives to the Unités d'Habitation, modern architecture had advanced the multi-story apartment as the prime urban house type. Yet it hardly justifies this devotion and dependence on the grounds of its modernity. Some reaction to this preoccupation and devotion to the flat has appeared within C.I.A.M., founder and prime protagonist of modern vertical living. At C.I.A.M. 10 the English members W. and G. Howell, J. A. Partridge state that "Even if and when we have built up a successful tradition and practice of multi-level living, which we are very far from having done—we feel that—there will always be a demand for a considerable proportion of (town) houses. And if the program demands it we must find ways of using them as elements in the city."

Although having a recurring role for two thousand years, the multi-story apartment has not built a successful tradition; it has found only limited acceptance and far from offering the key to a new and selective recentralization, is unable to arrest decentralization.

The realization must be all the more disheartening to the protagonists of vertical living in view of the fact that the concept has been advanced during a severe housing shortage when choice was severely restricted. The Unités,

Barbican, High Paddington, the Smithson concept, Gratiot all point towards improvement in multi-story development, and the tall apartment will continue to play an important role in central city housing. However, it is not a sovereign cure. The vocabulary urgently needs to be expanded; the court house constitutes an invaluable addition to the vocabulary of central housing. The court house can return the civilized, the urbane, and polite to the cities, offer the milieu for family life within the city, and provide an environment as urbane as it is delightful.

References

Benincasa, Eglo. 1955. "L'arte di abitare nel mezzogiorno: il colore." *L'Architettura Cronache e Storia* 1(B01, May-June):58–63.

Ecochard, Michael. 1955. "Habitat Musulman au Maroc." *L'Architecture D'Aujourd'hui* 26 (60, June):36–39.

Olsen, Donald. 1948. "The Contraspatial House." *Arts and Architecture* (April):32–37.

Pagano, P. G., I. Diotallevi, and F. Marescotti. 1940. "La casa unit=EO." *Costruzioni Casabella* XII (B0148, April):11–14.

Rapson, Ralph. 1948. "Case Study House No. 4." *Interiors* (September):116, 117–19.

12

Architecture in an Ecological View of the World (1970)

Ian McHarg spoke frequently at national architecture conferences and major architecture schools. Here, employing the device of fantasy, he attempts to show the architect "how the world really works" and demonstrates that it is difficult to separate what is environment from what is human. This AIA Journal *article is based on excerpts from an address delivered during the "Day of Awareness" at the 1970 American Institute of Architects meeting in Boston.*

The first proposition I have to make is that the attitude of man to environment which permeates the Western tradition is a fantasy. It has no correspondence with reality, no survival value, and it is the best guarantee of extinction.

Once upon a time, I met a scientist who was engaged in an experiment to send a man to the moon with the least possible luggage. This experiment was conducted ten years ago when it was thought that going to the moon was worthwhile and would take quite a long time. The experiment then had to be a recirculating process.

It consisted of a plywood capsule simulating a real capsule, in the lid of which was a fluorescent tube simulating the sun. Inside the capsule were some algae—microscopic, photosynthetic plants—some bacteria, some air, and a man. The man breathed in air, consumed oxygen, and breathed out carbon dioxide which the algae breathed and gave out as oxygen which the man breathed. The man became thirsty, drank some water, which, when he urinated, went into the water solution with the algae-bacteria. The algae transpired, the transpirations were collected, and the man drank. The man became hungry, ate some of the algae and defecated. The excrement went into the water medium with the algae and bacteria, the bacteria reconstituted the excrement into forms utilizable by the algae which grew, which the man ate. Now that's how the world works.

What we need to do is to recognize that that capsule is a beautiful simulation of the world-at-large. There is only one input: sunlight. There is only one output: heat. There is a closed cycle of water and food. We are plant parasites. We don't know how to accomplish photosynthesis; we have to depend upon microorganisms which know how to reconstitute the wastes of life. Our requirements are oxygen and food.

This little experiment absolutely changed my life ten years ago. It can change more lives. Let us use it here for instructional purposes.

What we need is a celebratory event which I will describe as "Fireworks at Cape Kennedy." We require a cast of characters for our Independence Day event.

We need to assemble a cast of arch-destroyers. We collect all of the ossified, calcified, implacable Generals Overkill, those people in the Defense Departments of all countries, for whom it is not enough to be able to kill every man, woman, and child in the world a thousand times, but who must devote their energies and half the treasury of the United States to killing every man, woman, and child in the world two thousand times over. We assemble them all and measure each one for an algal-bacterial waistcoat-capsule.

We also assemble the mutational retrogressionists of Atomic Energy Commissions—those people who attack the world at its gonads, who are unmoved by the knowledge that every increase in radiation is an increase in mutation. They began life, in my imagination, pulling wings from flies, gravitated to cherry bombs, made their way to high explosives and realized full gratification only by the accomplishment of atomic explosions. We must assemble them at Cape Kennedy and give them their algal-bacterial capsules.

Then we collect those particular putrescences, the scientists engaged in biochemical warfare who are not satisfied with the bubonic plague but must cultivate more virulent forms. And we move down to the "reign of death" people, those engaged in the business of selling death in the form of herbicides, pesticides, and toxins to satisfy stockholders, the great captains of industry who carelessly, cynically, void their excrement into the environment, who engage us in enormous gluttony by which six percent of the world's population consumes 60 percent of the world's nonrenewable resources. And we assemble, too, those negligent automobile manufacturers of Detroit who give the greatest amount of pollution for the least amount of transportation—those people who are engaged in the aphrodisiac business but should be in the business of transportation.

And so we have this vast array of all the destroyers, every one of them with a Saturn rocket and with an algal-bacterial waistcoat because they are going off into space. With 500,000 cheering schoolchildren waving American flags and with bands playing the national anthem, we send the lot of them into space—all these animated, planetary diseases who masquerade as men and whose best efforts are to inflict lesions on the world body. Bang! Bang! Bang! They are off in space.

If one listens intently, he will begin to hear an Aeolian hymn of regeneration. All the lesions inflicted by men on the world body will begin to heal; every single wound will generate new cells. But we can't wait because we have to follow the path of General Overkill; we have to follow him in space because his conversion is our conversion. We carry within ourselves, right from our mother's milk, this same implicit, explicit view of man and nature. We may not be to the same extent the destroyer General Overkill is, but even architecture has within itself a profound sterilizing power, an inordinate ignorance, malice, and arrogance.

General Overkill spends lonely weeks in space, and the earth is a distant orb. He is extremely lonely with only two companions to address: the algae and the bacteria. "I am divine," he says. Man is made in the image of God— no atoms, no molecules, no cells, no unicellular organisms, no plants, no animals, save one, is made in the image of God. This means there is only one moral arena: the acts of man to man. God looks carefully if you commit adultery; if you covet your neighbor's wife, He will rap you straight across the knuckles. But if you kill every whale in the world, kill every Ponderosa pine, devastate great areas, make Lake Erie septic, apparently neither God, the churches, the priests, nor the courts care about the acts of man to nature.

General Overkill says, "I am divine." The alga doesn't say anything, just holds its hand up to the sunlight. The General says, "I have dominion over you." That's what the Book of Genesis says, that man is given dominion over life and nonlife. And if you have any doubt about the intended meaning, the text continues, man shall multiply and subjugate the earth. Subjugate.

Five or six weeks pass, and the General, who went to West Point and knows about probability theory, realizes that this is a recirculating system. He realizes that the biomass of the algae and bacteria is equal to the biomass of the General. There's going to be a time, according to probability theory, when everything that had been algae and bacteria at the onset will be General; and everything that had been General at the onset will be algae and bacteria.

What's true of the capsule is true of the world—the same interacting, recirculating process. The General realizes it is an interacting system, and there is going to be a point in time when everything that had been algae and bacteria will be General. He contemplates the assumptions about exclusive divinity, dominion, and subjugation. He concludes that divinity is pervasive, not exclusive. The algae know how to accomplish photosynthesis; the General and modern science do not. The bacteria know how to reconstitute waste; neither the General nor modern science does. Any act of dominion or subjugation on the part of the General can only inhibit the capacity of the algae and bacteria to perform that which they can perform uniquely. If the General subjugates them, he will kill them. This, of course, involves him not only in self-mutilation but in suicide.

And so the General learns the lesson we all must learn: Any relationship which concludes that man is exclusively divine and everything else is rubbish is an illusion and a fantasy. The acts of man to man are sacramental, and the acts of man to nature must be sacramental also. There is absolutely no place for subjugation. The exercise of dominion and subjugation extended to the world can only mean self-mutilation, suicide, genocide, biocide—an absolutely profound lesson.

We have to know the way the world works. Architecture is a device to deny the student any possibility of understanding human physiology, psychology, human behavior, or the realities of biophysical processes. This is a horrifying thing to say but absolutely true. I speak as one who teaches in an architectural school and who has visited every important school of architecture in the United States.

Let us return to the General. He has learned that there is one system: nature. It is an extension of ourselves; we are an extension of nature. There is no division between man and environment; we are one thing. There is one world, one biosphere which shares one history of which we are present, sensate expression. There is only man/nature.

Recall that the Defense Department has an alliance with the Atomic Energy Commission. Yet it would be calamitous if this ally left some radioactive material in the capsule. Now any increase in radioactivity inside the capsule is likely to cause mutations in either the General, the algae, or the bacteria. So the General says, "In my capsule, no increase in the level of radiation." If that's good enough for the General it is good enough for us. Every increase in atomic radiation whether from atomic testing, reactors, Gas Buggy, or Alaskan harbors is going to show up in increased numbers of cases of leukemia, skin cancer, bone cancer, mutation deformations, still births; in sum, mutational retrogression.

It would be calamitous if any of the General's cohorts in biochemical warfare who are destroying Vietnam happened to leave some pesticides or herbicides in the capsule because the herbicides would kill the algae, the pesticides, the bacteria—and that would take out the General. The General says, "We've got a great thing going in Vietnam, but in my capsule there will be no agents of biochemical warfare, no pesticides, no herbicides." If it's good enough for the General, it is good enough for the world.

The question is, under what conditions do we let this man and all the others back? (There are tens of thousands of these arch-destroyers going through this same experience in space in my fantasy.) It's a great experiment because if you lose them, what have you lost? Nonetheless, we have to be decent enough to say, "No, you are arch-destroyers, but if you are indeed converted, we will let you back." Under what conditions? I would require a plain prayer.

The General would address the sun and say, "Shine that we may live." He would address the earth simply as "home." He would say to the oceans, "ancient home." He would speak to the clouds, rain, rivers, and say, "Replenish us from the sea, we erstwhile sea creatures who have escaped from the sea by only the length of a single cell." He would say to the atmosphere, "Protect and sustain us," knowing that the life-giving oxygen within that atmosphere was derived from all the breaths of long dead and now living plants. Then he would address the plants with inordinate deference, saying, "Plants, live, breathe, grow that we may breathe, eat, and live." He would say to all the decomposers—carrion-eaters, worms, and grubs—"Decomposers, please reconstitute the waste of life in life and the substance of life after death in order that life may endure."

When he says these things with understanding and deference, we can say to the General, "Come on home; welcome to the blue, green, glorious, wonderfully rich, diverse, ancient, and enduring world, where the evolution of life has persisted for 2 ½ billion years. Welcome back with this new deference, born of understanding, which allows us to say that you may now exercise your creative will upon this earth, and we may give you this freedom in the full certainty that your interventions will contribute to our possibility of survival and the more distant possibility of fulfillment."

In the capsule is a beginning of another view which says this is an interdependent, interacting world, and it is very difficult to decide what is environment and what is man and the difference between them. The only differences among the algae, the bacteria, and man are the apertures of the genetic code. They are united.

Almost all architects, planners, and landscape architects (although the latter are less criminal than the rest) should be handcuffed and their licenses taken away until they learn the way the world works. At the moment, one can toss a coin and decide the consequences of the acts of almost any architect or planner. The consequences of their interventions, honorable and passionate men though they be, have an equal chance of being neutral, detrimental, or beneficial. This is calamitous. So we must find another view which guarantees that simple, decent, and honorable men work within a context which corresponds to reality so that their small, modest interventions accrete toward something which is creative and enhances life.

There is something called creativity. Moreover, creativity has nothing to do with precious art. Creativity in fact has permeated all matter and all life in all time and does so now.

Creation can be defined as the employment of energy and matter in order to raise matter and energy to higher levels of order. Its antithesis is reduction or entropy which consists of matter and energy going from a higher to a lower level of order. You can envisage this reduction by thinking of a forest and measuring everything in it. Measure all the oxygen, carbon, nitrogen, phosphorus, macronutrients, micronutrients—everything. Then burn it and nothing will have happened. No matter has been created or destroyed, but the matter has gone from highly developed and ordered biological elements to inert and simple ones, heat, carbon dioxide, and water.

Evolution, of course, is the reverse of this, and so is creativity in which matter is raised from a lower to a higher level of order, like taking the inert world and suddenly covering it with a bioskin. All the creativity which has engaged all matter and all life in all time is represented by the orderings of matter, represented by the atoms in the periodic table, the evolution of compounds, life forms, ecosystems, and the biosphere. All of the ordering accomplished by all life in all time, all the potential represented by them in cells, tissues, organs, organisms, ecosystems, their apperception, symbiotic relationships, and a genetic potential—these constitute the sum of creativity which all evolution has accomplished in all time.

This conception, that matter and energy are creative, have been creative, and are now creative is a very different view from the one which assumes that nature is a sort of backdrop to a human play in which man plays his uniquely creative role. In the ecological view, we are uncertain about what creative role man has. We know that he is an arch-destroyer of geological dimensions, but his creative role in the biosphere is hard to discern.

We can't possibly believe in a malevolent God who would deny the possibility of any creative role to man. There must be a creative role for man. That is our challenge, prospect, and future. The conception of the biosphere as a creative process which engages all matter in all life in all time is a new, and for me, profoundly important conception.

Evolution has been both creative and retrogressive, but the sum of all the processes has been positively creative. This allows us to look at all the creatures which surround us and all the processes in quite a different way as creative process. If evolution has been creative, let us see what attributes evolution has demonstrated because these then reveal criteria for creativity. Evolution has proceeded from greater to lesser randomness, from simplicity to complexity, from uniformity to diversity, from instability to stability, from a low to a high number of species, from a low to a high number of cooperative mechanisms. Indeed, in sum, from the tendency to degradation, which is entropy, toward a tendency to increasing order, which is negentropy. That is a marvelous model.

When I went to Harvard, Dean Joseph Hudnut used to say of modern architecture, "simplicity at any cost." This was indeed the name of modern architecture. Simplicity in the biological world is a pejorative term because simplicity is the antithesis of complexity and evolution moves from simplicity to complexity. So when an architect designs a simple building, this probably reveals not the complexity of the situation he is trying to solve but simply his simple-mindedness.

We have a model of creativity which applies to any system whether it is a house, an individual, a family, a community, or an institution like the American Institute of Architects, or cells in an organism, or the ecosystems in the biosphere. We have a conception about creativity and the dynamics of the process. If we see a trend from complex to simple, it is retrogressing. If it goes from instability to stability, it is evolving.

There is another term which indicates the degree to which any process is evolving or retrogressing is being creative or reductive. And this term is the conception of fitness. Whether you know it or not, you are engaged in the business of fitting. Architecture should not be called architecture; it should be called fitting.

This verb "to fit" is of profound importance. Charles Darwin said that the surviving organism is fit for the environment. On the other hand, Lawrence Henderson has said that the actual world, with all the variability of environments constitutes the fittest possible abode for all life that has existed, does exist, or will exist.

You can think of yourself, your cells, your tissues, your organs, your institutions and consider all available environments for them. Among the multiplicity of environments, there are most-fit environments. There is a requirement, not only to find the most-fit environment but also to adapt that environment and/or yourself in order to accomplish fitting. The fit survive, according to Darwin.

So we are engaged inextricably in the process of finding fit environments and adapting them and ourselves. We are in this business of adaptation for survival. That is the real definition of architecture.

Where you find that most fit environment and adapt it and yourself to accomplish a fitting, you accomplish a *creative* fitting in thermodynamic terms. This is real creativity in which every organism and every ecosystem is intensely involved throughout all life.

You are engaged in a creative process, which has nothing to do with long hair, whether you wear sandals, whether you wash or don't wash. This is the implacable test which engages all creatures in all time and must engage all men in all time in order to ensure survival. When done, it is creative, and the measure of its creativity is survival of the process.

Because this whole system is in fact one system, only divided by men's minds and by the myopia which is called education, there is another simple term which synthesizes the degree to which any intervention is creative and accomplishes a creative fitting. And that is the presence of health. Wherever you find health—physical, social, mental in human societies, or physiological in nonhuman ecosystems—you have found absolute, explicit, irrefutable evidence of creative fitting. Any process which has found the fittest environment, which has been able to adapt that environment and itself to accomplish a creative fitting, is healthy. Wherever pathology is found at any level, in cell, tissue, organ, organism, institution, or ecosystem, there is evidence of a misfit, a reductive misfit; and the extension of this pathology will lead to the death of the species, the institution, or the ecosystem.

There is also the subject of form. Form and process are indivisible aspects of a single phenomenon. There is no such thing as abstract form; there is no such thing as capricious form or unmeaningful form. Form and process are indivisible. If one wishes to describe an atom, molecule, crystal, or compound, one can describe it only in formal terms. If one wishes to describe a cell, tissue, organ, organism, or ecosystem, one can do so only in formal terms. All form is meaningful. The degree to which meaning can be perceived is a function of the ability of the observer to perceive the meaning which is intrinsic. One can only understand what is in terms of evolutionary history—evolution of form and process.

The only way to understand the Appalachian Mountains is in terms of the fact that they once were an ancient sea; the only way to understand the molehills of the piedmont is to know that they were once 27,000 feet high. One can understand that which *is* only in terms of that which has been. That which is, has been and is in the process of becoming. It was process-form, is process-form, and will become process-form.

Every form reflects processes engaged in the business of creative adaptation toward the end of survival; form is only one superficial expression of the processes. Butterflies don't want to be pretty to make us happy. Sphagnum moss doesn't want to look like sphagnum moss. Sphagnum moss is, and as a process is, absolutely appropriate to the business of surviving while being sphagnum moss. Form and process are indivisible. Moreover there is generic form to cells, crystals, vascular processes, nervous systems, plants, and animals. All we have been talking about are processes—processes that have been subject to evolutionary tests over unimaginable periods of time and have been refined by the test of survival. The processes survive not only in terms of process but also in generic form.

There must be generic form in architecture, which leads us to something which must be called adaptive architecture—not architecture to gratify the muddy psyches of architects but architecture as a device by which man can adapt toward survival and the more distant prospect of fulfillment.

One has to think about the client, whether an individual, an institution, or a society. We must identify the organism and the environment because we are in the business of trying to accomplish a creative fitting, which creative fitting is inescapably involved in the business of form. There will be a form of fitting which is most fitting.

Homeostasis is a device which, without the intervention of the brain, is able to deal with the environment of energies and interpose various membranes and processes between these energies and the internal system. Without thought, we can maintain 98.6° F body temperature, and when we fail by a degree or two, we have a fever. Homeostasis is able to deal with environmental energies and through homeostatic controls maintain equilibrium. Architecture is in the same business but is dealing with a larger array of environmental energies. So we have the conception of the organism, its own homeostatic devices, and all the other energies which constitute the environment. We have all of environment variability, the organisms and their proclivities. We seek to find the most-fit environment of all.

That's not enough. We must adapt the environment and ourselves. We have to adapt in order to ensure survival and fulfillment of the system. We have to identify the environment, which brings me to my bailiwick because I am engaged in trying to find fit environments, to identify regions, as a range of opportunities and constraints for all prospective land uses and to fit these demands to available resources.

What I really do is called ecological planning and it simply consists of inventorying the environment so that one understands the way the world works, not only as biophysical process but also as opportunities and constraints for all prospective land uses.

First, you have to assemble those people who are competent. This is an outrageous novelty which architects don't ever consider. The great problem with ecological planning is that you are not allowed to speak in the absence of evidence. We'll start at the beginning, which, first and most important, is bedrock geology. That gives us 500 million years of evidence. We employ the man who knows about bedrock geology, and he describes the geological history and geomorphology of the region.

Then we hire the biometerologist who understands climate. Then we ask the two to get together because the interaction of climate and bedrock geology over the past million years is reflected in surficial geology. If you understand surficial geology, you then are in the process of understanding hydrology. That enables you to understand why rivers are and where they are; whether there is underground water or not.

Once you understand about groundwater and surface-water hydrology, you are able to understand about soils because they are only a byproduct of a process which can be explained in terms of the interaction of climate, bedrock geology, surficial geology, physiography, and hydrology. If you understand about soils, then you understand about plants because plants are variable with respect to environments, which variability is comprehensible in terms of climate, geomorphology, physiography, hydrology, and soils. If you understand about plants, you understand about animals because all animals are plant related, which leads you to understand about that special animal called man.

So one has to assemble those people to identify the region under study as phenomena, at the end of which you know why escarpments and caves and kettles and deltas are where they are. They are not only there, but their form and type explain what they are and what they have been doing and what they are in the process of becoming. Once you have identified the area as phenomena, you ask the same natural scientists to go over the same ground to reconstitute the region as processes. Then you assemble them all together to reconstitute the area as one single, interacting biophysical process, and then you have an ecological model.

Once understood as interacting biophysical process, the same data can be reconstituted as a social-value system. It is now possible to identify and locate all of the most propitious and the least detrimental attributes of air, land, water, life, and location for all prospective land uses.

So if you can identify what the land use is—whether it is a new town, an atomic reactor, a sewage plant, a highway, a single house, or garden—you can identify what is most propitious for that thing or that person, community, or institution in terms of factors of climate, bedrock geology, surficial geology, physiography, hydrology and limnology, soils, plants, animals, and land use. If you can identify all these needs, you can find the most propitious location. It can be done in a handcraft way or we can ask the computer to find these places where all these most propitious factors coexist. By this method we can solve the problem of location.

We can do this for every prospective land use—for agriculture, for urbanization, for recreation, for forests, all by type. Man identifies the most propitious factors which he requires and asks nature for the locations which provide them.

But we must identify those who ask nature for the most fitting environment. We have to find out what their needs and proclivities are. We must identify these in terms of social phenomena, social processes, and interacting social process. This allows us to enter the orthodoxy of city planning to assess the present and make projections into the future. These can be constituted into growth models, each associated with explicit hypotheses linked to the generating forces of growth. These are, then, demands in terms of land and resources. When demands can be matched to the opportunities and constraints which the region represents, there is then the basis for a plan.

Thus you have a creative fitting. And the most important conclusion for architects is that there are implications of form in fitting. There is no capriciousness in nature. The architect who believes that the white paper represents a site upon which he is going to invest his professional skill is mad. Written upon that white paper, whether he sees it or not, are 4 ½ to 6 billion years of physical evolution, 2 ½ billion years of biological evolution, a million years of human evolution and perhaps some thousand years of cultural evolution. All are written upon that land in biophysical and cultural processes having intrinsic form with implications for the form which he must give.

We are on the edge of time when we could, if we wished, feel the world's pulse, where we could use this ecological view to monitor the world. If instead of being so absolutely destructive, if we could abandon this cultural inferiority complex which is the base of our attitudes to nature—these poor, whimpering, puny creatures who were mute and defenseless in face of an implacable nature and in this impotence developed that bile of vengeance which explains the lesions and lacerations inflicted upon the life body of the world—if we could abandon all this and say we would like to be good stewards, we can develop ecological planning and design so that every honorable and decent architect may add his modest interventions to an enduring, cumulative, creative process.

We can, in fact, monitor the world from satellites continuously. We can augment this with high-level aerial photography. We can supplement this with ground truth. We can take this information from these sources and digitize it through high-speed scanners immediately to computers. And we can have an ecological model of the sort I have described, which actually simulates the ongoing biophysical processes. These can be consistently enriched and corrected. We can write programs asking for intrinsic suitabilities for all prospective land uses—for urbanization, for agriculture, for recreation. Anything we want to ask, we can have the world reveal to us.

This is a view of a working world of which we are a part. We can use this unique gift of human consciousness and be able to act as an enzyme, as an intelligent steward of nature. That possible destiny allows us to transform ourselves from geological destroyers to incipient creators.

Now this is a fantastic dream, and architecture must find a place in it. Architecture must absolutely reconstitute itself, as must all of society. You have traditionally assumed the leadership before. You have to reject the metaphysical symbol which has been ours for 2,000 years and replace it with another one: the ecological view. It exists for our use. It is marvelous because it does correspond to reality. It does offer the possibility of survival and a dream of fulfillment beyond dreams.

13

Nature Is More Than a Garden (1990)

Randy Hester of the University of California-Berkeley invited McHarg to read this paper at a conference on garden design. It appeared in the book The Meaning of Gardens *edited by Hester and Mark Francis of the University of California-Davis and published by MIT Press. McHarg views the garden as a device for human reassurance, a place for peace and tranquillity, an oasis in nature.*

I have found the aspiration for reassurance to be a useful consideration in examining the garden. In the home furniture, memorabilia, and books provide a familiar and reassuring environment. I believe that the garden is also a vehicle for reassurance. I have observed that the familiar is an important component of reassurance and often derives from the ancestral landscape. The English Quakers who left Buckinghamshire in England found familiar environments in Bucks and Chester counties in Pennsylvania. There they proceeded to make their environment even more familiar.

Reassurance may also derive from familiar conventions. Traditional English suburban gardens contain a formal vocabulary—lawn, herbaceous border, rose garden, rock and water garden, wild garden—annually celebrated at the Chelsea Flower Show. The equivalent in Philadelphia adds Colonial Williamsburg overtones and is annually presented at the Philadelphia Flower Show. Often, however, the convention is in conflict with the natural landscape, such as when East Coast and European gardens erupt in the desert.

Affirmation of values is linked to reassurance. I believe that the garden combines both explicit and implicit statements of affirmation. Perhaps the most dominant statement is that nature is benign. Usually docile, tractable, and floriferous plants are arrayed. Poisonous plants, animals, and weeds are stringently excluded.

The next affirmation of the garden is that nature is bountiful. Here vegetables, fruit, and herbs give testament. Within the garden, nature is represented as orderly. There is an accompanying belief that work outdoors, preferably in a garden, touching soils, plants, water, stone, confers not only physical but also mental health. And, finally there are the sentiments in doggerel: "A garden is a lovesome thing, God wot" and "A kiss from the sun for pardon, a song from the birds for mirth, I feel nearer God's heart in my garden, than anywhere else on earth." I have long believed that the garden is a better symbol of peace than the dove.

However true they may be of gardens, these representations are illusory when applied to nature. Nature is not always benign, inflicting volcanoes, earthquakes, hurricanes, tornadoes, floods, and drought. Nor is nature uniformly bountiful. Arctic, Antarctic, tundra, taiga, and deserts provide meager sustenance. Nature is indeed orderly, but with a complex expression quite different from garden forms, which surely represent an illusory order. Then is God more accessible in a garden than elsewhere, than in nature perhaps?

Far be it from me to deprecate the creation and cultivation of gardens. All congratulations to professionals and amateurs alike who create islands of delight, tranquillity, and introspection. These are surely among the most successful testaments to man's humanity, often islands in anarchic, cheerless environments.

My purpose is not to discount but to add. I have been moved by Ryoan-ji, Saiho-ji, the Alhambra, Vaux, but I seek more. Gardens, of necessity, are simplifications. They exclude much, not least time and change. They contribute only a fragment of what is known. Indeed, they have more in common with aquaria and terraria than with nature.

The most beautiful gardens I have ever seen are pristine coral reefs in the South Pacific. They are artifices, created by coral, transforming oceanic deserts into the richest biotic environments in the world. They are also benign, bountiful, and orderly. They are dynamic and they are natural. Perhaps coral should be exemplar to men who make gardens.

However, in terrestrial environments I prefer nature. Nature contains the history of the evolution of matter, life, and man. It is the arena of past, present, and future. It exhibits the laws that obtain. It contains every quest that man can pursue. It tells every important story that man would know. Therein lie its richness, mystery, and charm.

So for me it is not either garden or nature. I can accept the imperfect reassurance, simplicity of order, even the elimination of time and change that gardens represent. I accept the great pleasure that gardens give, but I will reserve my deeper quest and larger fulfillment for nature.

14

Landscape Architecture (1997)

In 1996–97, Ian McHarg undertook a speaking tour on behalf of the American Society of Landscape Architects (ASLA). Jim Dalton, then executive vice president of ASLA, sought to promote membership in the society but, even more, wanted to elevate the aspirations of the existing members. He selected McHarg for this task. As a result of the speaking tour, McHarg wrote this reflective essay for ASLA.

I know of no other profession which escalated as swiftly from oblivion to international significance nor one where so few persons have accomplished so much. Landscape architecture is unique in both respects. This should give us inspiration, confidence, and courage.

Law had its origins in courtiers selling access to power and spawned an army of lawyers; the master builders bequeathed us architecture, what a gift; artificers, sappers, and miners led to engineers; witch doctors, shamans, and in the West, barbers with leeches, led to medicine. Originally this was a mixed blessing. Until this century interventions were just as likely to be detrimental as beneficial. Medicine was no better than chance. Not until the Flexner Report, when medical schools were induced, perhaps better, bribed, to espouse biology, did medicine rise to its present august position. The medical experience contains a powerful lesson. Do we wish our efforts to be random, inconsequential, or indeed malevolent, or should we follow medicine and espouse science, biology, perhaps ecology and anthropology, and justify a more central and consequential role? I hope so.

The precise date when landscape architecture emerged is clouded. There were transitions. But in sixteenth-century Italy there appeared a singular expression. Popes and cardinals chose to leave Rome in summer and reside in Frascati and other nearby towns, where they built villas. These were not remarkable, but their gardens and outdoor spaces certainly were, particularly Villa D'Este and Villa Lante, works of excruciating beauty, a major threshold.

Were Pirro Ligorio, Jacopo Barozzi da Vignola, or Donato Bramante members of a new breed, or were they simply green architects? I think not, the originality and the dominance of the gardens demands a new signature. How proud we can be to have these illustrious founders as our own antecedents. Landscape architecture would seem to have developed in full bloom.

The locus of power, invention and art moved to France where a single figure, André Le Nôtre, dominated the next century. First with Vaux-le-Vicômte for Nicolas Fouquet, later for Louis XIV at Versailles, Le Nôtre designed the largest exercise of garden art in history. It still excites our astonishment. Masses of tractable, docile, and colorful plants, with clay, sand, and gravel, were assembled into a great symmetrical composition. Its purpose was to portray the sovereignty and power of Le Roi Soleil, king by divine right, demonstrating his dominion over all men and nature, his power to subjugate them. The composition was an enormous genuflection to his majesty and power, it consumed half of the royal treasury. Would that other monarchs and princes had emulated him with the creation of gardens, or, even better, protecting and cherishing nature. But that was not the message of Versailles which sought to demonstrate man's dominion over nature. This constitutes the worst possible admonition to those explorers who were then about to discover and colonize the earth. Anthropomorphism, dominion, and subjugation are better suited to suicide, genocide, and biocide than survival and success.

Was Le Nôtre a green architect? I think not, the sheer dominance of the garden suggests a different scope of concerns, interests, and interventions. The fact that the palace was simply an exclamation point in the composition, suggests a new role and profession. Le Nôtre was truly a landscape architect. His works were the zenith of art on the seventeenth century. Consider his accomplishments or of the Italian trio of Ligorio, Vignola, and Bramante.

The English landscape movement began as Versailles was being finished. The handful of men who would proceed to transform an entire nation were dedicated to the expression of a harmony of man and nature. Of them there is no doubt. A new view was born in the eighteenth century. Whence its antecedents? I have not been able to discover. But here was Walpole saying of Kent, "he leap't the wall and discovered all nature to be a garden" and again "he found in nature a new creation." In my opinion, these are most powerful statements, evidence of a new view, indeed the emergence of the modern view.

William Kent, Capability Brown, Humphry Repton, Uvedale Price, Richard Payne Knight, and William Shenstone accomplished a total transformation of what was then an impoverished agriculture, deforested landscape, attenuated fields, and created the fairest, most productive, and beautiful landscape in Europe in less than a century. This, I suggest, is the finest accomplishment of art in the Western tradition. It deserves our most profound admiration. It should be revered as an important precursor.

These six men led England to accept and display the unity of man and nature and in so doing, transformed a nation. Persuasive and effective as was this new view it, was unable to withstand the power of its successor which led to the industrial revolution. Coal, iron, steel, mines, factories, railways, canals, industrial cities assumed ascendancy. No longer was nature to be cherished, nurtured, and emulated but rather to be exploited. The world was now seen as a storehouse inviting plunder.

But the landscape ideal survived, absorbed by the father of the profession, that great American, Frederick Law Olmsted, who visited England, observed the first public park at Birkenhead by Joseph Paxton, and proceeded to apply and expand the eighteenth-century principles into nineteenth-century America. Certainly the creation of a system of national parks was an original conception—the identification, protection, management of regions equivalent to nation-states. The invention of the urban park was comparable—Central Park remains unmatched; Riverside and the American subdivision, Stanford and the college campus, even the highway overpass falls within the inventions of Olmsted who single-handedly equaled the entire production of the professions of architecture, planning, and engineering during the nineteenth century.

This extraordinary paragon, in addition to his other virtues, had the wit to identify his successor—Charles Eliot, son of Harvard's president. In 1880 Eliot determined to spend a productive summer. A student at Harvard, he enlisted six classmates who entitled themselves the Champlain Society and proceeded to undertake an inventory of Mount Desert Island in Maine. Over six years they performed what was the first ecological inventory ever done. It produced two products, "Outline of the Geology of Mt. Desert Island" and "Flora of Mt. Desert, Maine."

But Eliot expanded this purpose to invent the first ecological planning study in the United States or the world, for the Boston metropolitan region, the 1893 study which, to date, has neither been equaled nor surpassed. It included the entire region from Blue Mountains to the sea, it included rivers, forests, marshes, the offshore islands. Eliot and his invention—regional planning—could not have arrived at a better time. Here was the appropriate attitude to lead the colonization of the country, here was a visionary plan for the land, and the world. But, it was not to be, for Eliot died of cerebrospinal meningitis prematurely at 37, to the loss of the nation, the world, and to nature.

The eighteenth-century view envisaged an ideal landscape, first expressed by the painters Salvator Rosa, Nicolas Poussin, and Claude Lorraine, observed in the *campagna*. This effort of restoration required and received massive energies. This was not necessary in America. Here the pioneers had discovered a virgin continent. The task was not to represent harmony that existed in the systems which were being discovered. Here the task was to recognize, cherish, and protect first and also to develop with discrimination, employ art in accomplishing felicitous adaptations. This was a simpler task, but it was at odds with the explorer mentality, the extraction morality, be it of gold or silver, beavers and bison, timber or wheat, exploitation was its name.

Olmsted and Eliot had presented a better view, but Eliot had died even before Olmsted, and to our astonishment and loss, these extraordinary paragons did not reproduce themselves. The concept died in England at the end of the eighteenth century. Eliot died in 1897, Olmsted in 1903, and their movement stalled. It should have been enthroned at Harvard, spread to other leading institutions, and permeated the new profession of landscape architecture. To my continued chagrin, it did not. Indeed it declined from the elevated status achieved by Olmsted, promised by Eliot.

The time has come to rediscover and celebrate the accomplishments of our predecessors, not least Olmsted and Eliot. They should be enthroned at Harvard, represented by bronze statues, studied, admired, and emulated worldwide.

The traditions continued into this century. First in the person of the Brazilian polymath, painter, naturalist, designer of jewelry, floral decorations for state ceremonies in Brasilia, architect but, most of all, designer of gardens: Roberto Burle Marx. He was a man of such fame as to be known to cab drivers in Rio. He was also renowned as a belly dancer and singer of bawdy songs, and in several languages. Not least, he was a successful plant collector and created an elaborate arboretum.

Yet another is Lawrence Halprin, very much alive at 78, productive, notably in the United States and Israel. His reputation began with modern gardens, catapulted after the Portland Fountain, expanded with Sea Ranch, and had a fitting climax with the FDR Memorial in Washington, D.C., just completed and resoundingly appreciated. Halprin deserves inclusion in this pantheon.

These are emergents, hints of successors to this great lineage. First are the partners of Andropogon, Carol and Colin Franklin, Leslie Jones and Rolf Sauer; Jones & Jones of Seattle; Edward Stone of Florida; EDAW in San Francisco, Atlanta, and elsewhere; Jon Coe, Gary Lee, and their partners in Philadelphia; Design Workshop of Aspen, Tempe, and elsewhere; and, of course, there is A. E. Bye who disclaims scientific ecology, but whose works are of great beauty and very appropriate ecology. There is another figure, Jack Dangermond, President of ESRI in Redlands, California, who is the leader in spatial computation. Dangermond has drawn on his multidisciplinary academic training in landscape architecture, planning, and geography to create a new industry and lead it.

The giants who led the profession, Ligorio, Vignola, and Bramante, Le

Nôtre, the English Six, Olmsted and Eliot, Burle Marx and Halprin have been augmented not by practitioners, but by science and technology. Concern for nature in the Renaissance was limited mainly to princes and pontiffs. In England it was the province of the landed aristocracy, artists, and scholars. The audience widened in the nineteenth century but exploded at the end of the twentieth. Newspapers, magazines, film, but mainly television, contributed to this effervescence. PBS, *National Geographic, The Planet Earth, Nature*, the Discovery and Learning Channels, brought rich, sophisticated, and persuasive insights into nature to a rapt public attention.

Science, long immured in subatomic particles and molecular biology, emerged into the sensate world with plate tectonics, atmospheric physics, chemosynthesis, and a new understanding of microbes and of the importance of environment. Surely the greatest benefit from the diminution of the nuclear threat was the recognition of the environment as having primacy on the global agenda. In this evolution emerged new technological marvels, sensors, satellite imagery, geo-positioning systems, computers, and geographic information systems. We can feel the world's pulse. We can undertake not only national, but also global inventories. We can monitor the planet.

Who would have thought that the Christian church would address man's relation to nature through the garden at D'Este?

Who would have expected that the major energies of the most powerful monarch in Europe would be employed to create a metaphysical symbol of his rank and role as at Versailles?

Was there reason to expect that the most compelling philosophical investigation would be a new and benign view of the relationship of man and nature in eighteenth-century England?

Who could have expected that the environment would emerge as the most compelling subject confronting the world at the end of this century?

The profession of landscape architecture has a client, the earth and its creatures. In order to meet this challenge, to respond to our client in a sustainable manner, the profession must ensure that it forms an alliance with the environmental sciences and that we come to be seen by them and the public as their agents for achieving felicitous, ecological adaptations.

Professional education must recognize this relationship and incorporate environmental science. The American Society of Landscape Architects must become a spokesman for the environment and appropriate adaptations. We must become leaders, not only in understanding the environment, but also in planning ecological restoration, management, and design, that is, in sustainable development.

To this day, neither architects nor city planners have been required to study environmental science and thus bring only innocence and ignorance to bear. Engineers traditionally study physical environmental sciences, notably geology, and hydrology, but learn nothing of life or people. Landscape architects have a long association with botany, horticulture, and, more recently, ecology.

There is a vacuum of environmental competence which the profession should fill. Success is contingent upon landscape architects learning enough environmental science to be unerringly selected to answer all questions relating to its planning and design. When this comes to pass the profession will receive the appreciation, adulation, and rewards befitting to the descendants of our illustrious ancestors. We have increased our numbers a thousandfold. We have inherited an unimaginable expansion of capabilities. While problems have escalated with population, our scientific understanding and technological competence have more than kept pace. The canvas has expanded from site to region, to nation to now embrace oceans, atmosphere, and the planet earth.

The only necessary elements are confidence and conviction. I have long ago concluded that knowledge is the essential ingredient. Given this, then confidence will follow. Consider the example of Frederick Law Olmsted. Has anyone ever equaled his conviction of the salubrious effect of nature, particularly necessary for urban man?

What an extraordinary lineage we have inherited. It gives us example, confidence, and courage. Let us follow their example and proceed into the twenty-first century.

15

Ecology and Design (1997)

In 1992 Arizona State University (ASU) initiated a new degree in landscape architecture. In the process a Department of Planning became the School of Planning and Landscape Architecture. To celebrate the event George Thompson of the Center for American Places and Frederick Steiner organized a symposium and a book on landscape architecture theory. They received a grant from the National Endowment for the Arts for the symposium and the book.

The concept was to pull together the senior and junior theorists in the discipline around the theme of ecological design and planning. The senior figures had pioneered the use of ecology in landscape architecture. Several younger theorists had been critical of this use and noted that ecology had drained some of the creative juices from design.

Ian McHarg was the central figure at the symposium. Each of the other theorists referred to his influence in some way or the other. McHarg responded to the criticisms of ecology with this spirited essay. It appears in the book Ecological Planning and Design, *edited by Thompson and Steiner and published by John Wiley & Sons.*

I am unabashedly committed to the imperative *design with nature*, or ecological design and planning. Indeed, I conceive of nonecological design as either capricious, arbitrary, or idiosyncratic, and it is certainly irrelevant. Ecology, the study of environments and organisms, among them people, is totally inclusive. What falls outside this definition? Not content, perhaps only attitude. Nonecological design and planning disdains reason and emphasizes intuition. It is antiscientific by assertion.

There is no doubt about my attitude toward this topic. I invented *ecological planning* during the early 1960s and became an advocate of *ecological design* thereafter. This was explicit in *Design with Nature*; it was not only an explanation, but also a command.[1]

Ecological planning is that approach whereby a region is understood as a biophysical and social process comprehensible through the operation of laws and time. This can be reinterpreted as having explicit opportunities and constraints for any particular human use. A survey will reveal the most fit locations and processes.

Ecological design follows planning and introduces the subject of form. There should be an intrinsically suitable location, processes with appropriate materials, and forms. Design requires an informed designer with a visual imagination, as well as graphic and creative skills. It selects for creative fitting revealed in intrinsic and expressive form.

The deterioration of the global environment, at every scale, has reinforced my advocacy of ecological design and planning. Degradation has reached such proportions that I now conclude that nonecological design and planning is likely to be trivial and irrelevant and a desperate deprivation. I suggest that to ignore natural processes is to be ignorant, to exclude life-threatening hazards—volcanism, earthquakes, floods, and pervasive environmental destruction—is either idiocy or criminal negligence. Avoiding ecological considerations will not enhance the profession of landscape architecture. In contrast, it will erode the modest but significant advances that ecology has contributed to landscape architecture and planning since the 1960s.

Yet, you ask: What of art? I have no doubt on this subject either. The giving of meaningful form is crucial; indeed, this might well be the most precious skill of all. It is rare in society, yet it is clearly identifiable where it exists. Art is indispensable for society and culture.

Does art exclude science? Does art reject knowledge? Would a lobotomy improve human competence, or is the brain the indispensable organ?

There is a new tendency by some landscape architects to reject ecology, to emphasize art exclusively. This I deplore and reject. Such an approach is tragically ironic when so many world leaders are calling for sustainable development, when architects are issuing green manifestos, and professional associations in architecture and engineering are refocusing their attention on the environment.

We have been at this impasse before; it was not beneficial, and the result was calamitous. We have only to remember that, by the end of World War I, landscape architecture was firmly established at Harvard University. It was the world center for this subject. It had inherited the concepts and accomplishments of Frederick Law Olmsted and Charles Eliot, but all was not well: There was dissension.

It transpired that there were opposing camps within landscape architecture. The Olmsted disciples wished to emphasize conservation and regional and town planning. They included Henry Hubbard and Theodora Kimball, Harland Bartholomew, John Nolen, Warren Manning, and, later, Howard

Mennhenick. The remainder were oriented to Beaux Arts; they were self-proclaimed aesthetes, interested in designing estates for the rich and famous: Bremer Whidden Pond, James Sturgis Pray, Steven Hamblin, and Robert Wheelwright. The aesthetes defined landscape architecture design between the world wars at Harvard and elsewhere. Meanwhile the Olmsted disciples founded the field of planning during the 1920s, and inadvertently created a schism between design and planning that persists to this day.[2] Brains and knowledge abandoned landscape architecture, which experienced a massive decline from the peaks of Olmsted and Eliot to an abyss with little intelligence, skill, or passion.

This antagonism between art and science, as well as between design and planning, has lasted too long. It is now a serious obstruction to education and the earth's well-being. Both art and science have their antique, prepared positions, their mandarin advocates, their lines of competence defined, and their proprietary jargons. Yet, when stripped of pomp and pretensions, at root art merely means skill and science means knowledge. Can we imagine, in the challenging environment we occupy, the rejection of either art or science? Surely knowledge needs skill to give form and significance to our landscapes and our adaptations. Surely skill needs knowledge just as a solver needs a problem. Surely, once and for all time, art and science, skill and knowledge, ecology and design and planning should unite.

What the world needs from landscape architecture is an enlarged vision, greater knowledge, and commensurate skill. Landscape architects are engaged in the challenge of adaptation. They must acquire the accomplishments that can make a significant contribution to preserving, managing, planning, and restoring the biosphere, to designing human environments.

And, thanks to Charles Darwin and Lawrence Henderson, we have a theory. Darwin said: "The surviving organism is fit for the environment." Henderson, another biologist and author of *The Fitness of the Environment* (1913), wrote that Darwin's assertion was insufficient. He concluded that, as there are infinite environments and organisms, the evolutionary challenge for every participant is to seek and find the fittest available environment, to adapt that environment and the self to accomplish a better fit. Moreover, Henderson's writing defined a fit environment as one in which most of a consumer's needs exist in the environment as found, requiring less work for adaptation than for any competitor. The thermodynamic challenge implies that successful adaptation is creative.[3]

What are the instruments for adaptation? The universal adaptations—mutation and natural selection—while manipulated extensively for food, plants, and animals, are not widely applied to human breeding (thank goodness). Mutation and natural selection are slow processes. And innate behavior in living organisms is similarly difficult to manipulate. Cultural adaptation is the more pliant and useful. Language, philosophy, science, art, and technology are such instruments. If one is to ask which aspect of cultural adaptation most clearly meets the Darwin-Henderson challenge—to find the fittest environment and then to engage in adaptation—surely the most direct response is landscape planning and design.

But we need an appropriate criterion for guiding and evaluating landscape architecture in the twenty-first century. Art critics evaluate the contribution of painting, sculpture, dance, photography, and other art forms. Can their appreciation extend from the product to the source of creation, the painter, his or her brain, eye, hand, bones, sinews, arteries, and veins? Beauty alone is an inappropriate criterion for evaluating art or the organs that create it, so why should beauty be used exclusively to evaluate a landscape? Fitness, as explained by Henderson, for me is a thoroughly suitable criterion. We have, then, not only a theory, but also criteria for performance and fitness.

If one is fit, then one is healthy, and this applies equally to a landscape. Furthermore, if being healthy enables one to seek and solve problems, or provides the ability to recover from insult or assault, then fitness confers health. Therefore, fitness is an index of health. Extending this thought to landscape architectural theory and practice, do we have a method for accomplishing creative planning and design and, more simply, an ecological method for adaptation?

We live in a physical world, a biological world, and a social world, and our investigations must include them all. As matter preceded life and the human species was late in biological evolution, we can employ chronology as a unifying force. We can recapitulate events and retrace time. Thus, when we design and plan, we should begin with the geological history of a landscape, working in concert with an understanding of climate. Bedrock and surficial geology as well as climatic processes can be reinterpreted to explain geomorphology and hydrology. These processes set the stage for soil formation. Now, the relationships among the constituent parts of a landscape become clear: The past informs the present, and each feature is only comprehensible from understanding its earlier layers. After we learn about a landscape's geology, climate, hydrology, and soils, then vegetation patterns become more apparent, as does the resultant wildlife. At which point we can ask the human occupants who they are, how they distinguish themselves from others, how they view the environment and its occupants, and what are their needs and desires, their preferences and aversions.

I wish to emphasize my belief that ecological study includes natural and cultural processes. We will find that discrete value systems are associated with distinct human constituencies, and we can associate these groups with their needs and values. This approach allows landscape architects to interpret all phenomena in the light of these systems. With such vision and knowledge, we can plan, because we have developed the context for planning and design.

This is the biophysical model I developed more than three decades ago for ecological design and planning. This is the model I live by. It can be reinterpreted to explain social values, technological competence, an ethnographic history of human settlements—urban as well as rural. We then are able to see the primeval landscape successively modified, through history, in order to arrive at the present.

Ecological study is indispensable to planning, but it also produces a context for a regional design vocabulary. The settlements of Dogon, the Berbers in Morocco, the settlement of the Greek islands, Italian hill villages, and pueblo communities in New Mexico and the Colorado Plateau are fitting examples of ecological responses in planning and design. Contemporary examples of ecological designers are too few. I am able, however, to select three firms.

The first is Andropogon in Philadelphia, whose principals are Carol and Colin Franklin, Leslie Jones, and Rolf Sauer. These landscape architects possess unchallenged primacy in ecological design and restoration. Their science is impeccable, their applications cross the threshold of art, and their realizations of design and planning are wonderfully effective, fitting, and, even for the uninitiated, beautiful.[4] Coe Lee Robinson Roesch in Philadelphia is the second example; the third is Jones & Jones in Seattle. Both firms have built sterling reputations designing and building appropriate exhibits for zoos. Their science, too, is elegant, employing inventories of the native environments of animals, replicating these environments with consummate skill. Their creations include ecological and psychological factors never before employed, to my knowledge, for human habitations. It is more difficult to find other examples. These three exceptions simply prove the rule. Ecological design is still an aspiration, not yet a practice, within landscape architecture.

A major obstruction to ecological design is the architecturally derived mode of representation drawings. This is paper-oriented, two-dimensional, and orthogonal. In contrast nature is multi-dimensional, living, growing, moving with forms that tend to be amorphous or amoebic. They can grow, expand, interact, and alternate. Field design would be a marvelous improvement over designing on paper removed from the site. Yet new representations must be developed to supersede the limitations of paper-oriented, orthogonal investigations with their limited formal solutions. We should be committed in our work to designing living landscapes in urban, rural, and wild settings. Yet there are infinite opportunities afforded to those who would study natural systems, their components, rules, succession, and, not least, their forms. This should be the basis for an emerging ecological design.

This system does not need invention. Forms, materials, and processes have evolved by trial and error over eons of time and represent the finest solutions of materials and form that nature could invent. Such ecosystems are exquisitely adapted and provide an example for people to design and plan.

Strangely, the area where art and science have been most successfully employed is neither architecture nor landscape architecture. It is in the creation of prostheses. Here biological knowledge is indispensable, but skill produces the adaptation. The purposes are to amplify the performance of a biological function—to see small and far, we have the microscope and the telescope; to speak far, we have the telephone and the microphone; to move far and fast, we have the plane and the rocket. Our major prosthesis is the expansion of power from muscle to tools, mechanical equipment to atom bomb.

Consider the steps to improve sight—spectacles, bifocals, magnifying glasses, laser operations for cataracts and glaucoma, and soft contact lenses—a miracle of adaptive design. Or walking—first a shoe, then a crutch, a walker, the wheelchair, now titanium hips and Teflon knees. The computer may be the prosthesis for the brain.

Should we pursue this track we would reconsider membranes. The giant clam and nudibranch have incorporated chloroplasts; those animals can now photosynthesize. Why not build membranes, walls, and roofs? Could they do so? Consider vegetation on walls and roofs to add carbon, fixing and minimizing carbon dioxide. Consider creating calcium carbonate, with electric charges in seawater.

Membranes modulate freshwater and saltwater. They facilitate the transport of nutrients. Consider the adaptations to cold in plants, reduction in water content, hairy surfaces, corrugations, and color. Wastes in nature are often nutrients, not problems. The route that Andropogon, Coe Lee Robinson Roesch, and Jones & Jones have developed is superb but needs to be augmented. The example of prosthetic development is a fitting analog. It is indisputably ecological, without caprice.

Of course, the best example of successful adaptation is the coral. The ocean floor is generally sterile. Coral transforms such areas into some of the most fertile and beautiful environments on earth. Would that landscape architects could equal this.

When the training of landscape architects includes at least an introduction to all of the relevant natural and social sciences, as well as design proficiency, then a new proposal can provide them with an exceptional opportunity to design and plan ecologically and artfully.

There are moves afoot to initiate a National Biological Survey. I recommended this in 1974 to Russell Train, then of the U.S. Environmental Protection Agency (EPA). When William Reilly became EPA administrator in 1990, he asked me to advise him on the reorganization of the EPA, and the conduct of the Environmental Monitoring and Assessment Program (EMAP), the proposed inventory. EMAP was proposed to be a broadly conceived ecosystem inventory integrating regional and national scales, allowing for monitoring and assessment, and designed to influence decision making. With my colleagues John Radke, Jonathan Berger, and Kathleen Wallace, I produced a document, *A Prototype Database for a National Ecological Inventory* (1992). This recommended a three-part process, a national inventory at 1:2,000,000 with all natural and social regions delineated; a regional scale inventory at 1:250,000; and, finally, samples at the scale of 1:24,000.

Our first assertion was that the resolve to undertake a National Ecological Inventory should be recognized as the most important governmental action ever taken in the history of the American environment. This resolve contains implicit resolutions: That inventory, monitoring, and modeling are indispensable to the EPA and essential to the fulfillment of its regulatory roles.

This first requires the reconstitution of the EPA to include leadership from all environmental sciences. To provide such leadership, we recommended the creation of an executive committee composed of leading officers in all of the scientific societies. Regional groups of environmental scientists and planners would be assembled to undertake regional inventories. And landscape architects, being among the most competent professionals to decide on the appropriate data to be incorporated and its contribution to planning and design, would participate in the content of these inventories. For the crystalline piedmont and adjacent coastal plain in Pennsylvania and New Jersey, for example, we would assume that landscape architects and regional planners at the University of Pennsylvania, Rutgers University, and Pennsylvania State University would be part of a central group to that association of regional scientists. This model would be replicated throughout the country with other university landscape architecture faculties, professional designers, and planners contributing to the regional groups. By such an involvement the landscape architecture profession would vastly enhance its social contribution and academic reputation.

It is then necessary to produce a plan for the process to undertake the inventory as well as to monitor its progress. This would involve the recommended scientific committee, an expanded staff representing all of the environmental sciences, and an appropriate organizational structure. When the plan is completed, we advocate a massive public relations and advertising campaign to inform the general public, conservation groups, the scientific community, and government officials at all levels of the significance of the enterprise.[5]

Our proposed inventory must include physical, biological, and social systems. The last is indispensable for understanding human environments. We suggested a demonstration ethnographic survey to illustrate that these are crucial for understanding human ecology. In our recommendation to the EPA, we observed that the greatest problem lies not in data collection, but rather with integration, synthesis, and evaluation.

Now, there is a new development. Secretary of the Interior Bruce Babbitt announced, shortly after his appointment by President Clinton in 1992, his intention to undertake a National Biological Survey (NBS). This may supersede EMAP. There is another possibility: NASA, the Defense Mapping Agency, and the federal departments of defense and energy have collected global environmental data since the onset of the Nuclear Age, employing instrumentalism that is unavailable to civilians. There is discussion of declassifying these data, which, of course, could be included in a National Ecological Inventory or a National Biological Survey. There is, also, the possibility that this capability could be invested in the United Nations as the U.S. arm of the U.N. Environmental Program and employed for a global inventory. Others are recommending the creation of a National Institute of the Environment in which the inventorying and modeling might be invested.

Clearly massive data will soon become available, ultimately in digital form, globally and locally. Whoever has access to this cornucopia will have immense power. Landscape architects should become advocates for such ecological inventories and become primary users of these data for planning and design. Landscape architects must learn to lead.

In 1992 I received a signal honor from President George Bush, the National Medal of Art. The noteworthy aspect of this act was the inclusion of landscape architecture as a category eligible for this high honor. As preface to the award President Bush stated, "It is my hope that the art of the twenty-first century will be devoted to restoring the earth."

This will require a fusion of science and art. There can be no finer challenge. Will the profession of landscape architecture elevate itself to contribute to this incredible opportunity? Let us hope so. The future of our planet—and the quest for a better life—may depend on it. So let us resolve to green the earth, to restore the earth, to heal the earth with the greatest expression of science and art we can muster. We are running out of time and opportunities.

Notes

1. Ian L. McHarg. 1969. *Design with Nature*. Garden City, N.Y.: Doubleday, Natural History Press. 1992. Second edition, New York: Wiley.
2. Frederick Law Olmsted was an amateur farmer, familiar with science, and Charles Eliot consorted with the leading scientists of his time, but their influence was bred out of city planning, which became the applied social science department that I encountered as a student at Harvard University in 1946. The natural sciences were banished. It is barely credible that the accomplishments of that giant, Olmsted, and the opportunities presented by Eliot were disregarded—first, by landscape architecture and, then, by city planning at

Harvard. Nor were either replaced by a superior doctrine. We have yet to rediscover their significance.

3. I use the word *consumer* because the roots of *ecology* and *economics* both lie in the Greek word, *oikos*, or "a dwelling place." Henderson used terms such as *consumer* close to this root meaning.

4. See Carol Franklin, "Fostering Living Landscapes," in George F. Thompson and Frederick R. Steiner, eds., *Ecological Design and Planning*. New York: Wiley, pp. 263–92, as well as Leslie Jones Sauer, *The Once and Future Forest*. Washington, D.C.: Island Press, 1998.

5. It is worthwhile to remember that Charles E. Little and David Brower, among other leading conservationists, have for decades advocated the necessity of employing advertising and public relations techniques in the cause to inform the public, industry, government, and university officials about environmental matters. Also of note is Richard Beamish's important book, *Getting the Word Out in the Fight to Save the Earth* (Baltimore: Johns Hopkins University Press, 1995). Beamish is one of the unsung heroes of the modern environmental movement, especially for his work on saving the Adirondacks.

Part IV

Revealing the
Genius of the Place:
Methods and Techniques for
Ecological Planning

Ian McHarg provided an orderly procedure for ecological planning. Suitability analysis is the process of determining the fitness of a given tract of land for a defined use or set of uses. This procedure involves overlaying mapped information to reveal opportunities and constraints for potential land uses. "Consult the Genius of the place in all," Alexander Pope advised. Suitability analysis is a logical framework for making such a consultation.

Landscape architects began using hand-drawn, sieve-mapping overlays in the late nineteenth century. Pennsylvania State University professor emeritus Lynn Miller credits Charles Eliot and his associates in the office of Olmsted, Olmsted, and Eliot with pioneering overlays through sun prints produced on their office windows. Both Miller and McHarg acknowledge the early contributions of Charles Eliot, an Olmsted protégé, who worked with scientists systematically to collect and map information to be used in planning and design. Warren Manning, a protégé of both Olmsted and Eliot, used soil and vegetation information with topography and their combined relationship to land use to prepare four different maps of the town of Billerica, Massachusetts, in 1912. Manning's Billerica Plan displayed recommendations and changes in the town's circulation routes and land use (Steinitz et al. 1976; Manning 1913).

Eliot left the most explicit explanation about why and how the overlays were employed. After his death his father Charles W. Eliot, the president of

Harvard, wrote a biography-autobiography. *Charles Eliot, Landscape Architect* (1902) was the father's interpretation of his son's work. This work provides perhaps the first account of the overlay technique. The Boston Metropolitan Park work undertaken by Olmsted, Olmsted, and Eliot, with Eliot in charge, involved six months of "diligent researches" (1902, p. 496). Eliot used a variety of consultants including a Massachusetts Institute of Technology professor, as well as Olmsted staff, such as Manning, to conduct surveys of the metropolitan region's geology, topography, and vegetation. These maps provided the basis for the overlay process which Eliot describes as follows:

> By making use of sun-prints of the recorded boundary plans, by measuring compass lines along the numerous woodpaths, and by sketching the outlines of swamps, clearings, ponds, hills, and valleys, extremely serviceable maps were soon produced. The draughting of the several sheets was done in our office. Upon one sheet of tracing-cloth were drawn the boundaries, the roads and paths, and the lettering . . . ; on another sheet were drawn the streams, ponds, and swamps; and on a third the hill shading was roughly indicated by pen and pencil. Gray sun-prints obtained from the three sheets superimposed in the printing frame, when mounted on cloth, served very well for all purposes of study. Photo-lithographed in three colors, namely, black, blue, and brown, the same sheets will serve as guide maps for the use of the public and the illustration of reports.
>
> Equipped with these maps, we have made good progress, as before remarked, in familiarizing ourselves with the "lay of the land" (1902, p. 496).

After Eliot and Manning there are several studies in which the use of the overlay technique is apparent, but a theoretical explanation about the rationale for using the technique as an orderly planning method was missing. The city plan for Dusseldorf, Germany, in 1912 the Doncaster, England, regional plan in 1922 (Abercrombie and Johnson 1922) the 1929 regional plan of New York and its environment (Regional Planning Staff 1929) and the 1943 London County plan (Forshaw and Abercrombie 1943) incorporate typical characteristics of the overlay process (Steinitz et al. 1976). Thomas Adams, who directed the extensive 1929 New York regional planning study, addressed suitability in his 1934 *The Design of Residential* Areas, but mostly from an economic perspective. An academic discussion of the overlay technique did not surface until 1950 with the publication of the *Town and Country Planning Textbook* with an article by Jacqueline Tyrwhitt that dealt explicitly with the overlay technique. The book consists of a series of articles dealing with planning and design methods and issues and provides the first explicit discussion of the overlay technique (Steinitz et al. 1976, see also Collins et al. 1998).

In an example given by Tyrwhitt, four maps (relief, hydrology, rock types, and soil drainage) were drawn on transparent papers at the same scale, and referenced to common control features. These data maps were then combined into one land characteristics map which provided a synthesis, interpretation, and a judicious blending of the first four maps (Tyrwhitt 1950, Steinitz et al. 1976). This sieve-mapping, overlay method was widely accepted and incorporated in the large-scale planning of the British new towns and other development projects after World War II (Lyle and Stutz 1983, McSheffrey 1999). At the end of the war McHarg took a correspondence course offered by Tyrwhitt and others. McHarg was also involved in new town planning in the early 1950s in Scotland, so he was quite aware of the British new town program. As a result, he was introduced to the concept of suitability analysis early in his career.

George Angus Hills' plan for Ontario Province (1961) is a pioneering North American example that employed a well-documented data-overlay technique (Belknap and Furtado 1967, 1968; Naveh and Lieberman 1994; Ndubisi 1997). Hills was on the staff of the Ontario Department of Lands and Forests. His technique divides regions into consecutively smaller units of physiographic similarity based on a gradient scale of climate and landform features. Through a process of comparing each physiographic site type or homogenous land unit to a predetermined set of general land-use categories and rankings of potential or limitation for each use or activity, the resulting units were regrouped into larger geographic patterns called landscape units and again ranked to determine their relative potentials for dominant and multiple uses. The land-use activity with the highest feasibility ranking within a landscape unit was recommended as a major use (Belknap and Furtado 1967).

The year after Hills' Ontario plan, Philip Lewis, a landscape architect at the University of Wisconsin-Madison and principal consultant to the Wisconsin Department of Resource Development, applied an overlay analysis technique to evaluate natural resources for the entire state of Wisconsin. This work was a direct response to the growth and demand for outdoor recreation across the state. According to Ndubisi, "Unlike Hills, whose work was based primarily on examining biological and physical (biophysical) systems such as landforms and soils, Lewis was concerned more with perceptual features such as vegetation and outstanding scenery" (1997, p. 21). Lewis stressed the importance of the patterns, both natural and cultural within the landscape. He combined individual landscape elements of water, wetlands, vegetation, and significant topography through overlays onto a composite map depicting

Wisconsin's areas of prime environmental importance (Belknap and Furtado 1967, 1968; Steinitz et al. 1976). By combining resource inventory data and soil survey data, Lewis was able to create maps that identified intrinsic (natural) patterns. Once additional resources were grouped by patterns and mapped, points were assigned to major and additional resources and totaled to identify relative priority areas. Demand for planned uses and limitations of each priority area for specific uses were then combined to assign specific uses to each priority area (Collins et al. 1998).

In another early example of the overlay technique, Christopher Alexander and Marvin Manheim (1962) mapped a set of twenty-six decision criteria for highway location (Steinitz et al. 1976). The study was conducted at the Civil Engineering Systems Laboratory, Massachusetts Institute of Technology. Alexander and Manheim propose a hierarchical tree as a formal procedure for combining factors. Each map is shaded separately to show the better or worse areas for highway alignment. They proceed to identify areas of similarly shaded patterns and superimpose these different maps photographically on one print. In doing so, they assigned weights to each set of decision criteria that were then represented on the final composite print.

McHarg, Lewis, and Hills refined their approaches during the 1960s and built their work on all these earlier efforts. McHarg especially advanced previous methods significantly by linking suitability analysis with theory. He provided a theoretical basis for overlaying information. McHarg's approach focused on mapping information on both natural and human-made attributes of the study area and photographing them initially as individual transparent maps (Belknap and Furtado 1967, 1968; McHarg 1969; Gordon 1985). The transparent prints of light and dark values were superimposed over each other to construct the necessary suitability maps for each land use. These x-ray–like composite maps illustrated intrinsic suitabilities for land-use classifications, such as conservation, urbanization, and recreation for the specific planning area. These maps were then combined with each other as overlays to produce an overall composite suitability map (McHarg 1969).

McHarg's inventory process provides one of the first examples of methodological documentation for the overlay technique (with those by Hills and Lewis). McHarg was also the first to advocate the use of the overlay technique to gain an ecological understanding of a place. He noted that "a region is understood as a biophysical and social process comprehensible through the operation of [natural] laws and time. This can be reinterpreted as having explicit opportunities and constraints for any particular human use. A survey will reveal the most fit locations and processes" (1997, p. 321). As a result, he was explicit about the range and sequence of mapped information to be collected. McHarg also observed that the phenomena represented by the maps were *valued* differently by various groups of people and thus could be weighted differently, depending on the circumstance.

Ecology is a language for reading landscapes. McHarg notes, "written on the place and upon its inhabitants lies mute all physical, biological and cultural history awaiting to be understood by those who can read it." His 1967 *Landscape Architecture* article, "An Ecological Method for Landscape Architecture," outlines an ecological method and is one of McHarg's earliest published explanations of suitability. He advocates inventorying all unique or scarce features and environmentally sensitive areas. He also advances the notion of "communities of land use," that is, their ecologies or how uses interact with one another, how compatible or incompatible they are with each other. A place may be intrinsically suited for many uses, but some of these uses may fit with neighboring uses better than others.

According to McHarg, his method can be used in both urban and rural areas. He explains that "successive stages of urbanization" are adaptations to the environment, "some of which are successful, some not." He provides a model for urban human ecology by comparing urban systems regressing from health or evolving towards health. McHarg suggests that his model be used both for diagnosing the health of the city and for prescribing appropriate interventions.

McHarg's 1968 "A Comprehensive Highway Route Selection Method," is a specific example of the application of his method to highway route selection. According to McHarg, his method enables social and aesthetic values to be incorporated into the route selection process. His highway route selection work during the 1960s provided the methodological foundation for environmental impact statements and other types of environment assessments mandated by the National Environmental Policy Act (NEPA) and many similar laws enacted by the federal, state, and local governments in the United States during the "environmental decade" of the 1970s. Environmental impact assessment documents also have become mandatory in many other nations since the 1970s. NEPA's purpose is

> To declare a national policy which will encourage productive and enjoyable harmony between man and his environment; to promote efforts which will prevent or eliminate damage to the environment and biosphere and stimulate the health and welfare of man; to enrich the understanding of ecological systems and natural resources important to the Nation; and to establish a Council on Environmental Quality.

NEPA required federal agencies "to consider every significant aspect of the environmental impact of a proposed action" and federal agencies to "utilize a systematic, interdisciplinary approach which will ensure the integrated use of the natural and social sciences and the environmental design arts in planning and in decision making which will have an impact on man's environment."

Furthermore, NEPA instructed federal agencies to "identify and develop methods and procedures . . . which will ensure that presently unquantified environmental amenities and values may be given appropriate consideration in decision making along with economic and technical considerations."

NEPA was exactly what McHarg had been advocating during the 1960s, and he had been refining for a decade the "methods and procedures" for assessing environmental impacts. His best known pre-NEPA suitability work involved highways. During the 1950s and 1960s, interstate highways had been built at a rapid pace, providing an efficient transportation system but destroying many communities, much farmland, and significant amounts of environmentally sensitive lands in the process. Because of President Dwight Eisenhower's admiration for Hitler's *autobahn*, the interstate highway system turned its back on the earlier American, more gentile tradition of parkways and turnpikes (such as the Pennsylvania Turnpike). Whereas the parkways had been designed, at least in part, by landscape architects, civil engineers dominated the planning of the interstates, a situation that McHarg criticized vehemently.

McHarg sought to recapture the involvement of landscape architects. In this quest, he had a powerful ally in Lady Bird Johnson. His work on Interstate 95 between the Delaware and Raritan Rivers in New Jersey is an explanation of this alternative method for highway location. He suggested that "presently unquantified environmental amenities" be considered in the route selection process. Specifically, he advocated that traditional cost-benefit analysis be replaced with one that assessed "maximum social benefit and the minimum social cost." To accomplish this, the role of the highway needed to be expanded from its single-purpose function of moving traffic to a multipurpose perspective that contributed to community development.

Balance sheets were developed by McHarg for the location of I-95. These balance sheets reveal the highway alignments with the most social benefits with the least social costs. Maps were used to represent these benefits and costs which were then superimposed for interpretation to reveal the most suitable routes.

McHarg has been critical of both sanitation and traffic engineers. In 1976 in "Biological Alternatives to Water Pollution" he suggested alternative techniques for ensuring clean water supplies. He noted that, "The entire subject of water must be seen to be a problem of biology rather than engineering." Biologically based techniques to alleviate water pollution are purposed. In this case, he relied much on the knowledge and expertise of his colleague Ruth Patrick. Dr. Patrick, a leading limnologist, conducted research at the Philadelphia Academy of Natural Science and taught for many years in McHarg's department at Penn.

The article is also based on work he undertook for the U.S. Environmental Protection Agency (EPA) to help the agency implement NEPA. McHarg suggested an administrative structure to plan, manage, and regulate environmental quality, including water quality. Essentially, he suggested using physiographic regions in tandem with watersheds as the geographic basis for planning. McHarg's suggestions were consistent with EPA's response during the 1970s to clean-water legislation. Section 208 of the Clean Water Act mandated an "areawide" approach. In spite of the withdrawal of the federal commitment to Section 208 planning during the 1980s (in fact the overall hostility to the environment and planning by the Reagan administration), areawide, or regional, approaches continued to evolve within EPA. With the Clinton administration the agency was advocating the use of watersheds for planning, much as McHarg had advised two decades earlier.

It is interesting to note that in his 1976 biological alternatives paper McHarg had become a critic of environmental impact statement (EIS) procedures. His criticism was that EISs had become ad hoc project exercises divorced from the comprehensive understanding of regions. His approach for impact analysis was to build the ecological database on the scales of physiographic regions and watersheds, then to draw on that information to assess the consequences of possible actions.

One of the strengths of suitability analysis is its applicability to a broad range of planning situations. In the early 1970s, Wallace, McHarg, Roberts, and Todd was engaged in the planning of The Woodlands new community in Texas. In 1979 McHarg published an explanation of the method used in The Woodlands with his Penn colleagues Arthur Johnson and Jonathan Berger. The article, "A Case Study in Ecological Planning," is perhaps the best single description of suitability analysis and was included in a comprehensive book on land-use planning methods.

In addition to maps, matrices are used in suitability analysis. McHarg and his associates explain that these matrices can be used to explore relationships, such as those between land uses and development activities and those between development activities and the landscape. Maps and matrices are used to reveal both opportunities and constraints for various land uses.

For a new town, such as The Woodlands, the range of land uses is broad. The Woodlands site presented many constraints to development. It was flat, forested, and wet. The development principles that guided the new town planning included the minimization of disruption of the hydrological regime, the preservation of the woodlands, the preservation of wildlife habitats, the minimization of development costs, and the avoidance of hazards to life and health. Suitability analysis addressed all these principles.

The most serious constraint was the threat of flooding. New development was certain to alter an already delicate flood regime. The solution was to recognize natural drainage systems and to fit the development accordingly.

Flooding is a serious issue and new development frequently exacerbates the problem. The application of suitability analysis at The Woodlands by McHarg and his associates illustrates how new development can occur without endangering the health and safety of people or the environmental quality of a place. Health and safety are central to the methods and techniques for ecological planning developed by McHarg. He illustrated that decisions can be made in an environmentally responsible manner with methods that are replicable.

References

Abercrombie, P., and T. H. Johnson. 1922. *The Doncaster Planning Scheme.* London: University Press of Liverpool.

Adams, Thomas. 1934. *The Design of Residential Areas.* Cambridge, Mass.: Harvard University Press.

Alexander, Christopher, and Marvin Manheim. 1962. *The Use of Diagrams in Highway Route Location: An Experiment.* Cambridge, Mass: MIT Civil Engineering Systems Lab.

Belknap, Raymond K., and John G. Furtado. 1967. *Three Approaches to Environmental Resource Analysis.* Washington, D.C.: The Conservation Foundation.

———. 1968. "The Natural Land Unit as a Planning Base." *Landscape Architecture* 58(2):145–147.

Collins, Michael G., Frederick R. Steiner, and Michael Russman. 1998. " Land-Use Suitability Analysis: Retrospect and Prospects." Under revision for the *Journal of Planning Education and Research.*

Eliot, Charles. 1902. *Charles Eliot, Landscape Architect.* Boston: Houghton, Mifflin.

Forshaw, J. H., and Patrick Abercrombie. 1943. *County of London Plan.* London: Macmillan.

Gordon, Steven I. 1985. *Computer Models in Environmental Planning.* New York: Van Nostrand Reinhold.

Hills, G. A. 1961. "The Ecological Basis for Natural Resource Management." In *The Ecological Basis for Land-use Planning.* Ontario, Canada: Ontario Department of Lands and Forests Research Branch.

Lyle, John, and Frederick Stutz. 1983. "Computerized Land Use Suitability Mapping." In W. J. Ripple, ed. *Geographic Information Systems for Resource Management: A Compendium.* Falls Church, Va.: American Society for Photogrammetry and Remote Sensing and American Congress on Surveying and Mapping.

Manning, Warren. 1913. "The Billerica Town Plan." *Landscape Architecture* 3:108–18.

McHarg, Ian L. 1969. *Design with Nature.* Garden City, N.Y.: The Natural History Press.

————. 1997. "Ecology and Design." In George F. Thompson and Frederick R. Steiner, eds. *Ecological Design and Planning*. New York: Wiley.

McSheffrey, Gerald. 1999. *Planning Derry, Planning and Politics in Northern Ireland*. Liverpool, England: Liverpool University Press.

Naveh, Zev, and Arthur S. Lieberman. 1994, 1984. *Landscape Ecology: Theory and Applications*. New York: Springer-Verlag.

Ndubisi, Forster. 1997. "Landscape Ecological Planning." In George F. Thompson and Frederick R. Steiner, eds., *Ecological Design and Planning*. New York: Wiley.

Regional Planning Staff. 1929. *The Graphic Regional Plan, Regional Plan of New York and Its Environs*, Vol. 1. New York: Regional Plan Staff.

Steinitz, Carl, Paul Parker, and Lawrie Jordan. 1976. "Hand Drawn Overlays: Their History and Prospective Uses." *Landscape Architecture* 9:444–55.

Tyrwhitt, Jacqueline. 1950. "Surveys for Planning." In *Town and Country Planning Textbook*. London: Architectural Press.

16

An Ecological Method for Landscape Architecture (1967)

The editor of Landscape Architecture *magazine during the 1960s and 1970s was Grady Clay, a friend and admirer of McHarg. Clay published several of McHarg's early works, including this article proposing that landscape architects embrace an ecological model. No other discipline besides landscape architecture provides a bridge between the environmental sciences and the design and planning professions. McHarg observed that this situation offers landscape architects a unique opportunity for leadership, a role that they have only partially pursued.*

In many cases a qualified statement is, if not the most propitious, at least the most prudent. In this case it would only be gratuitous. I believe that ecology provides the single indispensable basis for landscape architecture and regional planning. I would state in addition that it has now, and will increasingly have, a profound relevance for both city planning and architecture.

Where the landscape architect commands ecology he is the only bridge between the natural sciences and the planning and design professions, the proprietor of the most perceptive view of the natural world which science or art has provided. This can be at once his unique attribute, his passport to relevance and productive social utility. With the acquisition of this competence the sad image of ornamental horticulture, handmaiden to architecture after the fact, the caprice and arbitrariness of "clever" designs can be dismissed forever. In short, ecology offers emancipation to landscape architecture.

This is not the place for a scholarly article on ecology. We are interested in it selfishly, as those who can and must apply it. Our concern is for a method which has the power to reveal nature as process, containing intrinsic form.

Ecology is generally described as the study of the interactions of organisms and environment which includes other organisms. The particular interests of landscape architecture are focused only upon a part of this great, synoptic concern. This might better be defined as the study of physical and biological processes, as dynamic and interacting, responsive to laws, having limiting factors and exhibiting certain opportunities and constraints, employed in planning and design for human use. At this juncture two possibilities present themselves. The first is to attempt to present a general theory of ecology and the planning processes. This is a venture which I long to undertake, but this is not the time nor place to attempt it. The other alternative is to present a method which has been tested empirically at many scales from a continent, a major region, a river basin, physiographic regions, sub-regional areas, and a metropolitan region to a single city. In every case, I submit, it has been triumphantly revelatory.[1]

First, it is necessary to submit a proposition to this effect: The place, the plants, animals, and men upon it are only comprehensible in terms of physical and biological evolution. Written on the place and upon its inhabitants lies mute all physical, biological, and cultural history awaiting to be understood by those who can read it. It is thus necessary to begin at the beginning if we are to understand the place, the man, or his co-tenants of this phenomenal universe. This is the prerequisite for intelligent intervention and adaptation. So let us begin at the beginning. We start with historical geology. The place, any place, can be understood only through its physical evolution. What history of mountain building and ancient seas, uplifting, folding, sinking, erosion, and glaciation have passed here and left its marks? These explain its present form. Yet the effects of climate and later of plants and animals have interacted upon geological processes and these too lie mute in the record of the rocks. Both climate and geology can be invoked to interpret physiography, the current configuration of the place. Arctic differs from tropics, desert from delta, the Himalayas from the Gangetic Plain. The Appalachian Plateau differs from the Ridge and Valley Province and all of these from the piedmont and the coastal plain. If one now knows historical geology, climate, and physiography then the water regimen becomes comprehensible—the pattern of rivers and aquifers, their physical properties and relative abundance, oscillation between flood and drought. Rivers are young or old, they vary by orders; their pattern and distribution, as for aquifers, are directly consequential upon geology, climate, and physiography.

Knowing the foregoing and the prior history of plant evolution, we can now comprehend the nature and pattern of soils. As plants are highly selective to environmental factors, by identifying physiographic, climatic zones, and soils we can perceive order and predictability in the distribution of constituent plant communities. Indeed, the plant communities are more perceptive to environmental variables than we can be with available data, and we can thus infer environmental factors from the presence of plants. Animals are fundamentally plant-related so that given the preceding information, with the addition of the stage of succession of the plant communities and their age, it is possible both to understand and to predict the species, abundance or scarcity of wild animal populations. If there are no acorns there will be no squirrels; an old forest will have few deer; an early succession can support many. Resources also exist where they do for good and sufficient reasons— coal, iron, limestone, productive soils, water in relative abundance, transportation routes, fall lines, and the termini of water transport. And so the land-use map becomes comprehensible when viewed through this perspective

The information so acquired is a gross ecological inventory and contains the data bank for all further investigations. The next task is the interpretation of these data to analyze existing and to propose future human land use and management. The first objective is the inventory of unique or scarce phenomena, the technique for which Philip Lewis is renowned.[2] In this all sites of unique scenic, geological, ecological, or historical importance are located. Enlarging this category we can interpret the geological data to locate economic minerals. Geology, climate, and physiography will locate dependable water resources. Physiography will reveal slope and exposure which, with soil and water, can be used to locate areas suitable for agriculture by types; the foregoing, with the addition of plant communities, will reveal intrinsic suitabilities for both forestry and recreation. The entire body of data can be examined to reveal sites for urbanization, industry, transportation routes, indeed any human land-using activity. This interpretive sequence would produce a body of analytical material, but the end product for a region would include a map of unique sites, the location of economic minerals, the location of water resources, a slope and exposure map, a map of agricultural suitabilities by types, a similar map for forestry, one each for recreation and urbanization.

These maps of intrinsic suitability would indicate highest and best uses for the entire study area. But this is not enough. These are single uses ascribed to discrete areas. In the forest there are likely to be dominant or co-dominant trees and other subordinate species. We must seek to prescribe all coexistent, compatible uses which may occupy each area. To this end it is necessary to develop a matrix in which all possible land uses are shown on each coordinate. Each is then examined against all others to determine the degree of compatibility or incompatibility. As an example, a single area of forest may be managed for forestry, either hardwood or pulp; it may be utilized for water management objectives; it may fulfill an erosion-control function; it can be managed for wildlife and hunting, recreation, and for villages and hamlets. Here we have not land use in the normal sense but *communities* of land uses. The end product would be a map of present and prospective land uses, in communities of compatibilities, with dominants, co-dominants, and subordinates derived from an understanding of nature as process responsive to laws, having limiting factors, constituting a value system, and exhibiting opportunities and constraints to human use.

Now this is not a plan. It does not contain any information of demand. This last is the province of the regional scientist, the econometrician, the economic planner. The work is thus divided between the natural scientist, the regional planner-landscape architect who interprets the land and its resources, and the economics-based planner who determines demand, locational preferences, investment, and fiscal policies. If demand information is available, then the formulation of a plan is possible, and the demand components can be allocated for urban growth, for the nature and form of the metropolis, for the pattern of regional growth.

So what has our method revealed? First, it allows us to understand nature as process insofar as the natural sciences permit. Second, it reveals casuality. The place *is* because. Next, it permits us to interpret natural processes as resources, to prescribe and even to predict for prospective land uses, not singly but in compatible communities. Finally, given information on demand and investment, we are enabled to produce a plan for a continent or a few hundred acres based upon natural process. That is not a small accomplishment.

You might well agree that this is a valuable and perhaps even indispensable method for regional planning, but is it as valuable for landscape architecture? I say that any project, save a small garden or the raddled heart of a city where nature has long gone, which is undertaken without a full comprehension and employment of natural process as form-giver, is suspect at best and capriciously irrelevant at worst. I submit that the ecological method is the *sine qua non* for all landscape architecture.

Yet, I hear you say, those who doubt, that the method may be extremely valuable for regional rural problems, but can it enter the city and reveal a comparable utility? Yes, indeed it can, but in crossing this threshold the method changes. When used to examine metropolitan growth the data remain the same but the interpretation is focused upon the overwhelming demand for urban land uses, and it is oriented to the prohibitions and permissiveness exhibited by natural process to urbanization on the one hand and the presence of locational and resource factors which one would select for satisfactory urban environments on the other. But the litany remains the same: historical geology, climate, physiography, the water regimen, soils, plants, animals, and land use. This is the source from which the interpretation is made although the grain becomes finer.

Yet you say, the method has not entered the city proper; you feel that it is still a device for protecting natural process against the blind despoliation of ignorance and Philistinism. But the method can enter the city and we can proceed with our now familiar body of information to examine the city in an ecological way. We have explained that the place was "because" and to explain "because," all of physical and biological evolution was invoked. So too with the city. But to explain "because" we invoke not only natural evolution but cultural evolution as well. To do this we make a distinction between the "given" and the "made" forms. The former is the natural landscape identity, the latter is the accumulation of the adaptations to the given form which constitute the present city. Rio is different from New Orleans, Kansas City from Lima, Amsterdam from San Francisco, because. By employing the ecological method we can discern the reason for the location of the city, comprehend its natural form, discern those elements of identity which are critical and expressive, both those of physiography and vegetation, and develop a program for the preservation and enhancement of that identity. The method is equally applicable when one confronts the made form. The successive stages of urbanization are examined as adaptations to the environment, some of which are successful, some not. Some enter the inventory of resources and contribute to the *genius loci*. As for the given form, this method allows us to perceive the elements of identity in a scale of values. One can then prepare a comprehensive landscape plan for a city and feed the elements of identity, natural process, and the palette for formal expression into the comprehensive planning process.

You still demur. The method has not yet entered into the putrid parts of the city. It needs rivers and palisades, hill and valleys, woodlands and parkland. When will it confront slums and overcrowding, congestion and pollution, anarchy and ugliness? Indeed the method can enter into the very heart of the city and by so doing may save us from the melancholy criteria of economic determinism which have proven so disappointing to the orthodoxy of city planning or the alternative of unbridled "design" which haunts architecture. But here again we must be selective as we return to the source in ecology. We will find little that is applicable in energy system ecology, analysis of food pyramids, relations defined in terms of predator-prey, competition, or those other analytical devices so efficacious for plant and animal ecology. But we can well turn to an ecological model which contains multi-faceted criteria for measuring ecosystems and we can select health as an encompassing criterion (table 3). The model is my own and as such it is suspect for I am not an ecologist, but each of the parts is the product of a distinguished ecologist.[3] Let us hope that the assembly of the constituents does not diminish their veracity, for they have compelling value.

The most obvious example is life and death. Life is the evolution of a single egg into the complexity of the organism. Death is the retrogression of a complex organism into a few simple elements. If this model is true, it allows us to examine a city, neighborhood, community institution, family, city plan, architectural, or landscape design in these terms. This model suggests that any

Table 3. Ecological Model for Healthy Systems

Retrogression	Evolution
Ill health	Health
Simplicity	Complexity
Uniformity	Diversity
Independence	Interdependence (symbiosis)
Instability	Stability (steady state)
Low number of species	High number of species
High entropy	Low entropy

system moving toward simplicity, uniformity, instability with a low number of species and high entropy is retrogressing; any system moving in that direction is moving towards ill health.

Conversely, complexity, diversity, stability (steady state), with a high number of species and low entropy are indicators of health, and systems moving in this direction are evolving. As a simple application let us map, in tones on transparencies, statistics of all physical disease, all mental disease, and all social disease. If we also map income, age of population, density, ethnicity, and quality of the physical environment we have on the one hand discerned the environment of health, the environment of pathology and we have accumulated the data which allow interpretation of the social and physical environmental components of health and pathology. Moreover, we have the other criteria of the model which permit examination from different directions. If this model is true and the method good, it may be the greatest contribution of the ecological method to diagnosis and prescription for the city.

But, you say, all this may be very fine, but landscape architects are finally designers—when will you speak to ecology and design? I will. Lou Kahn, the most perceptive of men, foresaw the ecological method even through these intractable, inert materials which he infuses with life when he spoke of "existence will," the will to be. The place is because. It is and is in the process of becoming. This we must be able to read, and ecology provides the language. By being, the place or the creature has form. Form and process are indivisible aspects of a single phenomenon. The ecological method allows one to understand form as an explicit point in evolutionary process. Again, Lou Kahn has made clear to us the distinction between form and design. Cup is form and begins from the cupped hand. Design is the creation of the cup, transmuted by the artist, but never denying its formal origins. As a profession, landscape architecture has exploited a pliant earth, tractable and docile plants to make much that is arbitrary, capricious, and inconsequential. We could not see the cupped hand as giving form to the cup, the earth and its processes as giving form to our works. The ecological method is then also the perception of form, an insight to the given form, implication for the made form which is to say design, and this, for landscape architects, may be its greatest gift.

Notes

1. Australia; Rhodesia; the United Kingdom; the Gangetic Plain, the Potomac River Basin; Allegheny Plateau; Ridge and Valley Province; Great Valley Province; Piedmont; Coastal Plain; the Green Spring and Worthington Valleys; Philadelphia Standard Metropolitan Statistical Area; and Washington, D.C. See Ian L. McHarg and David A. Wallace, 1965, "Plan for the Valleys vs. Spectre of Uncontrolled Growth," *Landscape Architecture* (April). (Reprinted in chapter 2.)
2. See Philip H. Lewis, Jr., 1964 "Quality Corridors for Wisconsin," *Landscape Architecture* (January).
3. "Simplicity, Complexity; Uniformity, Diversity; Independence, Interdependence; Instability, stability" thesis by Dr. Robert McArthur; "Stability, Instability," thesis by Dr. Luna Leopold; "Low and High Number of Species," thesis by Dr. Ruth Patrick; "Low and High Entropy," thesis by Dr. Harold F. Blum; "Ill-Health, Health," thesis by Dr. Ruth Patrick.

17

A Comprehensive Highway Route
Selection Method (1968)

This paper was presented at the 47th Annual Meeting of the Committee on Roadside Development in 1968. It was published in the Highway Research Record *by the Highway Research Board of the National Academy of Sciences-National Academy of Engineering.*

McHarg's method for highway route selection had considerable influence in the 1960s. In particular, it attracted the attention of Lady Bird Johnson. Mrs. Johnson presented McHarg's ideas to senior federal transportation officials. She even suggested that McHarg become director of the Bureau of Public Roads. McHarg helped locate several highways, including Interstate 95 through part of New Jersey, and the Richmond Parkway on Staten Island. Although some road locations were influenced by McHarg or his method, too many highway projects remain insensitive to environments and to human communities.

Abstract

The major deficiency in prevailing highway route selection method has been the inability to include social values, including natural resources and aesthetic values, within the criteria utilized. In this study, an attempt has been made to identify components of social value, natural resources, and scenic quality, and to locate these geographically. It is presumed that the area of lowest social value, if transected by a highway, incurs the least social cost. The normal determinants of highway route selection, topography, soils, etc., have been expanded to include management or impairment of groundwater and surface water resources, susceptibility to erosion, etc. When highway corridors of minimum social cost and minimum physiographic obstruction were revealed, they were tested against their effect on scenic values. The objective of providing an excellent scenic experience was considered as a social value created by the highway. The corridor of least social cost was next tested against the degree to which it could create new and productive land uses where these would be necessary and welcome. The sum of least social cost and highest benefit alignment was identified. It is described as the rate of maximum social benefit.

The method revealed the route of least social cost and least physiographic obstruction as a funnel of land parallel to Jacobs Creek, proceeding along the base of Pennington and Sourland Mountain and widening into a trumpet as it meets the Raritan River. This alignment has the added merit of permitting management of the aquifer-recharge area which it parallels to the benefit of groundwater resources in the Delaware–Raritan area. It provides an excellent scenic experience. It should additionally induce new and productive land uses in the West Trenton area and the Raritan River communities in New Jersey.

Introduction

The importance of highways is incontrovertible. They are essential components of the economy. The modern highway incorporates high levels of engineering skill in its geometric characteristics and traffic performance. Yet the increasing opposition to proposed highways reveals a fundamental weakness. The route-selection process has, to date, been unable to recognize and respond to important social and aesthetic values. As a result, the major highway is increasingly viewed as a destroyer, carving remorselessly through the hearts of cities, outraging San Francisco and Boston, humbling Faneuil Hall, destroying precious urban parks as in Philadelphia, offending great sectors of metropolitan population, and threatening resources and values such as Rock Creek Park and the Georgetown waterfront in the nation's capital. Examples abound. The major highway is increasingly regarded as a tyrant, unresponsive to public values, disdainful of the people it purports to serve.

The cause can be simply identified. It lies in the inadequacy of the criteria for route selection. These have been developed for rural areas where social values are scarce and engineering considerations paramount. These criteria have not been enlarged to deal with situations where social values hold a primary importance and engineering considerations are accorded a much lower value. The remedy lies in inverting the criteria to obtain a balance between social-aesthetic values and the orthodoxy of engineering considerations.

This study seeks to develop a more comprehensive route-selection method including social, resource, and aesthetic criteria for a section of proposed Interstate 95 (I-95) between the Delaware and Raritan Rivers.

Social Values in Highway Route Selection

The method utilized by the Bureau of Public Roads for route selection involves calculating the savings and costs derived from a proposed highway facility. Savings include savings in time and in operating costs and reduction in accidents through construction of a new highway facility. The costs are those of construction and maintenance necessary to obtain these savings with a minimum ratio of savings to costs of 1.2 to 1.0. Any qualitative factors are considered descriptively after the conclusion of the cost-benefit analysis.

The Bureau of Public Roads seeks to enlarge this method and develop a land-use model in which more parameters can be included in both cost and benefit calculations. The bureau was instrumental in initiating the Penn-Jersey Transportation Study which sought to advance the science of highway location. It seems reasonable to assume that it would welcome any serious effort to improve highway route selection method.

The objective of an improved method should be to incorporate social, resource, and aesthetic values in addition to the normal criteria of physiographic, traffic, and engineering considerations. In short, the method should reveal the highway alignment having the maximum social benefit and the minimum social cost. This poses many difficult problems. It is clear that many new considerations must be interjected into the cost-benefit equation and that many of these are considered nonprice benefits. Yet the present method of highway cost-benefit analysis merely allocates approximate money values to convenience, a commodity as difficult to quantify as health or beauty.

The relevant considerations will vary from location to location, with land and building values preponderant in central urban areas and scenic beauty dominant in certain rural areas. It should, however, be possible to identify a number of critical determinants for each area under consideration.

Criteria for Interstate Highway Route Selection

Interstate highways should maximize public and private benefits by (1) increasing the facility, convenience, pleasure, and safety of traffic movement; (2) safeguarding and enhancing land, water, air, and biotic resources; (3) contributing to public and private objectives of urban renewal, metropolitan and regional development, industry, commerce, residence, recreation, public health, conservation, and beautification; and (4) generating new productive land uses and sustaining or enhancing existing land uses.

Such criteria include the orthodoxy of route selection, but place them in a larger context of social responsibility. The highway is no longer considered only in terms of automotive movement within its right-of-way, but in context of all physical, biological, and social processes within its area of influence.

The highway is thus considered as a major public investment that will transform land uses and values and that will affect the economy, the way of life, health, and visual experience of the entire population within its sphere of influence. It should be located and designed in relation to this expanded role.

Positively, the highway can

- Facilitate safe, convenient traffic movement
- Provide key investment for urban renewal, and metropolitan and regional development
- Maximize the visual quality of movement
- Locate new, productive land uses
- Reveal the physical and cultural identity of the region it transects
- Provide access to existing inaccessible resources
- Link scenic and recreational resources

Negatively, the highway can

- Constitute a health hazard due to stress, anxiety, lead, hydrocarbons, ozone, carcinogens, positive atmospheric ionization
- Constitute a nuisance due to noise, glare, fumes, dust, danger, ugliness
- Destroy existing resources—scenic, historic, ground and surface water, forests, farmland, marshes, wildlife habitats, areas of recreational value, and areas of natural beauty
- Reduce property values by any of the above, plus division of property, creation of barriers, and loss of access
- Destroy existing communities and their hinterlands by transecting them, denying access, inconsiderate alignment, and dissonant scale, in addition to the preceding deleterious effects

It is clear that the highway route should be considered a multipurpose rather than a single-purpose facility. It is also clear that when a highway route is so considered, there may be conflicting objectives. As in other multipurpose planning, the objective should be to maximize all potential complementary social benefits and reduce social costs.

This means that the shortest distance between two points meeting predetermined geometric standards is not the best route. Nor is the shortest distance over the cheapest land. The best route is that which provides the maximum social benefit at the least social cost.

The present method of cost-benefit analysis as employed for route selection has two major components: the savings in time, operating costs, and safety provided by the proposed facility; and the sum of engineering, land and building purchase, financing, administrative, construction, operation, and maintenance costs.

On the credit side it seems reasonable to allocate all economic benefits derived from the highway. These benefits accrue from the upgrading of land use, frequently from agricultural to industrial, commercial, or residential uses. On the debit side, highways can and do reduce economic values; they do constitute a health hazard, a nuisance, and danger; they can destroy community integrity, institutions, residential quality, scenic, historic, and recreational values.

This being the case, it appears necessary to represent the sum of effects attributable to a proposed highway alignment and distinguish these as benefits-savings and costs. In certain cases these can be priced and can be designated price benefits, price savings, or price costs. In other cases, where valuation is difficult, certain factors can be identified as nonprice benefits, savings, or costs.

A balance sheet in which most of the components of benefit and cost are shown should reveal alignments having the maximum social benefit at the least social cost (see tables 4 and 5).

Considerations of traffic benefits from the Bureau of Public Roads can be computed for alternative alignments. The cost of alternative routes can be calculated. Areas where increased land and building values may result can be located, if only tentatively, in relation to the highway and prospective intersections. Prospective depreciation of land and building value can also be approximately located. Increased convenience, safety, and pleasure will presumably be provided within the highway right-of-way; inconvenience, danger, and displeasure will parallel its path on both sides. The degree to which the highway sustains certain community values can be described, as well as the offense to health, community, scenery, and other important resources.

Table 4. Components of Benefits and Costs Attributable to
a Proposed Highway Alignment

BENEFITS AND SAVINGS	COSTS
Price benefits	Price costs
Operating economies: Function of distance × volume × constant for operating economies and safety	*Costs*: Function of distance × engineering, land and building acquisition, construction, financing administration, operation, and maintenance
Economic values created: Increment of increased land and building values attributable to the highway within its sphere of influence	*Economic values lost*: Increment of reduced land and building values due to the same cause

(continues)

Table 4. (continued)

Nonprice benefits	Nonprice costs
Values added: Increased convenience, safety, and pleasure provided to drivers on the facility	*Values lost*: Decreased convenience, safety, and pleasure to populations and institutions within the sphere of influence; health hazard, nuisance, and danger
Price savings	Price costs
Construction economies: Propitious conditions of topography, geology, drainage foundations, and minimum structures	*Construction costs*: Inordinate costs due to difficult topography, geology, drainage, foundations, and necessity for many and/or expensive structures
Nonprice savings	Nonprice costs
Social values saved:	*Social costs:*
Community	Community values lost
Institutional	Institutional values lost
Residential	Residential values lost
Scenic	Scenic values lost
Historic	Historic values lost
Surface water	Surface water resources impaired
Groundwater	Groundwater resources impaired
Forest water	Forest water resources impaired
Wildlife	Wildlife water resources impaired

Application of the Comprehensive Method to I-95 between the Delaware and Raritan Rivers

This area under consideration is defined by a discontinuous ridge composed of Baldpate, Pennington, and Sourland Mountains to the northwest, and the Delaware–Raritan Canal to the southeast; the Delaware and Raritan Rivers form the remaining southwest and northeast boundaries. Urbanization is concentrated in and around Trenton to the southwest, New Brunswick-Bound Brook-Manville-Somerville to the northeast, with the intervening area substantially rural piedmont landscape with localized settlement in the town of Princeton and the villages of Pennington, Hopewell, and Griggstown. The majority of the area falls within the Stonybrook–Millstone watershed.

The entire area constitutes a segment of the Philadelphia–Trenton–New York corridor running southwest–northeast in the piedmont, paralleling the fall line dividing piedmont from the coastal plain.

This is an attractive landscape defined by wooded hills, drained by pleasant streams, and graced by decent farms. Princeton is its spiritual capital, and the quality of this institution and its surrounding landscape constitutes a prime locational value for the area. While terminated by industrial locations in Trenton and New Brunswick–Bound Brook and Somerville, the intervening valley is predominantly a rural-residential area. In such an area certain social values can be described, if only in normative terms—scenic beauty, residential quality, the integrity of institutions, towns, and villages. The diminution or impairment of these values can be described, again only in normative terms, as social costs.

Toward this end a number of maps have been prepared. They share the description of approximations as follows:

1. Sequence related to construction savings and costs
   a. Topography
   b. Land values
2. Sequence related to social values
   a. Urbanization
   b. Residential quality
   c. Historic value
   d. Agricultural value
   e. Recreational values
   f. Wildlife value
   g. Water values
   h. Susceptibility to erosion
3. Scenic value
4. Physiographic obstructions

In every case three values are allocated to each parameter. The presumption is that the corridor of maximum social utility will transect the zones of lowest social value and provide the major social benefit (see tables 4 and 5).

The method employed uses transparent overlays for each parameter. Each of these has three values, the highest representing the greatest physical and engineering obstruction to highway location. The highest value of obstruction is represented by a dark tone, the intermediate value by a light tone, while the lowest category is the residue and is fully transparent. When all of the parameters are overlaid on the base map, it is presumed that the maximum darkness represents the greatest aggregate physiographic and social value obstruction. In contrast, light areas, representing the least physiographic obstruction and the least social value, offer prospective corridors for consideration.

It is immediately conceded that not all of the parameters are coequal. Existing urbanization and residential quality are more important than scenic value or wildlife. Yet it is reasonable to presume that where there is an over-

Table 5. Suggested Criteria for Interstate Highway Route Selection

BENEFITS AND SAVINGS	COSTS
Price benefits	Price costs
Reduced time distance	Survey
Reduced gasoline costs	Engineering
Reduced oil costs	Land and building acquisition
Reduced tire costs	Construction costs
Reduced vehicle depreciation	Financing costs
Increased traffic volume	Administrative costs
	Operating and maintenance costs
Increase in value (land and buildings)	*Reduction in value (land and buildings)*
Industrial values	Industrial values
Commercial values	Commercial values
Residential values	Residential values
Recreational values	Recreational values
Institutional values	Institutional values
Agricultural land values	Agricultural land values
Nonprice benefits	Nonprice costs
Increased convenience	Reduced convenience to adjacent properties
Increased safety	Reduced safety to adjacent populations
Increased pleasure	Reduced pleasure to adjacent populations
	Health hazard and nuisance from toxic fumes, noise, glare, and dust
Price savings	Price costs
Nonlimiting topography	Difficult topography
Adequate foundation conditions present	Poor foundations
Adequate drainage conditions present	Poor drainage
Available sands, gravels, etc.	Absence of construction materials
Minimum bridge crossings, culverts, and other structures required	Abundant structures required
Nonprice savings	Nonprice costs
Community values maintained	Community values lost
Institutional values maintained	Institutional values lost
Residential quality maintained	Residential values lost
Scenic quality maintained	Scenic values lost
Historic values maintained	Historic values lost
Recreational values maintained	Recreational values lost
Surface water systems unimpaired	Surface water resources impaired
Groundwater resources unimpaired	Groundwater resources impaired
Forest resources maintained	Forest resources impaired
Wildlife resources maintained	Wildlife resources impaired

whelming concentration of physiographic obstruction and social value that such areas should be excluded from consideration; where these factors are absent, there is a presumption that such areas justify consideration.

This is not yet a precise method for highway route selection, yet it has the merit of incorporating all existing parameters, adding new and important social considerations, revealing their locational characteristics, permitting comparison, and revealing aggregates of social values and costs. Whatever limitations of imprecision it may have, it does enlarge and improve the existing method.

The preceding discussion has emphasized the identification of physiographic corridors containing the lowest social values as the preferred route for highways. In discussion of cost-benefit analysis, reference has been made to the role of the proposed highway in creating new values. This view deserves a greater emphasis. Within limits set by the points of origin and destination, and responsive to physiographic obstructions and the pressure of social values, the highway can be used as conscious public policy to create new and productive land uses at appropriate locations. In any such analysis, cost-benefit calculations would require that any depreciation of values would be discounted from value added. In addition, scenic value should be considered as possible added value. It is, of course, possible that a route could be physiographically satisfactory and could avoid social costs, create new economic values at appropriate locations, and also provide a satisfactory scenic experience.

The highway is likely to create new values whether or not this is an act of conscious policy. Without planning, new values may displace existing ones, but even if a net gain results there may well be considerable losses. An example would be a highway transecting a good residential area that then became used for industrial purposes. The increase in land and building values might well be destroyed. The same effect, adjacent to industrial zones in existing urban centers, would accomplish the same benefits without comparable social and economic costs.

Parameter Analysis

1. *Topography.* The area under consideration is a broad valley extending from the Delaware to the Raritan, limited by the Baldpate, Pennington, and Sourland Mountains and divided by Rocky Hill. It contains two major drainage systems, the Stonybrook, draining the area to the west of Rocky Hill, and the Millstone, draining the area to the east. As a result of this physiography, fans of tributaries run tangentially across any direct line between West Trenton and the northeast. Rocky Hill represents a major topographic obstruction.

   The two obvious topographic corridors are to the north and south of

Rocky Hill. The northern corridor follows Jacobs Creek, may proceed either north or south of Pennington Mountain, and then follows the base of Sourland Mountain and widens into a broad swath toward Somerville and New Brunswick. The southern corridor is less defined but falls south of Rocky Hill and parallels U.S. Route 1 and the Pennsylvania railroad.

2. *Land Values.* Land values reflect urbanization and residential quality in nonurbanized areas. Land values are highest in a swath of land including Trenton along U.S. Route 1 to New Brunswick, with an intrusion of high values in and around Princeton. Values tend to decrease generally from this base line to a band on the summit of Sourland Mountain and rise northward. Lowest land values occur in the northern corridor; highest in the southern corridor, influenced by Route 1.

3. *Urbanization.* Trenton, Princeton, New Brunswick, Bound Brook, Manville, Somerville, and Raritan constitute the major areas of urbanization. The villages of Hopewell, Pennington, Lawrenceville, etc., constitute the remainder. Thus urbanization is concentrated at the termini of the area under consideration—in Trenton at one end and the broad band of communities united by the Raritan River at the other. Princeton and the remaining villages are islands between these urban extremes. Southern alignments will affect Lawrenceville, Princeton, Rocky Hill, and recent subdivisions on Dead Tree Run Road, Willow Road, and Township Line Road; a northern alignment will affect the village of Hopewell.

4. *Residential Quality.* Princeton and its environs constitute the major concentration of residential quality as measured by value. Land and building values of $120,000 per acre exist in Princeton alone. An acre to the east contains average values in excess of $60,000. Values fall fairly regularly from the Princeton centroid. Destruction of residential quality will rise as Princeton and its environs are transected and will diminish as distance from Princeton increases. The northern corridor transects areas of lesser residential quality as reflected by value.

5. *Historic Value.* Only one value has been shown reflecting historic importance. Three areas are discerned: the first, Washington's Crossing, Delaware—Trenton; the second, Princeton and environs; and the third, the Millstone River corridor. Northern and southern routes avoid conflict with historic values. A central route does profoundly affect the historic values adjacent to the Millstone River.

6. *Agricultural Value.* The value of agricultural land is twofold: as a source of food and (even more so, in this area) as a land use that sustains an attrac-

tive landscape and maintains it. There is no prime agricultural land in the area, and intrinsic value is quite low, with the single important exception of the visual landscape quality provided by farming. Second-class agricultural land is limited to a triangle of Trenton–Princeton–Pennington. This is more accurately identified as scenic quality.

7. *Recreational Value.* Existing open space is a major constituent of recreational value. This is concentrated in the Stonybrook–Rocky Hill–Millstone–Six Mile Run Impoundment areas. These unite a crescent of land bordering Rocky Hill and the Millstone River. Within this area fall the major open spaces (public and private), the major rivers and streams, and the majority of the recreational potential, with the exception of the mountain ridge. These represent a major social value. Avoidance of these resources would divert the highway corridor to either the north or south of Rocky Hill and outside of the mountain ridge.

8. *Wildlife Value.* These values are concentrated on the forested uplands— Baldpate, Pennington, Sourland Mountain, and Rocky Hill; and the forests and large woodlands, the major rivers, and marshes. There are thus two major divisions of habitat, the forested hills and the water-related system of marshes, streams, and rivers, and their containing valleys. Highways constitute a major hazard to terrestrial wildlife; filling of marshes is a threat to fish-spawning and wildfowl. The forested uplands are concentrated in the defining mountain ridge and Rocky Hill. Both northern and southern corridors can avoid conflict with wildlife resources. The fissures of rivers and streams run tangentially across the major axis of the valley, and any central corridor will adversely affect these resources.

9. *Water Values.* Water resources fall into two categories: surface water and groundwater. As has been observed, the Millstone River is the major drainage, with the Stonybrook as secondary. Toward these run a number of tributaries, generally tangential to the long axis. A highway that follows the central axis of the valley will interfere with surface runoff and affect the behavior of existing streams. This will be exacerbated when the highway is either in cut or fill. It will have the effect of a trench interceptor drain in cut or of a dam in fill. This can be obviated in two ways. The first is by following ridge lines throughout its length, a proposal barely feasible. The second is to locate the highway near the source of the watershed where the effect is minimized. A northern alignment would accomplish this objective.

The inadvertent function of a highway in behaving like a trench drain or dam has an effect on groundwater resources. It can be utilized as a conscious device for management of groundwater. In the negative sense, the highway will cause least offense by passing over the least valuable aquifer—that of Brunswick shale. It will commit a minor offense by passing over the intermediate aquifer of Stockton sandstone. It will create the greatest offense by paving the major aquifer recharge areas.

Positively, the highway, in fill, acting as a dam, can be used to recharge the aquifer and as such would perform a supplementary service. A route south of, and parallel to, the aquifer recharge area at the foot of Sourland Mountain and north of Pennington Mountain would avoid a destructive role on the water regimen and perform a function in groundwater management.

10. *Susceptibility to Erosion.* Highway construction is a process which exacerbates erosion and sedimentation. Excavation and grading combined with hundreds of acres of bare soil guarantee that surface water channels will be surfeited with sediment. This increases the turbidity of streams and reduces photosynthesis, and thus reduces the biotic population. It is often unsightly. It raises flood plains and deposits alluvial silts.

The Stockton sandstone is least susceptible to erosion; Brunswick shale is intermediate; Argillite and Diabase are most susceptible. A southern route crosses mainly Stockton sandstone and Brunswick shale. A central route crosses bands of Lockatong Argillite, Brunswick shale, and Diabase. A northern corridor can follow either Brunswick shale or Stockton sandstone. A central corridor appears to produce the maximum erosion and sedimentation.

Interpretation of Superimposed Maps

Ten maps were prepared, representing a range in values for the selected parameters. Each of these has been analyzed independently. The method, however, suggests that (1) the conjunctions of social values represent an obstruction to a highway alignment, (2) the conjunctions of physiographic difficulties represent an obstruction to a prospective highway, and (3) the aggregate of these obstructions, social and physiographic, represents the sum of obstructions to a highway corridor.

In contrast, the lightest area, representing the lowest social values and the least physiographic obstruction, indicates the highway alignment of least social cost and least physiographic difficulty.

When maps of social values and physiographic obstructions are superimposed, it is immediately apparent that the concurrence of obstruction occupies a broad belt between the Delaware and Raritan Rivers, Trenton, and New Brunswick. This aggregate obstruction diminishes to the south, but the continuous area containing the least obstruction occurs as a trumpet with its northern limit at the base of Pennington and Sourland Mountains, narrowest at Hopewell, and widening eastward between Sourland Mountain and the Millstone River.

If social values are accepted as criteria for route selection, in addition to normal factors of topography, it is clear that the route of least social cost proceeds parallel to and west of Jacobs Creek, either north or south of Pennington Mountain, and thence along the base of Sourland Mountain. At the tail of this mountain the corridor widens, permitting a route to proceed either to I-187 near Pluckemin or to South Bound Brook.

In addition to providing an alignment of minimum social cost, this route, if located south of the major aquifer recharge, permits the highway to enhance the water regimen by permitting managed aquifer recharge.

Tests of the Area of Lowest Social Value against Physiographic Restraints

A map was prepared which showed three levels of physiographic obstruction:

- *Zone 1*. Areas having slopes in excess of ten percent. Areas requiring major rivers, highway, and railroad crossings
- *Zone 2*. Areas having slopes in excess of five percent but less than ten percent. Areas requiring minor river and highway crossings
- *Zone 3*. Areas having slopes of less than five percent. Areas without consequential bridge crossings

When the corridor of least social cost was tested against this finer-grain analysis, it was seen to follow a route of least physiographic obstruction.

Test of the Area of Least Social Cost and Least Physiographic Obstruction against Scenic Value

In order to measure the highway corridor against the scenic experience it could provide, a map of scenic value was prepared. Three values were determined as follows:

- *Zone 1*. A broad band embracing the Delaware River, Washington's Crossing, Pennington Mountain, Rocky Hill, the Stonybrook watershed, and narrowing to include the Millstone Creek and the Duke Estate
- *Zone 2*. In general, this zone includes the Sourland and the area of farmland on either side of the Millstone River
- *Zone 3*. Remainder of area

The valley of Jacobs Creek, Baldpate Mountain, the valley of Stonybrook and the Pennington Mountain, Rocky Hill, the Millstone River Valley, Beden Brook, and Sourland Mountain constitute the major elements of scenic value in the area. They fall into two major elements: the northern ridge as one, and the heartland, composed of Stonybrook, Rocky Hill, Millstone River, and Beden Brook as the second.

Scenic value can be considered in two opposing ways: as a value that the highway should avoid, or as a resource the highway should exploit. If avoidance is the objective, then the corridor should fall south of the Stonybrook and Millstone. It should positively avoid transecting the heartland or paralleling the Millstone River. If exploitation is the criterion, then two possibilities are apparent. The first would select the Rocky Hill Ridge and the Millstone River corridor. The other alternative is the northern corridor at the base of the Baldpate, Pennington, and Sourland Mountains.

The Rocky Hill–Millstone River corridor, while undoubtedly scenic, transects the area of highest social values and high physiographic obstructions. It does not correspond to a reasonable direction for the highway. The alignment on Jacobs Creek, skirting the base of Pennington and Sourland Mountains, equally offers an excellent scenic experience, but avoids areas of high social value and areas of physiographic difficulty—and it corresponds with the general direction of the prospective route.

The proposed corridor skirting the base of the mountain ridge not only satisfies the criteria of low social value and low physiographic difficulty, but offers an excellent scenic experience.

The Highway as a Conscious Device to Locate New and Productive Land Uses

If one assumes that cannot only the highway avoid unnecessary social costs but also create new productive land uses, then it becomes important to decide where these might best be located.

In the area under consideration, industrial and commercial land uses exist in Trenton and in the band of communities bordering the Raritan River. In the intervening area industry is sparse. The ethos of the heartland, Princeton-dominated, is residential and institutional. The creation of new industrial land uses would be unwelcome in the heartland but welcome at either end, in Trenton, New Brunswick, Bound Brook, Manville, Somerville. This being so, the highway corridor should be selected to locate new productive land uses at the extremities but avoid the creation of conflicting land uses in the central valley. In addition, any direct central route would inflict not only dissonant land uses but also a corridor of noise, glare, dust, health hazard, nuisance, and danger on the rural-residential-institutional land uses of the heartland.

If this analysis can be substantiated, the optimum highway corridor would follow an alignment and locate such intersections as to benefit both the Delaware River and Raritan River termini with new productive land uses and would avoid such conflicts in the intervening area. A northern route could induce new land uses adjacent to West Trenton and the Raritan River communities, where new industrial and commercial land uses would be both consonant and welcome.

18

Biological Alternatives to
Water Pollution (1976)

In the early 1970s McHarg established the Center for Ecological Studies in Planning and Design at Penn as the research program for the Department of Landscape Architecture and Regional Planning. The Center became engaged in several projects, including the landmark ecological plan for Medford Township, New Jersey, and the book Biological Control of Water Pollution *(1976), co-edited by two former students of McHarg's: Robert Pierson and Joachim Tourbier. Tourbier later directed the Water Research Center at the University of Delaware and is now professor of landscape architecture at the University of Dresden, Germany. McHarg contributed this chapter to* Biological Control of Water Pollution, *which helped introduce an alternative way to addressing the issue of water pollution.*

Any consideration of alternatives must begin from the datum of the status quo. It may then be useful to describe the assumptions and processes which now produce what is euphemistically described as drinking water. First let us consider the assumptions. The implicit assumption, the inalienable right governing water management, is that thou shalt defecate into thy neighbor's drinking water and, further, if for any reasons of delicacy, hygiene, or prudence you prefer not to do so, be assured that thy municipality shall do it for thee. So water treatment and sewage treatment are, for all practical purposes, synonymous. We can observe, parenthetically, that this rule does not hold for all primitive societies where often taboos seek to separate excrement from drinking water. Primitive, then, can also mean the capability of drinking water from rivers, lakes, streams, and springs. This is not the way of advanced technological societies. Beginning from a modest commitment to excrement as an essential component of water supply, with advancing technology there followed an enrichment of the attendant nutrients. The development of industry, not least the chemical industry, ensured a wide variety of new additives. Among the earliest of these were the nitrates and phosphates; the former, derived from sewage and fertilizer, is an essential ingredient for blue babies or cyanosis. But a wider population could be served by DDT, dieldrin, aldrin, and the organic phosphates. These are not benign, nor are arsenic, lead, cyanide, selenium, cadmium, or other benefits from modern industry. Until recently these additives to drinking water were uncoordinated, but with the commitment to regionalization of sewage treatment, industry was invited to contribute its toxins to the nation's resources of drinking water. This is advanced technology.

In the competition among major cities for reducing the time factor between the two critical orifices in the human water cycle, the City of Philadelphia assumes a high position, perhaps even primary. This success derives from the inspired location of the sewage and water treatment plants on the Delaware River. The sewage receives secondary treatment when it does not rain; it is poured into the Delaware River where the U.S. Geological Survey monitors the continued absence of dissolved oxygen, year after year, with meticulous instrumentation. As the Delaware is tidal, the sewage moves downstream until slack tide when it returns upstream, passing the sewage treatment plant, and proceeds to the intake basins of the water treatment plant which can only be filled at high tide. Thence follows water treatment in a fully computerized facility. This, we observe, is a modern facility utilizing these high-technology innovations of caged sedimentation, coagulation, filtration, and, finally, chlorination. Now we all know that sanitary engineers, valiantly fighting their way into the twentieth century, never accomplished water treatment. This was done by microorganisms. These creatures have been successfully engaged in water treatment for hundreds of millions of years. Their commitment to this endeavor is not related to the objective of cleaning water, but to eating and survival. One would assume that these indispensable creatures and their ways would be of the greatest significance to those engaged in treating water. Not so, for the sanitary engineer does not need to know these essential decomposers. His objective is to kill all organisms. How else can you drink a dilute soup of dead bacteria in a chlorine solution? And so hyper-, super-, extra-, ultra-chlorination ensues at such levels as to guarantee that the consumer at the end of the water line receives only dead bacteria with his toxins. And, not least among these toxins, as we have recently learned, are the carcinogens produced by the chlorine. This is modern technology at its best. Only when drinking water is delivered at 98.4°F will there be another significant advance.

But what of modern industry? It clearly operates on a modified version of the implicit inalienable right. Thou shalt poison thy neighbor's drinking water, and, if for any reason of delicacy, hygiene, or prudence, you prefer not to do so, thy regional sewage system shall do it for thee.

Once upon a time I was invited by *Fortune* magazine to address the presidents of fifty of the largest corporations in the United States at the Four Seasons Restaurant in New York. "Gentlemen," I said, "I wish to make a bargain with you on behalf of the American people. I know that this is presumption on the part of a Scottish immigrant, but hear me out. I have no doubt that you all bathed and changed your shirt and underclothes before coming here. I am sure you have a clean pocket handkerchief. I would not be surprised if many of you added a dab of underarm deodorant. Moreover, I have observed you at cocktails and dinner, noted your handling of knives, forks, spoons, table napkins, even finger bowls. I am sure that the American people would agree with me that your standards of personal hygiene are impeccable. But as my bargain requires concessions on your part, the American people, too, then must make concessions to you. On their behalf, I offer you a relaxation in these demanding standards of personal hygiene to which you subscribe. You may forego the changes of underwear, finger bowls, underarm deodorants; you may belch or even fart in public. This relaxation may be welcome to you and yet will not endanger the American environment. For this relaxation the American people require an improvement in your standards of corporate hygiene. We require that you now cease and desist from voiding thousands of millions of gallons and tons of your excrement into the American environment. The time has come for American industry to be toilet trained. You are incontinent. This condition may either be a sign of infantilism or senescence. Should it be the latter, we can only await your demise with impatience. If the former, we can help you into adult continence whereby you control the deposition of your excrement to minimize offense to the American people and the American environment, in particular, that you cease and desist from poisoning the nation's drinking water."

Of course, government is not immune to similar criticism. Indeed, the gravest threats to the nation's health and well-being are accomplished at public expense. Atomic testing, atomic reactors—notably accidents to these—contribute radioactivity to the atmosphere, to the hydrosphere, and to our drinking water. The government also contributes more modest toxins. An analysis of well logs in the Denver metropolitan region disclosed many wells with excessive levels of arsenic, cyanide, lead, and selenium. When these were mapped, they pointed like an arrow to the source and the culprit, the Rocky Mountain National Arsenal. It would be unfair to omit the United States Army Corps of Engineers, entrusted with the enforcement of the 1899 Refuse Act. They failed to initiate prosecutions under the act for over three score years and ten. They must be held responsible for the pollution of America's water systems. In other military societies the appropriate remedy for such celestial negligence is ceremonial disembowelment. Industry and government have been coequally negligent in the area of water treatment. Yet, it would be unfair and ungracious if the positive accomplishment of conventional water treatment and distribution were not recognized and applauded. It is precisely this system which has banished the major water-borne diseases, the pestilences of typhoid, gastroenteritis, cholera, dysentery, and others. It would be just as unfair to fail to note that many primitive societies are scourged by such diseases today and are less successful in solving these problems than the Western countries. Yet, the successes are long past and the processes for water and sewage treatment, long efficacious, are incapable of dealing with the products of modern industry and chemistry and, finally, the finest tool of the system, chlorination, is now accused of contributing carcinogens to our water supply.

Wherein lies the remedy? Surely it must begin with recognition of the fact that clean, potable water is a byproduct of biological systems. The entire subject of water must be seen to be a problem of biology rather than engineering. This would recognize that nature has been in the business of water and sewage treatment since the beginning of life, most effectively, and that solutions to the problems of water lie in understanding aquatic biology and, dominantly, limnology. But, knowing that water systems are affected by terrestrial processes (indeed water quality represents a synthesis of aquatic and terrestrial processes), then the scientific basis for the management of water resources must be ecology. In fact, we can say that the biological alternatives which concern us in this volume are ecological alternatives to nonecological existing methods. The definition of ecology is the study of the interaction of organisms and the environment, which includes other organisms. Applying this concept to the provision of potable water would suggest that, as such, water is ultimately a product of aquatic organisms, and as these organisms require specific environmental conditions to survive and prosper, the conditions of terrestrial and aquatic systems must be preserved or managed to maintain the survival and success of the essential organisms which produce potable water. We do not have to create or discover the model which would govern such an ecological approach. It is the limnological model. One of its creators and most effective practitioners, Ruth Patrick (and her colleagues at the Philadelphia Academy of Natural Science), has devoted several chapters in *Biological Control of Water Pollution* to an exposition of this theoretical concept. It is enough to say here that this model can identify water quality from the number of species and discriminate between levels of quality using certain organisms—their presence, absence, or relative abundance—as specific indicators. Moreover, the factors which determine these conditions of aquatic "health" are generally known and can be manipulated. I subscribe totally to the limnological theory as the essential perception for ecological planning for water quality. How could such a view be institutionalized? I will simply paraphrase parts of a research project which I undertook as an agent of the American Institute of Planners [now the American Planning Association] for the Environment Protection Agency (EPA) entitled, "Towards a Comprehensive Plan for Environmental Quality" (Wallace, McHarg, Roberts, and Todd 1973).

The first matter concerns an administrative structure for the planning, management, and regulation of water resources. Acceptance of ecology-limnology as the scientific basis for this objective implies an administrative structure. The unit of surface-water hydrology is the watershed, the unit of subsurface hydrology is the groundwater basin, a unit of ecological planning is the physiographic region—an area, homogeneous with respect to geological history and therefore homogeneous with respect to physiography, hydrology, soils, plants, and animals. The United States is subdivided into thirty-four such physiographic regions. The problem of selecting the appropriate unit is not simple. While the major groundwater basins are frequently within physiographic regions, the major rivers often transect several regions. A solution to the complex problem of an administrative structure for water planning and management, consonant with ecology-limnology, should first involve acceptance of the watersheds of the major rivers as the primary planning units. It would recognize the Continental Divide and thus divide the country into the two administrative units of east and west. Within each major subdivision the great rivers—for example, the Hudson, Delaware, Susquehanna, Potomac, and James in the east—would provide the major administrative elements. The next subdivision would be the physiographic region within the watershed or, as in the case of the coastal plain, the physiographic region itself. The smallest administrative unit would be the watershed within a physiographic region.

Applied to the Philadelphia area, the major administrative unit would be the Eastern Office. The Delaware River Watershed provides the next unit, subdivided into the physiographic regions of Allegheny Plateau: Valley and Ridge Province; Great Valley; Reading Prong; Triassic Piedmont Lowlands; Piedmont Uplands; and Coastal Plain. Each of these regions is homogeneous and has characteristic problems associated with hydrology, limnology, and land use. These regional problems cumulatively effect water quality in the watershed. The Allegheny Plateau, with the Catskills and Poconos, is primarily used for recreation and second homes. It has excellent water in lakes and streams. The problem here is preservation and enhancement. In the Valley and Ridge Province, transected by the Delaware and its tributaries and characterized by the location of coal mining, the overwhelming problem is acid mine drainage, and water management must seek to solve this problem. The next province, the Great Valley, is preponderantly limestone with significant groundwater resources. It is the location of extensive agriculture. Here the characteristic problems are pollution from fertilizers, herbicides, pesticides, sedimentation, and nitrates. The Reading Prong has little influence upon water quality, but the piedmont, site of extensive urbanization, contributes massive human wastes and concentrates industrial toxins. Finally the coastal plains constitutes the most valuable water resource of the watershed reposing in the aquifer system. It presents the problem of managing groundwater. This suggests that the characteristic problems of each physiographic region require an appropriate staff of scientists, planners, and administrators. Each region is specific, yet all are concerned with cumulative effects reflected in the entire watershed, its water quality and quantity.

Given an administrative structure consonant with the morphology of hydrologic-limnologic systems, it is then possible to plan and regulate within existing legislation. Sections 201 and 208 of the Federal Water Pollution Control Act Amendments (Public Law 92-500, commonly referred to as the Clean Water Act) provide effective vehicles for water planning and management, particularly the latter. Section 201 is devoted to the provision of sewage treatment facilities; section 208 is concerned with nonpoint sources of pollution and with the effects of urbanization and land use. If this latter legislative power required ecological planning, including the limnological model, and were such planning structured within watersheds and physiographic regions, there would be reason for confidence of ultimate success. However the process today is hampered by arbitrary political subdivisions and by an assumption that the objectives of the act can be satisfied by the orthodoxy of sanitary engineering. Acceptance of ecology as the scientific basis, limnology as the specific science for water management, hydrological units as administrative units, and ecological planning as the instrument for fulfilling the objectives of the Water Pollution Control Act would provide massive improvement but yet would still not be sufficient. The environmental impact statement procedure, while valuable, is ad hoc, adventitious, and can be negative. That is, the sum of environmental impact analyses for projects in a region does not contribute to an understanding of that region as an interacting biophysical system.

Planning and management of water resources require that the workings of the biophysical cultural region, in this case the watershed, be understood so that prediction can be made of the consequences of certain contemplated acts. Moreover, in accordance with the Clean Water Act, these contemplated actions must be assessed for their effect upon water quality and quantity. The primary requirement then is to understand the operation of the system, be it a major watershed or a physiographic region. This suggests that modeling of watersheds and regions must be undertaken to provide the necessary predictive capability. Such inventories and models then permit both positive planning towards established social ends and the avoidance of social costs. The avoidance of negative impacts, toward which the present procedures are oriented, would be complemented by a capability of inducing positive acts, i.e., development of propitious areas and positive steps to ameliorate water quality. It would require only an interpretation of Sections 201 and 208 to undertake such ecological planning studies involving both inventories of natural phenomena and processes, and the creation of predictive models, insofar as science can now provide these.

I would recommend a major improvement to existing planning method, that is, the uniform employment of a planning method having the attributes of being overt, explicit, and replicable. In other words, the data employed should be available to the public, the weights or values attributed to factors should also be overt and explicit so that the planning process is replicable. Such a planning method would then be employed east and west, in every watershed and physiographic region.

Yet another improvement to present processes would involve devolution of water planning and management to the smallest units of government, recognizing differences in perception of the environment, values attributed to its several aspects, and alternate forms of remedy. This suggests that municipalities produce ordinances regulating land use and management, based upon the health and welfare provisions of the U.S. Constitution, the provisions of the National Environmental Policy Act, and appropriate state legislation specifically related to place and people. This requires the same understanding and capability necessary for planning watersheds and regions. However, if Section 208 induced ecological inventories and models as central to ecological planning, these data could be made available to municipalities. If performance specifications can be written, local ordinances can be formulated specific to the municipality, the natural system it includes, and the needs, desires, expectations, and aversions of its population.

This returns us to the primary concerns of this book (Toubier and Pierson 1976): the biological control of water pollution. The insistence upon performance specifications is tolerant to alternatives. There are many simple and effective methods to be considered and employed. These range from preservation of existing resources to a wide range of remedial techniques. What distinguishes those techniques presented in this collection is their ecological-limnological basis. They recognize that organisms are essential for potable water in nature or by human management, that water planning and management must be ecological-limnological, that sanitary engineering cannot achieve the objectives of the nation.

The world of water and sewage treatment is dominated by the subject of waste. Yet this is a misnomer. There are no wastes, only matter in various states. Most of that named waste is better described as nutrients. We need to learn how to complete the cycle, notably the return stroke involving the decomposing microorganisms in water and soil and their symbionts. And it is these microorganisms who are the heroes of this book, the creatures who have been thoughtlessly engaged in water treatment for aeons and who continue to be indispensable. The EPA disclosure that carcinogens are produced as a product of chlorination is only the death knell to the concept of killing for water potability. It must be replaced by a biological alternative that utilizes the essential microorganisms. The future of water treatment lies in ecology-limnology, as this book so clearly affirms. Let us formally abandon our right to defecate in our neighbor's drinking water. Let us embark upon a national toilet-training program, and above all, let us make a formal commitment to limnology and ecology as the basis for this endeavor.

References

Toubier, Joachim, and Robert Pierson, eds. 1976. *Biological Control of Water Pollution*. Philadelphia: University of Pennsylvania.

Wallace, McHarg, Roberts, and Todd. 1973. *Towards a Comprehensive Plan for Environmental Quality*. Washington, D.C.: American Institute of Planners for the U.S. Environmental Protection Agency.

19

A Case Study in Ecological Planning: The Woodlands, Texas (1979)

with Arthur H. Johnson and
Jonathan Berger

A distinguishing characteristic of the Penn Department of Landscape Architecture and Regional Planning under McHarg's leadership was its interdisciplinary nature. Landscape architects and planners collaborated with ecologists, geologists, soil scientists, and anthropologists. Jon Berger, a planner, and Art Johnson, a soil scientist, were among the most enthusiastic of these collaborators. They were central participants in an introductory interdisciplinary studio that exposed graduate students to ecological planning. Suitability analysis was an important component of this studio.

This paper is one effort to provide a clear explanation of suitability analysis, as it was conceived by McHarg and refined by him and his Penn colleagues, including Johnson and Berger. It was published in Planning the Uses and Management of Land, *a comprehensive text on land planning and management, by the American Society of Agronomy, the Crop Science Society of America, and the Soil Science Society of America.*

Introduction

In reviewing the publications and reports in the regional and landscape planning literature and project reports from the profession, one finds a lack of uniformity in methodology, with ad hoc procedures "suited to the particular problem" a common approach. A method is presented in this chapter for determining the inherent suitability of a landscape for assimilating human activities and their artifacts. The approach is suggested in the writings of McHarg (1969) and exemplified by Juneja (1974) and has been applied professionally to a wide array of sites and locations. The method of landscape analysis described here is one part of a more comprehensive planning process which includes the social, legal, and economic factors which must be melded into a comprehensive plan that responds to the needs, desires, and perceptions of the people for whom the planning is being done. In developing an area, one would like to achieve the best fit between each human activity and that portion of the landscape to which that activity is assigned. As a starting point, a landscape may be thought of as being comprised of elements or components which may be labeled *geology, physiography, soils, hydrology, vegetation, wildlife,* and *climate.* Each landscape element may provide opportunities for certain land uses, and likewise, there may be constraints to each kind of desired land use imposed by components of the landscape. Areas which are most suitable for a specific use will have the greatest number of opportunities provided by the landscape and the least number of, or least severe, constraints imposed by the landscape on that particular use.

By using the approach of combining analyses of opportunities and constraints, the environmental impacts of the planned uses can be minimized, and the energy required to implement and maintain the proposed uses and artifacts can likewise be minimized. For example, areas where the water table is near the surface frequently or for extended periods provide an obvious constraint to subdivision housing in unsewered areas. This property of the landscape lowers the inherent suitability of such areas for that use. The situation can be ameliorated by the addition of sewers or by other engineering solutions, but costs, either economic or ecological, will be incurred, and additional energy will be required for installation and maintenance. This same area may provide little constraint to a golf course or park. Areas which are on the lee side of vegetative or physiographic barriers to winter winds provide a slight advantage for housing as energy costs for winter heating will be somewhat reduced. This same property of a site produces little opportunity for a park or golf course if the use is confined to the warm seasons. Thus the pattern of land uses assigned to the landscape could be controlled to a large degree by the characteristics and properties of the landscape. To this end, a careful analysis of the physiographs, geology, soils, hydrology, plants, animals, and climate-microclimate of an area should be carried out and the implications for specified land uses determined by trained scientists.

The approach outlined here is designed to be flexible. It has been applied to areas ranging in size from a few hectares to a few hundred square kilometers and to urban, suburban, and rural areas.

There are also mechanisms to incorporate new data which may be generated after an initial plan has been formulated. Although flexible, the method is designed to be as objective as possible. The solutions are replicable and the methods of analysis overt and explicit.

Additionally, the method may be used to derive performance requirements (i.e., conditions which must be met by the developers) for the development of areas of less than prime suitability. The impact of any use on the landscape (or the impact of the landscape on the land use) can be mitigated by engineering to have the same result as the same development in the most suitable areas. The areas of prime suitability thus may become a "meter stick" for specifying what additional measures should be taken to minimize impacts on the land use by the landscape, and on the landscape by the land use.

Outline of the Methods

A flowchart of the planning process, of which this method of landscape analysis is a part, is given in Figure 1. The stream of landscape analysis identified by the box in Figure 1 is the subject of this chapter. This part of the process is dependent upon the input of natural scientists. Clearly, the assembly of scientific data and its interpretation require the perceptions and expertise of soil scientists, geologists, meteorologists, hydrologists, and ecologists. For a plan to be sound, the interpretations for opportunities and constraints must be suitable for the level of information obtained. The judgment and experience of trained scientists is necessary in collecting and interpreting data from the landscape. It should be the planners' charge to combine the natural scientists' perceptions with those of social scientists and engineers to cast these into a comprehensive plan within a sound legal and economic framework.

The first step in this holistic approach to analyzing a particular landscape is to collect information and map the components of the landscape. Some representative inventory maps which have generally been proven useful are listed in table 6. The level of detail of the data will be determined by the avail-

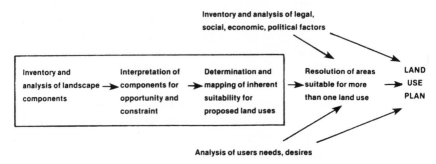

Figure 1. Flow chart of the ecological planning process. Box indicates the part of the process treated in this chapter.

Table 6. Some Useful Inventory Maps

1. Physiography	Elevation, slope
2. Geology	Bedrock or subsurface geology, surficial deposits, geologic cross-sections
3. Soils	Series or phases, drainage classes, hydrologic groups, capability group, depth to seasonal high water table, as applicable
4. Hydrology	Depth to water table, aquifer yields, direction of ground-water movement, recharge areas, water quality, surface waters (lakes, streams, wetlands), flood zones, drainage basins
5. Vegetation	Distribution of associations, communities, and habitats as identifiable, areas important as noise buffers, food supplies, for wildlife, nesting areas
6. Wildlife	Identification of species and their habitats and ranges, movement corridors
7. Climate	Macro- and microclimate parameters (temperature, moisture, wind). Ventilation and insulation may be determined in conjunction with physiography
8. Resources	Mineral or other valuable natural resources

able information, time, and available resources which are related to the size of the area.

An inventory of the landscape in a parcel of, say, ten hectares can be carried out in considerable detail, whereas for a 1,000-km^2 site published reports may constitute the bulk of the useable information. In general, as the size of the area to be planned increases, the level of detail decreases and the uniformity of information across the various categories listed in table 6 decreases.

The next step is to determine how the landscape functions as an interacting system of related components. For this purpose, a two-dimensional array like that shown in figure 2 may be used as a guide. Each element in the matrix identifies the possible interaction or relationship of two of the landscape components, and the sum of the bivariate relationships includes all of the major interactions and processes important in the landscape. Knowledge of how the various components of the landscape affect and are affected by one another leads to an understanding of how the whole system works. This should indicate chains of events which might occur because of some proposed land uses. The completeness of understanding will, of course, depend upon the level of information used and the perceptions and abilities of the scientists who contribute to the understanding of the natural system. It is safe to assume that a complete understanding of a landscape and its processes is never achieved—the planner must deal with incomplete information, and care must be taken that the inferences drawn from the data are justifiable given the detail and completeness of the database from which they are made.

The categories shown in figure 2 may be varied to suit the nature of the landscape and level of information used in the analysis. In a small area with detailed information, one can subdivide the categories to a more detailed level, producing a larger matrix. Increasing the detail of information used allows a better understanding of the processes which may be affected by development or other changes in land use.

To understand the links between landscape elements and proposed land uses the set of matrices shown in figure 3 may be useful if there are a number of land uses which need to be considered. Matrix I describes the relationship between land uses and development activities. Matrix II describes the relationship between development activities and the landscape. Matrix III is the same as figure 2. These arrays are one way of organizing the information which is brought to bear on the final land-use plan, helping to make the assimilation of a large amount of information orderly and explicit.

As an example of how this process may be used, consider the development of an area which requires a substantial amount of paving and impermeable surfaces such as roofs and roads with attendant drainage improvements. Consider high-density housing; one of the major impacts is on the hydrologic

	physiography	bedrock geology	surficial geology	soils	ground water	surface water	vegetation	wildlife	climate
physiography						11			
bedrock geology									
surficial geology									
soils					1	2	3	4	5
ground water							6	7	
surface water							8	9	
vegetation								10	
wildlife									
climate									

Figure 2. Simple version of a matrix arraying landscape components. The interactions or relationships identified by each element in the matrix are organized into this format which facilitates systematic evaluation of disruptions of natural processes which may accompany specific human activities. Numbers refer to the example given in the text.

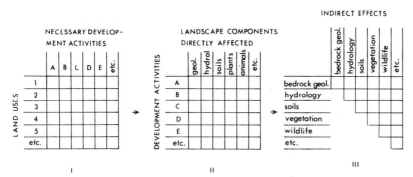

Figure 3. Organization of information for assessing the relationship between a set of desired land uses and the impacts they will have on the landscape.

regime. Portions of the landscape are rendered impermeable and other landscape components will also change in response to the new conditions. By using figure 2, the changes in other parts of the landscape may be evaluated by considering the components which interact with the hydrologic system. Many of the changes considered in this example are defined quantitatively by Leopold (1968). Groundwater recharge will be reduced and the depth to the water table may be increased (no. 1 in figure 2), marshes and seasonally wet areas may dry up, altering vegetation and wildlife (nos. 6, 7, 10), and surface water discharge will be increased. Flood peaks will be higher and bankfull stage will be more frequent, as will floods of a given magnitude (no. 2). As a result of the stream regime changes, stream channels will enlarge to adjust to the new flow regime (no. 11), suspended solids loads will increase at least during the period of channel enlargement, low flows will decrease, water quality will change, and stream communities will necessarily adjust to the new conditions (nos. 8, 9). The vegetation and wildlife will be changed (nos. 3, 4), and the energy balance of the site may be altered as transpiration may be reduced, the soil moisture balance altered, and the microclimate in the area may change considerably as observed in large conurbations.

The information assembled in the planning process amounts to someone's interpretation and synthesis of information compiled and arrayed in map and matrix form to define the landscape components. Given sufficient information of this type at an appropriate level of detail, there is a basis for interpreting the assembled information to understand the opportunities afforded by the landscape for specified activities, and the constraints imposed by the landscape.

Determination of opportunities begins with a specific set of land uses which are desired by the users. Such uses have optimal or prerequisite conditions for their implementation and these must be defined, i.e., swimming areas require good water quality, appropriate bottom material and topography, and accessibility. Houses optimally need stable material beneath, well-drained soils for on-site sewage disposal, gentle to moderate slopes, and perhaps a good view and protection from winter winds. For each desired land use, the geology, soils, vegetation hydrology, and/or other inventory maps are interpreted for the opportunities they afford, producing a set of opportunity maps which show the best areas for each land use individually based on the landscape components which afford opportunity. For each land use, the individual opportunity maps derived from each of the pertinent landscape components are combined by overlay techniques to produce a composite opportunity map which shows the opportunities afforded by the whole landscape for each desired land use.

In most cases the greater the number of concurrences of opportunities found in a particular environment, the higher the capability of that environment for the defined use. The trade-off between the environments of higher and lower capability will be increased capital costs of design and construction as well as increased energy costs for construction and maintenance if performance requirements are met. Users can decide between the possible trade-offs. Using the method outlined in figure 3, the consultant scientists can demonstrate the attendant environmental costs and benefits of any desired scheme.

Constraints, defined here as adverse impacts of the land upon the land use and adverse impacts of the land use upon the land, are best expressed using the vocabulary of the National Environmental Policy Act and the health and welfare provisions of the states' and federal constitutions (table 7). Some landforms because of the natural processes are "inherently hazardous to life and health." Examples would be flood-prone areas, areas subject to landslides, areas subject to collapse, and areas of fire-prone vegetation.

Other natural factors present "hazards to life and health through specific

Table 7. Types of Constraints

Legally Defined Constraints	Rules of Combination with Other Uses
Inherently hazardous to life and health	Preempts nearly all development
Hazardous to life and health through specific human action	Allows some land uses but not others
Unique, scarce, or rare vulnerable resource	Requires regulation through performance requirements

human action." Examples are the pollution of ground and surface waters from septic tanks in soils with a seasonally high water table, or the pollution of domestic groundwater supplies through construction or waste disposal on an aquifer recharge area. Certain landforms with associated vegetation and land use can be classified as "unique, scarce, or rare." Alteration of these areas through development would mean the loss to society of irreplaceable features. Social scientists (historians, ethnographers, archaeologists, folklorists, and art historians) and natural scientists value such areas. Finally, particular landforms may be "vulnerable resources" which need regulation to "avoid social costs." Depending on the environment under study, these would include prime agricultural soils, high-quality gravel deposits, and scenic features, among others.

Planners and their consultant scientists can evaluate every inventory map and determine from the categories of data the relevant set of constraints. These constraints are mapped. Unlike opportunities, the concurrence of numerous constraints may not be as significant as the existence of one constraint which represents a "hazard to life and health."

The next step in the procedure is a synthesis of opportunities and constraints for a selected land use to produce a suitability map which identifies a gradient of suitabilities for that prospective use. The areas with the greatest number of opportunities and least constraints are the most suitable for the specified land use. The method of combining the opportunities and constraints and ranking the suitability may be arbitrary but is explicit if an array is used to show how decisions of suitability were made. The matrix in figure 4 shows the determination of most suitable land and land of secondary suitability for housing with septic tanks. The example is oversimplified, but the method has been applied successfully to complex landscapes. The reliability and accuracy of the map overlay techniques this method employs are discussed by MacDougall (1975).

The suitability maps for the land uses that the landscape must accommodate are then assessed. Where there are areas which are of primary suitability for only a single use, that use should be allocated to the suitable areas if the other relevant social, economic, and legal factors are favorable. In many instances, multiple suitabilities will arise. That is, some areas will be highly suitable for more than one use. Clearly, prime agricultural lands will be suitable for housing, recreation, and other uses. In these cases, land uses are assigned based on the needs and desires of the users which can be determined by surveys and interviews (Berger 1978) or reflected in local officials or spokespersons for the users. Such allocations are also subject to legal and economic considerations which should also be incorporated into a land-use plan.

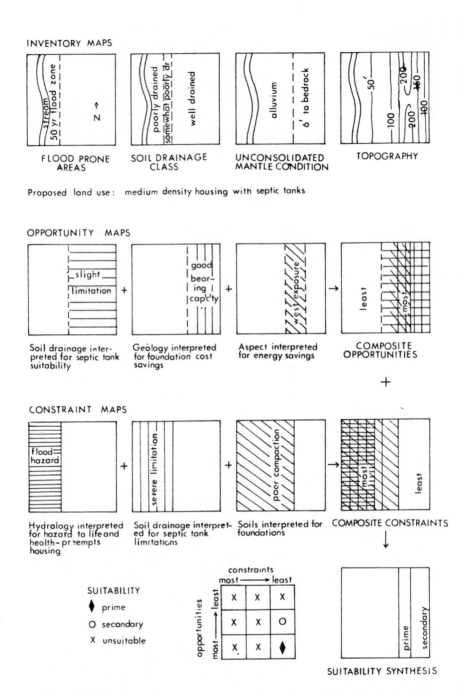

Figure 4. Overlay method for determining suitability of a specific land use by combination of opportunities and constraints.

Application

A simplified example is given below which is a summary of a portion of the plan for the new city called *The Woodlands* (Wallace, McHarg, Roberts, and Todd 1974), now being developed just north of Houston, Texas. A site map is shown in figure 5. The site presented many problems for such a development. It was entirely forest—a pleasant place to live, but a difficult environment to build in. It is extremely flat with few slopes greater than five percent. As a

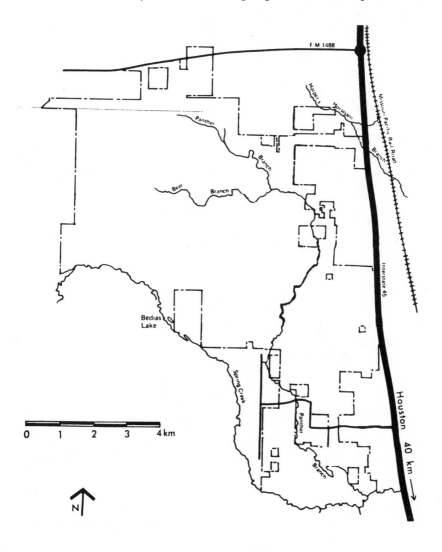

Figure 5. Regional location and site map of Woodlands new community.

result of the topographic and rainfall characteristics, nearly a third of the site is in the 100-year flood plain of Panther, Bear, and Spring Creeks. Drainage of storm runoff was poor. Many depressions exist on the flat terrain which is dominated by impermeable soils, and standing water was common. The determination of housing sites and housing densities in The Woodlands is used as an example of the method of landscape analysis outlined above.

Nature of the Site

The Woodlands is located in the Gulf coastal plain and is underlain by unconsolidated formations comprised of Quaternary and Tertiary age gravels, sand, silt, and clay, in various combinations and proportions. The formations strike northeast, roughly parallel to the coast, and dip southeast at 1 to 2 m/km. Several of the units are good aquifers and are sources of high-quality water. The bearing strength of the geologic units underlying the site is adequate for most development purposes. There are subsidence problems in the Houston area, but subsidence should not affect The Woodlands; groundwater withdrawals and recharge have been carefully determined in the planning for the area, as described in more detail below.

The hydrologic regime was an extremely important consideration in designing the plan for The Woodlands community. There were flooding and storm-drainage problems to be dealt with and a water supply to be developed.

Recharge of water was of primary importance to diminish the risk of subsidence on the site as well as down dip in Houston, which pumps from the same aquifers. Additionally, groundwater was planned as a means of augmenting baseflow in the creeks to enhance the amenity value of artificial lakes to be constructed on the site.

Spring Creek and lower Panther Creek are the only perennial streams within the site. The others are intermittent, flowing during periods of storm runoff. During low flow periods, discharge is low since baseflow is limited, but storm-periods produce large peak flows due to the heavy precipitation events and predominance of impermeable soils.

The soils on the site are mostly paleudults. Surface horizons are generally sandy or loamy with well-developed argillic horizons below. The Woodlands soils were grouped according to permeability and storage capacity in inches of water. The soil will store beyond field capacity above the slowly permeable layers or the seasonal high water table. Figure 6 shows the profiles rated according to the permeability of the horizons, and table 8 summarizes the pertinent properties.

Table 8. Some Properties of the Soil Series Present on The Woodlands Sites

Map Designation	Soil Series	Drainage	Depth of Permeable Soil, >5 cm/hour (cm)	Depth to Seasonal High Water Table
La, Eu	Lakeland, Eustis	Well	200	300
Br	Bruno	Well	200	75
Boh	Boy	Moderately well	125	75
Al	Albany	Poorly	120	75
Lu, Fu	Lucy,	Well	53	200
	Furquay	Well	58	75
Leh, Wi	Wicksburg,	Poorly	68	75
	Leefield	Poorly	86	38
Co, COG, Se Seg, Su, An, SS	Conroe, Segno, Susquehanna, Angie, Sunsweet	Poorly to moderately well	0	Variable
Sph	Splendora	Poorly	0	38
So-Bo, TK				
So	Sorter	Poorly	0	38
Cr	Crowley	Poorly	0	38
Wa	Waller	Poorly	0	38
Wap	Waller Ponded	Very poorly	0	38

The site is a mixed woodland dominated by loblolly pine. In mature stands, the pines are associated with oaks, sweet gum, hickories, tupelo, magnolia, and sycamore. The woodlands provide an amenity for development as well as limiting runoff and erosion. Additionally, the forest provides habitats for wildlife. Eight major vegetation associations were recognized: (1) shortleaf pine—hardwood; (2) loblolly pine—hardwood; (3) loblolly pine—oak—gum; (4) pine—oak; (5) mixed mesic woodland; (6) pine—hardwood; (7) flood-plain vegetation; and (8) wet-weather pond. Much of the forest has been logged at one time or another.

There are a multitude of types of wildlife present on the site. Those types which are abundant include songbirds, rabbits, raccoon, squirrels, opossum, armadillo, white-tailed deer, and wild turkey. The persistence of most of these types can be promoted by careful management and by maintaining suitable habitats and territories and movement corridors which are large enough to suit the species. Flood-plain areas in The Woodlands provide a diversity of

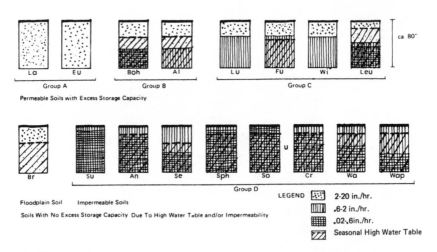

Figure 6. Soil profiles interpreted for permeability and depth to seasonal high water table. Map unit designations refer to Table 8.

habitats suitable for several desirable forms of wildlife, so that type of vegetation association has a high value for wildlife preservation. Forest edge conditions provide a diversity of habitats and also encourage a diversity of wildlife. These edge conditions occur around wet-weather ponds, which increases their value for wildlife protection. The ponds also serve as sediment traps and temporary shortage basins during storm periods, amounting to a significant value for the ponds.

The climate of the area is subtropical with warm, moist summers and mild winters. The climate factors were used in site planning but were not of overriding importance in determining suitability for development and so will not be discussed here.

Planning for Development

An overall plan for locating best areas for development, including high- and low-density residential, commercial, recreational, municipal, industrial, and open-space land uses was derived from the inventory of the landscape. Economic consultants produced a housing market analysis for the Houston metropolitan region which showed seven feasible housing types for The Woodlands New Town. Engineers and landscape architects described the attributes of each development type in terms of space occupied by buildings, space covered by other impervious surfaces and vegetation cleared (table 9).

Table 9. Development Types with Clearance and Coverage Requirements Determined by a Housing Market Analysis

Housing Type*	Clearing Required (%)	Coverage by Impermeable Surfaces (%)
Single family, 2.5 DU/ha (1 DU/acre)	37	24
Single family, 6.9 DU/ha (2.75 DU/acre)	70	36
Single family, 10 DU/ha (4.0 DU/acre)	50	43
Patio houses, 15 DU/ha (6.0 DU/acre)	90	51
Garden apartments, 37.5 DU/ha (15 DU/acre)	85	45
Townhouses, 25 DU/ha (10 DU/acre)	95	55
Elevator apartments, 100 DU/ha (40 DU/acre)	70	50

*DU = dwelling unit.

Relationship of Development Activities to Landscape Processes

The desired land uses and their attendant development activities would affect soils, vegetation, groundwater levels, stream flow, and stream-channel form. Modification of these landscape elements would affect the following processes: the balance between infiltration and overland flow, channel deposition and erosion, storage and movement of groundwater, and the regenerative capacity of the forest and wildlife communities. The effects on the hydrology of the site are essentially the same as identified in figure 2.

Given these forecasted impacts of urbanization, several interest groups wished to mitigate potential adverse environmental impacts. The regional water management commission wanted to maintain the recharge of the city of Houston's groundwater supply. The new town developers wanted to maintain a healthy forest as the prime marketing element of the new town. The U.S. Department of Housing and Urban Development had environmental guidelines for the processing of guaranteed loans. In response to these different interests the five guidelines listed below for the plan and design of the new town were established:

1. Minimize disruption of the hydrologic regime by creation of a natural drainage system which allowed removal of the low-frequency event runoff and recharged as much precipitation as possible from high- and low-frequency storms to maintain groundwater reserves
2. Preservation of the woodland environment
3. Preservation of vegetation providing wildlife habitats and movement corridors
4. Minimization of development costs
5. Avoidance of hazards to life and health

Requirements to Minimize Disruption of the Hydrologic Regime

Since The Woodlands site is a flat landscape with large areas of impermeable soils and streams of low gradient, conventional means of storm-water management called for site drainage through a large and expensive network of concrete drainage channels. These would decrease recharge to the groundwater reservoir, and call for the removal of vegetation. To avoid these environmentally and economically expensive problems a "natural" drainage system was devised.

Calculations of cleared area and impervious area for typical The Woodlands residential clusters indicated the magnitude of development impacts on surface runoff, soil storage capacity, and forest cover. The design aim was to promote infiltration of high-frequency, low-volume storm water (up to 25 mm of precipitation in six hours) to reduce the period of standing water and increase movement into the groundwater reservoir. For purposes of this design storm (25 mm in six hours), the soils were assumed to be at field capacity and flood plains were assumed to be left in their naturally forested state.

As a design tool to promote percolation, the most abundant soils were grouped according to their capacity to accommodate water from the high-frequency storm. Available storage capacity was calculated from the depth of the permeable soil layer, the depth to the seasonal high-water table, and the air-filled pore space at field capacity. The proportion of each soil map unit which needed to be left undisturbed to absorb runoff from the cleared portion was calculated (table 10).

Table 10. Tolerance of Soils to Coverage by Impermeable Surfaces Based on Ability to Store Storm Runoff from a 6-hour, 25mm Storm

Group*	Soil Series	Available Storage Capacity	Percent of Area That Can Be Made Impermeable
A	Lakeland, Eustis	High	90
B	Boy, Albany	Medium	75
C	Furquay, Lucy, Leefield Bruno, Wicksburg	Low	50
D	Angie, Crowley, Segno, Sorter, Splendora, Susquehanna, Waller	None	100 Effectively impermeable under present conditions

* The designation of A, B, C, and D is not related to slope or hydrologic group as defined by the Soil Conservation Service.

With the on-site recharge capacity of the soils known, the capability of any soil environment to handle any development type could be determined. In some cases higher densities on lower recharge capacity soils were possible if adjacent land had a moderate to high storage capacity to handle the storm runoff not recharged by the lower capacity soil. Housing densities could be increased in this case, since all of an area of high recharge capacity soil could be used as a sump for the runoff from adjacent areas developed on soils not suitable for storage of storm runoff.

Given the need to "borrow" recharge capacity from adjacent soils, the juxtaposition of soil types on the landscape became important in addition to the on-site recharge capability of a soil in determining housing suitability. Soil patterns based on drainage relationships were identified for their suitability for the different development types. figure 7 shows one example. For each

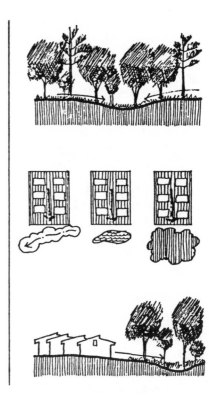

D Soils with slope greater than 1% are impermeable and therefore have minimal recharge capacity. When runoff from these soils cannot be recharged on A, B, or C Soils, it should be directed to a swale, water storage area, or area of uncleared D Soil with slope less than 1% which can be temporarily flooded.

Management Guidelines

The extent of clearing and the amount of impervious surface are not restricted except for limitations established by existing vegetation. (See vegetation guidelines.)

Housing Suitability

Since D Soils are already impervious they are especially suited to high density development.

Siting Considerations

Situate and design buildings, roads, and paths so as not to impound runoff.

Major pedestrian traffic should be on fill parallel to the line of slope, or raised on posts if traffic is perpendicular to the line of slope.

Figure 7. Management guidelines, housing suitability, and siting considerations for group D soils (no ability to store 6 hour 25mm storm).

drainage relationship, management guidelines, housing suitabilities, and siting considerations were specified.

Requirements to Preserve the Woodland Environment

Different vegetation types gave rise to different levels of clearing. Based on their desirability to the projected residents, their tolerance to disturbance, the soils on which they grow, and their regenerative requirements, the forest types were rated somewhat subjectively on a scale of allowable clearing. For example, large pure hardwood or nearly pure hardwood stands are relatively scarce in the region, attractive to the residents, intolerant of soil compaction and change in groundwater levels, better landscape shade trees, and slower to regenerate than pure pine stands which abound in the area. Clearing of hardwood stands was considered less desirable than clearing of pine stands. figure 8 is a summary of the recommended clearance percentages based on the amenity value of the various forest types.

The gradient of tolerance from pure hardwood to pure pine is a gradient of opportunity and constraint for the development types. The more tolerant the vegetation to clearing the greater the opportunity for higher density housing. The lower the tolerance to clearing the greater the opportunity for lower housing densities.

Movement Corridors

Wildlife needs cover, food, and water. The design objective was to provide for wildlife needs so that a maximum number of species present on the site could remain after development. Large areas offering diverse vegetation and water would make suitable wildlife refuges. These refuges would be connected by corridors of vegetation. Vegetation in refuges and corridors would be preempted from development. The corridors were provided by the design of a natural drainage system as described below.

Requirements to Avoid Hazards to Life and Health and Cost Savings for Construction

The ecological inventory of The Woodlands showed that flood hazard was the only natural hazard to life and health. Development in the area along major streams inundated by the projected 100-year flood (under development conditions) was preempted. In addition to the use of some soils as sinks for high-frequency storm drainage, a system of naturally occurring swales and stream corridors supplemented with man-made swales

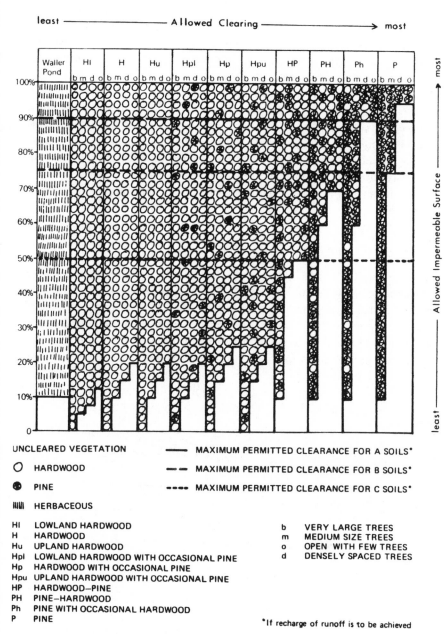

least ——————————— Allowed Clearing ——————————→ most

Figure 8. Suggested clearance percentages based on vegetation types.

was designed to carry storm runoff from the low-frequency events. Development in the 25-year flood zone of the smaller drainage ways was also preempted. The swales and stream corridors were left in a vegetated condition which helped preserve the woodland environment and maintain corridors for wildlife movement. Wherever possible, the drainage system was routed over permeable soils to further increase the infiltration of storm runoff. Coupling this with the siting plan for infiltration of storm runoff, the need for conventional storm sewers was eliminated. This saved an incredible $14 million dollars in development costs and raised land values due to the elimination of unsightly concrete ditches, in addition to minimizing the disruption of runoff-recharge relationships, helping to preserve the woodland environment, and helping to provide for the maintenance of wildlife on the site.

Opportunities and Constraints

The constraints to housing were the flood zones and restrictions placed on clearance by the vegetation analysis. This meant that areas prone to flooding, wetland areas, and hardwood areas were considered restrictions to development. Opportunities for various housing types were determined from the allowed clearance of vegetation and the impermeable surface permitted by the soil groups so as to allow infiltration of the high-frequency storm. figure 9 shows the distribution of soil groups and the vegetation types mapped with constraint factors for one portion of the new town site. The different soil groups of figure 9 are most suited to different types of housing,

Table 11. Housing Suitabilities Related to Runoff Holding Capacity of Soil Groups A, B, C, and D

Map Code	Housing Suitability
3A1	All types and densities suitable
3A2	A or B soils used for recharge of runoff from C or D soils should not be developed or cleared. C and D soils for which A or B soils have been provided to accomplish recharge have no development restrictions
3A3	Low-density housing
3B1	Suited to high-density housing with runoff carried by natural drainage system
3B2	All types suitable, but drainage will be required

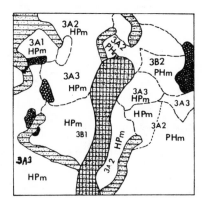

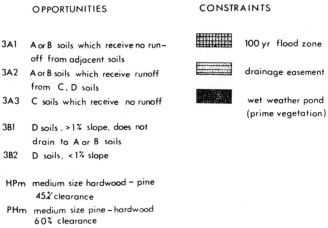

OPPORTUNITIES

3A1	A or B soils which receive no run-off from adjacent soils
3A2	A or B soils which receive runoff from C, D soils
3A3	C soils which receive no runoff
3B1	D soils, >1% slope, does not drain to A or B soils
3B2	D soils, <1% slope
HPm	medium size hardwood – pine 45% clearance
PHm	medium size pine – hardwood 60% clearance

CONSTRAINTS

- 100 yr flood zone
- drainage easement
- wet weather pond (prime vegetation)

Figure 9. Mapped opportunities (as determined by soils and vegetation). Suitability for the housing types is given in Table 11.

since the storage capacity of the soils for the 6-hour 25-mm event must not be rendered inadequate by too much impermeable surface. The suitabilities are identified in table 11. For those areas that are not restricted by the defined constraints, a certain percentage of clearance was allowed, based on the vegetation present, a maximum amount of coverage by impermeable surfaces was set by the water-holding capacity of soils, and a certain type of housing with its characteristic density could be accommodated. figure 10 shows the clearance, coverage, and allowed density for the area in figure 9.

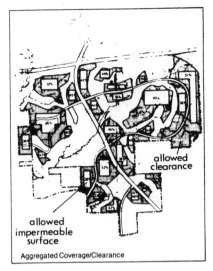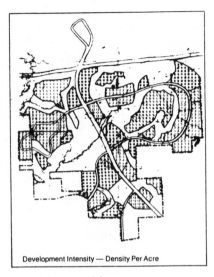

Figure 10. Clearance coverage and housing densities determined for an area.

Summary

The development will surely have impacts on the landscape and the natural processes occurring within it, but the development scheme allows for minimum disruption of the hydrologic cycle—recharge is maximized, exacerbation of flooding by development minimized, the groundwater and baseflow to streams augmented vis-à-vis conventional drainage, and erosion hazard reduced due to vegetated drainage ways. Desirable wildlife and vegetation are also preserved. Planning for The Woodlands encompassed far more. Site planning and phasing were considered in detail, as were the location of roads and industrial, commercial, and recreational areas. Engineering and economic considerations were incorporated into the overall development plan. Wildlife and the other components of the landscape were treated in much more detail than described here. The scope of the example is limited, as the inclusion of larger areas and more land uses greatly increases the complexity, and would require a great deal more space to describe.

An understanding of the features of a landscape, i.e., the soil, geology, hydrology, vegetation, and wildlife, as well as how they interact or are linked by natural processes, allows some understanding of the effects specified types of development will have on the whole ecosystem. Certain elements of the landscape may therefore become determinants of the pattern of planned land uses so as to minimize the adverse affects on the landscape. In The Woodlands example vegetation, soils, and the nature of the hydrologic conditions of the site were the most important determinants in the siting of residences. In other areas, certain other natural features may be more important determinants of planned land-use patterns. For instance, areas underlain by cavernous limestone bedrock, fault zones, or areas of vertisols may preclude building, or the ameliorative design strategies necessary to protect lives, property, or natural resources will be costly. Ecological planning as it is described here is sound in practice as well as in concept. In the case of The Woodlands, this type of planning saved the development corporation money in construction costs.

Presently [1979] there are 2,500 residents in The Woodlands, and the first phase of development is underway. The ecological plan was submitted to HUD in 1972 and led to a $50 million loan guarantee, the maximum under Title VII provisions.

References

Berger, J. 1978. "Towards an Applied Human Ecology for Landscape Architecture and Regional Planning." *Human Ecology* 6 (2):179–99.

Juneja, N. 1974. *Medford—Performance Requirements for the Maintenance of Social Values Represented by the Natural Environment of Medford Township, New Jersey.* Philadelphia: Center for Ecological Research in Planning and Design, University of Pennsylvania.

Leopold, L. B. 1968. *Hydrology for Urban Land Planning—A Guidebook on the Hydrologic Effects of Urban Land Use.* U.S. Geological Survey Circular 554. Washington, D.C.

MacDougall, E. B. 1975. "The Accuracy of Map Overlays." *Landscape Planning* 2 (1):23–31.

McHarg, I. L. 1969. *Design with Nature.* Garden City, N.Y.: Doubleday, Natural History Press. 1992. Second edition, New York: Wiley.

Wallace, McHarg, Roberts, and Todd. 1974. *Project Reports for the Woodlands New Community: (I) An Ecological Inventory, (II) An Ecological Plan, (III) Phase 1: Land Planning and Design Principles, (IV) Guidelines for Site Planning.* Philadelphia: Wallace, McHarg, Roberts, and Todd.

Part V

Linking Knowledge to Action

An important aspect of Ian McHarg's career is his involvement in numerous actual community design and regional planning projects. Throughout his career, he has been both a theorist and a practitioner. He straddled the academic and the professional worlds, blurring the distinctions between teaching, research, and service. Much innovation is captured in the professional reports produced by Wallace-McHarg Associates; Wallace, McHarg, Roberts, and Todd; and the Penn Department of Landscape Architecture and Regional Planning. These reports contain detailed lists of the project participants. McHarg always sought to give credit to all involved in each undertaking. Such acknowledgments were rare in the 1960s and, unfortunately, remain too infrequent. They reveal a multidisciplinary team approach to planning and design as opposed to a plan or a design produced by a single individual. An emphasis on process rather than a prescribed end-state plan or design is also revealed.

Among McHarg's many articles and papers, there are a few detailed accounts of his projects (I believe too few). Although even in his most theoretical papers actual projects are discussed; there are few detailed, reflective analyses of his plans. Included here are two descriptions of plans, a plan, plus one call for a more comprehensive planning framework. These four works were written in collaboration with professional colleagues.

The first description is McHarg's well-known plan for the Green Spring and Worthington Valleys in Maryland, written with his partner David Wallace. The planning study was not undertaken for a governmental jurisdiction; rather it was privately financed by local residents. In this 1964 study Wallace and McHarg addressed many of the problems resulting from suburbanization that are still prevalent and are likely to continue: How can prime farmlands be retained? Where are the best locations for new developments? How can growth be managed? How can environmentally sensitive lands be protected? How can the health and safety—the sustainability—of the area be ensured for current and future residents?

The Plan for the Valleys was, and remains, a unique combination of graphic presentation and economic analysis. Drawings were used to illustrate the deleterious consequences of uncontrolled growth as well as the prospects for imaginative planned growth. The economic analysis was used to illustrate that planned growth was as profitable as (and more fiscally responsible than) uncontrolled growth.

Central to the plan was McHarg's notion of "physiographic determinism," that is, the prospect that "development should respond to the operation of natural processes." This is, of course, McHarg's central message.

The plan was innovative in numerous ways. The attorney-planner Ann Strong suggested that a "real estate syndicate" purchase and transfer development rights approach be explored to manage growth. This idea was a precursor to both current land trusts as well as purchase and transfer of development rights programs. Today, Maryland leads the nation in farmland protected as a result of state and county purchase of development rights programs. Various zoning suggestions also pioneered subsequent performance-based, exclusive farm-use, large-lot, and environmentally sensitive lands zoning.

The Plan for the Valleys was a turning point for McHarg. He discovered a voice for vivid description of the environmental issues we face. In his PBS film, *Multiply and Subdue the Earth*, for example, he proclaimed, "if something isn't done—the future metaphysical symbol for the valleys will be a roll of toilet paper."

The Plan for the Valleys is thoroughly documented in *Design with Nature*. The Vermont and The Woodlands plans followed the publication of McHarg's landmark book. The 1972 Vermont study provides a comprehensive discussion of the ecological approach to planning. The study was conducted for Wilmington and Dover, Vermont; the Windham Regional Planning and Development Commission; and the Vermont State Planning Office. The study was undertaken at the time when Vermont was launching its innovative growth-management requirements.

The period following the first Earth Day and the publication of *Design with Nature* has been called "the environmental decade," when "a quiet revolution" in land-use regulation occurred (see Bosselman and Callies 1971). Land-use regulation is a state right and states generally had passed this authority on to local governments to protect the public's health, safety, welfare, and morals. During the "quiet revolution" states started to pull back some of their powers from local government and to require that specific environmental elements be addressed in local plans and ordinances. Hawaii was the first state to exert its authority, enacting statewide zoning. Even more far-reaching and influential state initiatives were adopted in Oregon and Vermont.

Ian McHarg influenced the growth control efforts in Vermont and produced one of the first plans in response to the state law. In 1970 he addressed the joint houses of Vermont legislature at the governor's invitation. McHarg entered the Vermont debate about state land-use initiatives and urged legislators to adopt what would become Act 250. Several local leaders from Wilmington and Dover heard McHarg address the Vermont legislature. "They liked what they heard and prevailed upon McHarg to undertake a pilot planning study" (Rushman 1997, p. 3).

The study was conducted with limited funding. As a result, all data were generated by the townspeople, then compiled, analyzed, and synthesized by regional planning graduate students at Penn. The Wilmington and Dover study, thus, is an example of citizen participation in what is normally considered a technical step in the planning process. Environment attorneys Victor Yannacone and Arthur Palmer provided legal assistance. McHarg's firm—Wallace, McHarg, Roberts, and Todd—was involved in this "philanthropic" effort. McHarg directed the study and was assisted by three of his most capable lieutenants from the firm: Michael Clarke, David Hamme, and Narendra Juneja.

Michael Rushman, who was a young planner in the northern Catskills during the early 1970s, has made a critical analysis of the Wilmington and Dover ecological planning study twenty-five years after its publication. Both a planner and a lawyer, Rushman asked, "Has Vermont stayed the course with ecologically-based planning?" He notes that Act 250 contains both a planning component and a regulatory component (Rushman 1997). The plan by McHarg and his colleagues addressed both, but emphasized the planning component. Rushman found that, since its promising beginnings, Vermont has favored the regulatory component over the planning component and, in the end, although developers, towns, and the attorneys of both must go through many procedural hoops, there is little substantive change on the ground. In fact, Rushman finds little difference with neighboring New Hampshire, well known for its local control and antipathy to government regulations.

Michael Rushman also studied the impact of the study on Wilmington and Dover themselves. The study by McHarg and his colleagues had some influence on the town plan of Wilmington but none on Dover. The overall local influence, however, has been minimal. Still Rushman indicates several recent planning initiatives in Vermont where the McHarg influence lingers and is perhaps resurging. These efforts involve the watershed-wide cooperative management efforts in the Connecticut River Valley and bioregionally based planning of the Northern Forest (Rushman 1997). In fact, Rushman holds more hope for ecologically based planning in these efforts "rather than with traditional jurisdiction-based comprehensive planning."

The Woodlands provides a more successful outcome, at least in the short term. The Woodlands new community was introduced in chapter 19 that summarized the suitability analysis. In this section McHarg and Jonathan Sutton provide a more holistic account. Like the Plan for the Valleys and the Wilmington and Dover study, the planning for The Woodlands was undertaken by McHarg's consulting company. Wallace, McHarg, Roberts, and Todd developed the ecological plan for The Woodlands near Houston, Texas, for the Mitchell Energy and Development Corporation in the early 1970s. The Woodlands was one of fifteen Title VII U.S. Department of Housing and Urban Development (HUD) sponsored new towns and the only one not to go bankrupt (Steiner 1981).

The Woodlands and the other HUD Title VII new communities were planned at a climax of American interest in new towns. During the 1960s Reston, Virginia, and Columbia, Maryland, both near Washington, D.C., created considerable interest among elected officials, developers, planners, landscape architects, and architects. New towns were viewed as a solution to America's urban woes, which were brought in sharp focus during the Civil Rights movement of the 1960s. In contrast to the suburbanization that occurred in the United States after World War II, a coordinated program of urban reconstruction and of new town development was undertaken in Europe with considerable success.

The HUD Title VII new communities were also planned following the passage of the National Environmental Policy Act (NEPA). As a result, the Title VII new towns were to address both social and environmental concerns. Private developers, mostly large homebuilders with little social or environmental planning expertise, received guaranteed loans of $50 million to plan and build these new towns. Eventually fifteen HUD Title VII new communities were initiated, including The Woodlands. George Mitchell, the developer of The Woodlands, was a Texas oil baron with deeper financial resources than the other HUD Title VII developers. Mitchell turned to McHarg because of Wallace, McHarg, Roberts, and Todd's environmental planning acumen. After all, who would better address NEPA requirements than the man who had helped to create its intellectual base and methodological framework?

McHarg and his colleagues with other consultants and Mitchell's staff planned the new community around the drainage and, as the name implies, the woodlands of the site. McHarg and Sutton note in their 1975 *Landscape Architecture* magazine article that the analysis of ecological processes "determined the form of The Woodlands." Computer technology was used in this analysis. In fact, the computerized soil and vegetation surveys conducted in the first planning phase represent one of the first actual applications of geographic information systems technology to a built project.

The Wallace, McHarg, Roberts, and Todd effort linked regional environmental information to detailed ecological design. The Woodlands is an important link in the American tradition of new town planning that began with the Spanish Laws of the Indies in 1573 and continued through the planning of Williamsburg, Philadelphia, Savannah, and Washington, D.C. The Woodlands can be viewed as part of the organic approach of that tradition that began with Olmsted's Riverside, Illinois, and was carried on by John Nolen, Henry Wright, Clarence Stein, and the Greenbelt New Towns of the New Deal. The neotraditional town planners, or new urbanists, of the 1990s (i.e., Elizabeth Plater-Zyberk, Andres Duany, and Peter Calthorpe) have rekindled this approach.

McHarg has undertaken both actual projects, like The Woodlands, as well as conceptual projects. After the publication of *Design with Nature*, McHarg focused largely on three overlapping interwoven idea projects: the understanding and application of human ecology, the application of computers to ecological planning, and very large-scale ecological inventories. He proposed these inventories, initially, at the national and, eventually, at the global scales. His premise was that ecological planning depended on a sophisticated database. If such comprehensive inventories could be collected, stored, updated, and made accessible, then accurate and fair environmental assessments of future activities could be undertaken.

McHarg's first opportunity to formally propose a national inventory came in 1972 when U.S. Environmental Protection Agency (EPA) administrator Russell Train asked him to propose a comprehensive plan for environmental quality. The EPA gave a grant to the American Institute of Planners (AIP) for the study. Gerald Mylroie then contracted McHarg through Wallace, McHarg, Roberts, and Todd. Mylroie also formed an AIP advisory group of prominent planners for the project, including Robert Einsweiler as chair, Alan Kreditor, James Park, Robert Paternoster, E. Jack Schoop, Paul Sedway, and Harold Wise. Einsweiler had previously helped to sponsor McHarg's ecological study for the Twin Cities region in Minnesota.

McHarg's resulting report *Towards a Comprehensive Plan for Environmental Quality* was quite influential within the EPA and helped to define the early development of environmental impact assessments. However, McHarg's central recommendation to establish a national ecological inventory was not followed by the EPA. Through the years the EPA did evolve a computer-based inventory that was not as comprehensive as McHarg's proposal.

The EPA's system is known as the Environmental Monitoring and Assessment Program (EMAP). McHarg had a second opportunity to propose his grander vision in 1990 when EPA administrator William Reilly sought

McHarg's advice on EMAP. McHarg responded with his colleagues John Radke, Jon Berger, and Kathleen Wallace with a proposal for a National Ecological Inventory. Radke is a geographer who was running Penn's geographic information system (GIS) lab at the time and is currently on the University of California-Berkeley faculty. Berger and Wallace were both graduates of McHarg's regional planning program. Jon Berger also holds a doctoral degree in city planning from Penn. The central chapter of their 1992 report "A Strategy for a National Ecological Inventory" is included here.

The timing of the release of their report in 1992 doomed its implementation. Their champion, William Reilly, left office with the defeat of George Bush. The recommended National Ecological Inventory was not pursued by the EPA. However, President Clinton's Secretary of Interior Bruce Babbitt proposed a National Biological Survey. McHarg continues to consult with the Department of the Interior about the design of the National Biological Survey. He also remains committed to both smaller-scale comprehensive GIS-based inventories, such as for the state of Alaska, and larger global-scale ecological databases. Eventually, national and global inventories will no doubt be conducted and hopefully become an ongoing element of planning and decision making at all scales. As McHarg and his colleagues note, such inventories could well be the most important acts to protect the environment in history, "indispensable for intelligent regulation and management, but moreover, capable of transforming both environmental research and education."

References

Bosselman, Fred, and David Callies. 1971. *The Quiet Revolution in Land Use Controls.* Washington, D.C.: U. S. Government Printing Office.

Rushman, Michael J. 1997. McHarg's *Ecological Planning Study for Wilmington and Dover, Vermont,* "Twenty-five Year's Later: Has Vermont Stayed the Course with Ecologically Based Planning?" (unpublished paper). Tempe: School of Planning and Landscape Architecture, Arizona State University.

Steiner, Frederick. 1981. *The Politics of New Community Planning.* Athens: Ohio University Press.

20

Plan for the Valleys vs. Spectre of Uncontrolled Growth (1965)
with David A. Wallace

Lewis Mumford summed up the importance of the Plan for the Valleys as follows:

> *This Plan for the Green Spring and Worthington Valley is brilliantly conceived and thoroughly worked out, down to the detailed demonstration of a better community pattern, based on the cluster instead of the row, for the individual housing development. In both method and outlook, this is the most important contribution to regional planning that has been made since Henry Wright's original 1926 report on the Development of the State of New York. McHarg and Wallace have shown by constructing an appropriate many-sided model what great opportunities for improving the human habitat actually exist once the forces that are now blindly despoiling the landscape and depressing every human value are guided with intelligence and imagination to more valid goals. The Plan for the Valleys in both its method of approach and its human aims should serve as a pattern for all future efforts to conserve life values in a growing community, where uncontrolled or misguided developments may, as in so many parts of California, obliterate the very natural advantages that stimulated this growth. This report should guide not only the farsighted Council that brought it into existence, but also communities all over the United States that are confronted with similar problems who have too often been frustrated and deformed by ill-conceived highway and residential settlement plans, and which can be saved or improved only following the strategy that the Plan for the Valleys has worked out.*

Mumford's forward to this Landscape Architecture *magazine article nicely intro-duces this important plan.* McHarg *discusses it more comprehensively in* Design with Nature.

The Plan for the Valleys is a privately financed planning study for 70 square miles of Baltimore County northwest of Baltimore undertaken by Wallace-McHarg Associates of Philadelphia. It examines a larger segment of Baltimore's rural hinterland, now sparsely populated and ripe for development. It is a study which has significance to many problems of metropolitan growth and suburbanization.

The basic originality of this study lies in the client and the problem itself. A large number of landowners of this 45,000-acre area constituted themselves into The Green Spring and Worthington Valley Planning Council. This private, nonprofit organization recognized that current planning powers could neither prevent destruction nor ensure wise development. It assumed the initiative for the preparation of a plan and the responsibility, with public powers, for its realization. This assumption of initiative and responsibility on the part of landowners is both remarkable and thoroughly commendable.

The Plan for the Valleys, the report submitted to the Planning Council, exists in two forms, a technical report of some 80,000 words and an illustrated synopsis designed for submission to each participant landowner (figure 11). This report contains five concepts which, while important to the study area, have a wider relevance as conceptual tools for planning for metropolitan growth.

If planning necessitates the posing of alternatives with the costs and benefits of each, it is necessary to be able to demonstrate the physical and financial consequences of the *status quo* extended into the future. This is the second element in the study with some claim to wider relevance. The existing population of 17,000 was predicted to increase to between 110,000 and 150,000 in thirty years by William Grigsby, housing market analyst for the study. An Uncontrolled Growth Model was developed by which the physical form of the future could be seen if no new planning powers were introduced. The physical form of this product is described as The Spectre. The profits from land sales under this process were calculated as a base line for comparison with other alternatives. The description of this process reveals the commonality with the rural fringes of all metropolitan areas.

One face of the future is revealed in the Spectre Map (figure 12). Uncontrolled growth, occurring sporadically, spreading without discrimination, will surely obliterate the valleys, inexorably cover the landscape with its smear, irrevocably destroy all that is beautiful or memorable. No matter how well designed each individual subdivision may be, no matter if small parks are interfused with housing, the great landscape will be expunged and remain only as a receding memory.

Yet this melancholy process produces enormous profits in land sales and development. In the study area these will total $33,500,000 in development value by 1980. Consequently, any alternative method of development must aspire to equal this level of development value.

The nature of prospective uncontrolled growth was represented in both graphic and financial terms. It was rejected as a spectre. Given the anticipated population to be accommodated and the development potential of the area, what principles can avert spoliation, ensure enhancement, and equal the development values of uncontrolled growth? The Plan for the Valleys depends exclusively upon *physiographic determinism* to reveal the optimum pattern of development. This concept is yet another aspect of the report having wide relevance to problems of development. In short, physiographic determinism suggests that development should respond to the operation of natural

BIRD'S-EYE PERSPECTIVE

Figure 11. Bird's eye perspective as proposed, the Green Valley and the Worthington Valley, Maryland.

SPECTRE OF UNCONTROLLED GROWTH

Figure 12. How the valleys will look if current sprawl patterns continue.

processes. These processes will vary from region to region. The application of the concept in the study area was circumstantial, but the concept is, however, general in its applicability.

As the name suggests, the Valleys contain three major features, the Green Spring, the Worthington, and the Caves Valleys. These broad, sweeping lands have been well farmed for 200 years. In pasture, with dairy and horse farms, these great valleys are beautiful and memorable. They are defined by wooded ridges to both north and south with a major, intervening wooded plateau.

The first test used is the *genius loci*, the genius of the site. This was revealed as the major valleys and their wooded, confining slopes. The initial conclusion suggested that, while these were vulnerable to development, easily destroyed, and attractive to developers, the maintenance of the pervasive character and beauty of the area required that the valleys be exempted from development. Subsequent physiographic analysis involved topography, sub-surface geology, surface and groundwater, the 50-year flood plains, impervious soils, slopes in excess of 25 percent, and forest cover.

Geological examination revealed that the valleys were coterminous with the major aquifer in the metropolitan area, groundwater used for wells and feeding city reservoirs. Development over this aquifer would constitute a hazard to health. Consequently development was prohibited in the valleys.

As surface water and groundwater are interacting, development was prohibited on riparian lands 200 feet from the edge of streams. For reasons of safety, development was prohibited on the 50-year flood plain; and impervious soils were identified and exempted from development requiring septic tanks. These features predominate in the valleys. In the next category, development was prohibited on all 25 percent slopes and on unforested valley walls. The last category, forest cover, was most abundant on plateau, ridges, and valley walls. Here development was limited to one house per three acres of wooded valley walls, one house per acre on wooded plateau. No restrictions were imposed upon the open plateau, and all restrictions as to density were waived for promontory sites suitable for tower apartments.

While the application of these criteria suggested prohibition of development in the valleys and restricted development on valley walls, the plateau exhibited few restraints upon development. Examination showed that development, conforming to physiographic determinism, could absorb all prospective population at densities consonant with market preferences. Without violating the *genius loci* of the great valleys, this development was located in a hierarchy of communities, a country town, and several villages and hamlets.

When this proposal was examined in terms of the development value produced, it was seen to create an anticipated value of $7 million in excess of the uncontrolled growth model.

Given a projection of population, the next question is how to carry out a development conception that satisfies both amenities and development values. The major innovation in this realm is the proposed real-estate syndicate developed for Wallace-McHarg by Ann Louise Strong. This device suggests that the landowners of the valleys constitute themselves into a syndicate and acquire, among other powers, the development rights of the land for either cash or stock. The syndicate is seen as a private planning and/or development instrument supplementary to public planning processes.

The syndicate can both develop land and preserve open space. It may acquire either development rights, options, first refusals, or title to land as a method of ensuring that development be in accord with the plan. For these rights, it pays either in stock or in cash, in full or by installments. It may also be the agent through which bilateral or multi-lateral agreements between landowners are negotiated in conformity with the plan. It may thereafter sell title or rights or lease land for development according to the plan or may act as developer itself, either singly or in cooperation with other agents. The profits from these transactions will be used to reimburse landowners whose property is not planned for development, and to finance additional purchases of rights or title or for outright development.

The basis for this proposal lies in the expectation that planned growth is likely to develop $7 million more land value by 1980 than uncontrolled growth, that land values will appreciate over time, particularly on the plateau, and, that a real estate syndicate can utilize this increasing value as the basis of its operation.

The final aspect of the Plan for the Valleys which may contain some wider relevance is the concept of an accumulation of powers. A sequence of both private and public actions, including the acquisition of new powers, is shown in a timed sequence.

The public powers necessary to realize the plan extend from the vigorous enforcement of present powers to entirely new controls requiring state legislation. It is a primary objective to obtain public acceptance of the plan in principle, reflected in directives to various agencies of county government. A most important defense of the area lies in the county intention to sewer the plateau but not the valleys. In the absence of sewers, the recent state health regulations prohibiting development on the 50-year flood plains, impervious soils, and steep slopes are of vital importance. These regulations should be rigorously enforced. Sewer and highway policy can be used strategically to guide development to the plateau and divert it from the valleys.

In addition, new public powers must be sought, mandatory cluster zoning, subsequently expanded to include deeding, minimum 3-acre zoning, promontory zoning, promontory zoning for highrise development, and minimum 25-acre zoning are all advocated. Natural resource zoning, including compensation where necessary, is recommended and would include floodplain zoning, forest and woodland zoning, steep slope zoning, and riparian zoning. Special assessment districts and public development corporations are less immediate objectives.

The Plan for the Valleys then contains these five aspects, private planning, the uncontrolled growth model, physiographic determinism, the real-estate syndicate, and the accumulation of powers. It has revealed a process whereby a beautiful landscape can absorb growth without destruction and a parallel process by which this may be realized. The report presents its thesis in the form of propositions from which the sequence of analysis and proposals are revealed:

- The area is beautiful and vulnerable.
- Development is inevitable and must be accommodated.
- Uncontrolled growth is inevitably destructive.
- Development must conform to regional goals.
- Observance of conservation principles can avert destruction and ensure enhancement.
- The area can absorb all prospective growth without despoliation.
- Planned growth is more desirable and as profitable as uncontrolled growth.
- Public and private powers can be joined in partnership in a process to realize the plan.

Fortune magazine reviewed the study and quoted from the report, "The United States awaits a large scale demonstration of a beautiful landscape developed with wisdom, skill and taste." Its comment, "This could be it."

21

An Ecological Planning Study for
Wilmington and Dover, Vermont (1972)
with Wallace, McHarg,
Roberts, and Todd

Especially after the publication of Design with Nature, *McHarg undertook numerous ecological planning studies for local, state, and federal agencies as well as private businesses and nonprofit organizations. These studies were conducted by the firm Wallace, McHarg, Roberts, and Todd or at Penn or, as in this case, some combination. During the 1960s and 1970s there were many interactions between the firm and the university. The founding partners of the firm were academics, and theories and methods generated at the university were often tested at the firm or vice versa. Many students and alumni worked at the firm. The Wilmington and Dover study was selected for inclusion here because it epitomizes that close relationship. It is republished here without the many detailed, colorful inventory maps that McHarg became well-known for.*

The study is also included because of its connection to the innovative state growth management (or growth control, as it was called then) efforts of the early 1970s. The Wilmington and Dover study was a partnership involving local citizens, the regional planning commission, the Vermont State Planning Office, Penn regional planning students, and Wallace, McHarg, Roberts, and Todd. The recommendations in the plan are closely linked to Act 250, Vermont's pioneering land-use and development control law. In total the study resulted in twenty-five recommendations. Some were followed, some not. From these suggestions it was clear that McHarg and his colleagues envisioned the study both as a beginning and as a reference point for decision making. Ecological planning is an ongoing process, one where information about a place is used to chart paths for its futures.

Preface

It began one snowy day in 1970, when Ian McHarg traveled to Vermont at the governor's invitation to address the joint houses of the legislature on the subject of an ecological planning study for the state. The address was received with mixed emotions, either limitless enthusiasm or equally intense aversion. One small group, already converted, was anxious to proceed immediately with a pilot plan for Dover-Wilmington, and so, in view of the State House, over many cups of coffee, Ellen Reiss, Robert McCafferty, Peter Zilliacus, and others initiated a process which reaches a certain culmination now with the publication of this study two years later.

It was Robert McCafferty of Wilmington who first suggested the study. He, with Ellen Reiss, William Schmidt, the executive director of the Windham Regional Planning and Development Commission, Ted Riehle, Benjamin Huffman, and Bernard Johnson of the State Planning Office, were the cadre which developed the idea and generated support for it. The planning commissions of both towns participated, notably Verne Howe and Merrill Haynes of Wilmington and Elva Turner, Peter Zilliacus, Rodney Williams, and Richard Joyce, all of Dover. After inordinate efforts by all concerned it became clear that a modest study would be financed, employing funds from the U.S. Department of Housing and Urban Development, the state of Vermont, the Windham Regional Planning and Development Commission, and the towns of Wilmington and Dover. A magnificent picnic meeting was arranged to be held, Peter Zilliacus cooked a gourmet meal, and the study was formally authorized. But the problems had only begun. It was immediately clear that the funds were totally inadequate for the study envisaged. It was as clear that the same dedication and generosity which had characterized the preparation must permeate the entire study. It would have to be a philanthropy, both from the citizenry and the consultant. In fact the operation of the study required that all data would be generated by townspeople, gratis. But, it should be noted, that while the data collectors were unpaid, they were not amateurs. As to the consultant, the partners [of Wallace, McHarg, Roberts, and Todd] agreed that the study would be done at cost, it would pay no overhead and produce no profit. But that was still not enough. It was impossible to pay prevailing salary scales and so graduate students of regional planning from the University of Pennsylvania were retained as the work force. Although students, the three staff members were considerably skilled. They were Karen Glotfelty, Richard Notzold, and James Wilson. Other staff engaged in producing the report were Ravindra Bhan, Susan Beatty, Carolyn Jones, and Margaret Dewey. The consultant also relied upon John Edinger of the University of Pennsylvania for his insights on sanitary engineering and water supply. Finally, enormous assistance was provided by attorneys Victor Yannacone and

Arthur Palmer who are well known for their devotion to writing and defending laws in support of ecological planning, whose special efforts will make the study especially valuable to the towns. The entire study was under the direction of Ian McHarg, assisted by Michael Clarke, the project manager, David Hamme, and Narendra Juneja.

In Vermont a much larger group had been assembled. The indefatigable Ellen Reiss was the local coordinator; Verne Howe, chairman of the Wilmington Planning Commission, supervised students who surveyed streams. Arthur Ball, a young forester waiting to join the Army, undertook the vegetation survey. Dr. Ralph Haslund, a physics professor, resident of Wilmington, invented a device for measuring stream flow. Dozens of residents from both towns cruised the area day after day recording land-use information. The tedious business of assembling data on property was undertaken by Peter Zilliacus, an erstwhile restaurateur now in public service. Dr. Charles Ratte, a geology professor, and his students assembled data on geology. As a result, a considerable segment of the population was actively engaged in finding out the nature of the region they inhabited. It was at once an educational experience and a significant accomplishment of community involvement in the planning process. While the more normal method of contracting a professional team may have produced more data, it would have produced neither the educational experience nor the planning commitment which did in fact result.

The data are imperfect, and this caused much anguish. Should the study halt and await better data or should it proceed? But, in fact, the study has revealed more and better data for Wilmington-Dover than may exist for any other area of Vermont. These data allow good first approximation judgments to be made on the destiny of the region. The process should continue, more and better information should be developed, but it is important to recognize that much has been accomplished; a small group of people know much of their region, they are competent to discuss their destiny and, not least, they have initiated a most remarkable and commendable planning process.

The objective of the study was to develop and apply an ecological planning method to the areas of Dover and Wilmington. This method should reveal the region to its inhabitants as a natural system which is at once a social value system. So understood, the region should be comprehensible as a system of opportunities and constraints for all prospective land uses. Moreover, the study was required to consider alternative dimensions for future growth, to relate these to the opportunities afforded, and to advise on a development structure which provided the maximum social benefit to the community at the least social cost. The areas hazardous to life and health, where high social values existed or where the environment was inordinately intolerant, were also to be identified as unsuitable for development.

Having identified the region and demonstrated alternative patterns of growth responsive to ecological realities, it was necessary to determine the degree to which its recommendations could be affected. This involved an examination of powers now reposing in state, regional, and local governments, giving particular attention to the extent to which they can be made mutually consistent. The study should be complementary to the objectives of both the Regional Planning Commission and the State Environmental Board. It should be seen as a pilot for the State Land Use Plan as well as for other Vermont towns, and the basis for the promulgation of Town Ecological Laws. We commend this report to your attention.

Summary of Recommendations

1. The study shall be employed as the basis for a continuing ecological planning process involving data collection and interpretation. However, the present data as identified herein shall be used as the basis for public and private action.

2. The study shall be examined in public hearings and, as amended, be adopted as a public planning document, as prescribed by the Vermont Planning and Development Act and by other legal devices ensuring its use in planning decisions.

3. All future town, regional, and state planning decisions shall be preceded by environmental impact statements of all alternatives considered.

4. In the absence of ecologically relevant local statutes, Vermont Acts 250 and 252 shall be employed as the major instruments for controlling land use.

5. In conformance with Act 252 and Act 250, Section 12a(1), no new locations shall be established for discharge of sewage into streams and lakes.

6. In conformance with Act 252 and Act 250, Section 12a(1), no increase in discharge of effluent volumes shall be authorized at existing sewage treatment plants prior to a detailed investigation of aquatic ecosystems.

7. Before granting a development permit under the water requirement provisions of Act 250, Section 12a(2), a developer shall provide a record of pumping tests as evidence of adequate water resources.

8. As prescribed by Act 250, Section 12a(3), any new development shall provide its own water supply, in that the present public water supply of Wilmington is unsafe, and Dover has no water supply system.

9. As prescribed by Act 250, Section 12a(4), flood plains and muck soils, sand and gravel aquifers, steep slopes over 15 percent, and areas above 2,500 feet elevation shall be prohibited from development.

10. As prescribed by Act 250, Section 12a(8), certain scenic areas, wildlife

habitats, and historic sites as identified in this study, shall be exempted from development.

11. The urban suitability and protection maps identified in this study shall be adopted as land capability plans under Act 250, Section 12a(9).

12. Full implementation of the intent of Act 250 shall be achieved at the town level by the enactment of ecologically sophisticated, environmentally responsible, socially relevant legislation, dealing with local development. Such legislation shall include zoning and subdivision regulations under Chapter 91 and a new class of environmental protection acts.

13. The present uniform commercial and one-acre residential zoning shall be revoked, and development be guided by new zoning categories in response to intrinsic suitability as defined by the study.

14. New taxation policies shall be adopted to provide benefits to long-term owners of rural lands through tax deferrals, homestead exemptions, and special assessments for properties under voluntary restrictive-use covenants.

15. A new Highway Route 100 proposed by the Vermont Highway Department shall not be accepted until it is demonstrated that improvements to the existing road system cannot accommodate traffic demands.

16. Sewage planning and management areas (now comprised of Fire Districts 1 and 2) shall be enlarged to include the aquatic ecosystem of Harriman Reservoir and its drainage area, and Rock Creek Watershed.

17. A development tax or a special capital gains tax shall be imposed on profits from the sale of land, the funds from which to be used for environmental protection programs.

18. The Green Mountain National Forest shall acquire certain lands within its jurisdiction.

19. Wilmington and Dover shall acquire or invite the state to acquire property rights to preserve regional resources and other natural and cultural features where private action or use of noncompensatory regulations is not effective.

20. The proposed Vermont Land Acquisition and Development Agency shall be activated and invited to take actions to induce future urban growth into suitable locations in Wilmington and Dover.

21. It is recommended that Wilmington and Dover create their own public corporations to acquire and improve suitable lands, and that they convey these lands to private enterprise for appropriate uses.

22. It is recommended that private foundations, trusts, and other civic organizations acquire and maintain those lands identified in this study as requiring protection.

23. Wilmington and Dover should invite landowners to constitute themselves into real estate syndicates to control the timing and location of future development.
24. Developers whose subdivisions are already platted shall revise their plans wherever possible to conform with the intrinsic suitabilities of their properties.
25. Certain land uses in conflict with intrinsic suitability shall be defined as non-conforming uses.

The Ecological Planning Method

The method employed is described as ecological planning. Simply, it means understanding Wilmington and Dover as a natural system, recognizing that the natural elements which compose regions are also social values. Certain places are better suited for towns, parks, farms, and ski slopes than others. If the towns can be described as a natural system, and if the elements that compose it can be seen as social values, then it becomes possible to plan. It is then necessary to identify places hazardous to life and health on the one hand, and areas which are intrinsically fitting for all of the prospective uses which are likely in the future. The region can be described under the titles of climate, geology, physiography, groundwater and surface water, soils, plants, and animals. The phenomena in each of these categories are variable: more or less stressful climates, rocks of different strength and stability, slopes obstructive or beneficial, water of varying quality and quantity, soils differing in properties and usefulness, vegetation comprised of different communities having distinct values, and similarly for animals.

But people have been responding to this natural system and continuously adapting it. We must then proceed to identify people, families, institutions as both phenomena and processes. This can best be done by invoking history and examining colonial subsistence agriculture in the last century and the resurgence of the present. So current land use can be seen in terms of cultural history, revealed in the pattern of settlements, villages, roads, farms, schools, and the like.

Natural environments are then variable, comprised as they are of variable rocks, slopes, soils, plants, animals, and microclimates. People, in turn, have modified those processes and phenomena and added variable environments of their own. Similarly, environmental needs also vary. The requirements for crop agriculture are different from those necessary for ski slopes or a new community. If we can identify the place as composed of different environmental attributes more or less suitable for human uses, we can then assemble all of the factors most beneficial for every prospective use. When we find locations which provide all beneficial attributes, and where the major detrimental factors are absent, we can describe such locations as intrinsically suitable for the land use in question. The summation of this exercise is the representation of the place as having variable intrinsic suitabilities for all prospective land uses. Such are its opportunities. The reverse image reveals those areas or processes hazardous or stressful to life or health, where environments are intolerant, or where significant social values exist.

Given this vantage, it next becomes necessary to examine alternative futures. A projection of the most likely future can be made, assuming that all current trends will continue. That may be compared to other options for growth which respond entirely to the towns' intrinsic suitabilities. Social costs and benefits can be approximated for all alternatives. It then becomes necessary for the towns to choose their own futures through public discourse and political and legal instruments. This will require citizens to participate in an active planning process using methods and data such as those employed in this study.

Geology

The Green Mountains are comprised of metamorphic rocks, most of which are derived from pre-existing mountains of the Pre-Cambrian period, dating back one billion years ago. This very early geologic history consisted of alternating sequences of mountain uplifts, erosions, submergences, sediment depositions, and volcanic activity. The Green Mountains were created at the close of the Ordovician period about 425 million years ago, the same time as the Taconic mountain-building sequence. Structurally, they are an anticlinorium, an arched complex of folds.

Unconsolidated surficial rock material overlies bedrock, derived predominantly from the Pleistocene Epoch, which occurred between 10,000 and one million years ago. During the Pleistocene, Wilmington and Dover experienced two glaciations, separated and followed by times of post-glacial erosion and deposition. Advancing ice scoured large areas over which it crossed, typically removing several feet of bedrock. Many stream valleys transversed by ice were probably filled with glacial debris, whereas parallel valleys were scoured and given a characteristic U-shape. During their advance, glaciers accumulated rock debris by exerting plucking stresses on bedrock underneath and along their margins. When the lower part of the ice became heavily laden with debris, excesses were deposited as ground moraine which were then overridden by the more active ice above. Toward the end of glacial advances, ice became stagnant and began to melt, leaving deposits that took various forms such as kames, kame terraces, eskers, and valley trains. The Pleistocene has thus left clear marks in the area.

Physiography

Physiography can be best understood from those natural processes responsible for its being. Following the Green Mountain episode, the landscape has continued to evolve through successive glaciations and subsequent fluvial processes. Physiography, then, is a product of the past. But it is continuing to change, although usually at imperceptible rates. Streams are downcutting their beds while reworking sediments in their flood plains. Weathering processes in the highlands are transporting materials downslope to new locations in the lowlands. People are contributing changes to physiography faster than nature, as evidenced by sand and gravel pits, road cuts, and landfills.

Our perception of physiography depends upon our proximity to the landscape. A geographer looking at the eastern United States would say that New England is comprised of the Appalachian Highland, but a Vermonter would describe his state as divided into at least five regions: the Champlain lowland, the Taconic Mountains, the Vermont Piedmont, the Northeastern Highlands, and the Green Mountains. And still, to say that Wilmington and Dover are within the Green Mountains, does not describe their physiography sufficiently. Actually, four subregional expressions of the Green Mountains can be identified in the towns: the Ordovician Highlands, the Pleistocene Highlands, the Pleistocene Lowlands, and the Pleistocene Valley. While their origins are speculative, their geographical identity is accurate.

The degree of slope constitutes savings or costs to building construction. Slopes exacerbate hazards of overlying soils. Physiography is the essential visual component of the landscape.

Soils

In New England, soils are derived from a soil-building process called podzolization. Decomposing organic matter on the ground surface produces acids which leach through the organic horizons downward through the mineral layers below, dissolving and removing carbonates of all kinds. This process produces soil horizons which from top to bottom are: a partially decayed organic zone where litter is decomposed into humus; a leached acidic siliceous zone (called the A horizon); and an accumulated zone containing carbonates and other soluble salts leached from above (called the B horizon). When fully developed, this is the profile of a true podzol soil.

Less developed variations of the true podzol, known as podzolic soils, characterize southern New England. Their organic, leached, and accumulated horizons are smaller. The towns are comprised of both podzol and podzolic soils. Soils data for Wilmington and Dover are limited to soils associations, constituting large groupings of soils related to one another. However, many are comprised of different combinations of the same soil types. Moreover, many soil types in the same association may be very different from one another with respect to their intrinsic suitability for different land uses. This means that association data for Wilmington and Dover cannot be interpreted for planning purposes. Other than identifying locations of alluvial, muck, and peat soils, the towns must ask the Soil Conservation Service to undertake a modern detailed soil survey, from which the data can be used in town planning.

Hydrology

Groundwater occurs in rock interstices. Consequently, thick deposits of glacial sands and gravels have the most consistent potential for groundwater storage. Few interstices were created during the metamorphic period creating the area's bedrock. Most of them are derived from secondary joints and fractures created after the rocks were formed. Mapping of surficial geology has just been initiated, and knowledge of bedrock fracture zones is very limited. However, a search for groundwater would initially seek deep sands and gravels in the Deerfield Valley in the vicinity of recharge sources such as streams, ponds, and bogs. The next choice would be the Wilmington gneiss (the most weathered rock with the most fractures), particularly in locations overlain by surficial deposits and near recharge sources. The amphibolites seem to be the least-probable groundwater sources. Little information is available on groundwater in the other bedrock formations, although they apparently are not as good as Wilmington gneiss or as bad as the amphibolites.

Of 53 inches of average annual precipitation, 25 to 30 inches become natural runoff in the streams. Highest flows occur with snowmelt, and thereafter decline continuously, reaching annual lows in August or September. During the fall and early winter streamflow gradually increases to another peak and remains steady or declines slightly until spring again. Harriman Reservoir receives all of the Deerfield's drainage, and is a closure to an otherwise open stream system. Conversely, Lake Raponda (in Wilmington) is located at the head of a drainage area, making it less vulnerable to pollution from entering streams.

Plants

Other than a generalized forest map and some field observations, little is actually known about the towns' plant communities. Present vegetation originates from the close of the Pleistocene over 11,000 years ago. Following the retreat of the last glacier, Wilmington and Dover were probably initially occupied by tundra, later by boreal trees, and then predominately by the hardwood forest. Early people, following not long after the last glaciation, are thought to have caused extensive burning. Their disturbances and, later, eighteenth- and nineteenth-century agriculture and twentieth-century logging, have continually rearranged the composition of the forest. Moreover, plant succession itself is a dynamic process, responsible for steady change in plant associations without human intervention.

The towns are comprised of both the northern hardwood and boreal forests. The hardwood forest is comprised predominately of American beech, yellow birch, and sugar maple, in association with eastern hemlock, sweet birch, red maple, basswood, white ash, and northern red oak. Pioneer species after cutting or fire include aspen, birch, spruce, or fir, depending upon site conditions. The spruce-fir forest is comprised of red, white, and black spruces and balsam fir. Pioneer associations after fire or cutting may include those same species or hardwoods, depending upon site conditions.

Stressful climates and thin, infertile soils above approximately 2,500 feet elevation are extremely unfavorable for all plant forms. Yet, plant life is necessary if this fragile zone is to contribute significantly to the water-holding capacity of the land.

Animals

Diverse and abundant populations of birds, mammals, and fish reside in the towns (figure 13). White-tailed deer, skunks, woodchucks, chipmunks, squirrels, red fox, rabbits, hare, porcupines, and grouse may be found practically anywhere. Bear, bobcat, and possibly coyotes live in the highlands. Ducks, woodcock, beaver, mink, muskrats, and probably otter live along streams and other wet areas. Streams and lakes contain brown trout, brook trout, smallmouth bass, perch, and many other species. Mappable data are limited primarily to white-tailed deer, beaver, and trout.

White-tailed deer are ubiquitous forest dwellers, but they are also found along forest openings, orchards, and farmlands where they forage. With few natural predators such as the bobcat, populations are controlled only by hunters, starvation, and disease. The major diet is twigs, although herbaceous plants and fruits are eaten in the summer. The towns have numerous colonies of American beaver, who build dams of sticks, mud, stones, and tree trunks to impound water to a sufficient depth to prevent its freezing to the bottom. Beavers build lodges in their impoundments with entrance chambers opening under water, thus protecting themselves from their enemies.

Most of the towns' streams are good trout waters, despite seasonal low flows, warm temperatures, and soft waters with low buffering capacities. Particularly good reaches are steep gradient streams mixed with riffles and pools having wooded streamsides protected from the sun. Harriman Reservoir is one of Vermont's largest lakes and is potentially a very important fishery resource.

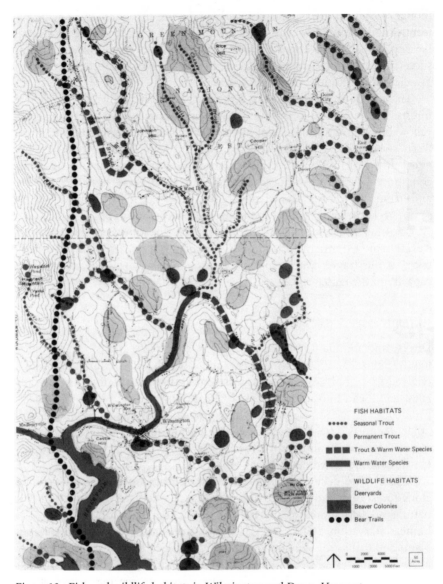

Figure 13. Fish and wildlife habitats in Wilmington and Dover, Vermont.

Climate

Adiabatic cooling of air masses rising across the Green Mountains causes higher precipitation on mountain slopes and valleys. Local observations suggest the occurrence of a very heavy snowfall zone at elevations above approximately 2,200 feet, whereas heavy snows occur throughout the region. Prevailing winds are from the northwest in winter and west or southwest in summer. Consequently in winter, exposure is maximum on west-facing slopes and minimum on east-facing slopes. Tops of ridges and hills are always windy. Local winds tend to be channeled down or up the Deerfield Valley.

Because of their high elevations, the towns' temperatures are as low as those of northern Vermont. Frost-free periods average fewer than 60 days annually. Local temperatures vary as much as 10 to 20 degrees, such extremes occurring between steep slopes facing the sun (south) and steep slopes oriented away from the sun (north). Fog and frost pockets tend to occur in low areas adjacent to the Deerfield River. Climatic categories identified are:

1. Heavy snow
   Leeward wind conditions
   South slopes, over 3%
   West slopes, over 8%

2. Heavy snow
   Moderately windy
   South slopes, over 3%
   West slopes, over 8%

3. Heavy snow
   Leeward wind conditions
   All slopes, 0–3%
   West slopes, 3–8%
   East slopes, over 3%
   North slopes, over 3%

4. Heavy snow
   Moderate wind conditions
   North slopes, over 3%
   East slopes, over 15%

5. Very heavy snow
   Leeward or moderately windy
   South slopes, over 8%

6. Very heavy snow
   Leeward or moderately windy
   All slopes but south, over 8%

7. Heavy snow
   Windward conditions
   All slopes, all orientations

8. Very heavy snow
   Windward conditions
   All slopes, all orientations

9. Fog areas
   All wind conditions
   All slopes, all orientations

Life Zones

As a sum of interacting natural processes, the place can be expressed in terms of the diverse environments it imposes upon people and other life forms. Employing available data on microclimate, surficial geology, physiography, hydrology, and soils, twenty terrestrial life zones were identified and ranked in a gradient of winter stress. Aquatic life zones were also identified. While the data are limited and imperfect, the life zones have considerable value as a first approximation of locations unfavorable or propitious for human habitation. The life zone data have been reviewed by a number of town residents, several of whom corroborated its general accuracy by agreeing upon its representation of winter stress conditions in areas with which they were familiar. Also seen is a coincidence of winter deeryards and locations of least winter stress.

The Place Is the Sum of Natural Processes

Natural processes and phenomena have been described thus far as discrete components: mesoclimate, microclimate, bedrock geology, surficial geology, groundwaters, surface waters, soils, plants, and wildlife. But the place must be seen synoptically as a single expression of all its parts. The science of ecology seeks this perspective, being derived from the Greek word, *oikos*, meaning house. Ecological planning in turn seeks to understand the place before it prescribes alternative futures.

The place can be described at various levels of sophistication. It can be mathematically modeled, either manually or with computers. Many hydrologic models, for example, have been developed to describe relationships among physical, chemical, and biological characteristics of streams and lakes. The place may also be seen through graphic techniques, using overlays indicating the coincidence, for example, of microclimate, geology, soils, plants, and animals. It can also be identified descriptively.

Most simply, the place can be described as a "layer cake." Its bottom layer is the metamorphosed rocks, the oldest of which are derived from Pre-Cambrian times dating back over one billion years ago. The Taconic mountain building sequences occurring at the close of the Ordovician period some 350 million years ago produced the Green Mountain anticlinorium.

The place's surficial geology is its next layer, derived from the Pleistocene period which occurred between one million and 10,000 years ago. During that time the place experienced two glaciations, separated and followed by times of post-glacial erosion and deposition, which plastered the pre-existing bedrock with unconsolidated sediments.

The third layer is the place's physiography, a product of geologic history, expressed as four subregions within the Green Mountain physiographic province: the Ordovician Highlands, the Pleistocene Highlands, the Pleistocene Lowlands, and the Pleistocene Valley.

Groundwater is interbedded within the geologic and physiographic layers of this conceptual layer cake. Only small quantities are found in the original interstices of metamorphic rocks. Most of it is in joints and fractures which have formed subsequent to the period of metamorphism and in the unconsolidated overburden deposited during the Pleistocene.

Surface waters are the next layer. The place's dendritic streams have steep gradients and variable flows. They are soft and slightly acid, making them especially vulnerable to change. Ecologically, Harriman Reservoir has created a closed system for nutrient movement.

Soils come next, derived from geologic parent material, physiographic characteristics and other layers above, i.e., climate, plants, and animals. The place's soils develop from podzolization, a natural acid-leaching process forming soil horizons of humus, silicates, and carbonates and other soluble salts.

Plants are the next layer, influenced by all of the physical characteristics of the place which produce a variety of sites appropriate for a diversity of species from two distinct forest associations. The northern hardwood forest is the predominant climax association. However, the northern boreal forest is also seen because of the place's high elevation physiography.

Animals are the next layer, depending upon all of the place's attributes for their habitats and survival. In addition to people, we see diverse and abundant populations of birds, fish, and other mammals, which include white-tailed deer, skunks, woodchucks, chipmunks, squirrels, red fox, rabbits, hare, porcupines, grouse, bear, bobcats, ducks, beaver, mink, muskrats, brown trout, brook trout, bass, possibly coyotes and otter, and many other species.

Micro- and mesoclimate comprise the top layers of the cake. Microclimate, i.e., the climate near the ground, varies with elevation, landform, slope, gradient and orientation, and vegetative cover. Wind is important, reaching its maximum on west-facing slopes, and the tops of hills and ridges. Insolation is equally so, reaching its minimum on steep, north-facing slopes. The place's mesoclimate is controlled principally by prevailing sub-arctic westerly winds and the frequent passage of warm, moist air coming up from the Gulf Coast.

This description of the place would be inadequate without emphasizing its dynamism. It is comprised of many systems involving energy movement through precipitation, erosion, deposition, transport, heating-cooling, freezing-thawing, evaporation-condensation, weathering, insolation, and countless other physical-chemical processes. These physical-chemical processes involve and affect all life forms, their birth, development, movement, reproduction, and death.

The Land and the People

A review of the historical development of the towns of Wilmington and Dover offers little insight into the future. The most probable form of development will have little relation to and will place small value on the history of these communities. Artifacts and structures which recall an earlier day abound in the area and are of interest to at least a portion of the present residents. Their value in the future, however, may be more in evoking a general American myth of a comfortable rural past rather than their specific relationship to the histories of the towns.

While the specifics of the past are of little interest here since they instruct little, the more general trends which have set the stage for the future deserve some attention. The towns were both first settled in the eighteenth century and grew predominately as farming and herding communities with such attendant industries as these activities would comfortably support. By the latter part of the nineteenth century, the farms were exhausted by questionable agricultural practices and were no longer able to support even a marginal level of production. At about the turn of the century, both communities turned to tourism to replace declining agricultural industries. The Village of Wilmington, the Handle Road area, and Lake Raponda became popular summer resorts. But the decline of the resident population, begun by the depletion of the meager soils, continued to the middle of the present century. These patterns meant that neither town ever went through a period of intensive urbanization. They have been, and they still remain essentially rural. This pattern is now threatened by recent development.

The Immediate Past

It is in the immediate past that the key to the future may be found. Following World War II, an increasingly affluent American population sought escape from the boredom and tension of routine daily life by increasing expenditures in a broad range of leisure activities. The entrepreneurial response was quick and is still continuing.

In Wilmington and Dover this response took the form of developing ski areas. Mt. Snow, Haystack, and Carinthia provide one of the most popular ski complexes in the State of Vermont. As a result, the ski industry, including the ski areas themselves and the supporting commercial activity, is the primary economic activity in the towns. In the last five years, the growth has assumed logarithmic proportions. During this period, Mt. Snow doubled its lift capacity, and plans are now afoot for even further expansion.

Significant to the future of the towns has been a shift in preferences of this tourist population. The original day and weekend skier has been joined by a vacationer of a less transient nature. This person, often not primarily a skier, is seeking a fixed vacation spot for both summer and winter in a pleasant rural environment. Satisfying this desire often requires the purchase of a second vacation home. The trend of second home ownership has gradually increased in Wilmington and Dover over the past ten years, culminating in Chimney Hills, a subdivision of about 800 lots. As of 1971, there were 539 second homes in Wilmington and 411 in Dover. An additional 2,000 acres have been sold throughout the two towns for second home development. The pattern of the future has been established (figure 14).

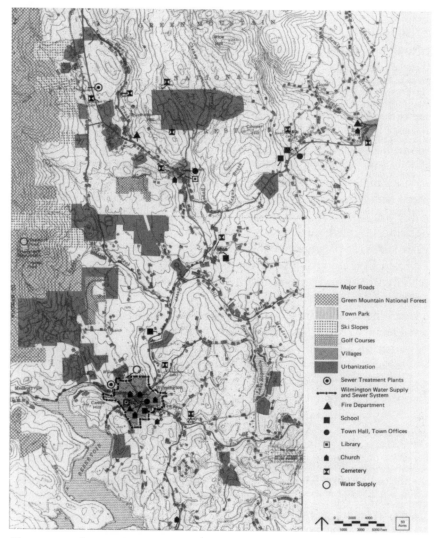

Figure 14. Facilities and development patterns in Wilmington and Dover, Vermont.

The Structure for Change

Presently the Village of Wilmington has a sewage treatment and a water supply system. A small private treatment plant serves Snow Lake Lodge at Mt. Snow, and a few of the subdivisions provide private central water supplies. The remaining developed areas rely on individual wells and septic systems. These services are inadequate to meet the needs of the anticipated growth of the area.

The provision of large-scale central sewer facilities in Fire Districts 1 and 2 (new sewer service areas in the Town of Dover) will dramatically alter the pace and the pattern of future development. Both of these sewer plans are in the proposal stage, and it remains to be seen whether or not either can satisfy the provisions of Acts 250 and 252. Without discussing the relative merits of the proposals, it is sufficient to say that, given the present market situation the two systems, if constructed, will attract development from elsewhere in the area in spite of other considerations of accessibility, land use, and environmental suitability.

The new population in Wilmington and Dover will be largely seasonal in nature. Employment and major purchases (cars, durable goods, etc.) will take place elsewhere. From the local communities these residents will require police and fire protection, road maintenance, trash and garbage disposal, occasional (probably emergency) health service, and general government services such as code enforcement. Sharp increases in town expenditures can be expected in these areas. These same residents will add little to the public school enrollment. They will not vote. They will pay property taxes. They will not support local churches or other institutions. In general they will establish a social life separate from that of the permanent residents. Finally, the seasonal population will add little to the human resources of the towns in terms of leadership or technically skilled personnel.

Regional access provided by the interstate system through Brattleboro is excellent. The decrease in travel time to major centers of population occasioned by this system is largely responsible for the development pressure upon Wilmington and Dover. It is doubtful whether further major improvements in travel time can be produced by additional construction in Vermont.

Travel between the interstate system and the destinations in the two towns can be made easier and thus more attractive by improvements to both Route 9 and Route 100. To maintain the desirability and the development demand of the area, Route 9 at least should be improved to ease traffic movement from Brattleboro to Wilmington.

Agents of Change

Wilmington and Dover are well located to exploit the second home market. The largest concentration of population in the United States lies within four hours' automobile travel of the area. This includes Boston, Providence, Hartford, New Haven, New York, and the northern part of New Jersey. Within six hours of travel lie Allentown, Trenton, and Philadelphia. While general population growth in this megalopolis is not high by national standards, the proportion of people moving into income brackets of $15,000 or more per year exceeds the general population growth rate. It is this higher income level that constitutes the market for second homes. As far as location is concerned, Wilmington and Dover can tap the largest potential market in the country.

The area is already well endowed with the kinds of large-scale recreation facilities for both summer and winter which provide the attraction for second home users. The three ski areas already mentioned provide a total of 19 cable lifts, and plans are underway to expand this total. Excellent snow conditions and good trails particularly at Mt. Snow, combine to ensure that Wilmington and Dover will retain or even increase their present share of the ski industry.

Summer facilities are less spectacular. Nevertheless, either actually or potentially, the elements for year-round recreation are well established. Two golf courses are already constructed. Lake Raponda offers limited swimming and boating. Lake Harriman is presently underutilized for summer water sports, but has an enormous potential. Molly Stark State Park in Wilmington and the Green Mountain National Forest in both Wilmington and Dover provide trails, picnic spots, and camp grounds. Both towns are laced with streams which offer good fishing in season.

As has been stated, Wilmington and Dover have been and are now essentially rural. The villages, the only population concentrations in the area, retain the patterns of public and publicly related uses which serve the communities. Suburban development, though increasing, is still too sparse to alter the general rural character of the towns.

This pattern means that the vast majority of land remains in relatively large holdings unencumbered by intrusion of public or institutional uses which tend to resist change. Land held in this pattern is relatively easy to assemble into even larger parcels if there is economic incentive to do so. This is precisely what has been happening in the two towns.

A number of landowners, corporate and private, in Wilmington and Dover have an avowed intent, either through direct development or sales to entrepreneurs, to subdivide the land for building lots. This pattern is already well underway.

As these owners continue to realize their intentions, more rural land will be converted to suburban residential patterns, and occupied mainly by second home purchasers. In addition to the 2,000 acres sold or developed since 1967, another 1,500 acres are in subdivisions which have been platted and approved but not yet sold. About 2,400 dwelling units will eventually be constructed in these areas. An estimated 7,500–10,000 acres are being held in lands whose owners intend to develop in the next ten years. Construction of this magnitude will change the existing environment and the established pattern of uses and functions.

The Spectre of Future Growth

From now through the next ten years, the full fury of the long developing storm will break over the two towns. The forces of market demand, land ownership, established recreation attractions, and accessibility will converge and mature to produce a holocaust of construction and change. Compared with the immediate future, the past, i.e., the period of preparation, will seem tranquil and benign.

It is possible to outline the dimensions of this change, given no new major effort on the part of the towns to control or direct growth to ensure the greatest local benefit. For clarity, new growth can be considered in two categories: the permanent population and the second home population. Totals can be expressed in terms of dwelling units because it is extremely difficult to assign population to seasonal homes. The actual number of occupants in a second home can vary widely from zero to a dozen or more during ski season.

Table 12 projects the permanent growth in terms of both population and population converted to households (so that it can be compared with the second homes).

Table 12. Resident Population and Households, 1970–1980

	1970	1975 High	1975 Low	1980 High	1980 Low
Population					
Wilmington	1,586	1,901	1,795	2,146	1,961
Dover	555	739	704	962	851
Total	2,141	2,640	2,499	3,108	2,812
*Number of Households**					
Wilmington	481	570	540	650	600
Dover	160	210	200	270	240
Total	641	780	740	920	840

*Based on existing average household size: Wilmington (3.3 people/household) and Dover (3.5).

The following set of assumptions were made to determine the total future growth:

1. Currently platted subdivisions will fill.
2. Reasonably certain proposals for new subdivisions will be platted, approved, and filled.
3. The national economy will remain expansive over the long term and

incomes in the eastern megapolitan area will continue to rise at or near the present rate.

4. At least one other major and one minor all-season recreation complex will be developed by the middle of the decade.

5. The expansion of the Mt. Snow ski trails will take place as planned.

6. Sewer plants will be constructed for Fire Districts 1 and 2.

7. Route 100 will be realigned and Route 9 will be substantially improved.

8. Major development corporations with well-trained and aggressive sales forces will continue to invest in the area.

9. National publicity will remain favorable for the southern Vermont area and particularly for the two towns.

It was assumed that certain other events would not come to pass.

1. No new major ski area will be built in or adjacent to the towns during this decade.

2. Somerset Reservoir and the Town of Somerset will not be opened up by improved or new roads.

3. Harriman Reservoir will continue to be used for limited recreation but no major residential development will be built on utility holdings.

4. No major new land use controls will be adopted nor existing ones rigorously enforced.

With these assumptions the total number of dwelling units in the towns can be estimated. Table 13 lists total dwelling unit count by 1980, existing and to be built, and permanent and second homes.

Table 13. Total Dwelling Units by 1980, by Town

	Existing Dwelling Units	Total Potential New Dwelling Units		Total Dwelling Units	
		High	Low	High	Low
Wilmington	885	4,322	3,436	5,207	4,321
Dover	534	7,478	5,684	8,012	6,218
Total	1,419	11,800	9,120	13,219	10,539

Table 14 identifies those units which are constructed to meet the demands of the second home market in Wilmington and Dover.

Table 14. Second Homes by 1980, by Town

	Existing Second Homes (1971)	New Second Home Development in Existing Subdivisions by 1975		Additional Potential Second Home Development by 1980		Total by 1980	
		High*	Low*	High†	Low†	High	Low
Wilmington	539	1,682	1,652	2,521	1,615	4,742	3,801
Dover	411	632	622	6,766	4,952	7,809	5,980
Total	950	2,314	2,274	9,287	6,567	12,551	9,791

* High = platted lots not developed, high permanent household projection.
  Low = platted lots not developed, low permanent household projection.
† High = high total dwelling unit projections, high permanent household projection.
  Low = low total dwelling unit projections, low permanent household projection.

Under the assumptions set forth above, the estimated growth by 1980 will be between 671 and 967 permanent households and between 9,791 and 12,551 vacation homes. Such is the likely face of the future for Wilmington and Dover, a 1,000 percent increase in dwellings. The process is visible, it has clear implications for the future. The prospect is a spectre of sprawl. How can it be resolved? What perceptions and powers proffer alternatives?

Powers to Preserve Natural and Social Values

The threat is imminent. It has catastrophic proportions. It is vitally necessary to devise a strategy. The first element is an ecological basis for a plan based upon substantial information and intelligent interpretations. This locates areas intrinsically suitable for all land uses. Next we must consider state regulatory powers. But they are not enough. Town ecological laws must be promulgated and passed. Nor is that enough. These will merely prohibit or refrain. It is necessary to develop positive inducements to ensure that development will occur on the most propitious locations. But first, let us examine social values and the powers of Vermont Acts 250 and 252.

Natural processes and phenomena have intrinsic values to the natural systems of which they are a part. Plants are used by animals. Flood plains accommodate floods. Natural processes also constitute social values to people. Geologic processes produce areas of scenic splendor. Skiers use the snow-covered slopes of Mt. Pisgah. Favorable soils and slopes are savings for construction. People have created their own values as seen in their villages, schools, roads, churches, and recreation areas. Once accepted that the place is a sum of social values, inferences can be drawn regarding its utilization to ensure optimum use and enhancement. These values can be identified in Wilmington and Dover, and they can be protected by the performance standards of Act 250.[1]

> ... a development or subdivision:
>
> 1. Will not result in undue water or air pollution ...
>
> 2. Does have sufficient water available for reasonably foreseeable needs ...
>
> 3. Will not cause an unreasonable burden on an existing water supply ...
>
> 4. Will not cause unreasonable soil erosion or reduction in the land to hold water ...
>
> 5. Will not cause an unreasonable highway congestion or unsafe conditions ...
>
> 6. Will not cause an unreasonable burden on municipal educational services ...
>
> 7. Will not place an unreasonable burden on local governments to provide services ...
>
> 8. Will not have an undue adverse effect on the scenic beauty ... aesthetics, historic sites, or rare and irreplaceable natural areas.
>
> 9. Is in conformance with a duly adopted land-use plan ...
>
> 10. Is in conformance with any adopted plan under Chapter 91 of Title 24.

These standards are used by district commissions in reviewing individual applications for subdivisions and developments. Clearly, these same standards must be seen in terms of their formal implications for entire towns and regions. Consequently, the evidence assembled for Wilmington and Dover must now be reconstituted as opportunities and constraints, employing standards 1 through 8 above. Thereafter, a synthesis of those values reveals intrinsic environmental and community structure, which can then serve as the basis for plans envisaged in standards 9 and 10 above.

Protection of Water Quality

Most tributaries of the towns are healthy, whereas the main stem of the Deerfield is becoming unhealthy as a result of treatment plants below Mt. Snow and the Village of Wilmington, septic tanks, and urban construction practices. An essential insight to any water quality management program for the towns is that Harriman Reservoir and the entire Deerfield drainage area above it represent an aquatic ecosystem and a single management unit. There is an immediate need to study the long-term effects of wastes entering this system. Fire Districts 1 and 2 are totally inadequate instruments for planning sewage disposal and should be so recognized. Vermont's water quality objectives have been stated:

> ... the waters be protected and used to promote the general public welfare and interest ... [and] maximum beneficial use and enjoyment of all the waters of the state; and . . . that all the waters of the state be of a quality conforming with or exceeding the classification standards for Class B water .. .[2]

No waste may be discharged into waters of the state without a permit from the Department of Water Resources.[3] Wastes are prohibited in certain streams.

> No new discharge of wastes, which will degrade in any respect the quality of the receiving waters, will be permitted above elevation 1,500 feet or ... at a rate of flow of less than 1.5 cubic feet per second at any elevation ... which waters are hereby described as pristine streams and tributaries.[4]

Except for the northeastern edge of Dover (below elevation 1500 feet), the towns' tributaries are pristine streams, meaning that no discharge permits will be authorized other than at locations already having permits, i.e., Mt. Snow and the Village of Wilmington. Discharges at those locations cannot exceed a dilution ratio of 30 to one at any time.[5] The capacity of Wilmington's treatment plant can be enlarged modestly only if a 30 to one dilution ratio is to be maintained at low flow conditions.[6] Interbasin transfer of wastes (outside of the towns) will probably not be permitted by the Department of Water Resources. Consequently, little if any increase in sewered population appears possible in the towns, using conventional treatment and stream effluent disposal methods. New sewered developments must employ advanced technologies for treatment and disposal which do not use streams. Recycling should be considered as a serious alternative. Disposal methods through lagooning, spray irrigation, and subsurface recharge and other devices may be feasible, some of which are being explored by the Water Resources Department.

However, the burden of proving that a proposed waste solution will not degrade water resources must be borne by the developer.

State laws also protect groundwaters and surface waters from pollution by septic tanks.[7] No landowner may subdivide prior to obtaining a permit from the Department of Health. A permit is granted only after an applicant demonstrates that site conditions are suitable, accounting for soil percolation rates, lot size, proximity to water supplies, ground slope, elevation above flood plains, the groundwater table, and bedrock conditions.[8]

Both towns have severe limitations for septic tank systems because of seasonal high water tables, presence of an impervious fragipan (24–30 inches below the soil surface), shallowness to bedrock, and steep slopes. All of these conditions cause sewage to appear on the ground surface from flooding or downslope flows, thus contaminating surface waters and constituting a serious health threat. Without adequate soils data, only some of the alluvial and muck soils can be actually identified as locations where septic systems should be prohibited, despite general knowledge that large areas of the towns are unsuitable for such use. The towns must obtain a detailed Soil Conservation Service survey. Local experience suggests that slopes approaching 15 percent and higher should be avoided in the interest of public health.

Provision of Water Supplies

In the absence of detailed groundwater survey data, a water budget was developed to quantify the towns' water resources.[9] A water budget simply is an accounting method to indicate amounts of water arriving, stored, and leaving an area over a given time period. It is derived from the following equation of hydrologic equilibrium:

> Surface + subsurface inflow + precipitation + imported water + decrease in ground and surface storage

> Equals

> Surface and subsurface outflow + consumptive use + exported water + increase in surface and groundwater storage

Safe yield or the annual quantity of water which can be withdrawn on a sustained basis was chosen as 25 percent of base flow or that portion of stream flow coming from groundwater.[10] Base flow estimates were made for different times of the year, and expressed in safe yields per acre.

Safe Yield Season	Persons/Acre at Gal/Day/Acre	100 gpd/Person
July, August, September	50.6	0.5
October, November, December	286.0	2.9
January, February, March	233.0	2.3
April, May, June	410.0	4.1

Water availability during the low-flow periods of August and September suggests that an all-season home with a domestic well should be located on a six-acre lot.[11] Conversely, a ski-season chalet used only in winter would require a 2.5-acre lot.[12] These calculations are guides and are not reliable for small areas where hydrologic conditions will vary. Nor are they substitutes for detailed hydrologic surveys. Yet, they suggest that development cannot be accommodated forever, solely using groundwater or free-flowing streams.

Harriman and Somerset Reservoirs are potential solutions to all future water supply problems in the towns, although both projects are currently operated for hydroelectric power generation. Some gross calculations show that Harriman could serve both purposes. Assuming a tenfold population increase in the next 15 years, about 2 percent of Harriman's storage would be required for water supply. Aside from the fact that it already exists, Harriman Reservoir is inherently better for large water supplies than those studied by the Soil Conservation Service for the Wilmington-Dover Area. Such small upland reservoirs are less reliable and floods fill them with cobbles. Today's most distressing water supply problem is Wilmington's public system, declared unfit to drink for reasons still unknown.[13] Future demands will rely upon new systems utilizing Wilmington gneiss, Deerfield sands and gravels, and Harriman or Somerset Reservoirs as the most promising sources.

Erosion and Water Retention

Erosion sediments shorten reservoir life spans, destroy fish habitats, increase floodstage levels, and clog drainage ways. Eroded soils have little utility for agriculture. Water infiltration, percolation rates, and storage capacity of eroded soils are diminished and, therefore, so is groundwater recharge. Erosion is exacerbated by surface runoff from rainfall, which loosens or picks up material by turbulence or eddy currents, aided by sediments already in solution which provide a scouring action. Slope gradients, as they increase, accelerate flow velocity, increasing the erosional force of running water. Surface runoff traveling over exposed soils, dislodges particles more easily than over vegetated surfaces where velocities are reduced and the soil surface is protected.

Most soils of Wilmington and Dover are inherently erodible because of their simple structures and fine grain textures, particularly on steep slopes. Inadequate soils data prohibit identifying locations of the towns' most hazardous soils. Removal of vegetation and prolonged exposure of soil surfaces on slopes should be accompanied by a management plan to restore vegetation and trap sediments. Soil disturbance should be avoided especially during nongrowing seasons of the year when immediate re-establishment of vegetation is impossible. Removal of forest vegetation in heavy snowfall zones (e.g., above elevation 2,200 feet) should be minimized to maintain snowpack conditions as long as possible for sustained groundwater and stream recharge. Excavation of sand and gravel aquifers should be prohibited to protect their storage capacities. Erosion hazard districts should be established from detailed soil and slope data.

Particularly fragile areas which are important sources of water are the upper Green Mountain zones, typically above elevations of 2,400–2,500 feet, where the sugar maple or beech hardwood forest is replaced by a transitional forest dominated by yellow birch, white birch, or red spruce. These areas have been described by Vogelman et al.

> Mountain soils with their high organic content hold large quantities of water which come from the high rainfall and fog moisture collections of forest trees. The water filters through the soils and eventually adds to stream flows, springs, and groundwater supplies in the valleys . . . the severe climatological environment of the upper mountain slopes imposes great physiological stress on plants growing in these areas. Removal or even disturbance of these fragile plant communities opens the soil to severe erosion and irreparable damage. The vegetation returns to these disturbed areas very slowly and with great difficulty.[14]

Vogelman has recommended that ecological disturbances in any form should be kept to an absolute minimum. Roads, structures, and septic tanks should be prohibited. Activities should be restricted to hiking and skiing. Vegetation openings and trails must be designed and maintained not to impede natural drainage, organic matter cycling or cause erosion. Vegetation on ski trails and lift line areas must be intensively managed to avoid soil loss.

Highway Congestion and Safety

The spirit of Section 12(5) of Act 250 is that no use will be permitted which will cause increase in traffic volume or interference with traffic flow which may result in highways becoming inadequate or unsafe, unless an applicant shares proportionate costs for improvement, expansion, or construction of highway facilities required insofar as such costs exceed the amount budgeted or planned by responsible agencies for such work in and about the area of the proposed use.[15] This principle becomes complicated in Wilmington and Dover, where Highway Routes 9 and 100 are already heavily congested and unsafe at times during ski months and occasionally during the summer and fall tourist seasons. Consequently, any new developments exacerbating those existing problems should be prohibited prior to improving present conditions. Yet, new Route 100 proposed by the Highway Department (Line FP) could be a disaster for both towns. The highway, proposed solely as a device to solve the traffic problem, presumes that the towns wish to encourage population growth. The proposed highway will attract vehicles which otherwise would not be in the towns, and could ultimately increase traffic congestion on town roads. Moreover, such an alignment will be a blight on the towns' scenic character and stimulate new developments in locations unsuited to such uses. Prior to accepting the proposed alignment, other options must be examined: improving existing roads, and facilitating traffic flow by removing certain obstructions, creating new turning lanes, and making roads one way at peak hours.

Schools

The ease by which the towns can provide education services as population increases is determined largely by capacities of present facilities, numbers of vacant seats, and the rates that those seats will be filled. The rates at which the schools will be filled in the years to come are hard to assess because of the difficulty of projecting increases in permanent population in a second home housing market.

The spirit of Section 12(6) of Act 250 is that no development or subdivision should be permitted which will increase the number of students attending public schools beyond their capacities in terms of space, facilities, instructional, and administrative staff, transportation, and other school-related services, unless the applicant can ensure that such uses will return their proportionate share of expected costs.[16] This will require a developer to prepare an impact statement indicating numbers of dwelling units and bedrooms, price ranges of units, age distribution of children, percentage of seasonal and permanent populations, and other information necessary to determine the tax return to the community from units he is producing, and the number of children he will be adding to the school system. The towns, in turn, must have a reasonable program for expanding their school facilities. Should the proposed development put more students into the school system than it can take, the towns can insist on adjustments such as delayed construction, rearrangement of housing mix, or monetary contributions to the school system.

Governmental Services

Section 12(7) of Act 250 states that a proposed subdivision or development shall not place an unreasonable burden on the ability of a town to provide services such as police and fire protection, highway maintenance, storm drainage, refuse and garbage collection and disposal, and sewage and water systems. Otherwise, an applicant must ensure that his proposed use will return to the town its proportionate share of the costs for expanded services, or provide the services himself.

A 1964 study of Vermont towns examined relationships between size and efficiency of operation, and concluded that larger communities (6,000 persons average) did achieve economies of scale and provided more and higher quality services than smaller towns.[17] However, that study also found numerous exceptions to its general conclusions. Moreover, a 1965 study suggests that Dover's property tax burden per capita is much lower than the average Vermont town of similar size, whereas Wilmington's is much higher.[18] These phenomena are determined by the pattern of urban development, although their relationships are poorly understood. For example, whether the towns' economy of skiing and second homes really pay back in tax revenues what they cost is not actually known. However, there is little doubt that forecasted sprawled growth will exacerbate the problem of public services, and that much better land-use options exist for the towns.

Aesthetics, Natural Areas, Historic Sites

Section 12(8) of Act 250 requires a developer to consider his project's impact on scenic and natural beauty, aesthetics, historical sites, and rare and irreplaceable natural areas. Wilmington's and Dover's scenic values are comprised of many geophysical forms as described below in six categories:

1. *The mountain range and its base.* Mt. Pisgah and Haystack comprise the range, with gentle sloping lands at the base.
2. *Ridge tops, steep slope highlands, highland plateaus, and terraces.* Rice Hill, Whites Hill, Cooper Hill, Johnson Hill, and others are part of a high ridge system of ridge tops and steep slope highlands. Interspersed are highland plateaus and terraces.
3. *Hillock-knoll-terrace, prominent hills.* Wilmington's southeastern corner has a complicated low-relief topography comprised of hillocks, knolls, and terraces. Just north of this area, prominent hills such as Castle Hill accent major valley walls and lowland plateaus.

4. *Lowland plateaus and terraces, gentle regular slopes.* Lowland plateaus and terraces are found above major valley walls and below the mountain range. These are bounded or interlaced by gentle regular slopes isolated from other stronger geophysical forms.
5. *Valleys.* Tongues of small, V-shaped valleys are in the northeastern corner of Dover. Small but broader, U-shaped valleys are best developed in a band across the southeastern corner of Wilmington. The Deerfield Valley with its walls and rims is a major valley in both towns.
6. *Water.* Harriman Reservoir, Lake Raponda, Haystack Pond, smaller ponds, and the Deerfield River comprise this category.

Landscapes vary both in eminence and continuity, e.g., the mountain range and ridge tops are strong, whereas gentle regular slopes and terraces are weak. But, the strongest landscape is not always the most enduring. It may be vulnerable to human presence, as along ridge tops where even scattered residential subdivisions create broken teeth along the ridge line. To maintain the towns' natural landscapes, their tolerances to urbanization must be recognized.

- *Mountain range, major valley walls, rims.* Intolerant of urbanization. Any development would be broadly visible from miles away. The valley's continuity is highly vulnerable.
- *Ridge tops, steep slope highlands.* Visible from distant locations. All but very low-density development would destroy their continuity.
- *Gentle, regular slopes.* Not identified with other strong landscapes. Often, the immediate landscape near which many residents live. Very low-density development allowed as a conditional use if their identity can be maintained.
- *Prominent hills, V-shaped valleys, Deerfield Valley.* Modestly tolerant of low-density development, although their utilization must be designed to retain eminence and continuity.
- *Highland plateaus and terraces, U-shaped valleys.* Tolerant of urban development if sited carefully to be unobstrusive.
- *Hillock-knoll-terrace.* Tolerant because if properly utilized, they can conceal developments from one another.
- *Lowland plateaus and terraces.* Ideal locations for urban settlement. Their identity cannot be easily lost, and their relationship to adjacent landscapes offers diverse visual experiences.

The towns' spruce-balsam-fir forests, taken for granted by many Vermonters, are amenities cherished especially by non-Vermonters for their northern evergreen qualities. Existing stands deserve protection. Additionally, they are valuable winter wildlife cover, and are frequently underlain by wet soils. Consequently, these forests are poorly suited for urban development.

White-tailed deer are an amenity. In the winter they yard, i.e., they congregate in relatively protected areas with a food supply and where their movements are not hindered seriously by deep snow. These yards must be protected if white-tailed deer are to survive the winters. Similarly, other wildlife amenities are beaver colonies, streamside furbearers such as mink and otter, and sport fish, particularly trout.

Although Nell M. Kull has provided a beautiful account of Dover's history,[19] neither town has a documentary study identifying the degree to which history is reflected in existing buildings and places. An architect-historian should be enlisted to produce a documented inventory. Yet, considerable anecdotal information on the history of individual dwellings resides in town residents, which should be recorded before it is lost permanently. The villages of both towns appear strongly reminiscent of the way they looked over 100 years ago, and they should be considered as special historical preservation districts.

The Towns' Carrying Capacities

An approximation of the towns' carrying capacities can be expressed according to the populations supportable under stated conditions of sewage treatment and water supply (figure 15). Had adequate data been available, similar estimates would have been made for highways, education, and other social services.

Sewered Populations. Stream flow conditions in major tributaries were estimated for different times of the year. Of particular concern is late summer–early fall when stream flow is lowest and the allowable quantities of sewage in streams is most restricted by Act 252. During that period the towns can accommodate approximately 4,400 persons (at 100 gallons per day per capita) if a 30-to-1 dilution ratio is maintained. Stream flow is so low during that period that a relaxation of the dilution ratio to 15 to 1 still could not accommodate the forecasted 1975 population. This means that recycling and other innovative conservation measures are absolutely necessary to sustain a future permanent population with centralized sewage treatment systems. Yet, during the ski season when stream flows are near peak, perhaps 30,000 persons could be accommodated with a conventional sewage system without violating the 30-to-1 standard. Consequently, the concept of carrying capacity using a minimum dilution ratio becomes complicated by variable flows, indicating an immediate need for further research, particularly of the Deerfield and Harriman Reservoir, to determine the long-term effects of human wastes in the area's aquatic ecosystems.

Town Carrying Capacities Compared to Population Forecasts

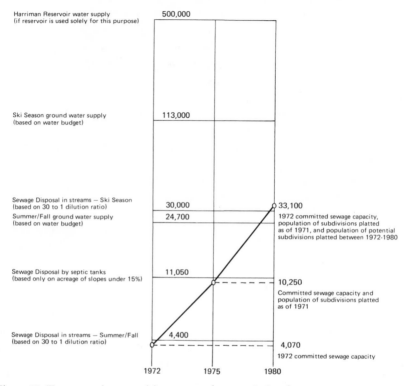

Figure 15. Town carrying capacities compared to population forecasts.

Septic Tank Populations. Town carrying capacities based upon exclusive use of septic tanks and leach fields depend upon dwelling unit lot sizes which, in turn, are determined by soil/slope characteristics and system design. In the absence of adequate soils data, calculations must be based upon the extent of vacant private land with slopes under 15 percent, which is approximately 13,000 acres. Assuming one half of that acreage is used for residences (the remainder needed for dedicated open space, streets, utilities, etc.), a net density of one-acre lots (at 3.4 persons per dwelling unit) gives a carrying capacity of 22,100 persons. However, local experience suggests that large, one-acre lot subdivisions would contaminate ground and surface waters, and that two acres should be a minimum lot size, thus indicating a population of 11,050. Obviously, all estimates are speculative in the absence of detailed soils data.

Water Supply Populations. The largest potential single sources of water are Harriman and Somerset Reservoirs. Harriman could possibly support

500,000 people if it were used solely for water supply. Water-budget cal-culations show how groundwater recharge rates vary throughout the year, determined mainly by temperature and evapotranspiration, since monthly precipitation remains about constant. Consequently, the carrying capacity of groundwater supplies also varies, being lowest in late summer and early fall (about 24,700 persons at 100 gallons per capita) and much higher during the January through March ski season (about 113,000 persons). Spring groundwater supplies are highest (over 200,000 persons) while fall–early win-ter conditions are slightly higher than ski season. These figures are approxi-mate, indicating magnitude of carrying capacity and not absolute limits. Both towns need a detailed hydrologic survey of groundwater, and should request immediate assistance from the Vermont Department of Water Resources.

Intrinsic Suitability

It is now possible to assemble all of the spatial values previously identified with performance standards 12(1) through 12(8) of Act 250, to invoke a sin-gle expression of the towns' intrinsic suitabilities for prospective land uses. This final step constitutes what in effect is a local land-capability plan cited in paragraph 12(9) of Act 250, with which Act 250 applications must conform to receive a permit. Moreover, such a synthesis will represent an essential component of a local or regional plan cited in paragraph 12(10) of Act 250, the final requirement of an Act 250 application.

A summation or synthesis of spatial values reveals two sets of potential structures for Wilmington and Dover. One represents a structure for the nat-ural or given environment, comprised of locations where nature is hazardous, stressful, or performing work for people. These locations should be managed in the interest of the public health, safety, and welfare of present and future generations. The other is a community structure, comprised of locations pro-viding the maximum concurrence of propitious factors for human habita-tion. Future population growth should be induced into these locations by appropriate incentives and land-use controls. Finally, the towns' committed structure must be acknowledged, comprising both natural and community elements such as the Green Mountain National Forest and the Village of Wilmington. That structure must be considered as permanent and irrevoca-ble. If the town residents, in fact, concur with the spatial values portrayed in the synthesis, they may then seek those measures by which the two inter-twining environments of community and natural process can actually be realized.

Based upon available data, a potential structure for the natural environ-ment is derived from the geographic distribution of primarily physiographic phenomena and scenic values. Ten districts are identified below in order of their need for preservation.

- Region 1. The fragile ecosystem above 2,500 feet and alluvial or muck soils, all located in landscapes (cited in the other regions below) intolerant to urban uses in varying degrees.
- Region 2. The fragile ecosystem above 2,500 feet, alluvial and muck soils, wherever they occur outside of the intolerant landscapes cited in Region 1.
- Region 3. Slopes over 15 percent located in landscapes very intolerant to urban uses, i.e., the Mountain Range and the walls and rims of the Deerfield Valley.
- Region 4. Landscapes very intolerant to urban uses, i.e., the Mountain Range, and walls and rims to the Deerfield Valley (excluding slopes over 15 percent of Region 3).
- Region 5. All slopes over 25 percent except those above elevation 2,500 feet on the Mountain Range, and the walls and rims of the Deerfield Valley, which are accounted for in Regions 1 through 4.
- Region 6. 15 to 25 percent slopes in landscapes intolerant to urban uses, i.e., ridge tops, steep slope highlands, and gentle regular slopes.
- Region 7. Landscapes intolerant of urban uses, i.e., those given in Region 6 (excluding 15 to 25 percent slopes of Region 6 and slopes over 25 percent of Region 5).
- Region 8. 15 to 25 percent slopes in landscapes moderately intolerant of urban uses, i.e., the Deerfield Valley floor, minor V-shaped valleys, and prominent hills.
- Region 9. 15 to 25 percent slopes in landscapes tolerant to urban uses.
- Region 10. Landscapes moderately intolerant of urban uses (cited in Region 8) without any other known restrictions.

Some of the phenomena given in the regions above are already committed to preservation when located in relatively permanent undeveloped areas such as the Green Mountain National Forest and other public open spaces, golf courses, and ski slopes. Finally, it must be recognized that the ten regions are based upon scant data and can be expanded enormously with better information on the towns' natural phenomena and processes.

Given a choice, new or expanding communities would seek those locations with plentiful groundwater, favorable microclimates, good soils and slopes opportunity, and within convenient reach of available governmental services such as fire protection and health facilities. Available data suggest six suitable urban districts, described below in order of their desirability.

- District 1 (most desirable). Locations which are very accessible (i.e., within one-half mile of a village center), with slopes under 15 percent, favorable life zones, the highest probability for finding ground-water, and near an existing recreation area.

- District 2. Locations generally very accessible, or within one-half mile of a major or secondary road, with slopes under 15 percent, and adjacent to, or within one-half mile from an existing recreation area. Either groundwater or life zone conditions may be restrictive.
- District 3. Conditions same as District 2, but with added restrictions. Includes locations adjacent to a recreation area but with groundwater or life zone conditions are restrictive. Accessible locations, not adjacent to a recreation area, which have good groundwater and life zone conditions.
- District 4. Conditions similar to District 3, with added restrictions. Very accessible locations but having no other attributes except slopes under 15 percent. Accessible locations with variable site conditions and distances from existing recreation areas. Poor access locations with other conditions as good as District 1.
- District 5. Locations which may or may not be accessible or adjacent to an existing recreation area, with slopes under 15 percent. Ground-water and/or life zone conditions are restrictive.
- District 6 (least desirable). Locations accessible or adjacent to an existing recreation area, without any other attributes except slopes under 15 percent. Locations with poor accessibility and variable site conditions.

These urban districts are based upon scant data and should be developed further with better information on natural processes and phenomena. Yet, they are sufficient to constitute a new urban structure for the towns whose benefits will exceed those of uncontrolled growth. Recent subdivisions have not chosen urban suitable locations, nor is it likely that future development will be more responsive. Therefore, a strategy must be devised to guide future growth.

Concepts for Growth

The towns' economic health will continue to depend upon the second home and recreation market mainly because alternatives such as extractive indus-tries, farming, logging, and most forms of manufacturing are not good prospects, at least during the next ten years. Specialized and finished product manufacturing aimed at markets on the East Coast may look favorably at Wilmington or Dover. However, these industries are also aggressively sought by other communities having larger labor forces and closer to metropolitan areas. Therefore, both towns must depend upon a recreation economy which, in turn, requires a beautiful unspoiled environment. This means that all future growth must conform to the towns' intrinsic suitabilities and that the pattern of trend growth as identified in this study must be avoided.

The next concern is how much growth should occur in Wilmington and Dover? It was Verne Howe, a member of the steering committee for this study, who finally gave focus to discussions between the committee and the consultant on the kinds of futures Wilmington and Dover residents really wanted. The issue, she said, was population growth, on which three conflicting opinions prevailed. One viewpoint is to minimize growth and keep Vermont rural. Another is to accommodate growth, since it seems inevitable. The third viewpoint is to encourage growth to improve the local economy.

Although it was beyond the study's scope, the consultant examined two of these viewpoints, i.e., to minimize or accommodate population growth as two different concept plans. An encouraged growth plan was not considered in that the population forecasts in both towns are so high that the differences between accommodating and encouraging growth is only a matter of degree.

A Concept to Minimize Growth

Population growth can be minimized by restricting town services, by preventing increases in the towns' carrying capacities, and by discouraging the creation of new recreation opportunities which attract people. This means limited snow-removal services and road maintenance, no new highways, no new sewage systems, no enlargement of existing sewage treatment plants, no new public water-supply systems, no new ski areas, very restrictive town ordinances, and acquisition of development rights on lands imminently subject to urbanization. Rigorous enforcement of Act 252 is essential because it can stop high-density developments unable to use septic tanks or discharge wastes into surface waters. However, Act 252 will also indirectly stimulate low density sprawl if developers build septic tanks to avoid the high costs of sophisticated sewage disposal or recycling systems. Consequently, actions to minimize growth must also consider impacts upon settlement patterns. Settlement can take the form of sprawl, where development is discouraged everywhere but may happen almost anywhere, or be nucleated, where development is discouraged almost everywhere save for a few selected prime locations.

A sprawl settlement pattern resembles trend growth, previously identified, although it would not be quite so disastrous. The nucleated settlement pattern is far more preferable even for a minimize growth concept. It would bring the least disturbance to the landscape and would be much less of a burden on town services. However, it would require enormous public control or private self-restraint and cooperation to ensure that all lands conform with a nucleated plan. This concept is most feasible when only a few large landowners are involved. Wilmington and Dover have large landowners, but they also have many small landholdings. This plan also presents the problem that the few fortunate landowners holding lands identified as prime urban suitable can profit from development, whereas all other owners of unsuitable lands are deprived of such gains. A private real estate syndicate comprised of any number of landowners is one device whereby all participants can share in the profits from development. Landowners benefiting from the plan would share their profits with those who give up their rights to development.

To demonstrate the minimize-nucleated concept, two prime urban-suitable locations were selected, one north and the other south of the Village of Wilmington. These sites, totaling about 350 acres, are appropriate locations for new village centers accommodating some 6,500 persons, assuming the availability of waste recycling, or advanced techniques for sewage disposal. Other good locations having the same acreage could also be selected in a minimize growth plan. However, the two sites chosen appear to have more attributes than any other locations in the towns. They have extensive edges along adjacent areas proposed to remain in a natural state, high sewering efficiency, superior scenic value, and favorable life zones.

A Concept to Accommodate Growth

This plan must accommodate a forecasted growth of about 9,000 to 12,000 new dwellings during the next ten years. The arguments for nucleating a major portion of that growth are even stronger than for the minimize growth plan. Moreover, if new construction relied exclusively on septic tanks, contamination of groundwaters and surface waters would be almost certain. Therefore, the density of a major part of this new growth must be sufficiently high to justify a new centralized sewage system. Expanded highway capacity, new public water supplies, and more town services are also implied.

Locations in the two highest categories of urban suitability were selected as centers for new growth to demonstrate an accommodate-nucleated growth concept. These locations reveal a new western corridor for future growth. It traverses both towns, situated between the Mountain Range and the Deerfield Valley, and extends from Mt. Snow to Harriman Reservoir. This corridor seems propitious for a year-long recreation economy based upon winter skiing and summer activities related to Harriman Reservoir. The developable area identified in the corridor includes 2,150 acres capable of supporting some 40,000 persons, assuming the availability of waste recycling or advanced techniques for sewage disposal.

Any plan to regulate and distribute population growth can only be so described if it contains the powers to realize its stated objectives. Therefore, an enumeration of those powers constitutes the essential ingredient of the planning process, i.e., a strategy for success.

A Strategy for the Future

Recent urban development has been increasingly destructive to the towns' natural resources and ignorant of their intrinsic suitabilities. In the absence of new powers which can regulate growth, both towns will experience large increases in population which, in spite of existing state and town regulations, will select locations mainly in response to the real estate market. Positive values to human location, such as good slopes and soils, plentiful groundwater, favorable climates, scenic beauty, and proximity to recreation opportunity and municipal services may be ignored, while locations unsuitable for development may be utilized. This can only worsen town problems of polluted streams and reservoirs, inadequate water supplies, soil erosion, despoliation of scenic beauty and historic village centers, degradation of natural plant and animal communities, congested highways, rising costs of municipal services, and higher taxes.

But other options exist. Future growth need not be destructive. Once understanding the towns as composed of natural systems constituting values either favorable or unfavorable to human location, two intertwining fabrics emerge. One is a natural structure where nature is hazardous, stressful, or performing work for people. The other is a community structure where nature beckons people and offers in varying degrees those environmental attributes from which they can benefit. This being the case, Wilmington and Dover with assistance from the State of Vermont and the Windham Regional Planning and Development Commission, must discourage future development from occurring in those locations which should remain in a natural or near-natural state, while inducing it to select those locations suited for such purposes. That can be achieved only through a strategy employing every device available in both the public and private sectors.

An Explicit, Replicable Public Planning Process

The first essential component of such a strategy is an explicit, replicable public planning process, as has been initiated by this study. It rests upon the simple proposition that good judgment requires good evidence. That is, given adequate information on the climate, geology, physiography, groundwaters and surface waters, soils, plants and animals, and equivalent socioeconomic data, it becomes possible to discern the place's opportunities and constraints and its intrinsic suitabilities for all prospective uses. This study was produced with a paucity of such evidence. Much better data are urgently needed. The four highest information priorities are: a new U.S. Geological Survey map (at 1:24,000 scale) to be used for plotting slopes and existing land uses; a modern Soil Conservation Service soil survey to identify opportunities and constraints of all soil types; a survey of urban tolerances of the aquatic ecosystem comprised of Harriman Reservoir and its drainage area; and a detailed groundwater investigation to identify the towns' groundwater resources and their management needs.

However, this study has produced sufficient evidence to make important judgments about the towns' futures. It reposes in maps and accompanying text which must be declared as public documents which, over time, can be enriched and corrected as better information becomes available. They can be recognized as elements of town plans as prescribed by the Vermont Planning and Development Act or by any other device that assures their prominent recognition in planning decisions.

All future planning must be the product of an explicit and replicable procedure existing at all levels of Vermont government which honestly appraises the social costs and benefits of all land-use proposals. Such a procedure has already been initiated by the federal and state governments through the National Environmental Policy Act and Vermont Act 250, both of which require environmental impact statements. Clearly, an equivalent system must be established at the town level. These decision-making procedures must be integrated at all government levels and employed to take a fresh look at highway and sewage problems and other land use issues requiring immediate solutions in the towns.

A new Highway Route 100 as proposed by the Vermont Highway Department should not be accepted until it is demonstrated that local improvements to the existing road system cannot satisfactorily increase carrying capacities. If the new highway can be justified, its alignment must conform to the intrinsic suitabilities of the towns, as identified in this study.

Fire districts should be abandoned as sewage planning areas, and a larger district encompassing the ecosystem of Harriman Reservoir should be established. In the absence of better information on the urban tolerances of that ecosystem, existing sewage discharges should be phased out in favor of recycling.

Regulation by the State

The State of Vermont administers a large group of environmental regulations to protect the health, safety, and welfare of the public. Those regulations set certain performance standards as a condition for obtaining a permit.

Waste discharge, land-under-water, and stream alteration permits are the responsibility of the Department of Water Resources. A storage permit for flammable liquids must be obtained from the Department of Public Safety. The Department of Highways gives permits for junkyards and highway access. Dam permits are obtained from the Water Resources Board. Operation of restaurants, hotels, and sanitary landfills are licensed by the Division of Environmental protection. Subdivision permits are administered by the Board of Health, while public water supply permits are provided by the Division of Health.

Vermont Acts 250 and 252 affect Wilmington and Dover more than any other state regulations. In the absence of town statutes which consider ecological realities, those acts should be employed as the major instruments for environmental protection. Act 252 and Section 12a(1) of Act 250 can be employed to prevent sewage effluents from being discharged into locations other than those which already have discharge permits. Those same acts can be employed to prevent increases in discharge volumes at locations having such permits, prior to a detailed investigation of the urban tolerances of the Harriman Reservoir ecosystem. Quality of sewage treatment should be upgraded immediately to meet state standards.

Under Section 12a(2) of Act 250, no developer using groundwater for his supply of water should be issued a permit prior to providing a record of pumping tests indicating yields per foot of drawdown of the groundwater table. This is necessary because of the inherent limitations of the region's groundwater resources to provide sustained yields, as well as the quality limitations of Wilmington's public supplies. Flood plains, peat and muck soils, sand and gravel aquifers, steep slopes over 15 percent, and ecologically fragile areas above 2,500 feet elevation, as identified in this study, should be prohibited from most developments, under Section 12a(4) of Act 250. This is necessary to prevent soil erosion and maintain the towns' water-holding capacity.

Areas scenically intolerant to urban uses should be exempted wherever possible from future development, employing Section 12a(8) of Act 250. These include the mountain range comprised of Mt. Pisgah and Haystack Mountain; the major valley walls and rims of the Deerfield Valley; the high ridge system comprised of Rich Hill, Whites Hill, Cooper Hill, Johnson Hill, and others; gentle regular slopes separated from other strong landscapes, prominent hills; and V-shaped valleys, Section 12a(8) of Act 250 should also be used to prevent future developments from destroying winter deeryards and beaver colonies, and places of historical significance such as the old village centers of Wilmington, West Dover, Dover, and East Dover.

The intrinsic suitability and synthesis maps produced by this study complement and enrich the interim capability plan prepared by the State Planning Office. They should be adopted as local capability plans by Wilmington and Dover, and, thereafter, adopted by the Windham Regional Planning and Development Commission. They may then be used by the District Environmental Commission to require conformance by all applicants, in accordance with Act 250, Section 12a(9).

Regulation by Wilmington and Dover

An inherent conflict must be recognized between sophisticated state regulations, such as Act 250, and the strong desires of towns to determine their own futures. Given the findings of this study, it is now possible for Wilmington and Dover to make their own laws to prevent material, irreparable, and permanent damage to their natural resources. These laws should be prepared by attorneys experienced in the field of environmental legislation and litigation.

A proposal to draft town statutes has been prepared by Victor J. Yannacone, Jr., Esq., of Patchogue, New York, and Arthur Palmer, Esq., of Cold Spring Harbor, New York, in collaboration with the consultant. Their proposal, already submitted to Wilmington and Dover, recommends the enactment of a new group of town laws derived from this study, which would preserve the ecologically fragile elements of both towns and those natural resources of regional significance. Initially, it is suggested that the towns enact an environmental policy resolution, followed by an environmental protection ordinance designating those town officials responsible for carrying out the policies enumerated in the policy resolution. The ordinance would require certain future developments to be authorized on the basis of a statement of environmental impact, to be submitted to the town. Additional town statutes would then be drafted and enacted individually to cover specific environmental subjects such as water quality, water supply, fragile areas, soils and erosion, plants, and animals.

These protection statutes would, in turn, be followed by a building code incorporating ecological factors and subsequent ordinances to direct future growth. They may include a system of penalties and credits wherein development responsive to natural processes is permitted multiple land uses and higher density, whereas development which contravenes ecological values be required to build remedial works and be constrained as to land use and density. Similarly, existing zoning ordinances prescribing one-acre and commercial districts bearing no resemblance to the towns' natural geometry should be superseded by new land-use districts. Regulations for the new districts should provide for flexibility in design, building coverage, and combinations of building types to reflect intrinsic suitability.

Tax Policies

Gerald Witherspoon, former Vermont Commissioner of Taxes, has offered several recommendations in his 1969 report on Vermont Tax Policy, which should be adopted.

Every permanent housing unit employed as a principal place of residence should be entitled to a $4,000 homestead exemption, as a means of reducing property taxes. Newly constructed housing units would be qualified for this exemption only if they conform to a voter-approved land-use plan. Agriculture should be encouraged by allowing double household exemptions to farmers.

Rural landowners forced to sell their lands because they are in an area of changing land use and rising taxes (e.g., on the fringe of an expanding ski area) should have an option of deferring, with interest, the excess tax attributable to the changing conditions until such time as their properties are sold. A special capital gains tax should be applied to profits from the sale of land, in which the tax rate decreases with the number of years the property is held. Proceeds from the tax would be earmarked for land-use planning and conservation purposes.

Individual property owners should be eligible for a preferential assessment if they restrict their lands from development by entering into restrictive use convenants with the towns.

Public Land Acquisition and Disposition

The Green Mountain National Forest should be invited to acquire lands within its jurisdiction, identified as requiring environmental protection. Both the state and Wilmington and Dover are empowered to acquire lands in fee simple, less-than-fee, and by lease. This method should be employed to preserve prime resources such as streamside areas and lakeshores, and other features requiring environmental protection where the use of noncompensatory regulations is not feasible. Towards that end, the towns should accept and manage gifts of land and historic buildings. The proposed Vermont Land Acquisition and Development Agency should be pursued by the towns as a vehicle to induce urban growth into urban suitable locations. Should that be unfruitful, the towns may create their own public corporations to acquire and improve lands, conveying these to private enterprise for appropriate uses.

Private Action

The final component of the strategy is concerted action by the private sector. Private foundations, trusts, and other civic organizations must be encouraged to acquire and maintain lands and buildings for public purposes. In their own interests landowners should undertake multi-lateral voluntary agreements to save their properties from despoliation. Landowners should consider establishing real estate syndicates to control the timing and location of future development and to secure an equitable distribution of profits from development, while concurrently protecting the towns from the ravages of uncontrolled growth. This private organization would purchase and develop lands especially suited for urban purposes. Part of the profits from this enterprise would be devoted to purchasing development rights of those properties which should remain in a natural state as identified in this study. Developers whose subdivisions are already platted must be urged by the towns and citizens groups to revise their plans wherever possible in conformance with the intrinsic suitabilities of their properties.

In conclusion, the future of Wilmington and Dover must not rest upon traditional zoning and subdivision regulations. These controls are insufficient. Both towns must undertake a new strategy, utilizing a new group of public and private devices to direct urban growth.

Epilogue

Wilmington and Dover are on the edge of disaster. The second home invasion threatens to engulf them, destroying as it goes. A few will benefit at the expense of many. But you did not need a study to discover this, although it may have given more authority and precision to the dimensions of the threat. Perhaps a thousand new permanent households and ten thousand new vacation homes!

What can we do about it? The first step was a good one. Make a plan. Moreover, the planning process includes a large number of townspeople who learned much of the region in developing data for the study. There is now an informed electorate. It has participated in a study which now emerges as a document. What does it say? Where now? First, it has revealed the towns as a natural system with supervening values both in nature and in human activities. It has revealed areas where there is a hazard to life and health, intolerant areas and those of high social value. The powers reposing in Acts 250 and 252 have been invoked to ensure that development be so regulated as to protect people and land.

Next, it assembles all of the factors, which together constitute the best places for development, and locates these in the towns. If development will occur here these are the locations where it can cause at once the least despoliation of natural resources, provide the best place to live and play, and add the greatest enhancement to the towns. But law operates best to constrain. Can development be deflected from sprawl, from poor areas into nucleated communities in the most propitious situations? Acts 250 and 252 can be used to exclude development from unsuitable locations. Town ordinances can give these areas greater precision and power. Moreover, positive actions based upon public expenditures on highways, water, sewers, and treatment plants can be expressly designed to induce development into preferred areas. The plan designating areas intrinsically suitable for development can also have a positive effect. Those who wish to develop, can identify locations where such development will receive public support, where it will not be destructive and may be enhancing. This too should act as a positive inducement.

Where should development be located? The sites are clearly revealed. They provide the maximum edge to recreational opportunity and scenic value, the best climate areas, the most propitious factors of slope, soils, water, and accessibility. Here people can build new complementary communities, employing the best sites in the towns, enhancing them with buildings, places, and spaces consonant with the land, the people, and their history.

It takes no high intelligence to accomplish this, no great art to locate this marriage of people and the land. Modest architecture, landscape architecture, and planning should be able to achieve this end. Much more difficult is the task of halting the wave of despoliation, stopping "hit and run" development, initiating ecological ordinances, and enforcing them, indeed, changing the image of the towns as tolerant to inchoate, shabby building, to that of an effective community which insists upon the best practices of development.

The approval of this plan in public meetings and the invocation of Acts 250 and 252 to realize it are a splendid beginning. The formulation of town ordinances regulating development and prohibiting it from unpropitious areas is the right step, one of enormous significance. The continuous enrichment of data and their interpretation is a further objective. Reorganization of sewer districts, expansion of the National Forests, intelligent planning for highways and sewers, can all provide beneficial results. But the most important task is the gradual transformation of the image of the towns as a vulnerable place for casual second home sites, to a highly organized community where only excellence is permitted. This requires greater vigilance, dedication, and persistence in the planning process than has been required in the decision to initiate a study or to conduct it. The benefits are great—the maintenance of a beautiful landscape and stable communities. The threats are greater—a rich, diverse, and beautiful landscape quickly transformed into Sprawl City, U.S.A. It is unthinkable, yet it is a most likely future. The postwar decades are testimony to the numberless cases of good people on beautiful landscapes who have been engulfed and destroyed by growth. What reason is there for Dover and Wilmington to succeed where failure is normal fate? There is reason, an informed electorate, a plan, regulating powers, and a powerful instinct to establish a landmark for the nation to see. Good new communities placed on beautiful landscape—people and nature. We have been proud to share in this adventure, we wish it well. America needs an example of intelligent planning, responsive to nature's values, deferential to her constraints. Dover and Wilmington may indeed be a landmark. We hope so.

Credits

Principal Project Advisors: Benjamin Huffman (State Planning Office), William Schmidt (Executive Director, Windham Regional Planning and Development Commission)

Project Coordinator: Ellen Reiss (Windham Regional Planning and Development Commission)

Project Steering Committee: Laura Heller, Verne Howe, Robert McCafferty (Chairman), Henry Meyer, Elva Turner, Wesley Ward, Albert White, Rodney Williams, Peter Zilliacus

Wilmington Planning Commission: Denise Allen, Peter Barton, Philip Davis, Verne Howe, Michael Kimack, Lynd Kimball (former position), Henri Logher (former position), Robert McCafferty (former position), John McLeod, Henry Meyer, William Palumbo, Lee Rich (former position)

Dover Planning Commission: Donald Albano, Dwight Blakeslee, John Christie, Robert Jalbert, Richard Joyce, John Nisbet, Ellen Reiss, Elva Turner

Wilmington Selectmen: Ervine Bishop (former position), Kingsley Dumont, Robert Grinold, Merril Haynes, Earle Howe (former position)

Dover Selectmen: Rexford Bartlett (former position), Stephen Chontos, Richard Joyce, Henry Sweeney

General Advisors: Robert Davidson (Extension Service), James Edgerton (Extension Service), Schuylar Jackson (Agency of Environmental Conservation), Bernard Johnson (State Planning Office), Forest Orr (Interagency Council), John Plonski (Town Manager, Wilmington), Alden Rollins (former Town Manager, Dover), William Stone (Extension Service), Joseph Teller (Windham Regional Planning and Development Commission), Charles Trebbe (former Town Manager, Wilmington), Robert Williams (Agency of Environmental Conservation)

Office and Administration: Janet Anderson (Secretary, Windham Regional Planning and Development Commission), Karen Davis (Summer Intern), Riley Robinson (Student Aide), Ellen Skelton (Secretary, Windham Regional Planning and Development Commission), Lucy Walkonen (Secretarial Assistant)

Climatic Data and Analysis: Frances Bond, John Christie, Guido Cimonetti, Ernest Gay, Robert Lautenheizer, John McArthur, Phyllis Shippee, Morey Storm, Oscar Tenenbaum, Philip Wagner, Marshall Witten, Esq.

Soils Data and Analysis: Frances Bond, Robert Brigham, David Gilman, David Grimwood, Larry Hamel, Earle Howe, Jasper Howe, Marshall Howe, Ray Pestle, Al Tallerico, Charles Turner, Elva Turner, Bruce Watson

Geology Data and Analysis: Charles Doll, Grant Moyer, Charles Ratte

Hydrology Data and Analysis: Robert Aiken, William Albert, Chris Allen, Joseph Anderson, Thaddeus Betts, Klaus Boettcher, David Coburn, Barbara Cole, Bruce Cole, Dean Davis, Bob Dufresne, Helen Dumont, David Gavett, George Gordon, Ralph Haslund, Mary Horan, John Howe, Verne Howe, Wesley Howe, Jim Hudson, Rachael Hurlbutt, Gerry Jenkins, Gerald James, Martin Johnson, Richard Joyce, Joseph King, Karen Larson, Joseph Lassiter, John McCloud, Ted Nelson, Charlotte Peck, Pat Potter, Richard Rader, Charles Ratte, Edward Rice, Tonia Rolf, Winifred Sargent, Tim Sockett, Charles Towle, Robert Wernecke

Wildlife Habitats: Richard Ackerman, Arthur Ball, Gilbert Cameron, Kenneth Davis, Helen duMont, Russell Hanson, Halsey Hicks, Alonzo Hodgedon, Roy Hood, Al Johnson, Peter Johnson, Eugene Keenan, Edward Kehoe, Richard Kenyon, Floyd Marieta, James McMartin, Charlotte Peck, John Poor, Wayne Rowell, John Stevens, Hubert Vogelman

Socioeconomic Data and Analysis: Stephen Anderson, Robert Augenstern, Emerson Baker, Justin Brande, Elizabeth Brown, Lensey Cole, W. Thompson Cullen, Gale Day, Jefferson Eaton, Thomas Farmer, Esq., Porter Farwell, Margaret Garland, Arthur Goss, John Gray, Margaret Greene, Russell Hanson, Hugh Henry, Rufus Horton, Ralph Howe, Wayne Kivi, Arthur Knight, Nell Kull, David Lyons, John Marshall, Robert Matteson, Howard Mitchell, James Monahan, Elbert Moulton, Richard Nicholls, Gerald Osier, William Palumbo, Ivor Pelsue, Peter Plastridge, Arthur Ristau, David Rockwell, Fred Sargent, Olin Stephens III, Robert Steward, Richard Thomas, Clarence Truesdell, Elva Turner, Jack Ware, John Williams, Robert Wilson, Betty Wolf, Lawrence Wright, Peter Zilliacus

Report Photographs: Alan Seymour, West Dover

Notes

1. A development is the construction or improvements on a tract of land for any purpose other than residential farming, logging, or forestry. It applies to properties one acre or over in a municipality not having permanent zoning and subdivision regulations, and ten acres or more for municipalities having those permanent regulations.
2. Rule 1: Policy. Regulations covering Water Classification and Control of Quality, State of Vermont Agency of Environmental Conservation and Water Resources Board, May 1971
3. 10 V.S.A., Chapter 33, paragraph 910(a).
4. Ibid. Rule 10(a).
5. Ibid. Rule 10(3).
6. WMRT examined a stream disposal waste credit system, assuming that every landowner had an equal right to put wastes in the streams at a 30 to 1 dilution ratio. To exceed that amount, a landowner would have to buy pollution rights (or credits) from other landowners in his sewage disposal district.
7. 18 V.S.A., paragraphs 102 and 1203, and Vermont Health Regulations, Chapter 5, Sanitary Engineering.
8. Other conditions must also be met. See Vermont Health Regulations, Chapter 5, Subchapter 10.
9. Under the supervision of Dr. Charles Ratte of Windham College, groundwater studies were initiated during the summer of 1971. However, important data such as well yields/unit time/feet drawdown, were not available for this study.
10. Twenty-five percent is a judgmental figure. The consequences of slightly higher or lower percentages are not known.
11. Assuming 100 gallons per day per person, and three persons per house: 300 gallons per day divided by 50.6 gallons per day per acre equals approximately six acres.
12. Assuming 100 gallons per day per person, and six persons per house, 600 gallons per day divided by 233 gallons per day equals about 2.5 acres.
13. National Community Water Supply Study for the State of Vermont, by the Public Health Service, 1970, p. 21.
14. Vogelman, H., J. Marvin, and M. McCormack. 1969. "Ecology of the Higher Elevations in the Green Mountains of Vermont." A report to the Governor's Commission on Environmental Control, Burlington, Vermont (7 pages, mimeo).
15. Agency of Environmental Conservation Memorandum, "Development of Criteria," Section 12, Act 250, October 30, 1970.
16. Ibid.
17. LeSourd, David A. and Sinclair, Robert O. 1964. *State and Local Taxation and*

Finance in Vermont. Burlington: Agricultural Experiment Station, University of Vermont.

18. Sinclair, R. O. 1965. *Procedure for Comparing Vermont Towns in Terms of Local Tax Base, Taxes Paid, and Effort.* Burlington: Agricultural Experiment Station, University of Vermont.

19. Kull, Nell M. 1961. *History of Dover.* Brattleboro, Vt.: Book Cellar.

22

Ecological Plumbing for
the Texas Coastal Plain (1975)
with Jonathan Sutton

The Woodlands is one of McHarg's most influential projects. It is the best example of ecologically based new town planning in the United States during the 1970s. Today the approach might be called "sustainable development." As with current efforts toward sustainability, The Woodlands' plan sought not only environmental sustainability, but also economic and social balance. In fact, the two latter objectives may have been achieved better overall in The Woodlands. Ecological values have faired somewhat less well, outside the initial development with the especially strong McHarg imprint. The Woodlands remains an important model for new community planning.

In 28 square miles of forest, north of Houston, a new city—The Woodlands, Texas—is taking shape (figure 16). It is a unique experiment. The plan of the new city is based on a comprehensive ecological study; indeed, it is the first city plan produced by ecological planning. Yet, its uniqueness will not be immediately visible. The housing groups contain pleasant and decorous homes set in the forest. The only exceptional fact is that the trees and shrubs will be so close to homes. Although not immediately apparent, the unique qualities of The Woodlands are pervasive and they derive from its ecological plan.

The planning process for The Woodlands presented a novel experience for Wallace, McHarg, Roberts, and Todd (WMRT) since the initiation of work in 1971 as part of a team of consultants planning an 18,000-acre new town for the Mitchell Energy and Development Corporation. It consisted of a four-year relationship beginning with a study of the region, selection of the new town site, and the development of principles applicable to a single house or

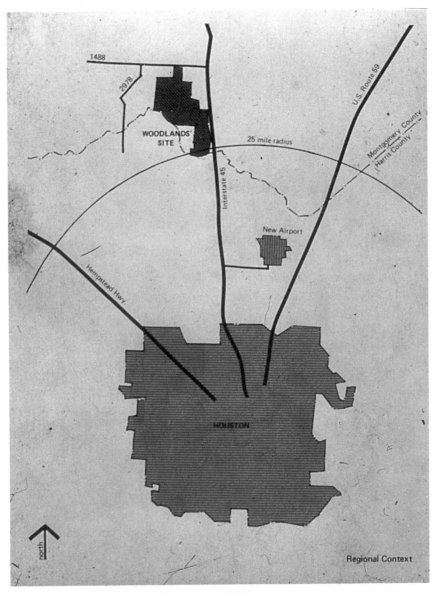

Figure 16. Regional context of The Woodlands, Texas.

lot. The Woodlands job presents a planning method, developed during the project which is overt, explicit, and replicable.

Having accumulated and interpreted the biophysical data describing the region and the 18,000-acre site, a method was developed which ensured that anyone who employed the data and the method would reach the same conclusions. Moreover, the data and method were printed in four technical reports, describing the ecological inventory and interpretation as well as the ecological plans and consequential principles to be employed in land and site planning. Thus any engineer, architect, landscape architect, developer, and the client himself were bound by the data and the method.

Because of its comprehensive analysis from the region to the residential setting, The Woodlands project represents a generic study with broad application to the entire physiographic region of the coastal plain from Long Island, New York, to Florida and Texas. In this region there is a wide commonalty of geophysical and biological phenomena.

Challenges of The Woodlands Site

The Woodlands site presented many problems. First, it is almost entirely forest—at once attractive, but also a difficult environment in which to build. Secondly, it is flat, indeed, so flat that local wisdom holds that you cannot predict where water will run unless you know which way the wind is blowing. Next, a high percentage of the soils are poorly drained. And finally, the site's streams are characterized by very low base flow and very high peak flows causing excessively broad and shallow flood plains in the flat topography. Nearly one-third of the site is within the 100-year flood plains of Panther, Bear, and Spring Creeks.

A crucial ecological concern was how to preserve the woodland environment while draining the land for the new community. Orthodox drainage would have required destruction of the forest in order to lay drain tiles.

As most landscape architects and planners know, engineering principles related to storm drainage throughout the United States were largely developed in the northeastern cities and were appropriate to conditions of the crystalline piedmont on which these cities were located. These principles emphasize accelerating runoff and disposal of this runoff in piped systems. An elaborate vocabulary of equipment and techniques composes this drainage technology.

The coastal plain, a great groundwater resource, requires the opposite approach, often inviting retardation of runoff to maximize recharge. Ecological planning for the coastal plain suggests solutions contrary to the orthodoxy of engineering. This was dramatically true of The Woodlands. It therefore became necessary not only to create an ecological planning method appropriate to this unique and difficult region but also to demonstrate its efficacy and economy to dubious engineers. Its effectiveness has now been clearly demonstrated. The elimination of a piped storm-water drainage system as anti-ecological and excessively expensive was an important factor in the engineers' conversion to ecological planning. The development of an inexpensive natural drainage system was a necessary corollary (figure 17).

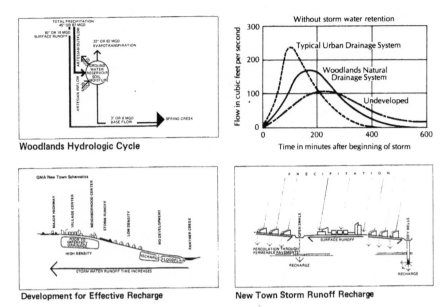

Figure 17. The Woodlands hydrological cycle.

The economic benefits of this approach were clearly demonstrated in the first engineering cost estimates for the storm drainage system of the new city. The costs of a natural drainage system were compared by the engineers with those of the conventional method of site drainage (Turner, Collie and Braden, Houston). The construction cost calculations for the storm sewers required for the conventional system were $18,679,300 while the natural drainage system costs were $4,200,400, an impressive saving of $14,478,900. Such figures accelerate conversion to ecological principles. There is no better union than virtue and profit.

The First General Plan

In 1970 WMRT was retained to undertake an ecological study for The Woodlands New Town. Gladstone Associates were retained to prepare market analyses. Richard Brown provided engineering studies and William L. Periera was responsible for land-use planning. Robert Hartsfield was the coordinating planner for the client. It is fair to say that the ecological studies were contracted less with a profound conviction of their necessity than as a concession to public environmental consciousness. The immediate objectives were threefold: to ascertain market feasibility, to design a plan consonant with the market and environmental opportunities of the site, and to apply for a U.S. Department of Housing and Urban Development (HUD) Title VII loan guarantee of $50 million.

The solution to these problems became so critical to the feasibility of the project that the ecological study moved from inconsequence to dominance. It determined the form of The Woodlands. Moreover, the HUD review process concentrated upon environmental factors. The ecological study was conducted simultaneously as a planning and environmental impact analysis and this contributed largely to the guarantee of $50 million in 1971.

All program allocation evolved from the ecological imperative that required maximizing recharge, protection of permeable soils, maintenance of water table, diminution of runoff, retardation of erosion and siltation, increase in base flow of streams, and the protection of natural vegetation and wildlife habitats. The satisfaction of these requirements provided the major structure of the plan and became influential at the smallest scale of development.

In the general plan for The Woodlands, arterial and collector roads were sited on ridge lines away from drainage areas. Development density was generally most intense near major roads and intersections and decreased with distance from these locations. Intensive development was located on areas of impermeable soils (for example, the Metro Core). Minor residential streets were used as berms perpendicular to the slope of the site to impede flow over excessively permeable soils. Design solutions such as the installation of permeable paving were recommended to increase the storage of storm water. (An experimental parking lot with porous paving has been constructed at the Commercial Leisure Center—the village focus for The Woodlands' First Phase—and is part of a monitoring program established by Rice University with grants from the U.S. Environmental Protection Agency and The Woodlands Development Corporation.)

Phase I Planning

The next engagement of WMRT in The Woodlands involved the first phase of development—an area of approximately 2,000 acres which was called Grogan's Mill Village. Detailed soil and vegetation surveys were computerized, from both field surveys and false infra-red photography, and one-foot contour interval topographic maps were prepared.

At this point three members of WMRT refined the concept of natural drainage, their objective to develop a method utilizing the attributes of the existing drainage system—streams, swales, ponds, natural vegetation (with its litter layer), the storage capabilities of soils—and to enhance this network by designing all infrastructure to satisfy water management objectives.

Impoundments, settlement ponds and basins, berms to encourage recharge, golf course construction, highways, roads, and streets were all considered as adaptive strategies to meet demands of a natural drainage system.

Having determined the structure's essential concept, it became necessary to quantify it. Elaborate studies were conducted to ascertain the contribution of each soil/vegetation type to the proposed water regimen. This investigation developed into the description of coverage/clearing ratios.

Determination of Landscape Tolerance as Established by Coverage/Clearing Ratios

Landscape tolerance is an index based on the requirements of the natural drainage system and the quality and adaptability of vegetation types. The measure of landscape tolerance is the percentage of a given soil and vegetation type which may be covered by impervious surfaces or cleared.

Permissible coverage is that fraction of an area which can be rendered impervious without affecting the ability of the remaining soil to absorb local runoff from high frequency storms (one inch in six hours). The amount of permissible coverage was derived from the excess storage capacity of each soil (down slope), which in turn was based on the depth of the upper pervious layer, its percolation rate and the height of the seasonal high water table and direction of slope (table 15).

Soil groups A and B were termed "Recharge Soils" and depending on their

Table 15. Coverage Disturbance Percentages

Soil Group	Soil Types	Capacity	Percentage of Area That Can Be Made Impermeable
A	Lakeland, Eustis	High	90
B	Boy, Albany	Medium	75
C	Fuquay, Lucy, Leefield, Bruno, Wicksburg	Low	50
D	Angie, Crowley, Segno, Sorter, Splendora, Susquehanna, Waller	None Effectively impermeable under present conditions	100

location were recommended for protection. Permissible clearing for each vegetation type reflects its quality and landscape value, its importance as a wildlife food source, and its tolerance to compaction and development activities. Permissible clearing is expressed as a percentage of area which may be cleared. Since both permissible coverage and permissible clearing are expressed as percentages, they were readily combined on one chart which served as an index of landscape tolerance.

Determination of Land-Use Impacts as Measured by Coverage/Clearing

Commercial uses, residential types and densities, golf courses, and roads were examined for their landscape impacts. Each use was evaluated in terms of the amount of impervious surface and clearing involved. Expressed as a percentage of a given unit of land, this coverage-to-clearing ratio measured development impact.

A study of the areas of impervious coverage and minimum clearing of 5, 10, or 15 feet around all building types (depending upon number of stories and construction technique for different densities) shows that coverage and clearing generally rise per unit area with higher densities. In order to check this conclusion against a wider sampling of developments, coverage and clearing as a percentage of total development area were taken from 22 representative site plans. The plans were published in various forms, and densities varied from 1 to 20 dwelling units per acre. All schemes analyzed relied on at-grade parking.

Design Synthesis

In order to match landscape tolerance with development impact a design synthesis base was created to illustrate the distribution of landscape tolerance. In addition, this base kept the land-planning process up-to-date and made it site-specific. A base map was developed which included a composite of all the salient ecological data. The synthesis involved a method of adding ecological factors in stages so that the contribution of each stage could be properly understood. The data were added to the map in sequence:

1. Field topography (1-foot contours)
2. Drainage pattern (watershed boundaries)
3. Soil types
4. Vegetation types
5. Adaptive strategies

Adaptive strategies include minimum open-space corridors associated with the 25-year flood plain or the minimum of 300-feet-wide drainage easements and storm water storage areas, which for the most part take the form of Waller ponds (shallow ponds, predominantly open, occasionally forested, which are situated on the impermeable Waller soils). Degrees of permissible coverage/clearing were established, based on the coincidence of soil types, vegetation types, and drainage patterns. These ranged from preservation to nearly total modification. The four steps leading to delineation of tolerance ranges in the design synthesis are illustrated:

1. Natural drainage system
2. Recharge soils
3. Prime vegetation
4. Impermeable soils, flat land less than 1 percent, and permeable soils and sloping land greater than 1 percent (to be developed according to the percentages indicated on the Coverage/Clearing Chart, Table 15)

Step 4 makes a distinction between land which is relatively well drained (because it has either permeable soils or slopes greater than one percent) and flat, poorly drained, impermeable areas. One percent slope was adopted as the limit for positive drainage in a forest with a little layer. Therefore, impermeable soils on slopes less than one percent are considered poorly drained. The soil's ability to drain affects directly the permissible coverage/clearing percentages. The Design Synthesis Map shows the essential structure of Phase I on which the various program elements were subsequently tested.

Matching Development Impacts with Landscape Tolerance

The combination of landscape tolerance (permitted coverage/clearing) of given soil and vegetation types with land-use requirements (required coverage/clearing) yielded an allocation of development impacts in a gradient from complete protection to extensive modification. Development types having extensive coverage/clearing impacts were matched with soils of low permeability and vegetation of low quality, and development types having slight coverage/clearing impacts were matched with soils of excess storage capacity for surface water and/or vegetation of high quality.

Each level of constraint required some additional development cost such as for increased drainage improvements, fill, or landscape treatment. An opportunity implied a decreased or normal development cost. The costs were then compared with the anticipated value created by both natural and human-made amenities. The final synthesis revealed the least cost/greatest benefit solution on the basis of the existing landscape characteristics.

There were persuasive social or economic factors that modified the design synthesis—altering locations of roads, golf courses, and shopping areas. Detailed vegetation studies caused us further to modify the plan. We calculated the acreage of each soil and vegetation type within each watershed to find its "development capacity"—i.e., the maximum area that should be covered and cleared. For example, the Grogan's Mill Village center was located directly upon impermeable soils—rather than over one of the absorptive recharge areas. We put all golf courses to a similar test—balancing development opportunities against costs to the environment.

Such were the steps leading to the land-use plan, which was derived from these structural elements: (1) drainage ways; (2) road net; (3) golf courses; (4) community facilities; and (5)pedestrian paths.

This plan showed us those areas suitable to become development parcels. To each of these parcels we assigned a "program module" depending on their aggregated landscape tolerance, surrounding amenities, physical configuration, marketing potential, and staging strategy. The exercise of matching "program modules" or density types with specific sites in Phase I (1,947 acre) suggested 4,350 dwelling units on 1,255 developable acres, including community facilities, a business park, and the commercial leisure center (note this reserved 692 acres as open space). In order to ensure a sufficient pace and market response in Phase I much of the program called for single-family lots.

Plan for the Village of Grogan's Mill

The residential areas of The Village of Grogan's Mill are organized around the Community Leisure Center (CLC), which includes commercial and office facilities, a community conference center, and sites for recreational activities. This large package of leisure facilities will give the CLC a catchment area well outside The Woodlands. It will supply the community focus and marketing impetus for Phase I.

The neighborhood in Zone I relates to the championship golf course, country club, tennis courts, and conference center. The neighborhood in Zone 3 is focused on the Sawmill Community Center at the corner of Grogan's Mill and Sawmill Roads. The public golf course, the existing Lamar Elementary School, with adjacent Tamina Mill Community Center and proposed park, provide neighborhood facilities and identity in Zone 4.

The three neighborhoods will be linked to the CLC by six miles of pathways for pedestrians and bicycles. The rights-of-way of the pedestrian system will provide at some future point the option of an alternative mode of vehicular transportation to the automobile. Grade separated crossings of Grogan's Mill Road are planned at the CLC and at the Sawmill Community Center to reduce conflict between the pathways and the arterial road.

Guidelines for Site Planning

In order to carry out the actual "fitting" of development types to specific site conditions, a decision tree was devised. Using summary sheets for hydrology, limnology, soils, vegetation, wildlife, and climate, the method reviewed the critical site conditions revealed during the ecological inventory. It also suggested the environmental objectives and physical adaptations related to each natural phenomenon. The main concern of the manual, though, is with the natural drainage system and the preservation of the woodland environment. This is to be achieved through careful organization and communication of site planning information for each development parcel.

The key method was developed to identify specific site conditions and relate them to design strategies. Ecological data related to soils and vegetation have been organized in a form which can be readily utilized by planners and designers. A manual outlines the step-by-step process of applying selected criteria to a particular site. Given the criteria and the procedure, all consultants who employ the method can produce a variety of designs, all of which will satisfy the stated environmental objectives. The outcome of the process provides only the framework for the plan or design. The quality and character of the final product will still depend on the ingenuity of the individual site planner.

Site Design

The execution of a site plan for two parcels in Grogan's Mill Village illustrates how the key method of the guidelines is employed (figure 18). The parcels in question contain a total of 48 acres, separated by a residential collector road and bounded by golf fairways and a primary drainage easement.

Taken together the sites were to form a sub-community of distinctive high- and medium-priced homes. Of the total acreage all except the 50 feet

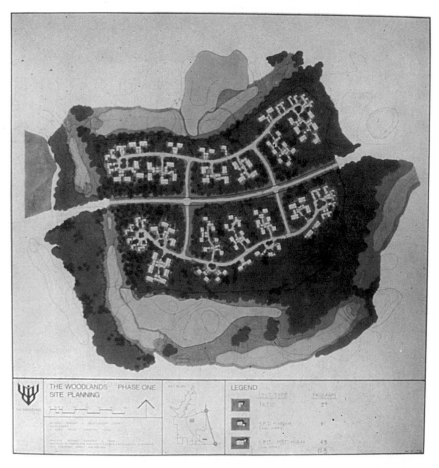

Figure 18. After guidelines were applied to two parcels of 48 acres, the above site plan resulted. The drainage system has been designed so that the roads perpendicular to the slope of each parcel intercept and direct runoff to points easily drained.

vegetation easements along Millrun Drive (to be assigned to the community association) and the land required for internal streets was to be converted to deeded home-sites. A preliminary scheme called for sites for a total of 113 units consisting of 43 single-family detached high (SFD-H) and 70 single-family detached medium high (SFD-MH) (figure 19). Up to 20 percent of this total could be planned as clustered patio-type units. The patio option was exercised to achieve the necessary match between program impact and permissible coverage-to-clearing ratios.

Figure 19. Typical new town houses in 1975.

Dwelling Unit Prototypes

Several housing prototypes were recommended as a response to specific site conditions identified in the "Guidelines for Site Planning." Each site condition suggested a different design approach with respect to foundation type, setback requirements, access, parking, yardspace, and housing configuration. A representative group of unit prototypes indicates the range of creative responses to specific site conditions.

General Plan Revisions

Since 1972 changes in the first general plan have been made as more detailed ecological, marketing, transportation, and design studies have been completed and the 1,947-acre first construction phase begun. In 1973, the following consultant team was assembled to prepare a revised general plan. In addition to WMRT, Land Design Research was responsible for land-use planning; LWFW for marketing, Turner Collie and Braden for engineering, Green Associates for transportation; and Espey and Winslow for hydrology.

The methods that had been developed in Phase I were used in revising the general plan. A design synthesis base was established for the whole new city, indicating degrees of permissible coverage/clearing, ranging from protection to nearly total modification. Levels of landscape tolerance are shown on the map by a range of colors. The map also gives an indication of the broad, open-space framework and the distribution landscape thresholds which structure the revised general plan. Three major zones, each with a range of appropriate land uses, are defined by the map.

Primary Open Space—At the Townwide Scale

Primary natural open space for the whole town of The Woodlands is conceived of as a conservation zone incorporating the ecologically valuable areas with respect to hydrology, wildlife, and vegetation. These areas would include the 25-, 50-, and portions of the 100-year flood plains of existing streams as well as preserves of highly diverse vegetation suited for conservation, passive recreation, and wildlife food and cover.

Secondary Open Space—At the Development Zone Scale

Secondary open space includes components of the natural drainage system not included in primary open space: secondary swales, storm-water impoundment sites, and storm-water recharge areas. The remaining wet-weather ponds, some of which may be impounded, are included as parts of the storm-water control system and for their natural and aesthetic value. Wooded fringes outside of the primary open space system are part of this category as are greenways, large stands of trees selected for preservation, and uncleared areas between development parcels.

Tertiary Open Space—At the Development Parcel Scale

Tertiary open space is important at the scale of the individual development parcel. Based on detailed vegetation mapping and analysis, this open-space system is comprised of those areas of vegetation not cleared for development purposes: small natural green spaces among detached houses or in open areas in higher density development (vegetation buffers along roads or in traffic islands). The on-lot drainage system would also be incorporated into the uncleared areas which make up tertiary open-space.

The hierarchy of open spaces just described will provide a multi-purpose network integral to the maintenance of natural drainage, of the forested environment and of certain species of indigenous wildlife. High-intensity recreation areas such as golf courses and playgrounds are situated to complement the basic structure of the natural open-space system but do not infringe upon it.

Test of Land Availability

In order to test how the development program could be adapted to the open-space system, three alternatives of land availability were examined. Alternative A respected all elements of the design synthesis in terms of primary natural open space, and recreational open space. The acreage outside of the open-space zone was divided into areas which could accept low, medium, or high coverage in terms of development intensity, based on the coverage/clearing guidelines of the design synthesis.

However, the available buildable acreage and the no-proceeds open space of alternative A did not balance with the projections of the economic model. To achieve a larger buildable area, Alternative B developed certain areas of the vegetation preserve and 100-year flood plain. Alternative C increased the open-space area over Alternative B in order to restore the balance between open-space priorities and the need for an adequate economic return, while permitting selected recreational and low-density residential uses within the secondary open-space system.

Alternative C formed the basis for the general plan revision, suggesting the overall capacity of the site for development, and establishing guidelines for land-use allocation. When an evaluation of coverage/clearing was applied to this alternative, the analysis suggested a "carrying capacity" of 33,000 dwelling units and 9,972 developable acres, given the assumptions of the economic model.

The primary objective of the revised general plan was to provide the direction for up-to-date development decisions that would be realistic as well as innovative. The plan will remain flexible in order to respond to changing conditions brought on by such concerns as energy crisis or new market preferences. However, the site-specific basis of the plan will ensure the attainment of certain fundamental environmental goals.

Community Structure

Once the open-space network was established for the new city, the areas with highest priority for development were defined. The activity focus of these development zones and the business hub of the new community was the Metro Center. Residential villages of approximately 2,000 acres each were organized around the Metro Center. The Village of Grogan's Mill was the first of these to be developed, and University Village will follow in the next phase.

The revised general plan intermixed employment, residential and community facilities at all scales. The higher density residential areas were related to the major roadways, to areas of maximum coverage/clearing, and to convenience shopping at the village center and Metro Center. The medium-density residential areas (town houses, quads, and patio units) were generally located near the major roads for easy access. These units allow for more flexibility in site planning, screening, and orientation than do single-family lots. The single-family dwellings were generally related to the smaller-scale streets, neighborhood collectors, loops, and cul-de-sacs. Since about 60 percent of the proposed residential land is for single-family detached housing, the edges of major roads will be protected by vegetation easements, landscape improvements, and special fencing.

Lessons Still to Be Learned from The Woodlands

Much of The Woodlands story remains to be told. The opening day for the new city was October 17, 1974. However, the first three years of its development may be critical to the success of the new community. The ecological, social, and economic objectives of the new city will be greatly influenced by initial decisions and commitments. The objectives of The Woodlands plan over the next 19 years are to minimize ecological and social costs while achieving economic goals. As each new area is considered for the next phase of development, the current benefits and costs as well as feasible alternatives will be considered.

Underlying such an evaluation is the continuing process of evolution in ecological planning initiated over the last three years. It has established a set of analytical methods and vocabulary of adaptive form responsive to the hydrology, limnology, soils, vegetation, wildlife, and climate of the coastal plain.

However, it is the quantitative capabilities of the method which deserve the greatest attention and refinement. While the data and the hypothesis employed in formulating the conclusions await testing, they represent a dimension of causality and quantification not heretofore accomplished in any projects by WMRT.

As the building of the new city is carefully monitored by the environmental planning staff of The Woodlands Development Corporation and several outside research groups, an in-depth understanding of this physiographic region will be gained. During the course of this research, the ecological planners' understanding of man's impact on the natural system of this area and of the manner in which these impacts can be mitigated will be greatly enhanced.

In fact, the construction of the first phases has already given testimony of the effectiveness of the natural drainage system. James Veltman, director of environmental planning for The Woodlands, reports "that despite 13 inches of rain in three days, and four inches of rain in one hour, there was no surface water within six hours and that during this period there was effective operation of detention ponds which filled when it rained and reverted to their normal level within six hours."

The results of this planning and such observations should be immediately communicated to The Woodlands residents. They should understand the drainage function of wet-weather ponds and temporarily wet lawns. They should realize that the presence of water in their yards is critical to the survival of The Woodlands themselves. They should be aware of the special characteristics of their environment, their community, and the exciting experiment of which they are a part.

If such a level of environmental awareness was reached in a new community, it would be unique. During the period when Reston and Columbia were being planned, environmental issues had hardly been voiced and ecological planning was at a rudimentary stage. It would be fair to say that no ecological planning, as it is now understood, was employed in the initial design of either of these new towns. The planning of The Woodlands occurred in a much different social climate during a peak of environmental sensitivity and in a particularly intolerant landscape. Moreover, the environmental impact analysis composed a major requirement for the HUD Title VII application.

The effort to achieve increased public (not just professional) awareness of the generic qualities and resources of the coastal plain landscape is one of many new directions in the ecological planning work for The Woodlands not touched on in this chapter. These new directions are the logical extensions of what has already been achieved. The next steps in the planning process are as follows: monitoring the development of a new city; understanding social processes in The Woodlands; energy conservation as a community design determinant; transportation as a design determinant; and adaptive architecture in The Woodlands. All these new directions, if vigorously and carefully pursued, will lead to an increasingly successful adaptation of the human-made to the natural environment.

Epilogue

The Woodlands site is a mute record of ancient seas and the deposition of clays and sands which underlie the forest. The seasons of the year, the hydrologic cycle, and the recycling of vital nutrients continue. Hurricanes sweep over from the Gulf of Mexico and produce intense storms. Incident precipitation enters the ground and in time replenishes the stream flow. Vegetation holds the sandy erodible soil in place and provides food and cover for wildlife. It is critical to recognize the dynamism of these physical and biological processes, for they affect man and are affected by his intervention.

As projects such as The Woodlands are planned, built, and monitored throughout the country, many lessons will be learned from each, thereby increasing the collective knowledge of the landscape architecture profession. Such knowledge of each physiographic region should be thoroughly documented and understood. This resource, if exploited with creativity and imagination, will usher in a new era of environmental design.

23

A Strategy for a National
Ecological Inventory (1992)
with John Radke, Jonathan Berger,
and Kathleen Wallace

We are surrounded by information. A few clicks on the Internet can produce a flood of data about a place. This situation poses both great opportunity and peril. Can we convert this information into knowledge to help us to create a more sustainable future? Or, will we be drawn into the sea of data, unable to make connections to a shore?

McHarg has steadfastedly advocated means for connection. First in the early 1970s, then in the early 1990s, he proposed to the U.S. Environmental Protection Agency a comprehensive national ecological inventory. The latter proposal resulted from the 1990 request from EPA Administrator William Reilly for advice from McHarg about the agency's computing system. With his Penn colleagues John Radke, Jon Berger, and Kathleen Wallace, McHarg suggested a three-scale inventory in 1992 that would incorporate the "entire spectrum of environmental science." They noted that the inclusion of appropriate social scientists was "essential" and "necessary to understand human environments." Their suggestion emphasized the centrality of the need to integrate and synthesize data. They recommended a shift from a focus on data collection to the synthesis of information. They proposed that the work be undertaken by teams of regional scientists rather than a centralized bureaucracy. Finally, they noted that "the establishment of a national ecological inventory be seen as the most important act protecting the American environment in history, indispensable for intelligent regulation and management, but moreover, capable of transforming both environmental research and education."

The National Ecological Inventory

Some years ago a realization emerged within the U.S. Environmental Protection Agency (EPA) that the agency was unable to provide an appraisal of the quality of the environments which comprise the nation for the President, Congress, the American people, or for its own use in regulating the environment.

In 1972 Russell Train, then administrator of EPA, asked Ian McHarg to describe a process for undertaking a national ecological inventory. His proposal (Wallace, McHarg, Roberts, and Todd 1973) recommended that an environmental laboratory be established in each of the nation's 40 physiographic regions, plus one national laboratory in Washington, D.C. Each would be constituted with the appropriate scientists and charged with undertaking inventories and performing monitoring. While the proposal was warmly received, it transpired that existing computer capabilities were inadequate to the task. Dramatic advances in computation have since developed and an increasing body of digital data is now available for the scientific community and is denoted as geographic information systems (GIS).

The proposal for a national ecological inventory persisted, and in 1988 the EPA Science Advisory Board again recommended a program to inventory and model the environment to ensure that agency policies were maintaining or improving environmental quality. The program mandate was to initiate a national inventory of ecosystems along with their status and trends. This required assessing the health of ecosystems and the effectiveness of existing regulation in protecting or enhancing those systems. The method selected consists of applying a hexagonal grid, each of 40 km^2, over the United States from which sample sites will be identified and studied. This effort came to be entitled the Environmental Monitoring and Assessment Program (EMAP).

The governmental decision to undertake a national ecological inventory may well be the single most important act in the field of the environment. Since World War II, when the greatest environmental transformations have ensued, it is accurate to state that the vast majority of these occurred without reference to the environmental consequences of contemplated actions. However, it should be observed that the culprit is not the absence of data. These are abundant, although of variable quality. The major deficiency derives from the fact that data are generated by distinct agencies for their internal purposes—EPA, NOAA, the U.S. Geological Survey (USGS), the Soil Conservation Service [now the Natural Resources Conservation Service] the U.S. Army Corps of Engineers, DMA, and CIA—and they have not been integrated as a result of which their utility is diminished.

Environmental research has been fragmented, partial, uncoordinated, and underfunded. An elaborate indictment is contained in the documents produced by the National Institutes of the Environment and need not be elaborated here. Undoubtedly, the generation of new data will play an important role in the national ecological inventory, but it is reasonable to assert that the integration, synthesis, interpretation, and evaluation of existing data may be one of its most valuable contributions. Clearly additional data must be developed, if for no reason other than to ensure that data are current, but the largest energies should be devoted to integrating available data. *It cannot be overstated that we are swamped by available data but they are not being utilized. The major commitment to data should be integration of existing resources.*

Ignorance of environmental data, partial information, or the inability to predict the consequences of modifications, all culminate in bad judgments. The contemplated inventory should dispel this ignorance and permit more knowledgeable and sensitive environmental adaptations. The product should lead to preservation, conservation, intelligent planning, management, regulation, and, not least, restoration.

We must learn how the world works. The national ecological inventory is a direct response to this resolve and an unequaled instrument for applying this understanding to the face of the nation.

However, it is important to recognize that the current EPA program, EMAP, does not occupy this important role, neither in the scientific community, the conservationist fraternity, nor the public. Indeed it has received little attention from scientists who at best view the enterprise with little interest, at worst with skepticism and opposition.

It is intolerable that such a vital objective should be so lowly regarded. The remedy for this situation constitutes our primary recommendation.

Executive Committee

It is recommended that the most distinguished scientists of the environment be constituted into an executive committee to advise the EPA administrator on the conduct of the enterprise. This act alone should provide legitimacy and authority to the inventory. Members should be selected from officers in all of the relevant scientific societies. By this decision, not only the scientist officers in these societies, but also the membership will be co-opted into the national inventory.

The creation of such a committee will assure the scientific community that the enterprise will benefit from the most august minds in environmental science. It will also provide the leadership which this monumental task deserves.

The composition of the EPA Science Advisory Board contains over forty persons with the largest component derived from medicine, epidemiology, and toxicology. Next in size is environmental science and engineering, with the smallest contingent representing environmental science. This composition may well be appropriate for the agency's regulatory function but it is not suitable for designing the national ecological inventory.

A useful comparison can be found in the composition of the Advisory Council for the National Institutes of Health. This body of forty-five members includes such luminaries as Carl Sagan, Kenneth Boulding, Paul Ehrlich, George Woodwell, Edward Wilson, George Wald, and the presidents of Harvard, Texas, and Notre Dame. The composition of the recommended executive committee for the national ecological inventory should aspire to a comparable caliber but it must be distinguished by the representation of all of the environmental sciences.

The organization of the EPA long preceded the determination to undertake a national ecological inventory. The question is whether it requires reorganization to fulfill this role. The current elements engaged in the EMAP process are invaluable but, it is suggested, insufficient. The small staff in Washington, D.C., the bio-statisticians at Corvallis, competence in remote sensed imagery in Las Vegas, air photography, and landscape ecology at Warrenton, together with the diffuse groups engaged in research, represent rich resources but, in sum, do not constitute the essential elements for the task. However, these small, scattered groups lack the resources and the leadership capable of comprehensive integration and synthesis of environmental data, which is essential for the achievement of the objective.

It is recommended that the executive committee identify the constituent roles in the inventory and monitoring processes and advise on the identification and selection of the staff. This contemplated staff should include representation of all of the environmental sciences. Physical science should include meteorology, physical oceanography, geology, hydrology, and soil science. Plant and animal ecologists, limnologists, marine biologists would be included in the biological sciences. Ethnography, anthropology, resource economics, geography are conspicuous among the social sciences. Biostatistics, remotely sensed imagery, and computation should be represented. The staff should be selected, not alone for their competence within their discipline, but for their demonstrated experience in interdisciplinary and multi-disciplinary research.

The current organization includes research on agroecosystems, arid lands, forests, estuaries, surface water, wetlands, Great Lakes, air deposition, and more. We observe that while arid lands are an appropriately ecological descriptor amenable to research, the same cannot be said of the phenomena of surface water, wetlands, and estuaries, all of which are interdependent elements in continuous processes. Forests as a title include so many types as to diminish their validity as a research subject. *We recommend for consideration the replacement of the current reductionist phenomena-based research by a regional/ecological approach employing physiographic regions, Kuchler's eco-*

regions and, perhaps including metropolitan regions among others (Kuchler 1964). As a consequence we recommend that the executive committee review and advise on existing and contemplated research.

A Title

We are of the opinion that one of the reasons why EMAP is so cavalierly dismissed or ignored is its title. EMAP is just another bureaucratic acronym of which there are far too many. Certainly this title will not evoke passions and commitment yet, given the signal importance of enterprise, arguably the most important single act in the history of the American environment, it does deserve a better title, capable of attracting supporters, advocates, enthusiasts, participants from the public at large, conservationists, governmental committees, and the scientific community.

In order to stimulate discussion on the matter we offer examples for consideration:

"The Face of the Nation"
"The State of the Nation"
"The American Landscape"
"The National Environment"
"The Health of the Land"

At that time when the executive committee is formed and it produces a report on the plan for the national ecological inventory and identifies operational structure, staff, plans, objectives, time table, budget, and anticipated benefits, there should be a concerted public relations effort. This should involve title, logo, a published report, and these should be presented to the American people with appropriate fanfare. There should be a continuing effort to keep the objectives and accomplishments of the venture in conspicuous public and scientific view and to engender widespread debate.

Basis for Recommendations

The recommendations for a national ecological inventory are based in part on the authors' experience with colleagues and students at the University of Pennsylvania since the early 1960s. This group has engaged in ecological planning studies for the Potomac and Delaware River Basins, their physiographic regions and selected sample sites within each of these. For the past four decades, sample sites in the Philadelphia metropolitan region have been examined. McHarg in his partnership (Wallace, McHarg, Roberts, and Todd) undertook elaborate planning studies in Iran and Nigeria and for many of the metropolitan regions of the United States. This association of physical, biological, and social scientists was described by the magazine *Science* as the most interdisciplinary and multi-disciplinary academic department in the United States (Holden 1977). Thus these observations and recommendations derive from extensive experience (see American Institute of Architects 1965–1966; Development Research Associates and Wallace, McHarg, Roberts, and Todd 1972; International Planning Associates 1979; The Mandala Collaborative and Wallace, McHarg, Roberts, and Todd 1975; University of Pennsylvania 1963; and Wallace, McHarg, Roberts, and Todd 1969, 1972, 1974, 1976, 1978).

In these exercises, notably of river basin studies, a three-part analysis was performed. The first study addressed the entire river basin, the second level concentrated upon the constituent physiographic regions, the final step involved examination of specific sites. Scales ranged from 1:250,000, 1:100,000, and 1:24,000. In this process sites became comprehensible within physiographic regions (Fenneman 1931, 1948; Hunt 1974), river basins, and in certain cases, metropolitan regions.

So, while we subscribe to the sample method of inventory, we suggest that while necessary, it is insufficient. A medical analogue identifies blood, urine, sputum, and tissue samples. Each can be analyzed within the characteristic attributes but as samples of an organism. So too with inventory samples; they should be selected from meaningful contexts.

For example, samples from Alaska and Florida, California and Maine, Minnesota and Texas, even adjacent Pennsylvania and New Jersey, will reveal dramatic differences. Are these normal, or abnormal? In the last example the explanation for profound distinctions lies in the observation that one sample reposes in the Crystalline Piedmont, the other in the Inner Coastal Plain. As all of the environmental sciences have developed taxonomies, it would be cavalier not to employ them. There are climate zones, geological and physiographic regions, river systems and groundwater basins, soils regions, bio-climatic zones, ecosystems, habitats, metropolitan regions, and more.

A six percent sample would be unable to ascertain boundaries of regions, yet the identification of samples, within the appropriate regions, will vastly facilitate analysis and evaluation.

Three-Part Inventory

So, we recommend that the contemplated national ecological inventory be performed at three scales: national (at 1:2,000,000), regional (at 1:250,000), and site (at 1:24,000).

The national inventory should extend to include contiguous regions which affect the environment—adjacent areas in Canada, Mexico, the Caribbean, oceanic and atmospheric processes. At this scale all regions should be delineated—climatic zones, geological and physiographic regions, rivers and groundwater basins, soil regions, big-climatic regions, biomes, ecosystems, and wildlife habitats. These should also include metropolitan, agricultural, energy regions among other social descriptors.

The regional inventory at the scale of 1:250,000 should include all environmental data nationwide which can be utilized for all regional analyses and provide the basis for sample selection in a stratified sampling process.

The final component, sites at 1:24,000 is provided by the hexagonal lattice. Thus, the national inventory would present data in its most aggregated form, appropriate for examination and resolution of large-scale problems. Regional data would amplify resolution and be amenable to analysis of homogenous areas. The sample at site scale would provide the richest data, highest resolution, and permit the most discriminating analyses.

It would take sixteen years of 6 percent samples to complete the inventory, an intolerable delay. As more digital data are currently available for both regional and national scales these inventories could be completed within a few years. Moreover, the role of samples should be limited to areas of crucial importance. They would not comprise the building blocks for the national inventory. However, employment of this method gives great importance to the criteria employed in selecting samples.

An Ecological Inventory

The questions to be addressed in landscape characterization are: What are the environments which comprise the nation; how did they come to be; what processes characterize them; what tendencies do they exhibit; what has been the effect of human use; what is their current status; and, most of all, what should we do?

The first prerequisite to an adequate characterization is an inventory of environments and their status. This step has long been needed and has been long awaited. It is commendable that the initiative has begun, but it is important to recognize that it is still in the process of design.

Given the mandate to undertake a national ecological inventory, as we have seen, the EPA concluded in favor of the sample method using a national hexagonal lattice, each of 40 km^2, and sampling within those hexagons. This permits resolution at a scale of 1:24,000 and is perfectly suitable for landscape characterization. However, adoption of such a general method does not resolve the issue of what data are to be employed nor does it inform which samples should be selected.

If the environment must be inventoried, there is no problem in identifying data sources. The environment has been dissected by science. Distinct subjects are proprietary to discrete fields and this relationship has been formalized in the sciences, university departments, and government agencies. Each major discipline—meteorology, geology, oceanography, hydrology, pedology, plant and animal ecology, limnology, marine biology, and others—

has its own academic and bureaucratic constituency. Science remains obdurately reductionist and shows no sign of change, yet the process of characterization demands multi-disciplinary and interdisciplinary exercises. Above all, it demands the kind of integration and synthesis which are inseparable from the ecological method of landscape characterization.

We note that the current process of the characterization in EPA has emphasized landscape ecology and placed large reliance on remotely sensed data. We consider this necessary but insufficient and recommend a comprehensive data set to include:

Meteorology	Limnology
Geology	Physical oceanography
Surficial geology	Marine biology
Groundwater hydrology	Ethnography
Physiography	Cultural anthropology
Surficial hydrology	Cultural geography
Soils	Archeology
Plant ecology	Planning
Animal ecology	

Chronology as the Structuring Device

The task of characterization requires that landscapes be understood as the product of processes, laws, and time. The exercise should identify meaningful processes and phenomena. To accomplish this, a structure of data organization should be employed which assimilates incremental data and which culminates in understanding and in meaningful representation.

The process of characterization needs to incorporate data from many disciplines. Given the fact that the normal circumstance will reveal, not a paucity of data, but a surfeit, there is a large premium in employing an organizing structure which absorbs data and expands meaning to culminate in a rich expression of the region under study. Chronology is just such an organizing structure.

The chronological method can be employed as the structural basis of characterization, used to reveal cause and effect as described by process and pattern. This suggests that characterization begin with the history of geological evolution, involving 500 million years of evidence in the case of the Pre-Cambrian. This geologic history begins to describe and explain the regions under study and reveal their dynamism. Meteorology follows with some 50 million years of climatic evidence, culminating with the major events of the Pleistocene. These can be employed to describe the glacial processes and events of this period. These data, comprising geology, meteorology, and geomorphology, provide the major bases for the phenomena of groundwater and for physiography. The addition of physiography provides the essential data to explain surficial hydrology. By this point, the cumulative nature of the evidence becomes manifest—no layer is comprehensible without reference to the antecedent layers, each building upon the previous one's stratum. Data assembled can now be reinterpreted to explain soils with their variable characters and distribution—derived from bedrock, affected by climatic conditions, transported by glaciation, alluvial or aeolian processes. All of the foregoing—geology, physiography, hydrology, and soils—can be reinterpreted as vegetative environments described as bio-climatic zones, biomes, or ecosystems. This addition of vegetation provides the final component to explain the region's wildlife.

This method, which we call the layer-cake approach, employs data in chronological sequence to progressively provide meaning to a landscape and to ultimately reveal the historic processes which explain contemporary phenomena characterizing regions and sites. Mountains and oceanic abysses, valleys and coastal plains, rivers, streams, wetlands and deltas, soils with variable characteristics, boreal and deciduous forests, prairies and deserts, sundry niches and habitats, all become comprehensible when viewed through the lens of chronology. Each place is *because*; natural history explains natural systems, and ecology is employed as the unifying science. Processes, laws, and time reveal the present. Therefore, characterization must not only represent spatial patterns as they exist today, but also identify the critical processes which have determined prior landscapes and which are inexorably converting the landscapes of the present into those of the future. The ecological inventory method of landscape characterization is ideally suited to this task.

This permits examining the nation, regions, and sites to disclose probability, causality, and meaning. It is an exemplary method. However, there are certain qualifications: data must be extensive, including all relevant environmental data, and must be of a consonant degree of resolution and time scale. If these characteristics are met, the method is a device for accomplishing integration and synthesis. As no data layer is comprehensible without reference to underlying layers, the accumulation of layers itself constitutes a synthesizing process. This ecological inventory method will explain climate, rocks, water, soils, plants, and animals; alone, however, it will be incapable of addressing human interventions and the realities of existing human environments.

This introduction of the subject of human intervention requires a further step, a more recent field which is less well developed than environmental science but which is nonetheless crucial to the process of landscape characterization. It can be described as human ecology (see, for example, Bennett 1983, Berger and Sinton 1985, Meinig 1979, Wiken et al. 1981). This begins with the primeval environment and its aboriginal population. Like ecological inventories, it employs chronology as its structuring device and it requires reference to a variety of disciplines, but here they include cultural and political geography, regional planning, history, ethnography, and anthropology to supplement physical and biological sciences.

Starting with the primeval landscape and its aboriginal inhabitants, human ecologists identify resources, technology, values, and resultant settlement patterns and land uses. The arrival of Europeans to America brought new values and technologies, thereby changing the definition of important resources and yielding new settlement patterns and land uses. Massive social events such as the Revolutionary War, the Civil War, the great migrations, the industrial revolution, and the World Wars were all influential. As important to the changing landscape was the introduction of technology: water transportation, water power, iron, coal, steam power, roads, canals, railroads, and the automobile with its associated interstate highways and suburbanization.

As history proceeds the environment is continuously modified, reflecting fundamental changes in the values of the inhabitants and the resources and technology available to them. The process is inexorable, with some landscapes being transformed, others neglected, and still others returning as forest succession; the changing landscape reveals the perceptions and values of past and present, its patterns gravid with meaning.

As with the biophysical layer-cake analysis, historic land-use maps reveal the changing human environment so that an informed viewer can observe the marks and changes resulting from earlier activities, fit them into the contemporary scene, and make predictions of the future landscape. The product is a synthetic view of a dynamic landscape continuously shaped by biophysical and social processes.

Regions and Stratified Sampling

Regional structures are indispensable for selecting samples. The first decision must be to select controls—pristine or near pristine environments representing the full range of regions, ecosystems, and varied habitats (lakes, forests, prairies, deserts) located presumably in national parks, national forests, wilderness areas, refuges, and conservancies. Pristine or near pristine environments constitute the upper limits of quality; similarly, samples should also be selected in the most debased environments. Among these would be U.S. Department of Energy installations—Hanford, Savannah River, Oak Ridge, Brookhaven, Rocky Flats, and nuclear test sites in Nevada; the most notorious toxic sites—such as, Love Canal and Times Beach; and also the most depraved urban sites revealing dereliction, abandoned buildings, brickbat soils, water in gutters and catch basins, virtually no vegetation, and wildlife of rats, mice, lice, fleas, cockroaches, sparrows, and starlings.

A subsequent structure for selecting further samples is afforded by the major physiographic regions as subdivided into aquifers, river basins, soil regions, bio-climatic zones, and faunal regions. In urbanized regions, an additional level of structure must be applied based upon both demographic and socioeconomic data.

Geographers have identified urban regions—central business district, zones of transition, inner city residential neighborhoods; inner suburbs; suburbs; outer suburbs; and the urban–rural fringe. Each of these may be associated with specific data on air quality, urban heat sink, degree of permeability, runoff, water quality, vegetative cover, and wildlife. Employment of socioeconomic data suggests that other regions be identified. While resources originate from natural history which explains their location, exploitation has specific consequences. Thus coal regions are associated with environmental degradation and acid mine drainage; cereal production relates to ancient prairies and is now associated with groundwater pollution, notably of nitrates. Economic minerals (iron ore, bauxite, limestone, sand and gravel, etc.) have regional locations and attendant environmental problems, as do other extractive land uses such as forestry, fishing, and grazing. There is a systematic relationship between regions, resources, exploitation, and environmental effects.

Data collected for hexagons within the context of larger physiographic regions and river basins would permit an analysis of the effects of cumulative environmental and social processes. For example, the Delaware River transects the Allegheny Plateau, the Ridge and Valley Province, the Great Valley, the Reading Prong, the Crystalline Piedmont (including the Triassic Basin), and the coastal plain. The changing water quality of the Delaware River reflects the regions transected. Headwater streams in the Allegheny Plateau are of high quality. Tributaries in the Ridge and Valley Province, a long-term locus of coal mining, contribute a massive burden of acidity from mine drainage. These tributaries and the main stem of the Delaware are effectively neutralized as they pass through the limestone Great Valley, but receive a large assault of sediments and fertilizers from agricultural activities, among others. When the river reaches the Crystalline Piedmont and concentrated urbanization, it receives an engorgement of urban sewage and industrial wastes. Thereafter, the river encounters the coastal plain where it impacts extensive aquifers and experiences estuarine processes.

How many samples would be required to evaluate the Delaware River; how many for the Schuylkill River, its largest tributary? Could the contemplated resolution permit comment on Wissahickon Creek, a small tributary which is nonetheless a major feature in the landscape of Philadelphia?

The physiographic regions enumerated above are transected by the Delaware, Susquehanna, Potomac, and James Rivers. A useful comparison could be undertaken between each of these rivers and their samples within each physiographic region. This method could be applied to comparative evaluations not only for physiographic regions and river basins, but also for climate zones, aquifers, soil regions, forest types, wildlife habitats, and, of course, for metropolitan areas.

The major purpose of this discussion on the basis for the selection of samples is, first, to emphasize the taxonomic regional structures which are employed by the environmental sciences and should be incorporated. Secondly, the opportunity of comparative, stratified samples, as for instance, for between river and groundwater regions in similar physiographic regions, or as between urban regions ranging from central city to the rural fringe, in their regional contexts.

Regional Expertise

Much knowledge exists about the ecology of the nation, not only by the distinguished scientists of the environment, but also of regional groups wherein repose the major perceptions and data. This is an important observation, that the largest body of knowledge required for inventories reposes in the knowledge, data, and repositions of existing scientists and institutions. As important, they are likely to possess not only current but also historic data. As a result we recommend that the conduct of both regional and hexagonal samples be devolved to regional groups. However, we recommend that EPA assume the responsibility for the national characterization, possibly in concert with the USGS and NASA.

This proposal would invest the effort in persons and institutions familiar with the relevant sciences and regions and avoid the necessity of creating a large bureaucracy.

A centralized computing facility should be installed in EPA to support the regional groups generating data. This would ensure quality assurance and quality control of data and would be the most cost-effective way to process specialty data sets. Furthermore, it is not necessary to know the study regions in order to process the data. Centralization of data processing allows the assembly of a highly skilled group, the development and updating of software to solve problems, and an economy of scale in setting up the facility. This economy of scale is quite significant because of the very large data sets involved, so large that even high-end workstations cannot efficiently process the data.

Synthesis

The nature of science is reductionist. This is reflected in the separate disciplines, journals, university and government departments devoted to individual specialties. Occasionally the investigation of ad hoc problems produces interdisciplinary and multi-disciplinary research, but such efforts remain an aberration. Yet, it is incontrovertible that a valid landscape characterization requires that all of the environmental sciences be involved and engaged in integration and synthesis.

We are not fundamentally committed to clouds, rocks, rivers, soils, plants, or animals; instead, we are interested in the quality of the human environment which partakes of all of these and more. The particular attribute which is crucial to the characterization process is synthesis.

Synthesis involves both science and art, two views thought to be dramatically opposed in traditional philosophy. When each is viewed with its larger pretensions, the conflict between rationality and intuition appears irreconcilable. However, when both nouns are reduced to their root meanings, reconciliation seems possible. Science means knowledge, art means skill. Knowledge without skill has limited utility, while skill without knowledge is incomplete. At this level it would appear that each is essential to the other. This is certainly valid in the synthesis required for characterization.

The scientist searches for irrefutable knowledge and refrains from making statements when such evidence is incomplete. Yet management of the environment will always include imperfect knowledge, and so government must employ the best available knowledge and act prudently with respect to it.

In spite of these difficulties it is possible to undertake landscape characterization. The first problem to be resolved results from the fact that no person exists who is coequally informed in all of the environmental sciences, particularly at threshold levels. It thus becomes clear that the exercise must be multi-disciplinary. From the physical sciences of meteorology, geology, physical oceanography, hydrology, and soils it is possible to find scientists who, while identified with one discipline, are conversant with the other physical sciences of the environment. But more important is the agreement that while physical processes have been dominated by plate tectonics, these and other processes are manifested in geomorphology. Physiography provides the initial synthesis for landscape characterization.

It transpires that biological systems synthesize both physical and biological conditions so that the organisms in an ecosystem represent a second level of synthesis, certainly prior to human intervention. This investigation is simplified by agreement on ecological principles espoused by plant and animal ecologists, limnologists, and marine biologists. It has also been enhanced by the perceptions of the emergent discipline of landscape ecology (Forman and Godron 1986).

The last function of producing a physical, biological, and social model is the least understood process and faces the serious problem that social scientists are generally uninformed in natural science. The reverse is equally true. Yet the natural environment is intertwined with human society. Values and attitudes toward the environment, combined with available resources, capital, and technology, constitute the basis for landscape history. If the combined socio-natural ecological inventory proceeds carefully, the current situation of the environment will become comprehensible, as will the population, its economy, the values they espouse, the institutions they select to fulfill their objectives, and their settlement patterns and land uses. There are a few precious people who possess the rare combination of skills to complete this integrative process of landscape characterization (Hills 1974, for example). From their work come the frames of reference for synthesis.

Ecological planning provides a means for synthesis (McHarg 1969). Ecological planning can be augmented by an immersion in cultural anthropology (Berger and Sinton 1985).

The key questions which must be addressed for each inventory and characterization are: What is the place? How did it come to be? What processes characterize it? What is its status? Where is it going? There is an equally important sequence of questions: Who populated the region, historically? Who today? How did they utilize its resources? How do they evaluate the environment? What issues do they perceive? What are their responses?

This interface between nature and people deserves extended treatment. It is indispensable for understanding human environments. Moreover this concern has not been conspicuous in the history of EPA which has tended to concentrate on biophysical environments. It cannot be too strongly stated that the EMAP process must address human environments.

The world is a single interacting biophysical-social system. There are no physical systems unaffected by life, no biological systems impervious to matter, no biophysical systems uninfluenced by people. Yet the world is subdivided by science and language, specific realms are jealously guarded as proprietary by the discrete sciences.

Traditional ecological inventories do not include ethnographic histories or historic analyses of economic and social processes. From our extensive and evolving experience, we assert that such historic analyses are absolutely crucial to landscape characterization. Jonathan Berger and John Sinton (1985) provide an example of such an ethnography in their book about the New Jersey Pinelands.

Conclusions and Recommendations

1. Create an executive committee drawn from the most distinguished leaders in the fields of environmental science.
2. Charge the executive committee to design the entire national ecological inventory process, determine the structure necessary to realize the objective, identity staff, computer operation, inventory, monitoring, and characterization procedure.
3. Design and implement a public relations campaign.

4. Investigate and appropriate scales of inventory, including national, regional, and site specific.
5. Investigate and resolve requirements for each scale of investigation.
6. Develop criteria to be employed in selecting sites.
7. Investigate the subject of an appropriate title for the enterprise.
8. Consider chronology as a suitable rubric for the characterization process.
9. Consider the utility of the layer-cake mode of representation.
10. Determine the obligatory contents of the inventory.
11. Discuss and resolve the matter of historical and ethnographic data to be incorporated into the inventory.
12. Investigate regional groups with the appropriate range of competence in physical, biological, and social science, competent in integration and synthesis.
13. Review the current research operation and determine whether or not this reductionist, phenomenon-based approach should be continued or replaced by a more integrated structure.

References

American Institute of Architects Task Force on the Potomac; Wallace, McHarg, Roberts, and Todd; and the University of Pennsylvania. 1965–1966. *The Potomac*. Washington, D.C.: U.S. Government Printing Office.

Bennett, John. 1983. "The Micro-Macro Nexus: Typology, Process, and Systems." 1981 Annual Meeting of the American Anthropological Association.

Berger, Jonathan and John Walter Sinton. 1985. *Water, Earth, and Fire: Land Use and Environmental Planning in the New Jersey Pine Barrens*. Baltimore, MD: Johns Hopkins University Press.

Development Research Associates and Wallace, McHarg, Roberts and Todd. 1971. *Ecological Studies of the Regional Transportation District, Denver, Colorado*. Interim Technical Memorandum, Task 5 of the Joint Venture. Denver: Regional Transportation District.

———. 1972. *Ecology-Natural Suitabilities for Regional Growth*. Denver: Regional Transportation District.

Fenneman, N. M. 1931. *Physiography of Western United States*. New York: McGraw-Hill.

———. 1948. *Physiography of Eastern United States*. New York: McGraw-Hill.

Forman, Richard T. T., and Michel Godron. 1986. *Landscape Ecology*. New York: Wiley.

Hills, G. Angus. 1974. "A Philosophical Approach to Landscape Planning." *Landscape Planning* 1 (4):339–81.

Holden, Constance. 1977. "Ian McHarg: Champion for Design with Nature." *Science* 195 (4276, 28 January):379–82.

Hunt, Charles B. 1974. *Natural Regions of the United States and Canada*. San Francisco: W. H. Freeman.

International Planning Associates. 1979. *The Master Plan for Abuja, The New Federal Capital of Nigeria*. Lagos, Nigeria: The Federal Capital Development Authority.

Kuchler, A. W. 1964. *Potential Natural Vegetation of the Conterminous United States*. Special Publication 36. American Geographical Society.

The Mandala Collaborative/Wallace, McHarg, Roberts, and Todd. 1975. *Pardisan, Plan for an Environmental Park in Tehran*. Prepared for the Department of Environment, Imperial Government of Iran. Philadelphia, Penn.: Winchell Press.

McHarg, Ian L. 1969. *Design with Nature*. Garden City, N.Y.: Doubleday, The Natural History Press. 1992 Second edition, New York: Wiley.

Meinig, D. W. 1979. *The Interpretation of Ordinary Landscapes*. New York: Oxford University Press.

University of Pennsylvania. 1963. *Metropolitan Open Space from Natural Processes*. Philadelphia: Urban Renewal Administration and the States of Pennsylvania and New Jersey.

Wallace, McHarg, Roberts, and Todd. 1969. *Ecological Study for Twin Cities Metropolitan Region, Minnesota*. Prepared for Metropolitan Council of the Twin Cities Area. Philadelphia: U.S. Department of Commerce, National Technical Information Series.

————. 1972. *An Ecological Planning Study for Wilmington and Dover, Vermont*. Brattleboro, Vt.: Windham Regional Planning and Development Commission and the Vermont State Planning Office.

————. 1973. *Towards a Comprehensive Plan for Environmental Quality*. Washington, D.C.: American Institute of Planners for the U.S. Environmental Protection Agency.

————. 1974. *San Francisco Metropolitan Regional Environmental Impact Procedure Study, California*. San Francisco: Bay Area Council of Governments.

————. 1976. *Lake Austin Growth Management Plan*. Austin, Texas: City of Austin, Department of Planning.

————. 1978. *Ecological Study for Northwestern Colorado Council of Governments*. Frisco, Colorado: Northwestern Colorado Council of Governments.

Wiken, E. B., J. P. Semyk, and E. Oswald. 1981. "Inventorying Land Resources through an Ecologically Based Approach." In *In-Place Resource Inventories: Principles and Practices*. Orono: University of Maine Press.

Prospectus (1998)

My battle began almost fifty years ago with a tentative presumption in favor of nature that became explicit in the 1960s. I employed this view wherever opportunity was afforded—in small sites and in metropolitan regions, in urban areas and rural landscapes, and across North America and abroad. By applying increased knowledge and developing a powerful model and method, I engaged a large army of practitioners: first, students, next, readers of *Design with Nature*, then, viewers of *Multiply and Subdue the Earth*, and finally, audiences throughout the country and the world.

This commitment recognized the enemy to be those devoted to anthropocentrism and anthropomorphism, those who believed that man was the justification of evolution, that he exclusively shared divinity and was given dominion over the earth, that he was licensed to subjugate nature and empowered to treat the planet as a storehouse awaiting plunder.

So there was a war between those who would treat the world and its creatures with, at least, deference, and perhaps better, with reverence, and those who would destroy without care or remorse. I resolved to mobilize all of my energies on behalf of the stewards.

For over a quarter of a century, I have been a strong advocate of ecological inventories at all scales, from the site to the whole earth. If we are to undertake a global ecological inventory and engage in continuous monitoring, the questions will quickly arise: what, where, and how should we restore? In brief, do we select areas massively destroyed or, in contrast, select the pristine which merely needs protection? Whatever course we follow will require a massive rediscovery of the earth in times of good health. For the West, that would be before the industrial revolution. For most of the developing world the time span would be much shorter, possibly only half a century. But we must describe the primeval world and consider how to restore it, how to green it, how to heal it.

Of course the greatest agency involved in this process is natural succession, regeneration, that process which is most dramatically portrayed on the slopes of recently active volcanoes but occurs worldwide. We must do more than sustain the planet, we must design regenerative communities and landscapes. Or we must get out of the way and let the earth regenerate itself.

A dramatic example of this is the demilitarized zone in Korea, which is

250 kilometers long, 4 kilometers wide, and is bordered by a high fence that has succeeded to forest, where many species of plants and animals once thought to be extinct are now abundant. Where are the healthy tissues of the world life body, the virgin areas—Arctic and Antarctic ice caps, miles of deep ocean trenches, mountains as high as they are deep, deserts, forests, bare rock, snow and ice, but, above all, water?

We know that succession is a real phenomenon. The example of regeneration after volcanic eruptions alone is persuasive. How fortunate we are to have such an ally. But let us consider the possibility that there exists a process, which might be called "infectious health," whereby pristine areas contribute to the regeneration of disturbed neighbors.

Could infectious health enable healthy systems to cause adjacent lands to recover? Then we should not only protect the pristine, but also their recovering neighbors. We would see pristine colonies expanding whereby species, microorganisms, and seeds initiate regeneration. We would see pristine realms coalesce, wounds and welts shrink. We would see the descent of health from elevated islands spreading symmetrically. We would see carbon being fixed on coral reefs, benthic limestone, and old-growth forests, and gas made palpable, changed from threat to inheritance.

And so I've advocated using ecology, employing all the environmental sciences, to understand our world and guide design and planning decisions. The determination to undertake national, digital, ecological inventions awaits us. It would be beneficial if this were performed successfully by a large country. Recent experience has been limited to small nations and regions, including New Zealand, Western Australia, and Taiwan. There is, of course, the most successful inventory performed anywhere—the environmental atlas of Alaska, led by Lidia Selkregg, but it is not yet in digital form. Selkregg's marvelous work consists of maps, diagrams, photographs, and tables, all of which should be digitized to constitute an exemplar for this nation. Because Alaska is perhaps the most pristine environment in North America, it is the most appropriate candidate for the first comprehensive, digital statewide ecological inventory.

If the primary objective of healing the earth were to begin with inventories to identify the pristine and near pristine environments which should be preserved to contribute to infectious healing and regeneration, there emerges the problem of cities. Conventional economic thought places cities at the apex of human achievement, followed by agriculture, while wild lands and native ecosystems are held at the lowest value.

An ecological perspective would reverse this hierarchy. Cities, rather than an ecological apex, would be considered to be a catastrophe. As the major sources of pollutions and toxins, particularly greenhouse gases, they exclude the vegetative contribution of fixing carbon. Agriculture makes a contribution to deterrence of the greenhouse effect but also contributes to excessive water use, soil erosion, and climatic extremes. Its carbon fixing falls far below that achieved by rain forests. Wild lands, lakes, oceans, and coral reefs, least valued in conventional wisdom, are, in contrast, the primary agents for fixing carbon and for climatic amelioration.

Present urbanization constitutes a major global ecological challenge with the maximum costs to the environment and none or few benefits. This suggests that cities, particularly megacities that can number up to thirty million in population, should be greened to diminish environmental costs.

In South America and Southeast Asia vegetation is profuse and can grow in unlikely places. In Honolulu parking garage roofs and walls are covered with ficus. In Singapore overpass structures are covered in vegetation. But this remedy should not be limited to tropical regions; temperate rain forests are admirable fixers of carbon and produce rich and beautiful environments and high biodiversity. Green roofs and walls should be investigated to reduce urban impacts on the environment.

New knowledge about our environments and new theories will continue the advance of ecological design and planning. There is nothing so practical as a good theory, or so the saying goes. Landscape architects and ecological planners should become the physicians of the land. We should be healers, but we should also be practitioners of preventive medicine. Medical doctors need to know human biology to practice their art. Similarly, we should be well-versed enough in landscape ecology to be able to make diagnoses and describe interventions.

The goal of earth medicine should be the support and the creation of healthy places. Health is the ability to recover from injury or insult. Our planet and its landscapes have suffered many injurious and insulting actions—the work to be done is cut out for us. The process of making landscapes healthy involves diagnosis, prescription, and intervention. As a medical doctor uses knowledge of anatomy during the checkup, so too must an ecological designer or planner understand natural and cultural processes in order to identify the nature of the illness.

Design and planning should be arts based on a body of knowledge built from case studies of practice. We should undertake actual projects and then assess our work through writing. This is the path to reflective practice and theory-building. Physicians learn their art from a solid foundation of literature, and they then build upon that foundation in the form of new research and papers. Surgery on the brain or heart or any other vital organ takes courage. So too does intervention in an urban neighborhood, a degraded wetlands, or any of the other tissues of the living landscape. To heal places, landscape architects and ecological planners must not only have the knowledge and skill to make reasonable diagnoses and to prescribe sound actions, but also the courage to take on difficult challenges.

Acknowledgment of Sources

Most essays and articles in this collection have been revised and reprinted with the kind permission of the original publisher. The following papers were published in these original sources:

"Man and Environment." In Leonard J. Duhl and John Powell, eds. *The Urban Condition*. New York: Basic Books, pp. 44–58 (1963).

"The Place of Nature in the City of Man." *The Annals of the American Academy of Political Science* (Urban Revival: Goals and Standards) 325 (March):1–12 (1964).

"Ecological Determinism." In F. Fraser Darling and John P. Milton, eds. *Future Environments of North America*. Garden City, N.Y.: The Natural History Press, pp. 526–38 (1966). From *Future Environments of North America* by Fraser Darling and John P. Milton. Copyright © 1966 by the Conservation Foundation. Used by permission of Doubleday, a division of Bantam Doubleday Dell Publishing Group, Inc.

"Values, Process and Form." In The Smithsonian Institution. *The Fitness of Man's Environment*. New York: Harper & Row, pp. 207–27 (1968). Used by permission of the publisher.

"Natural Factors in Planning." *Journal of Soil & Water Conservation* 52 (1, January–February):13–17 (1997).

"Regional Landscape Planning." In A. J. W. Scheffey, ed. *Resources, the Metropolis, and the Land-Grant University*. Proceedings of the Conference on Natural Resources, No. 410. Amherst: University of Massachusetts, pp. 31–35 (1963). (Comments by others on McHarg's remarks continue through p. 37.)

"Open Space from Natural Processes." In David A. Wallace, ed. *Metropolitan Open Space and Natural Process*. Philadelphia: University of Pennsylvania Press, pp. 10–52 (1970). From *Metropolitan Open Space and Natural Process*, edited by David A. Wallace. Copyright © 1970 by the University of Pennsylvania Press. Reprinted with permission of the publisher.

"Must We Sacrifice the West?" In Terrell J. Minger and Sherry D. Oaks, eds. *Growth Alternatives for the Rocky Mountain West*. Boulder, Colo.: Westview Press, pp. 203–11 (1975).

"Human Ecological Planning at Pennsylvania." *Landscape Planning* 8:109–120 (1981).

"Ecological Planning: The Planner as Catalyst." In Robert W. Burchell and George

Sternlieb, eds. *Planning Theory in the 1980s* (2d edition, 1982). New Brunswick, N.J.: The Center for Urban Policy Research, Rutgers University, pp. 13–15 (1978). Reprinted with permission of Rutgers University, Center for Urban Policy Research, from *Planning Theory in the 1980s: A Search for Future Directions,* edited by Robert W. Burchell and George Sternlieb. Copyright © 1978 Rutgers University.

"The Court House Concept." *Architectural Record* 122 (September):193–200 (1957). Reprinted with permission from *Architectural Record,* Vol. 122 (1957).

"Architecture in an Ecological View of the World." *AIA Journal* 54(5):47–51 (1970).

"Nature Is More Than a Garden." In Mark Francis and Randolph T. Hester, Jr., eds. *The Meaning of Gardens: Idea, Place, and Action.* Cambridge, Mass.: The MIT Press, pp. 34–37 (1990).

"Ecology and Design." In George F. Thompson and Frederick R. Steiner, eds. *Ecological Design and Planning.* New York: Wiley, pp. 321–32 (1996). Copyright © 1996. Reprinted by permission of John Wiley & Sons, Inc.

"An Ecological Method for Landscape Architecture." *Landscape Architecture* 57(2):105–7 (1967).

"A Comprehensive Highway Route Selection Method." *Highway Research Record* 246:1–12 (1968). In *Transportation Research Record 246,* Transportation Research Board, National Research Council, Washington, D.C. (1968).

"Biological Alternatives to Water Pollution." In Joachim Tourbier and Robert W. Pierson, Jr., eds., *Biological Control of Water Pollution.* Philadelphia: Center for Ecological Design and Planning, University of Pennsylvania, pp. 7–12 (1976).

"A Case Study in Ecological Planning: The Woodlands, Texas." In Marvin T. Beatty, Gary W. Petersen, and Lester D. Swindale, eds. *Planning the Uses and Management of Land.* Madison, Wisc.: American Society of Agronomy, Crop Science Society of America, and Soil Science Society of America, pp. 935–55, chap. 38 (1979).

"Plan for the Valleys vs. Spectre of Uncontrolled Growth." *Landscape Architecture* 55 (4, April):179–81 (1965).

"An Ecological Planning Study for Wilmington and Dover, Vermont." The study was prepared by Wallace, McHarg, Roberts, and Todd for Wilmington and Dover, Vermont, the Windham Regional Planning and Development Commission, and the Vermont State Planning Office, April 1972.

"Ecological Plumbing for the Texas Coastal Plain." *Landscape Architecture* 65 (1, January):78–89 (1975).

"A Strategy for a National Ecological Inventory." In *A Database Prototype for a National Ecological Inventory.* Washington, D.C.: U.S. Environmental Protection Agency, pp. 6–26, chap. 2 (1992).

Index

DATE DUE
